Klaus Schwab the World Economic Forum & the Coming Mark of the Beast

FIRST PRINTING

Billy Crone

Copyright © 2023
All Rights Reserved

Cover Design:
CHRIS TAYLOR

*To my family, Church family,
and all those around the world
who have had loved ones
murdered from this viral agenda.*

*God will have the last word
on this evil and suffering
and satanic behavior.*

*If these people
do not ask for forgiveness
and get saved
through Jesus Christ,*

*Hell will be there
awaiting them
with open arms.*

Contents

Preface vii

1. Klaus Schwab & the New World Order 9
2. Klaus Schwab World Economic Forum & Brain Chips 21
3. World Economic Forum & Global Leaders… 49
4. World Economic Forum & Global Finances 93
5. World Economic Forum & Global Health 125
6. World Economic Forum & the Great Reset 175
7. World Economic Forum & Agenda 2030 221
8. World Economic Forum & Fourth Industrial Revolution 231
9. World Economic Forum & the China U.N. Connection 253
10. World Economic Forum & the Ten Horned Kingdom 265
11. World Economic Forum & the Mark of the Beast 317
12. World Economic Forum & the Global Conditioning 343
13. World Economic Forum & Chip Implants 387
14. World Economic Forum & Digital Currency 395
15. World Economic Forum & Digital Scoring Systems 417
16. World Economic Forum & CBDC Currency 433
17. World Economic Forum & Global Biometric Passports 453
18. World Economic Forum & the Ultimate Losers 499

How to Receive Jesus Christ… 499
Notes… 501

Preface

Just when you thought things couldn't get even worse, here we go. If you read our last book on Klaus Schwab and his evil behavior, we not only exposed his family ties to Hitler and the Third Reich, but we also saw how Klaus is simply picking up where Hitler left off. That is, he is implementing, on a global basis, the Third Reich, only now relabeled as the Fourth Industrial Revolution. It's all the same. Then we also witnessed how, just like Hitler, Klaus is also directly involved in the new massive modern-day Holocaust called Covid-19, and the shots that are killing multiple millions of people around the globe, even more than what Hitler did with the Jewish people. As bad as that is, in this book, we expose the even more horrible and shocking news that Klaus has also been planning for a long time now through this outfit he created called The World Economic Forum, new leadership for the world that he has trained, that have pledged to do his bidding, and are now systematically placed all over the world in basically every developed country, including in the United States of America. The plants by Klaus are not only scattered throughout virtually all political offices around the planet, but they've also infiltrated the media, businesses, corporations, finance, health, you name it. Simply put, Klaus Schwab and his evil gang of Hitlerian puppets are now in virtually every sector of society implementing his sick Hitlerian nightmare. And with the help of the manufactured Covid-19 plandemic, Klaus Schwab and the World Economic Forum are preparing the planet for what the Bible warned about nearly 2,000 years ago. That is, the coming satanic Antichrist kingdom, a cashless society, and full implementation of the Mark of the Beast. And just so we don't realize the obvious connection, all Klaus and the gang have done is once again relabel this satanic regime that they're building as the new digital currency and the Great Reset. One last piece of advice; when you are through reading this book, will you please READ YOUR BIBLE? I mean that in the nicest possible way. Enjoy, and I'm looking forward to seeing you someday!

Billy Crone
Las Vegas, Nevada
2023

Chapter One

Klaus Schwab & The New World Order

In our last documentary, Klaus Schwab, the Third Reich and the Covid 19 Holocaust, we exposed the historical roots of Klaus Schwab, his family, and their obvious ties with Hitler and the Nazis, as well as Klaus Schwab pushing for what he calls The Fourth Industrial Revolution, which is really a rehashed, relabeled, and repackaged version of Hitler's Third Reich. The agendas and behavior are completely the same, and all Klaus and his evil gang of Global Elites have done is just change the name.

And this is why our future is radically changing right before our very eyes, and in a not-so-good fashion. In fact, it's being changed rapidly in a horrible, rotten fashion. The reality is this. If Klaus and his buddies get their way with their revamped Hitlerian agenda, soon this will be our experience when applying for a loan.

Here is a parody of a man going into the National Bank to apply for a loan:

Bank Manager: *"Hi, my name is Bryan, my pronouns are "He/Him"* (as he points to his nametag). *I hear you are seeking a small business loan, but you are having problems with your E in your ESG scores."*

Customer: *"I was denied."*

Bank Manager: *"What's your business?"*

Customer: *"I operate drilling equipment, oil, and gas."*

Bank Manager: *"Ah ha, the E in the ESG stands for environmental, you're in a dirty industry."*

Customer: *"So, I can't get no loan?"*

Bank Manager: *"Well, let's take a look at your company's social policies. Tell me about your plan to pay social justice."*

Customer: *"Social Justice?"*

Bank Manager: *"Do your employees get paid time off for abortion? And tell me about your diversity, equity and inclusion plan."*

Customer: *"Well, I ain't got none of that. I'm a driller and just hire good people to work."*

Bank Manager: *"Maybe there's one more thing that we can check. Do you have any female co-owners?"*

Customer: *"No, just me."*

Bank Manager: *"Have you ever identified as a woman? Or just non-binary? This could really help your score."*

Customer: *"What? Ewwwww!"*

Bank Manager: *"Your loan is denied."*

And all kidding aside, that's exactly where Klaus Schwab and his Hitlerian gang of evil Global Elites are taking us, whether we want it or not, and it's even worse than that!

It won't just be issues that determine whether or not we can get a loan, but even our attitude towards the government. And that also includes if you say anything negative against this so-called regime on social media, and any other public platform, anywhere, including who you hang out with, and how well you obey their orders, just to name a few of their admitted criteria!

This is simply a massive micromanaging of the planet that Klaus Schwab and his evil gang of Global Elites are bringing to us whether we want it or not, and they call it The Fourth Industrial Revolution and/or The Great Reset.

But as we saw in our last documentary, **Klaus Schwab, the Third Reich & the Covid-19 Holocaust**, it's simply what the Bible calls The Antichrist Kingdom. Let's revisit that passage again.

Revelation 13:2,3,4-6,7,8-9,11-18: "And I saw a beast coming out of the sea. He had ten horns and seven heads, with ten crowns on his horns, and on each head a blasphemous name. The dragon gave the beast his power and his throne and great authority. The whole world was astonished and followed the beast. Men worshiped the dragon because he had given authority to the beast, and they also worshiped the beast and asked, 'Who is like the beast? Who can make war against him?' The beast was given a mouth to utter proud words and blasphemies and to exercise his authority for forty-two months.

He opened his mouth to blaspheme God, and to slander His name, and His dwelling place, and those who live in Heaven. And he was given authority over every tribe, people, language and nation. All inhabitants of the earth will worship the beast – all whose names have not been written in the book of life belonging to the Lamb that was slain from the creation of the world. He who has an ear, let him hear. Then I saw another beast, coming out of the earth. He had two horns like a lamb, but he spoke like a dragon.

He exercised all the authority of the first beast on his behalf and made the earth and its inhabitants worship the first beast, whose fatal wound had been healed. And he performed great and miraculous signs, even causing fire to come down from Heaven to earth in full view of men. Because of the signs he was given power to do on behalf of the first beast, he deceived the inhabitants of the earth. He ordered them to set up an image in honor of the beast who was wounded by the sword and yet lived.

He was given power to give breath to the image of the first beast, so that it could speak and cause all who refused to worship the image to be killed. He also forced everyone, small and great, rich and poor, free and slave, to receive a mark on his right hand or on his forehead, so that no one could buy or sell unless he had the mark, which is the name of the beast or the number of his name. This calls for wisdom. If anyone has insight, let him calculate the number of the beast, for it is man's number. His number is 666."

So, the Bible warned and predicted nearly 2,000 years ago that an unthinkable evil empire would emerge upon the whole planet. And it's unthinkable and evil because first, it's satanic. The beast, or Antichrist, is empowered by the dragon that is defined in the Bible as none other than satan himself.

Then this beast, or Antichrist, would work together with a False Prophet, or global religious figure, who would then help deceive the whole planet into merging everyone on earth under their authority.

Then they would institute a One World Government (he was given authority over every tribe, people, language, and nation) a One World Religion (he exercised all the authority of the first beast on his behalf, and made the earth and its inhabitants worship the first beast), and a One World Economy, mixed with some sort of electronic Mark of the Beast type system (he also forced everyone, small and great, rich and poor, free and slave, to receive a mark on his right hand or on his forehead), that will then control all the buying and selling across the whole planet (so that no one could buy or sell unless he had the mark, which is the name of the beast or the number of his name.)

It also implies a huge global Big Brother system that knows everything about anyone (you know like the ESG video you just saw), including whether or not people are obeying and if they don't, they know exactly where they are so they can be killed. (He ordered them to set up an image in honor of the beast…and was given power to give breath to the image of the first beast, so that it could speak and cause all who refused to worship the image to be killed.)

So, as you can see, and as we exposed in our last documentary, Klaus Schwab and his so-called Great Reset agenda, pushed by the World Economic Forum, along with the help of all these Global Elites, are simply laying the foundation for what the Bible prophesied would come in the Last Days. And this is the Antichrist Kingdom.

And all these guys are in on it. All countries, virtually all politicians, both sides of the fence by the way, from all over the world, are all part of this satanic agenda, as this man shares.

Narrator: *"In every Western country today there are three clearly identifiable mega trends, shaping the policies of mainstream political parties across the board. Whether you are looking at Germany, or France or Britain, the U.S., Canada, or Australia. Whether you look to the left or the right, all mainstream parties support firstly, the ongoing immigration into our countries. They all ridicule the defensive borders and the idea of* *building walls or fences, while maintaining that strict border controls and immigration laws are somehow unfeasible.*

Secondly, they support a gradual build-up of global government structures such as the United Nations, the European Union, and transnational legislation in the name of human rights.

Thirdly, they all support far reaching global policies to combat supposed climate change, immigration, supranational legislation and climate policies. Those are the three grand projects that define the political undercurrent of Western mainstream parties, of both the left and the right.

It all represents a transition from one type of society to supposedly another type of society. They stem from the vision of a New World. A world in which we would no longer be divided into different nations, different peoples, a world without Parliaments that may decide things as one country alone. And in doing so, might greatly diverge from Parliaments of other countries.

It's a vision of a world in which we will supposedly all be growing towards one humanity, governed by common rules that are to be centrally administered on a global level. This would be a world in which a global superstate increasingly controls every tiny aspect of our lives, because everything we do, supposedly, affects the climate.

Senior aid, Congresswoman, Alexandria Ocasio-Cortez says, and I quote, 'We don't view the Green New Deal as a climate thing. We view it as a change-the-entire-economy thing.' But that is exactly right. We are in the midst of a structural remaking of the world as we know it. Our nations, our cultural, political, and spiritual homes are being dismantled. Slowly, but surely, our societies are becoming so diverse that a shared common identity will no longer be feasible. We are losing our democracies because Parliaments get to decide less and less, as well as our freedom because all of our lives are increasingly being regulated by the 'change the entire economy project' that masquerades as saving the planet.

It's crucial to understand that the fundamental idea behind these major threats is in fact, Marxist. These three grand projects embodied in their entirety, in their orchestrated position towards a supposedly higher utopian, peaceful, and egalitarian stage of existence. The long promised, post-capitalist era. The results alas will be dystopia. This is because we are beings in need of a sense of community, a sense of hope.

Mass migration, global governance and new climate control measures to take these things away. They alienate us from our actual lives. They make us 'nowhere' creatures inhabiting a land with which we will have lost all connection. Living with people to whom we feel no relationship and administered by bureaucrats over whom we have no control. We all experience this every day.

The New World Order is upon us. Europe has already gone further down this path of course, than America, but it is happening in the United States as well. It's a phenomenon that we are witnessing across the Western world. And it is the greatest danger of our life."

And it's what the Bible calls the rise of the Antichrist Kingdom! And like that gentleman, some of us are catching on and exposing this! This so-called utopia of these global, evil, megalomaniacs is simply to become the Antichrist nightmare that the Bible warned about. And the same evil, wicked, Global Elites, who are working with Klaus Schwab to pull all this off, to also control the media, the various media platforms that we use to share information, they admittedly filter, block or ban others from warning people about their New World Order ruse, the so-called Great Reset, The Fourth Industrial Revolution, whatever you want to call it.

And they're vilifying anyone who doesn't go along with their satanic ruse, making us whistleblowers out to be the bad guys, the crazy ones, and they further brainwash people into thinking that they shouldn't listen to us because we're just a bunch of wacky conspiracy people, as this man shares:

Neil Oliver Live, CBN Reports: *"Here's what I make of the bigger picture, of what some of us, so called covidiots, anti-vaxxers, Putin-apologists, fascists, far-right extremists, swivel-like loons want to talk about next. Whatever is happening in Ukraine, to that country and to its people, both are undoubtedly being used by those who also need something and someone to make their own populations look the other way.*

The horror show in Ukraine is being exploited. Here at home, last week, Boris Johnson implied that, while only lesser mortals are fretting selflessly, selfishly about heat and food, his attentions are focused on the lofty heights of saving the world. The little people of Britain must endure cold and hunger for guess what? The greater good.

Anyone with even the faintest grasp, or at least an interest in geopolitics knows it's utterly bogus, and he is a fraud along with Biden, Trudeau, Macron, Van der Layne, and the rest of the list so long I don't have time to read it out. The imminent cold and hunger were made inevitable, not by Putin in 2022, but years ago by the adoption of ruinous, ideologically driven nonsense presented as world-saving environmental policies that denied us any hope of energy independence, the profitable exploitation of all the resources beneath our feet and seas and condemned much of Europe to dependence on Russia.

What we are paying is the cost of going green when those policies are not green at all, but predicated upon some of the most destructive and toxic practices and technologies ever conceived. Wind and solar will never provide the energy we need to keep thriving as societies, to grow and flourish. The situation is so insane I find it easiest to conclude we're simply meant to do without. Stop thinking we're all going to have cars and international travel and warm homes, just different than before.

What seems obvious is that we're being groomed to live small lives. To make way for the grandiose expectations and entitlements of the elites that are working so effectively to gather up the last of the wealth. Smaller lives, colder lives, may actually be the best we can hope for, given the plans evidently laid out for us by those with hands on the levers of power. Our leaders used to tell us we needed them in order to be free. In the future, they will have us believe we need them to be safe. Caged animals are safe, but it's not much of a life.

Energy prices will keep going up. This will obviously hurt the poorest countries and the poorest people first and worst. What is obvious about the green warriors making war on affordable reliable energy, is that they do not care a jot about the poor. At least not the actual poor alive in the world today. Those real flesh and blood people are to be sacrificed by the millions. Utterly denied energy that might have lifted them out of poverty.

So, the imaginary people, as yet unborn, might thrive in a utopia that exists only in the imaginations of pampered protesters. China will just burn more coal to compensate and seize more control but best not to mention it. That corrupted thinking comes from communism or perhaps communism's idiot cousins, socialism. Green warriors don't care about the poor in the same way socialists don't care about the poor. They just hate the rich, which is ironic, given it was their infantile protests, they're doing the work of the very richest for them.

Ukraine produces a fifth of the wheat crop required by the poorest. Don't mention this though. Whatever has been grown will be hard to store and harder to export, so that hunger and full-blown famine become a looming threat for hundreds of millions of the world's hungriest people. In richer countries, life is being made deliberately impossible for farmers. Spiking costs of fertilizers and fuels are one thing, but governments in the Netherlands, across Europe, in Canada, and elsewhere around the world, are persecuting those who grow our food.

Farmers are made to endure restrictions that destroy their businesses, being driven off the land altogether. They'll have to watch as fuels they have known and cared for over generations are gathered up by transnational organizations with other ideas about what that land might be used for.

If you think mass migration and immigration are difficult problems now, wait until the unavoidable famines cause a hemorrhage of humanity out of the poorest countries of Africa and the Middle East. Perhaps hundreds of millions of people with nothing more to lose, where do you think they'll go?

And here's another inconvenient truth. Money and weapons keep flowing into Ukraine, but despite months of war and sanctions, the Russian Ruble remains strong and the end to hostilities seems as far away as ever. Maybe no one wants that war to end. Wars don't determine who's right anyway. Wars determine who's left. Ultimately, this is all about wealth and power. Not money, remember. Money is to wealth as a menu is to a steak.

One is a worthless bit of paper; the other is something that can keep you alive. This is about actual wealth and its acquisition. It's about the already super rich getting hold of even more of the real things, land, buildings, natural resources, gold. Well, we are supposed to be frightened out of our wits, squabbling among ourselves and just hoping that one day it will all be over. A relative handful of others are gathering up all the wealth as planned. Whichever way you slice it, an economic and societal shock on a scale that had not happened in lifetimes, if ever, is on its way.

The world we live in is built in its entirety upon unimaginable and now unsustainable levels of debt. Trillions, quadrillions of dollars worth. There's always much more debt in the world than money so that it's never possible to settle the debt. Now that debt, all that created money, is about to come crashing down. Don't be fooled by Sunac and the rest and their about-face, their pretense that they were with us all along. Covid and lockdowns carried them only so far, but they planned to go much further. Disease, war, famine, and death. The same people always ride on the same four horses. Now is not the time to take our eyes off the ball, not by a long shot. Keep watching the usual suspects. As I say, you ain't seen nothing yet."

Wow! We need news like that over here in America! But what he mentioned, what's coming next, you ain't seen nothing yet, with these power-hungry, global, evil megalomaniacs, is exactly what the Bible says as well!

The Scriptures declare that once the Antichrist Kingdom begins, and the whole planet gets snookered into his evil twisted agenda, the next thing that's coming after that is war, famine, disease, just like he said, just like these sickos are planning on doing. It's almost like somebody's following a script or something, go figure! But here's that text:

Revelation 6:1-8: "I watched as the Lamb opened the first of the seven seals. Then I heard one of the four living creatures say in a voice like thunder, 'Come!' I looked, and there before me was a white horse! Its rider held a bow, and he was given a crown, and he rode out as a conqueror bent on conquest. When the Lamb opened the second seal, I heard the second living creature say, 'Come!' Then another horse came out, a fiery red one. Its rider was given power to take peace from the earth and to make men slay each other. To him was given a large sword. When the Lamb opened the third seal, I heard the third living creature say, 'Come!' I looked, and there before me was a black horse! Its rider was holding a pair of scales in his hand. Then I heard what sounded like a voice among the four living creatures, saying, 'A quart of wheat for a day's wages, and three quarts of barley for a day's wages, and do not damage the oil and the wine!' When the Lamb opened the fourth seal, I heard the voice of the fourth living creature say, 'Come!' I looked, and there before me was a pale horse! Its rider was named Death, and Hades was following close behind him. They were given power over a fourth of the earth to kill by sword, famine and plague, and by the wild beasts of the earth."

You know, because the wild animals are going to be hungry too! I don't know, maybe it's just me, but I'm kind of thinking that doesn't sound like a good time to me! Anyone else?

Yeah, and that's what you get when you cut a deal with the actual Antichrist that the Bible warned about nearly 2,000 years ago, which is exactly what these Global Leaders, including Klaus Schwab, are doing right now, before our very eyes! They're laying the groundwork for it all!

The Bible says their so-called utopia quickly descends into an Antichrist nightmare very quickly! You immediately go into a global war, global famine, and global death of one-fourth of the population of the planet dying, nearly two billion people, which is precisely what these sick twisted people want! It's murderous and satanic.

Chapter Two

Klaus Schwab World Economic Forum & Brain Chips

But my question is, "How in the world did we get here, especially in such a short amount of time? What is this World Economic Forum that seems to be a part of this? What does this have to do with Klaus Schwab and the Global Elites around the world who are working with him to create this wicked, evil satanic agenda?

And what is this Great Reset utopia vision they keep talking about? Is it really a wonderful man-made utopia? Or is it simply, as we saw in our last documentary, a rehashed, repackaged, relabeled, Hitlerian nightmare, preparing the way for the actual Antichrist himself, which will make Hitler look like chump change?"

Well, that was a mouthful, so let's begin with that first question concerning Klaus Schwab and the World Economic Forum. In our last documentary, **Klaus Schwab, the Third Reich & the Covid-19 Holocaust, w**e left off in our historical journey, to the time that Klaus got married to his wife Hilde. It revealed that both of their children are now grown up and are a vital part of Klaus's cadre of global megalomaniacs, helping to institute this new and improved Hitlerian agenda across the whole planet.

But what also helped him to begin the process of global transformation was a global economic think tank he created, called, The World Economic Forum. So, let's see how that began, as this researcher exposes:

"Born in Ravensburg, Germany in 1938, Klaus Schwab is a child of Adolf Hitler's Germany, a police-state regime, built on fear and violence, on brainwashing and control, on propaganda and lies, on industrialism and eugenics, on dehumanization and 'disinfection,' on a chilling and grandiose vision of a 'new order' that would last a thousand years."

Schwab seems to have dedicated his life to reinventing that nightmare and to trying to turn it into a reality, not just for Germany, but for the whole world.

Worse still, as his own words confirm time and time again, his technocratic fascist vision is also a twisted transhumanist one, which will

merge humans with machines in 'curious mixes of digital-and-analog life,' which will infect our bodies with 'Smart Dust,' with which the police will apparently be able to read our brains.

And, as we will see, he and his accomplices are using the Covid-19 crisis to bypass democratic accountability, to override opposition, to accelerate their wicked agenda, and to impose it on the rest of humankind, against our will, in what he terms a 'Great Reset.'

This new fascism is today being advanced in the guise of global governance, biosecurity, the 'New Normal,' the 'New Deal for Nature' and the 'Fourth Industrial Revolution.' Schwab, the octogenarian founder and executive chairman of the World

Economic Forum, sits at the center of this matrix like a spider on a giant web.

The original fascist project, in Italy and Germany, was all about a merger of state and business, using the state to protect and advance the interests of the wealthy elite.

Schwab was continuing this approach in a post-WWII context, when in 1971 he founded the European Management Forum, which held annual meetings at Davos in Switzerland. Here he promoted his ideology of 'stakeholder' capitalism in which businesses were brought

into closer cooperation with the government.

And where 'businesses' or 'stakeholders,' would design everything to meet the needs of all 'stakeholders' and 'privately shovel money to themselves and executives, while maintaining a public front.'

In other words, businesses and governments control it all without any public voice or approval. This is why the 'stakeholder' concept is nefarious because it discards any idea of democracy, or rule by the people, in favor of rule by

corporate interests. Society is no longer regarded as a living community but as a business, whose profitability is the sole aim of all human activity.

And Schwab set out this agenda back in 1971 in his book 'Modern Enterprise Management in Mechanical Engineering' where his use of the term 'stakeholders' effectively redefined human beings not as citizens, free individuals or members of communities, but as secondary participants in a massive commercial enterprise.

We're just a cog in the wheel who exist for them!

The aim of each and every person's life is 'to achieve long-term growth and prosperity' for this enterprise – in other words, to protect and increase the wealth of the capitalist elite.

This all became even clearer in 1987, when Schwab renamed his European Management Forum, the World

Economic Forum.

The WEF describes itself on its own website as, 'the global platform for public-private cooperation,' and describes how it creates 'partnerships between businessmen, politicians, intellectuals and other leaders of society to define, discuss and advance key issues on the global agenda.'

These 'partnerships,' that the WEF creates, are aimed at replacing democracy with a global leadership of hand-picked, unelected individuals, whose duty is not to serve the public, but to impose the rule of the 1% on that public, with as little interference from the rest of us as possible.

Everything in this world is to be reduced to economic challenges, economic imperatives, and economic benefits for the ruling capitalist class. And it is this economic imperative that Klaus Schwab enthusiastically shares that will provide, 'a revolution that is fundamentally changing the way we live, work, and relate to one another' and he insists it will be, 'unlike anything humankind has experienced before.'

Then he gushes over this dystopian fascist nightmare by gleefully saying, "Consider the unlimited possibilities of having billions of people connected by mobile devices, giving rise to unprecedented processing power, storage capabilities and knowledge access.

Or think about the staggering confluence of emerging technology breakthroughs, covering wide-ranging fields such as Artificial Intelligence (or AI), robotics, the internet of things (IOT), autonomous vehicles, 3D printing, nanotechnology, biotechnology, materials science, energy storage and quantum computing, just to name a few. Many of these innovations build on and amplify each other, in a fusion of technologies across the physical, digital and biological worlds."

Which is why he has repeatedly called for people to get used to the idea of getting microchipped themselves, just like all our products.

Klaus Schwab is the founder and chairman of the World Economic Forum in Davos which annually brings together the heads of state of the world's major countries to discuss the future of world affairs. In this interview on January 10, 2016, with the Swiss channel RTS, he explains that human beings will soon receive a chip in their body in order to merge with the digital world. People who see this excerpt from the interview should remember that Klaus Schwab is the designer and promoter of the Great Reset, officially launched at the Davos Forum in January 2021.

In 2020, Klaus Schwab said that Covid-19, is a "rare but narrow window of opportunity to rethink, reinvent, reset our world." We won't be able to say I didn't know…

RTS Channel Interviews Klaus Schwab: *"Today at the end of this, we are talking about chips that can be implanted. When will that be?"*

Klaus Schwab: *"Certainly in the next ten years. At first, we implant them in our clothes. And then we could imagine that we will implant them in our brains, or in our skin. And in the end, maybe there will be a direct communication between our brain and the digital world."*

Boy, of all places for him to suggest we humans get microchipped. Just like all other "products" on the planet, it just happens to be in the head. Again, it's almost like somebody's following a script.

Because it just so happens, that that's exactly where the Bible says people will be taking the Mark of the Beast, under the Antichrist's coming global nightmare, in the 7-year Tribulation. It's either the right hand or the forehead.

Revelation 14:9-10: "If anyone worships the beast and his image and receives his mark on the forehead or on the hand, he, too, will drink of the wine of God's fury, which has been poured full strength into the cup of His wrath."

In other words, you're doomed if you take that "mark", which is why you need to get saved *now* through Jesus Christ so you can escape this horrible timeframe that we see being built right before our very eyes, by Klaus and the gang! Jesus Christ is the only way out of this mess! I didn't say it, He did!

John 14:6: "Jesus answered, 'I am the way and the truth and the life. No one comes to the Father except through Me.'"

But Klaus' words and behavior get even worse! He then goes on to describe this sick satanic vision for the whole planet to be microchipped on a massive scale, creating a type of surveillance state for all the people left behind at the Rapture.

"Klaus also looks forward to even more chips or sensors 'installed in homes, clothes and accessories, cities, transport, and energy networks, and to smart cities, with their all-important data platforms.

"All things will be smart and connected to the internet, says Schwab, and this will extend to animals, as sensors wired in cattle can communicate to each other through a mobile phone network."

He also loves the idea of, "smart cell factories, which could enable the accelerated generation of vaccines and big-data technologies."

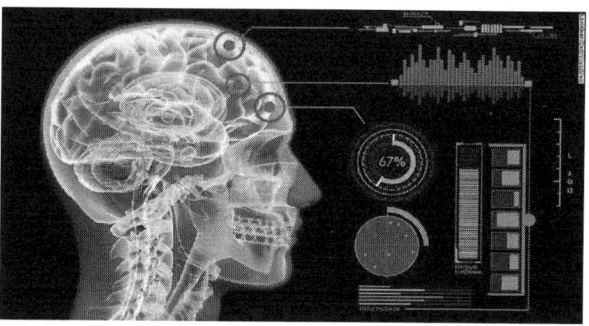

And he assures us it will, "deliver new and innovative ways to serve citizens and customers," and we will have to stop objecting to businesses profiting from and harnessing and selling information about every aspect of our personal lives. As he insists, 'Establishing trust in the data and algorithms used to make decisions will be vital.'"

But at the end of the day, it is clear that all this technological excitement revolves purely around profit, or 'value' as Schwab prefers to put it, with blockchain technology becoming the 'driving force behind massive flows of products and services, providing secure digital identities that can make new markets accessible to anyone connected to the internet.'

In general, the technologies of the 4IR, or The Fourth Industrial Revolution, for the ruling business elite, rolled out via 5G, pose unprecedented threats to our freedom, as Schwab concedes, "The tools of the Fourth Industrial Revolution enable new forms of surveillance and other means of control that run counter to healthy, open societies."

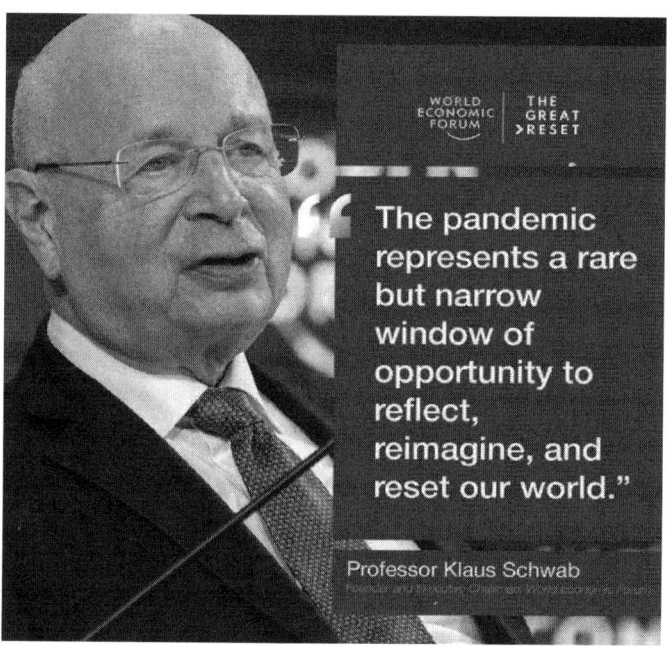

But he spins it in a positive light, saying, *"Public crime is likely to decrease due to the convergence of sensors, cameras, AI and facial recognition software."*

Then he even goes on to describe, while relishing how these new technologies, *"Can intrude into the private space of our minds, reading our thoughts and influencing our behavior."*

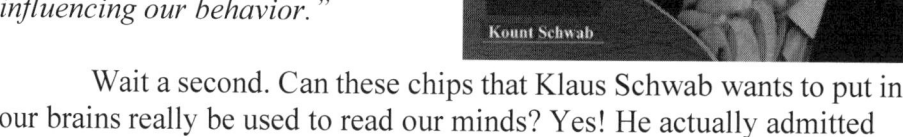

Wait a second. Can these chips that Klaus Schwab wants to put in our brains really be used to read our minds? Yes! He actually admitted that's exactly what those brain chips will allow him to do, as seen here in this next interview:

It features Klaus Schwab interviewing Sergey Brin at the World Economic Forum in 2017, the very next year after he mentions putting brain chips in people's heads as we saw before.

And, by the way, Sergey Brin is one of the co-founders of Google, the other one being Larry Page, who are also helping to create the AI, or Artificial Intelligence system needed to run the backend of Klaus' Antichrist system that will help micromanage the whole planet as outlined in the dystopian vision we just saw of Klaus Schwab.

But watch how Klaus Schwab admits what these brain chips will allow him to do to us, because as he puts it, "We're all going to get them."

Klaus Schwab: *"Can you imagine, that in ten years, when we are sitting here, and we all have implants in our brains? I can immediately feel, because you all,* (he waves his hand across the audience) *will have implants. I can measure your brainwaves, and I can immediately tell you how people react to your answers. Is that imaginable?"*

Sergey Brin: *"I think that is imaginable, I think, ummm..."*

I don't know about you, but to me, it's almost like Sergey Brin is stumbling, pausing, like he's saying in his head, "Dude, I can't believe you just let the cat out of the bag, in public! You're not supposed to do that! Are you nuts?! People aren't supposed to know all this, they'll freak out!"

But either way, as you can see, they really have plans for all of us getting these "brain chips," so they can read our minds! Talk about a Prison Planet. No wonder Jesus said to avoid this time frame by getting saved through Him now before it's too late!

But this is also what the Book of Revelation implies that the actual Antichrist and the False Prophet will be able to do in the 7-year Tribulation.

Revelation 13:15-18: "He was given power to give breath to the image of the first beast, so that it could speak, and cause all who refused to worship the image to be killed. He also forced everyone, small and great, rich and poor, free and slave, to receive a mark on his right hand or on his forehead, so that no one could buy or sell unless he had the mark, which is the name of the beast or the number of his name. This calls for wisdom."

Wisdom is right! But how are the False Prophet and Antichrist going to know who obeys their order to worship the image of the Antichrist all over the planet, all at the same time?

Simple. If you can get everyone to get these brain chips, Klaus Schwab and the gang and Sergey Brin are talking about, they would instantly know anybody's thoughts, anywhere on the planet, whether or not they obeyed, all at the same time, in real time, with AI running the whole system!

And again, if you have not seen our massive study on Artificial Intelligence, I encourage you to get it as well.

It's called **The AI Invasion** and we expose how these Global Elites really are invading the whole planet with AI, or Artificial Intelligence, just in time to create this Antichrist system that Klaus Schwab is envisioning and implementing for us.

But that's still not all he's working towards. Schwab also predicts, *"As capabilities in this area improve, the temptation for law enforcement agencies, and courts, to use these techniques to determine the likelihood of criminal activity, assess guilt or even possibly retrieve memories, directly from people's brains, will increase.*

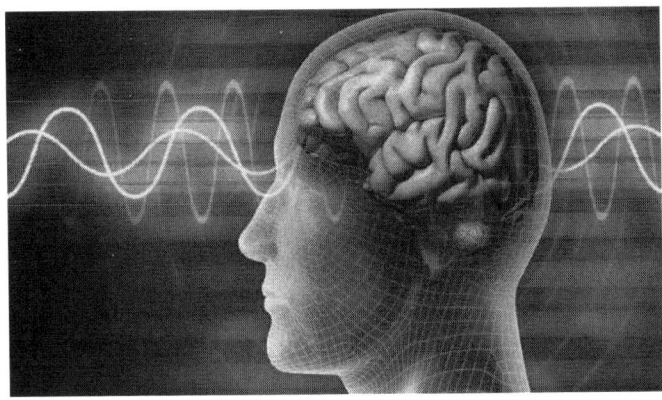

Even crossing a national border might one day involve a detailed brain scan to assess an individual's security risk."

Now wait a second. This is starting to sound like another movie premise. You know, like the one Tom Cruise was in, called "Minority Report." Let's take a look at what was going on in that movie premise for those of you who may not have seen it.

This is a clip from the *Minority Report* movie which is called Pursuit:

Tom Cruise, the main character, strolls down a hallway in what might be a shopping mall. There are advertisements on each side of the walkway. One is advertising Lexus. As he walks through the hallway, there are voices coming from each advertisement screen. It is a mixture of voices so heavy that you can't really understand anything they are saying. When he passes each ad, it scans his eyeball and validates who he is. He hears his name being called out, and then on the screen, he sees his name spelled out in large letters, "John Anderton, member since 2037." And these ads call out to him, "have a beer, take a vacation, how'd you like those gap tank tops you bought?" And he keeps walking as if he is on a mission.

Meanwhile in the office, men are watching as he walks through the mall. Tom Cruise has come up on their monitor as "Eyedentiscan Match."

He, (Tom Cruise) is headed to the Department of Precrime in Washington, D.C. He passes a very pregnant lady that he knows, greets her, hands her his jacket, and then asks if she is having any contractions. And she replies, *"Only the ones you give me."* And he then proceeds to go up to the next floor. This is the year 2054.

The next scene is of what looks like a young person's head that is underwater. While it is breathing underwater, a red ball slowly rolls down a small ramp and stops at the end with the word, 'Perpetration,' written on the globe that is enclosing the red ball. We later find out that the things in the water are called, "the twins," and they are the ones that tell of the crimes that are going to happen, the victims, and the one committing the crime. When the red ball drops, the person's name will be spelled out on the globe.

As he (Tom Cruise) walks into the office he greets the men and asks them, *"Hey Jan, what's going on?"*

Operator of the computer: *"Red ball, a double homicide, one male, one female. The killer is male, white, 40. Actually, they nailed the time at 8:04 am. The twins are a little fuzzy on that, so we need confirmation. The location is still uncertain. The remote witnesses are plugged in. This case will be 1108."*

He takes a hand controller from the globe containing the red ball and proceeds to go to the screen.

John Anderton: *"Case number 1108, previsualized by the pre-cogs, recorded on the hollow sphere by pre-crimes Q stacks. My fellow witnesses for case number 1108 are Dr. Katherine James and Chief Justice, Frank Pollard. Good morning."*

Witnesses: *"Good Morning."*

John Anderton: *"Would the witnesses preview and validate number 1108 at this time?"*

Chief Justice Pollard: *"Affirmative, I will validate."*

Dr. Katherine James: *"Go get 'em!"*

Time of murder 8:04 am, that is 24 minutes, 18 seconds from now. Tom Cruise is looking at the large screen while calming music is playing in the background. He raises his arms as if directing an orchestra. As he waves his arms higher, the visualization of the murder is presented on the screen. A very brutal murder. Not only is he seeing the murder take place, but he has a facial recognition of who is doing the brutal act. A white man, 40 years old. Just as the twins had told them. As he moves his hands at different angles, he can look around the room to try to pick up something that will tell where these murders will take place. They find the drivers license with the owner's name and address.

John Anderton: *"We got 'em in the foxhole. CPCD blue and white, set up a perimeter and tell them I'm enroute."*

While kids are playing in the playground, police start falling out of the sky from the helicopter above. They start running towards the address.

When they reach the address of where the murders are to take place, the police crash down through the glass ceiling, catching the two people on the couch by surprise. The police grab the man and woman and start to pull them out of the apartment while John Anderton reaches in the closet and drags the murderer to be out and throws him on the bed. It is the man with glasses, white and 40.

John Anderton: *"Look at me, look at me."*

He scans a ray of light into the man's eye and then reports what the handheld remote reads.

John Anderton: *"Positive for Howard Marks. Mr. Marks, by the mandate of the District of the Pre-Crime Division, I am placing you under arrest for the future murder of Sarah Marks and Donald Dubin, which was supposed to take place today, the 22nd at 0800 hours and 4 minutes."*

Howard Marks: *"No, I didn't do anything. Sarah..."*

John Anderton: *"Give the man his head."*

Howard Marks: *"Don't put that halo on me. Sarah, help me!"*

Danny Witwer: *"Let's not kid ourselves. We are arresting individuals that have broken no law."*

Fletcher: *"But they will. The commission of the crime is itself absolute metaphysics, precognitive future and never wrong."*

Oh yeah, computers are never wrong! Remember that movie? Remember those scenes? They knew wherever you went, wherever you walked, they could identify you and pinpoint your exact location anywhere, anytime. And they could even predict what you would do in the future, based on this constant electronic monitoring.

And as crazy as this sounds, I'm here to tell you, now with AI, Artificial Intelligence, that science fiction movie is about to become our everyday reality if Klaus gets his way! This is the system that Klaus Schwab and his evil gang of Global Elites are building for us, whether we want it or not!

And getting people microchipped in the head or the hand, along with everything else on the planet, you know, the so-called "Smart Cities" that Klaus is promoting, is how the Minority Report becomes our daily report or reality.

And if you don't think this system would ever be put into play, it already has, all around the world in these so-called "Smart Cities." Here's just one easy example.

TYTLIVE, Newscaster #1 reports: *"A Florida teenager has been insensibly harassed by local police after they decided to start using this predictive policing method, in order to essentially accuse people of committing crimes before they have even committed them. It's insane, and it's insane that it is being used already without any real national backlash."*

Newscaster #2: *"Now this is one of the most outrageous things, and now it is spreading like cancer throughout the country. But this case is amazing. So, I want to read you one thing here. They said, 'No, no, no, this is not a precrime. This is intelligence-led policing.' Even though that sounds like precrime. They say that 'this is for people who are destined to a life of crime.' That's a precrime! You say that they are destined for it. They're not destined to a life of crime."*

Newscaster #1: *"And you want to know how invasive their collection process is? They look into everything, like school records. School records were used to allocate students one of four labels: on track, at risk, off track or critical. Getting a D grade, or having a parent or sibling go to prison could be enough to put a child in the 'at risk' category, according to Pasco's own 83-page 'Intelligence-Led Policing Manual.'"*

Newscaster #2: *"Now, guys, just think about that for a second. Did you ever get bad grades in school? They are going to put you on a list for getting bad grades. The police came to this house – they said multiple times throughout the day, almost every day, they were coming in the middle of the night. And then they burst into the house. Insanity, right?!*

Bad grades, then crimes of the brother may be passed on to you. Your brother is on the list, your sister is on the list, now you're all on the list."

Newscaster #1: *"This is actually far worse than what we have experienced in our already terrible justice system. This isn't justice. This is the kind of stuff you would expect in some sort of authoritative government, dictatorial regime. And it just happened and it's not a top news story."*

Newscaster #2: *"No, it's just begun. It's like those science fiction movies where they look for proclivities in your DNA and your background, etc. It's literally begun. This is an NBC News report on it. Florida is an example of one, but it's a police manual that is being spread all across the country."*

DW Reports: *"Right now, somewhere, someone could be giving you a score. A number that would estimate how likely you are to break the law. Which tells the police if they should zero in on you and which could forever change your life and the lives of those around you. And this someone might not be a human being, but a computer.*

So, how do machines try to predict crime? And is it okay to do that? "Techtopia – Predictive Policing."

No, it's not okay, but they're still doing it anyway! And that's just with the information they collect on us with these huge databases they have on us from all aspects of life, like our financial transactions, Social Media posts and interactions, education and medical records, employment or incarceration status, likes, dislikes, political or religious affiliation, as well as our habits and lifestyles. All being constantly monitored on anything computer related, as well as the whole giant CCTV camera systems around the world, spying on us like rats in a cage wherever we go.

Now add to that, a precise microchipping of people in the hand or forehead that will give up not only your precise location, but access to your very thoughts. And as they admitted, with a computer, or Artificial

Intelligence, or AI constantly monitoring it all, it will even be able to predict what we'll do in the future and then deal with us accordingly.

What does that sound like? It's exactly like the *Minority Report* being built right before our very eyes by Klaus and the gang! Once again, Hollywood has prepared us for it, who by the way, also works for Klaus.

In fact, speaking of preparation, Klaus Schwab even then goes on to share his passion for where these brain chips could lead to and how this

new trending business model would involve someone "trading access to his or her thoughts for the time-saving option of typing a social media post by thought alone." Wow! A whole new version of laziness there!

In fact, it continues, "The further one progresses into the world depicted in Schwab's books, the less of a laughing matter it all seems." The truth is that this highly influential figure, at the center of the New Global Order, currently being established, is an out-and-out transhumanist who dreams of an end to natural healthy human life and community.

And believe it or not, Klaus Schwab actually repeats this message time and time again, as if to be sure we have been duly warned by saying, *"The mind-boggling innovations triggered by The Fourth Industrial Revolution, from biotechnology to AI, are redefining what it means to be human.*

The future will challenge our understanding of what it means to be human, from both a biological and a social standpoint. Already, advances in neurotechnologies and biotechnologies are forcing us to question what it means to be human."

And then he spells it out in even more detail in the book, "Shaping the Future of the Fourth Industrial Revolution," where he states, *"The Fourth Industrial Revolution technologies will not stop at becoming part of the physical world around us – they will become part of us. Indeed,*

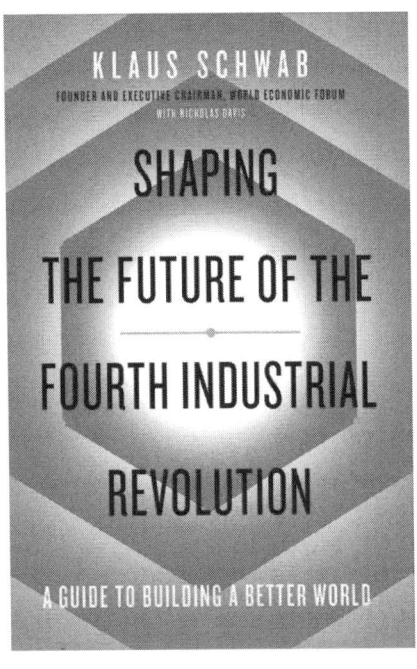

some of us already feel that our smartphones have become an extension of ourselves."

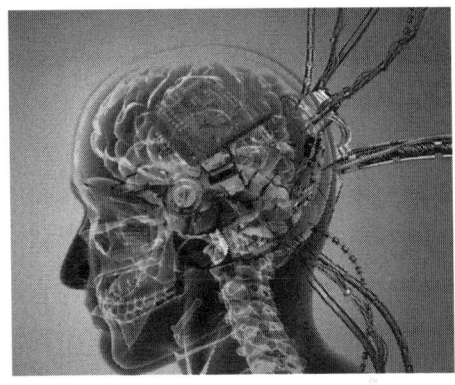

Today's external devices, from wearable computers to virtual reality headsets, will almost certainly become implantable in our bodies and brains.

Exoskeletons and prosthetics will increase our physical power, while advances in neurotechnology will enhance our cognitive abilities. We will become better able to manipulate our own genes, and those of our children. These developments raise profound questions: Where do we draw the line between humans and machine? What does it mean to be human?'

In fact, a whole section of his book is devoted to the theme, 'Altering the Human Being,' as he drools over, "The ability of new technologies to literally become part of us," and invokes a cyborg future involving, "mixing digital and analog life that will redefine our very natures. These technologies will operate within our own biology and change how we interface with the world. They are capable of crossing the boundaries of body and mind, enhancing our physical abilities, and even having a lasting impact on life itself."

Then Schwab dreams of "active implantable microchips that break the skin barrier of our bodies, smart tattoos, biological computing and custom-designed organisms." He is delighted to report that "sensors, memory switches and circuits

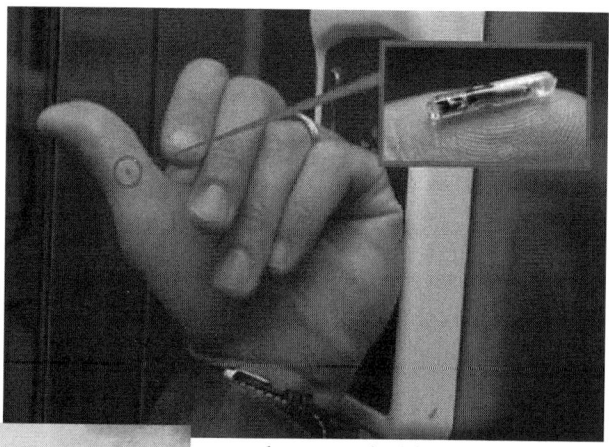

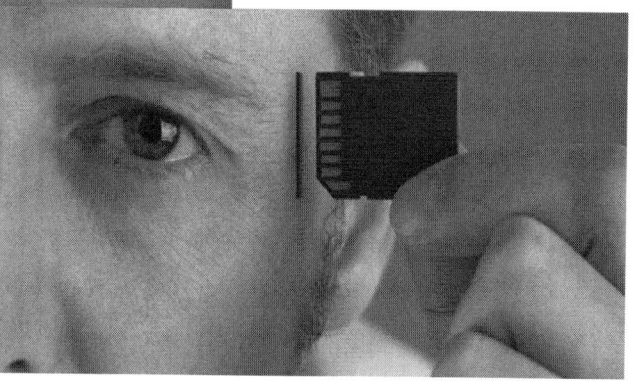

can be encoded in common human gut bacteria, and that Smart Dust, full computers with antennas, each much smaller than a grain of sand, can now organize themselves inside the body, and that implanted devices will likely also help to communicate thoughts, normally expressed verbally through a built-in smartphone, and potentially unexpressed thoughts or moods by reading brain waves and other signals."

And he adds something called, 'Synthetic Biology,' to the horizon of Schwab's Fourth Industrial Revolution world, which will give the technocratic capitalist rulers of the world, 'the ability to customize organisms by writing DNA' and 'neurotechnology's in which humans will have fully artificial memories implanted in the brain.'

This vision of the future is enough to make some of us feel sick. Ethical objections, anyone?

But it gets even worse. Schwab happily announces, *"The day is coming when cows are engineered to produce in its milk a blood-clotting element, which hemophiliacs lack, and pigs will grow organs suitable for human transplantation."*

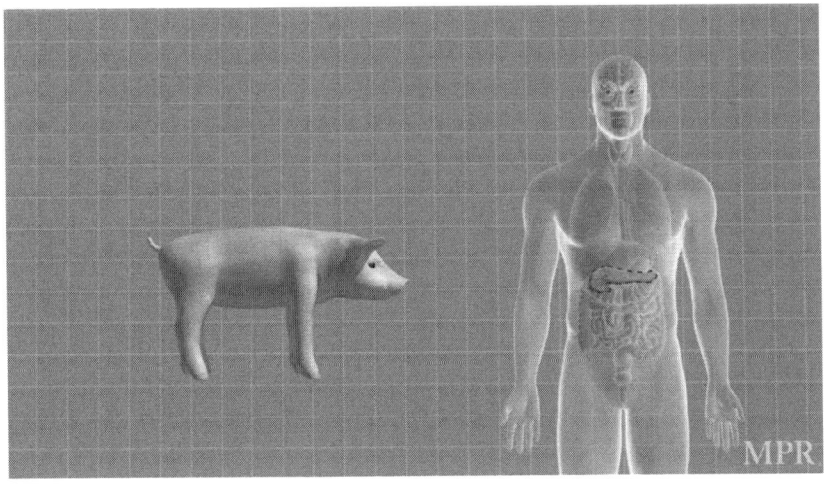

This genetic mixing of humans and animals in the very near future is disturbing, when one considers that the sinister eugenics program of Nazi Germany into which Schwab was born, used to be considered evil and deemed beyond the pale by human society, but now Schwab evidently feels eugenics is due a revival, announcing with regard to genetic editing,

"That it is now far easier to manipulate with precision, the human genome within viable embryos, so that we can have designer babies in the future who possess particular traits, or who are resistant to a specific disease."

And we are even warned by these sick Global Elites that, *"Those who remain as humans are likely to become a sub-species. They will, effectively, be the chimpanzees of the future."*

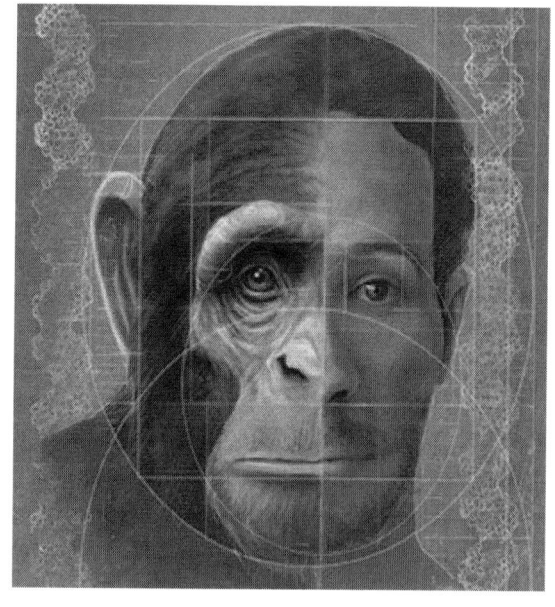

Or as Schwab puts it in his book, The Fourth Industrial Revolution, *"We are at the threshold of a radical systemic change that requires human beings to adapt continuously. As a result, we may witness an increasing degree of polarization in the world, marked by those who embrace change versus those who resist it.*

This ontological inequality will separate those who adapt from those who resist – the material winners and losers in all senses of the words. The winners may even benefit from some form of radical human improvement generated by certain segments of The Fourth Industrial Revolution (such as genetic engineering), from which the losers will be

deprived. These risk creating class conflicts and other clashes unlike anything we have seen before."

Schwab was already talking about this great 'transformation' back in 2016 and is clearly determined to do everything in his power to bring about his eugenics-inspired Transhumanist world of Artificial Intelligence,  surveillance, control, and exponential profit as is outlined in his annual World Economic Forum meetings in Davos, Switzerland."

And to pull this off, "Schwab has become one of the most well-connected men on Earth.

And uses, as the driving force behind this dystopian vision, the World Economic Forum, where Schwab has courted heads of state, leading business  executives, and the elite of academic and scientific circles into the Davos fold for over 50 years, and he is the front man of the Great Reset, a sweeping effort to remake civilization globally, for the express benefit of the Global Elite, the World Economic Forum and their allies."

Chapter Three

World Economic Forum & Global Leaders

So, the question is, "How did he pull this off? How did Klaus Schwab, a German born, Nazi influenced guy, get so many Global leaders and Elites and Governments around the world, to join him in creating this sick, evil, twisted, satanic Hitler revived, dystopian vision, this New World Order, The Fourth Reich, which he tries to pacify us by calling it The Fourth Industrial Revolution also known as The Great Reset?"

Well, the **first way** he did it was by controlling **WORLD LEADERS**. Believe it or not, many years ago, Klaus Schwab knew he couldn't pull this sick, twisted, satanic, dystopian, nightmare off for all our futures by himself. No way, not even close. So, this is why he created a group, years ago, basically a Global Recruitment Camp within the World Economic Forum called, "The Young Global Leaders Program."

There he groomed these future worker bees to aid him in implementing his evil, wicked, dystopian, global agenda upon the whole planet. But of course, you're not supposed to know or see that, so they pitch themselves as some sort of altruistic group of goody-two-shoes, who are only here to help lead us into a time of modern Utopia, as you can see falsely being promoted here.

Helena Leurent, World Economic Forum: *"We recognize that the world is changing at an incredible pace. What the World Economic Forum does is bring together leaders from all different backgrounds, and from all different walks of life. That creates a unique space for new ideas and new solutions to flourish."*

WORLD ECONOMIC FORUM – OUR STORY

Sarita Nayyar, World Economic Forum: *"It's really a very unique place. It's a place where industry comes together to work with the government, to work with NGOs, Academics, to truly make a difference in the world."*

David Aikman, World Economic Forum: *"Leaders come together because of their own personal commitment to one another. To seek follow-up to the discussions that they had at our meetings."*

Jeremy Howard: *"I am generally really skeptical about panels and debates and presentations and what not. But I was actually surprised to discover, in the last year, it makes a huge difference."*

HOW MUCH CAN WE GIVE FOR THAT WE GET?

Klaus Schwab, Founder and Executive Chairman, World Economic Forum: *"Suppressing challenges in a complex, interconnected, fast moving world cannot be met by one stakeholder group alone. It needs collaborative efforts."*

Saadia Zahidi, World Economic Forum: *"Magic moments happen all the time at the World Economic Forum, where the right kind of constituent unexpectedly will come together with somebody else who's looking for exactly that expertise."*

"Not only do the multi-stakeholder groups that we bring together, talk, they also make changes."

Katherine Milligan, World Economic Forum: *"A lot of the answers reside with practitioners, civil society voices, social entrepreneurs, young people and others who are on the ground, working with these populations at the front lines and finding solutions."*

Sanjana Govindani Jayade, Global Shaper, Banglador Hub, India: *"It challenges all your assumptions about your existing worldview, regardless of which part of the world you're from and how much experience you have."*

Indra Nooyi, PepsiCo, USA: *"Nowhere in the world is there another forum which brings together governments, NGOs, corporate leaders, activists, artists, musicians, to all come together and talk about the biggest issues facing the world."*

See, it's just a group of Elites from all walks of life working with Klaus Schwab to talk about the issues of the world for our own benefit. Really? Or is it Global Elites from Governments, Businesses, Hollywood, Entertainment, Media, Politicians, Billionaires and Tech Moguls around the world helping Klaus Schwab to take over the world? I think the answer is obvious, as you'll clearly see as we continue to progress.

But this is how they pitch themselves, as they literally meet on an annual basis, to take over the planet, remove our individual sovereignty and freedom, replace it with the Elites being served by the rest of us, who they allow to serve them as worker bees for their New World Order, the Great Reset, Fourth Industrial Revolution, whatever you want to call it. And they got it set up so that the average Joe, you and I, will never be able to join them in their meetings as Elites.

For instance, Schwab keeps the annual WEF meetings exclusive by limiting the Forum's memberships to 1,000 of the world's biggest corporations, which pay $39,000 a year for the privilege. Admission to the annual meeting is an additional $20,000. But those who work for governments, non-profits, and media outlets, get to go for free.

Schwab also bans those who have been indicted or whose companies are bankrupt. And if you're retired, you can't go either, no matter who you used to be.

Schwab is also the master scheduler, who has to juggle the lineups to accommodate egos, Bill Clinton won't attend unless he gets a primo speaking slot.

Arnold Schwarzenegger canceled an event in 2007 after breaking his leg in a skiing accident.

And no one really knows who will succeed Schwab. A survivor of prostate cancer, he had hoped that José María Figueres, one of the Forum's chief executives and a former president of Costa Rica would

take over. That idea was abandoned though, after Figueres had to resign upon failing to disclose $900,000 in consulting fees."

So again, unless you've got big bucks or big connections, you'll never step foot in these meetings that gather annually to discuss and plan out how best to take over the planet, because we're not Elites like them.

And fortunately, people are starting to catch on to the real motives of Klaus Schwab, the World Economic Forum and these Global Elites, as this investigator shares:

"If you think that the COVID-19 'outbreak' was an accident, think again.

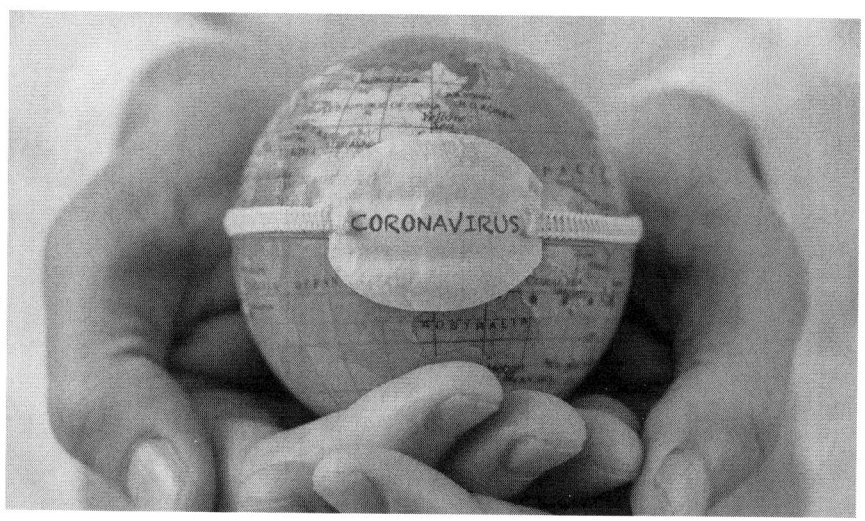

This has been in the works for decades, just waiting for the right reason to initiate it.

The great minds of the world's elite, who believe they are smarter than the peons that work for them, and they have the right to rule everything you do, have decided that it is time for the serfs to give up what

freedoms they now have and just do what they are told.

The World Economic Forum (WEF), has taken on the role of overseer of the whole world, believing that they need to be the ones who decide what you do, when you do it, and how you do it, and if they even think you should be allowed to do it. They also believe that because of their high intelligence and wisdom, they will be able to avoid world disasters and even pandemics.

I think we heard this same rhetoric garbage about the United Nations. They would stop all wars and control rogue nations. How'd that work out for us?

Saddam Hussein invaded Kuwait, and most Arab countries, are continually attacking Israel. But Israel is the one the UN sanctions. The Russia-Ukraine war, nothing to see here, move along. The WEF is just another attempt at global control by the global elite. Prove me wrong.

The WEF was initiated in 1971 by Klaus Schwab, with the goal of raising up world leaders, to look at only the globalist point of view, and seeing the average citizen as 'useless eaters.'

Another important piece of information through the WEF, initiated by Klaus Schwab in 1971, Mr. Global has been training his own puppets since 1992, through the Young Global Leaders Program.

Angela Merkel and Bill Gates were among the first class to graduate in the class of 1992. Even a large number of current leaders, politicians, predominantly weak personalities, with mostly well-trained rhetorical skills, also come from this program, including Justin Trudeau in Canada.

We can see what these so-called leaders are striving for, the New World Order (NWO). The WEF firmly believes that there are too many people on the planet. Isn't it funny that God didn't see that happening?

These arrogant fools think they have the answers to their made-up problems. Liberals always seem to invent a problem, and then try to convince you that they have the answer to solve that problem. Can you say climate change?

Dr. Reiner Fuellmich has been exposing the real agenda of the WEF for a while and believes that it must be stopped as quickly as possible. Their goal is to hold those who are responsible for this pandemic accountable

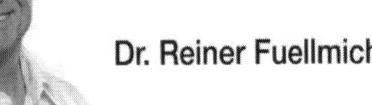

Dr. Reiner Fuellmich

under both civil and criminal law.

The Berlin Corona Committee now has extremely incriminating evidence proving that this Corona Plandemic never had anything to do with health. Rather, Mr. Global's (Klaus Schwab's) actions are aimed solely at these goals – destruction of regional economies to make the population dependent on Mr. Global's global supply chains, shifting the wealth of the world's population from the bottom to the top, to the super rich, to Mr. Global's population reduction.

No matter what word was being used to describe the pandemic and the fallout from the government overreach, Dr. Fuellmich concluded, *"You can call it genocide, as well as Mr. Global gaining total control over the remaining population, and the installation of a world government under the UN, which is now in control of the World Economic Forum. We are dealing with megalomaniac psychopaths and sociopaths who must be stopped, and in fact should have been stopped a very long time ago."*

The WEF doesn't stand on the mountain top and shout their intentions, but they aren't silent about it either. One of the major funders of the WEF is George Soros.

Anything that Soros is involved with is not good for America or the American people.

When it comes to those that have endorsed the WEF that are in our government, it is a list of who's who:

Bill Keating Congressman from Massachusetts (D), Daniel Meuser Congressman from Pennsylvania (R), Madeleine Dean Congresswoman from Pennsylvania (D), Ted Lieu Congressman from California (D), Ann Wagner Congresswoman from Missouri (R), Christopher A. Coons Senator from Delaware (D), Darrell Issa Congressman from California (R), Dean Phillips Congressman from Minnesota (D), Debra Fischer Senator from Nebraska (R), Eric Holcomb Governor of Indiana (R), Gregory W. Meeks Congressman from New York (D), John W. Hickenlooper Senator from Colorado (D), Larry Hogan Governor of Maryland (R), Michael McCaul Congressman from Texas (R), Pat Toomey Senator from Pennsylvania (R), Patrick J. Leahy Senator from Vermont (D), Robert Menendez Senator from New Jersey (D), Al Gore Vice-President of the United States (1993-2001) (D) just to name a few.

As you can see, the traitors to the American way of life are from both political parties. And I think you can see now why the WEF believes that this is the time for the Great Reset. The world population has shown its willingness to be shoved

in a box and do what we are told.

Americans aren't quite ready for this though. Some are, but we still have that God-given desire to be free, and we still have guns at our disposal to make sure it stays that way.

And for those that have read the book, "1984," you will recognize many of its features in the UN's and WEF's Agenda 2030: The World Economic Forum's Agenda 2030, is a dystopian nightmare that's chalk full of evil agendas, such as population control, eradicating livestock (save for the Elites), and replacing it with synthetic meat, forcing the masses to consume insects and live in pods  (you will own nothing and be happy), a digital takeover of everything, achieve total surveillance control, and consolidating power within a multinational globalist body that supersedes all other governments.

Essentially, once all institutions are razed to the ground, it will be the all-out technocratic reign of the elitists.

Any American politician that supports this organization can only be classified as a traitor. The WEF is an organization that we must stop, and we must stop it now!"

And I would wholeheartedly agree. Which is another reason why we're doing this study. But so much for being a simple, kind-hearted group of altruistic goody-two-shoes, only here to help us, for our highest good. Yeah, right! What a joke!

Yet, this is what Klaus Schwab, the World Economic Forum, and all his Young Global Leaders are all about! He groomed and planted all these Young Global Leaders around the world, and they do the bidding of Klaus and the gang, advancing his sick, twisted, evil, globalist agenda, as you can see here.

Ezra Levan, Rebel News Reports: *"So what is the World Economic Forum? It's the oligarchs who meet in that luxury town of Davos. The scheme about this plan is, it's for your world. They are the ones who talk about the great reset, all the time. The ones who fly on private jets all the time, but they tell you that you can't even drive a car. They are the ones that tell you to eat bugs while they dine on steaks. They are the ones that say, 'You'll own nothing. And you'll be happy.' While they gobble up billions of dollars. They are the ones that believe in transhumanism. It's a hacking of human beings and controlling them."*

Yuval Noah Harari: *"By hacking organisms, at least they gain the power to reengineer the future of life itself."*

Ezra Levan: *"It's just creepy. But their influence is everywhere. Politicians in every country seem to take their talking points from the WEF. Take a look."*

Barack Obama: *"And build it back better."*

Joe Biden: *"It's my plan to build back better."*

Sadiq Khan, Mayor's office London: *"Building back better, our economy."*

The Royal Family Channel: *"Build back better."*

Justin Trudeau: *"This pandemic has provided an opportunity for a reset."*

Ezra Levan: *"So, who is the World Economic Forum? Why do they talk like that? Who is their boss? Klaus Schwab, who looks and sounds like a James Bond supervillain."*

Klaus Schwab: *"The effect will be similar to a World War. And actually, all countries in the world are affected."*

Ezra Levan: *"Why does Justin Trudeau go there so often? What does he talk about with George Soros when they meet there? Politicians in every country are loyal to the World Economic Forum. What's that all about?"*

Klaus Schwab: *"When I mentioned names like Angela Merkel, even Vladimir Putin and so on, all have been young global leaders of the World Economic Forum. But what we are really proud of now, this young generation like Prime Minister Trudeau, the president of Argentina, and so on, so that we penetrate the cabinets. So, yesterday, I was at a reception for Prime Minister Trudeau, and I know that half of his cabinet, or even more than half of his cabinet are actually Young Global Leaders of the World Economic Forum."*

Commentator: *"And that's true in Argentina too."*

Klaus Schwab: *"It's true in France now. I mean the president with the young global leader."*

Narrator: *"Now this is a bit awkward. But during the debate during the Canadian Parliament, an MP asked the inconvenient question and as you can see for yourself, it wasn't exactly welcomed."*

Member of Parliament: *"I have a constituent asking the question about outside interference of our democracy. Klaus Schwab is the head of the World Economic Forum, and he bragged how his subversive WEF has quote 'infiltrated governments around the world.' He said that his organization had penetrated more than half of Canada's cabinet. I was wondering, in the interest of transparency, could the member please name which cabinet ministers are on board with the WEF's agenda? My concern is ...."*

Speaker of the House: *"I know that the member had a really good question there, but the audio was really, really bad."*

Narrator: *"The audio was bad. It really sounded good to me. But it wasn't enough for the MP to be silenced, he had to be discredited too."*

Member of Parliament #2: *"Mr. Speaker, that member is promoting open disinformation, that is not debate, we have to call out this information. We'll get into debate again."*

Narrator: *"Disinformation. Disinformation to say that Klaus Schwab is bragging about the World Economic Forum is infiltrating, or in his words, penetrating the government. No, it isn't, here's Klaus Schwab saying exactly that."*

Klaus Schwab: *"When I mentioned names like Angela Merkel, even Vladimir Putin and so on, all have been young global leaders of the World Economic Forum. But what we are really proud of now, this young generation like Prime Minister Trudeau, the president of Argentina, and so on, so that we penetrate the cabinets – so we penetrate the cabinets."*

Narrator: *"Yes, Dr. Strangelove 2.0 is quite proud of penetrating the cabinet in Canada. In fact, diverse media has found at least a dozen Canadians in a position of influence who are on the forum for Young Global Leaders created by the World Economic Forum. Is that disinformation too? These profiles are taken directly from the Young Global Leaders, the old website. So, it's not disinformation, it's* *completely true. You're the only one engaging in disinformation by claiming it is. Bear in mind that three years after Schwab spoke, he said directly, that the pandemic represents an opportunity for a great reset. I think I remember hearing someone else saying something quite similar."*

Justin Trudeau: "*This pandemic has provided an opportunity for a reset."*

Narrator: *"And it wasn't judged by the behavior of the Trudeau regime. The great reset will be achieved with the aid of police using horses to try and pull people in walkers and wheelchairs who protest against it. But I guess that's all just disinformation too, right?"*

Sky News.com AU Reports: *"Somewhere else that seems to be sliding into dictatorship, is Holland, which may not be entirely a coincidence. The similarities between Holland and Canada are as startling as they are disturbing. Here is Canadian Prime Minister Justin Trudeau and Dutch Prime Minister Mark Rutte, leader of the laughingly and ironically named People's Party for Freedom and Democracy. Apart from obviously sharing the same wacky, lefty sense of humor, those two are both of course, 'Golden Pinup Boys' for Klaus Schwab and the Globalist Fanatacists of the World Economic Forum.*

Only a few months ago it was the Canadian government that attacked its own citizens. And in the most grotesque and terrifyingly, authoritarian manner, during the so-called, 'Truckers Convoy Revolts.' When the government actually froze the bank accounts, and basically starved out any individuals involved in what was a legitimate, peaceful, democratic opposition to the Covid mandates. That ended badly for Trudeau, particularly after this shameful incidence in which Canadian mounted police trampled over a peaceful woman protestor."

The video shows several horses being ridden through a thick crowd, pushing people aside with the horses. When the horses had passed the person recording the scene, it came into view that a woman was laying on the ground. The horses had just walked over her. The crowd rushes over to see if she is hurt.

One man in the crowd: *"They just trampled that lady!"*

Sky News.com AU Reports: *"Hold on, I think I saw something like that before. That reminds me ... Oh yes, Melbourne under Dan Andrews."*

This video clip shows hundreds of protesters in the streets of Melbourne. Photographers are scattered around to record just what is going on. Suddenly there is what sounds like machine gun fire. And yelling and screaming, and people running.

Sky News.com AU Reports: *"But I digress. Let's go back to Prime Minister Mark Rutte at the World Economic Forum in Davos last year, boasting about Holland's involvement in the World Economic Forum's global food innovation hubs, which is busily 'transforming food systems and land use.'"*

Mark Rutte: *"I'd like to highlight a World Economic Forum initiative in this regard to the World Economic Forum Food Innovation House. And these Houses, in Africa, and Asia, and South America and Europe, will allow businesses to connect regional stakeholders to Skill Innovations. Because this is key, as Skill Innovations can address Food Systems challenges. Here I am particularly proud to announce that the Netherlands will host the Global Coordinating Secretariat of the World Economic Forum Food Innovation House."*

Sky News.com AU Reports: *"The Houses are set up to transform food systems and land use, eh? I wonder what that means, exactly? Well, your guess is as good as mine. But, as I mentioned last night, currently the Dutch government is embarked upon insane efforts to slash greenhouse gasses and reduce the amount of nitrogen ammonia in the soil by 30-70 percent by 2030, or even up to 95 percent in some places, in order to meet green EU climate change targets that Holland has signed up to. This means literally turfing people off their farms. I guess that's one way to* *transform land use and food systems. Well, the Netherlands House of Representatives has released a statement which said, 'the honest message is that not all farmers will continue in business. Those who do, will have to farm differently.' Wow! Just think about that.*

Everyday, hard-working Dutch family farmers and others are now involved in massive and growing protests. Hardly surprising, with tractor blockades, manure being dumped on government buildings or places, and there are accusations of the Dutch secret police infiltrating the protesters. The same playbook used by Trudeau, allegedly. What a coincidence. And overnight there are even accusations of shots being fired.

This, by the way, is what happens when your national government gets penetrated by globalist activists from the World Economic Forum. Oh, does that sound like a conspiracy theory? Yes, it does, but alas, it's not me saying it, it's dear old Klaus Schwab, back in 2017, fessing up to what the World Economic Forum is really up to."

Klaus Schwab: *"When I mentioned names like Angela Merkel, even Vladimir Putin and so on, all have been young global leaders of World Economic Forum. But what we are really proud of now, this young generation like Prime Minister Trudeau, the president of Argentina, and so on, so that we penetrate the cabinets. So, yesterday I was at a reception for Prime Minister Trudeau, and I would know that half of this cabinet or even more than half of this cabinet, are actually Young Global Leaders of the World Economic Forum."*

Bright Light News Reports: *"What does the everyday, average woman, man, child, how do they fight this? You know, how do they stop this?"*

Robert Malone: *"So, one of the things we tried to do, and I've invested thousands of dollars in this. We are teamed with a group in Sweden which is about to come out with a book on the World Economic Forum. It is currently in Dutch, so we have to get it translated into English and available in the United States. What we have done is compiled a massive spreadsheet of World Economic Forum trainees. Because they are* *everywhere. They are all over America, industry, government, big media, tech, okay? The starting point is that people need to know who they are dealing with. We need to out these people. The term is used, 'doxing.' As far as I'm concerned, with these folks, doxing is good, let's go get them!"*

And that's also what we're doing in this study. We're going to get them, "outing" or "doxing" them so we know what and who we are up against. It's a globally coordinated effort from Klaus Schwab and the World Economic Forum. And Covid, admittedly, was their time to strike and put all their evil, global, sick, twisted plans into place.

And when Schwab laughed and admitted he's got his "puppets" in place, secreted all over the world, he wasn't joking. What you just saw was the tip of the iceberg, as this researcher continues:

"How is it, that more than 190 governments from all over the world ended up dealing with the COVID-19 pandemic in almost exactly the same manner, with lockdowns, mask mandates, and vaccination cards now being commonplace everywhere?"

The answer may lie in the Young Global Leaders school, which was established and managed by Klaus Schwab of the World Economic Forum, and that many of today's prominent political and business leaders passed through on their way to the top.

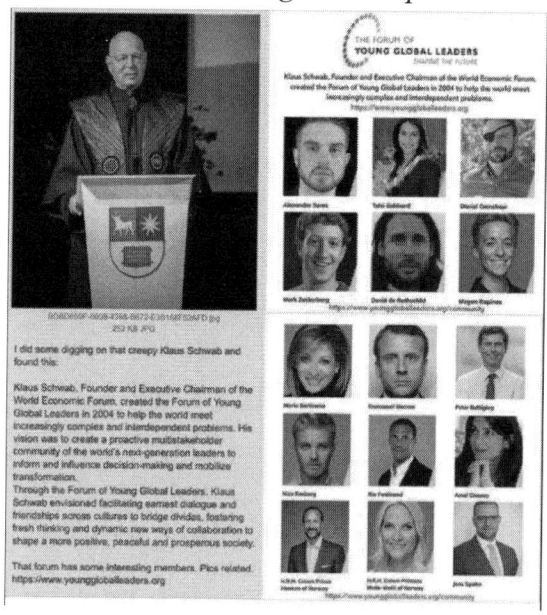

The story begins with the World Economic Forum (WEF), which is an NGO founded by Klaus Schwab, a German economist and mechanical engineer in Switzerland in 1971, when he was only thirty-two.

The WEF is best-known to the public for the annual conferences it holds in Davos, Switzerland each January, that aim to bring together

political and business leaders from around the world to discuss the problems of the day. Today, it is one of the most important networks in the world for the globalist power elite, being funded by approximately a thousand multinational corporations.

The WEF, which was originally called the European Management Forum until 1987, succeeded in bringing together 440 executives from 31 nations already at its very first meeting in February 1971, which was an unexpected achievement for someone like Schwab, who had very little

international or professional experience prior to this.

The reason may be due to the contacts Schwab made during his university education, including studying with no less a person than former National Security Advisor and Secretary of

State, Henry Kissinger. While Schwab was there, the Harvard Business School had been in the process of planning a management forum of their own, and it is possible that Harvard ended up delegating the task of organizing it to him.

The Forum initially only brought together people from the economic field, but before long, it began attracting politicians, prominent figures from the media (including from the BBC and CNN), and even celebrities.

In 1992, Schwab established a parallel institution, the" Global Leaders for Tomorrow" school, which was re-established as "Young Global Leaders" in 2004. Attendees at the school must apply for admission and are then subjected to a rigorous selection process. Members

of the school's very first class in 1992 already included many who went on to become important liberal political figures, such as Angela Merkel, Nicolas Sarkozy, and Tony Blair.

There are currently about 1,300 graduates of this school, and the list of alumni includes several names of those who went on to become leaders of the health institutions of their respective nations, including former and current health ministers.

Other notable names on the school's roster are Jacinda Ardern, the Prime Minister of New Zealand, whose stringent lockdown measures have been praised by global health authorities; Emmanuel Macron, the President of France; Sebastian Kurz, who was until recently

the Chancellor of Austria; Viktor Orbán, Prime Minister of Hungary; Jean-Claude Juncker, former Prime Minister of Luxembourg and President of the European Commission; and Annalena Baerbock, the leader of the German Greens, who was the party's first candidate for Chancellor in this year's federal election.

We also find California Governor Gavin Newsom on the list, who was selected for the class of 2005, as well as former presidential candidate and current US Secretary of Transportation, Peter Buttigieg, who is a very recent alumnus having been selected for the class of 2019.

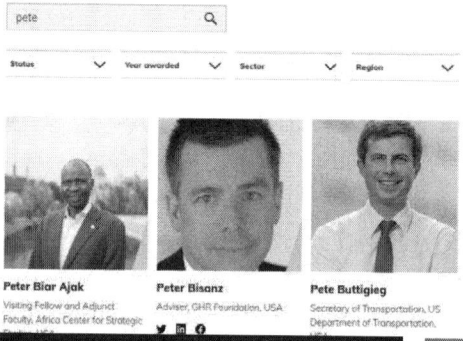

All these politicians who were in office during the past two years have favored harsh responses to the COVID-19 pandemic, and which also happened to considerably increase their respective government's power.

But the school's list of alumni is

not limited to political leaders. We also find many of the captains of private industry Including, Microsoft's Bill Gates, and Amazon's Jeff Bezos, Virgin's Richard Branson, and the Clinton Foundation's Chelsea Clinton.

Again, all of them expressed support for the global response to the pandemic, and many reaped considerable profits as a result of the measures.

The people behind the WEF and the Global Leaders school are the ones who really determine who will become political leaders, and the school's alumni include not only Americans and Europeans, but also people from Asia, Africa, and South America, indicating that its reach is truly worldwide.

Nicolas Sarkozy
Bono
Jorma Ollila (Shell Oil)
José Manuel Barroso (President of the European Commission 2004–2014).
Crown Princess Victoria of Sweden
Crown Prince Haakon of Norway
Crown Prince Fredrik of Denmark
Prince Jaime de Bourbon de Parme, Netherlands
Princess Reema Bint Bandar Al-Saud, Ambassador for Saudi-Arabia in USA
Jacinda Arden, Prime Minister, New Zealand
Alexander De Croo, Prime Minister, Belgium
Sanna Marin, Prime Minister, Finland

Carlos Alvarado Quesada, President, Costa Rica
Faisal Alibrahim, Minister of Economy and Planning, Saudi Arabia
Shauna Aminath, Minister of Environment, Climate Change and Technology, Maldives
Ida Auken, MP, former Minister of Environment, Denmark
Annalena Baerbock, Minister of Foreign Affairs, Leader of Alliance 90/Die Grünen, Germany
Kamissa Camara, Minister of the Digital Economy and Planning, Mali
Ugyen Dorji, Minister of Domestic Affairs, Bhutan
Chrystia Freeland, Deputy Prime Minister and Minister of Finance, Canada
Martín Guzmán, Minister of Finance, Argentina
Muhammad Hammad Azhar, Minister of Energy, Pakistan
Paula Ingabire, Minister of Information and Communications Technology and Innovation, Rwanda
Ronald Lamola, Minister of Justice and Correctional Services, South Africa
Birgitta Ohlson, Minister for European Union Affairs 2010–2014, Sweden
Mona Sahlin, Party Leader of the Social Democrats 2007–2011, Sweden
Stav Shaffir, Leader of the Green Party, Israel
Vera Daves de Sousa, Minister of Finance, Angola
Leonardo Di Caprio, Actor and Climate Activist
Mattias Klum, Photographer and Environmentalist
Jack Ma, Founder of Alibaba
Larry Page, Founder of Google
Ricken Patel, Founder of Avaaz
David de Rothschild, Adventurer and Environmentalist
Jimmy Wale, Founder of Wikipedia
Jacob Wallenberg, Chairman of Investor
Niklas Zennström, Founder of Skype
Mark Zuckerberg, Founder of Facebook

All of these people and more are "advancing a future-oriented global agenda." (In other words, they're working for Klaus).

Then, in 2012, Schwab and the WEF founded yet another institution, 'The Global Shapers Community,' which brings together those identified by them as having leadership potential from around the world who are under thirty. Approximately 10,000 participants have passed through this program to date, and they regularly hold meetings in 400 cities.

This is yet another proving ground where future political leaders are being selected, vetted, and groomed before being positioned in the world's political apparatus.

Given the growing discontent with the anti-Covid measures put into practice by the school's graduates who are now national leaders, it is possible that these people were selected due to their willingness to do whatever they are told.

And they are being set up to fail, so that the subsequent backlash can be exploited to justify the creation of a new global form of government.

This has been especially evident in most countries' response to the pandemic, where politicians who knew nothing about viruses two years ago suddenly proclaimed that Covid was a severe health crisis that justified locking people up in their homes, shutting down their businesses, and wrecking entire economies.

The WEF's current Board of Trustees includes such luminaries as Christine Lagarde, former Managing Director of the International Monetary Fund and President of the European Central Bank; Queen Rania of Jordan, who has been ranked by Forbes as one of the 100 most powerful women in the world; and Larry Fink, CEO of BlackRock, the largest investment management corporation internationally, and which handles approximately $9 trillion annually.

The ultimate conclusion one must draw from all of this, is that democracy as we knew it has been silently canceled, and although the appearance of democratic processes is being maintained in our countries, the fact is, that an examination of how governance around the world works today, shows that an elite of super-wealthy and powerful individuals, effectively control everything that goes on in politics, as has been especially evident in relation to the pandemic response.

The best way to combat their designs, is simply to educate people about what is happening, and for them to realize that the narrative of the "super-dangerous virus" is a lie that has been designed to manipulate them into accepting things that run contrary to their own interests.

If even 10% of ordinary citizens become aware of this and decide to take action, it could thwart the Elite's plans.

And perhaps open a window for ordinary citizens to take back control over their own destinies.

Again, this is another reason why we're doing this study, to educate you and get as many as we can around the world equipped with what these sick, evil, twisted, megalomaniacs are doing.

And for those of you here in America wondering, yes, Joe Biden is also clearly working with Klaus Schwab and the World Economic Forum.

Biden Confirms He's a Puppet of His Globalist Masters: 'There's Going to Be a New World Order'

You must be a conspiracy theorist if you think our leaders believe in a "New World Order" of globalist government, economy, and religion. Yet time and again, they admit it.

by JD Rucker — March 21, 2022 in Conspiracy Theory, News and Opinions

Around the Web

Nevada Seniors Rush To Try Powerful New Cannabis Discovery (Best Pain Relief)
HealthlineNews

What May Happen to Your Manhood if You Have Prostate Problems
Trending Reports

Doctor: "When Wrinkles Get Too Strong, Start Doing This"
HealthSectorNews

We saw this from the very beginning when Biden announced his campaign slogan, "Build Back Better," and the other phrase he used to scare us into voting for him, that of, "We're heading for a Dark Winter." Remember those phrases? Both of them come from the World Economic Forum and Klaus Schwab.

Ukrainian President Zelenskyy is tied to Klaus Schwab, Justin Trudeau, and other global elites

Other "puppets," would also include Ukrainian President Zelensky, which tells you the whole Russia-Ukraine issue is being used by these same globalists to further their agenda. And they're so bold in their global takeover since Covid, that they even bluntly warn us:

"Hand Over Your Sovereignty to the Elite or Die"

"World Economic Forum henchman Yuval Noah Harari warned humanity on Friday that if they refuse to hand their sovereignty over to the Elite, they will face extermination."

They really think they've got us now and there's nothing we can do to stop them, which is not true by the way, and we'll expose the lie in greater detail, Lord willing, in a future study.

And lest you think this is some wacky conspiracy theory, this is all clearly broadcasted on their own website as seen here, where you can search the whole giant database of the World Economic Forum's

Young Global Leaders and see where they're operating, as we speak, in your area, and country, and all over the planet! And this is why we're treated like this. **"Here's how every single government of the westernized world said, I love you."** They're all in it together folks. And this is why they're all speaking the same language.
**"This is when you know your

country is in trouble when your Prime Minister, Justin Trudeau, is paraphrasing Hitler," as you can see there. "Why do we tolerate these people taking up space."

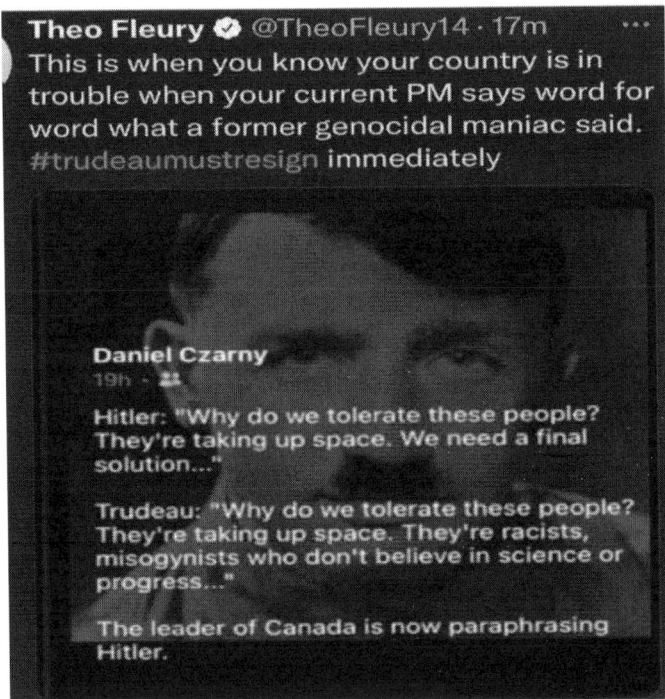

This is also why they keep getting elected.

"What a coincidence that the chosen leaders of the World Economic Forum keep winning elections even though they are absolutely despised by all their citizens?"

And this is why any new positions that come up in the governments around the world are refilled with World Economic Forum plants. Like the latest one in the UK.

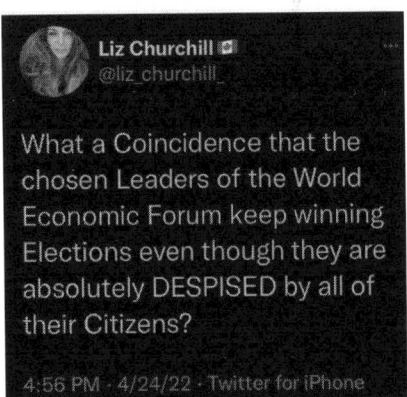

Coup Complete: Globalist Rishi Sunak Installed as Prime Minister of the United Kingdom." And, **"The Free Market Experiment Is Over' – Time for a 'Reset' with Sunak as PM, Says Top Tory."**

And I quote, "The 'reset' comments piqued particular

interest, given Sunak's connections to Klaus Schwab's World Economic Forum (WEF) with Sunak's father-in-law, N. R. Narayana Murthy, the billionaire founder of Indian tech giant, InfoSys, being a listed partner of the Davos-based group." In fact, this picture tells it all.

"The UK now has: WEF King. WEF Prime Minister. WEF Government. WEF Leader of Opposition. WEF Opposition Party. WEF Media.

And don't think this Klaus Schwab and World Economic Forum infiltration has escaped the United States. We just saw after 15 tries Kevin McCarthy finally getting appointed as the Republican Speaker of the House.

But as you can see here he too has direct ties and connection with the

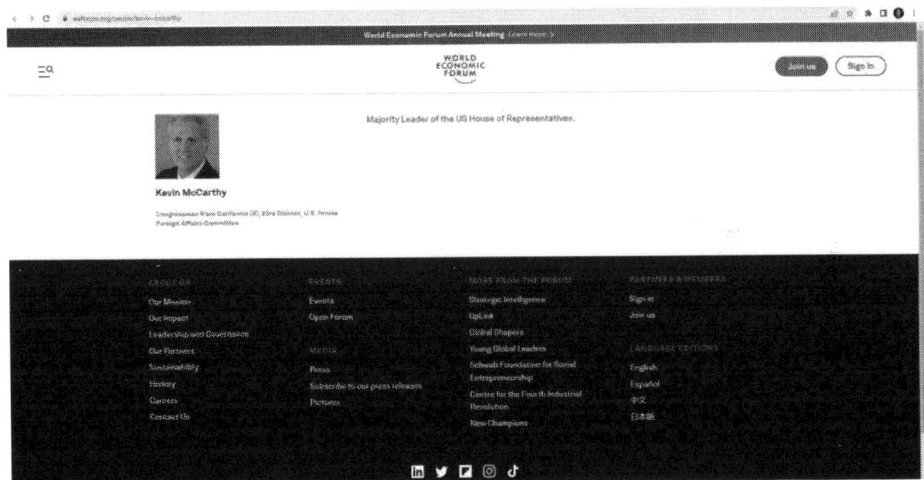

World Economic Forum. Now you know why they kept trying to vote him in after repeated failed attempts, the most in U.S. history. They had to have their WEF guy in place!

And this is also why, "The WEF has argued in favor of governments implementing socialist-style policies, such as wealth taxes and the green agenda. Following the outbreak of the Chinese coronavirus pandemic, founder Klaus Schwab argued that governments around the world, 'must act jointly and swiftly to revamp all aspects of our societies and economies,' and that there is a need for a, 'Great Reset of capitalism.'"

Sound familiar? This is why they were all working together to shut down any and all resisters, social media, bank accounts, your personal life, your transportation, your land, we're all threatened if you

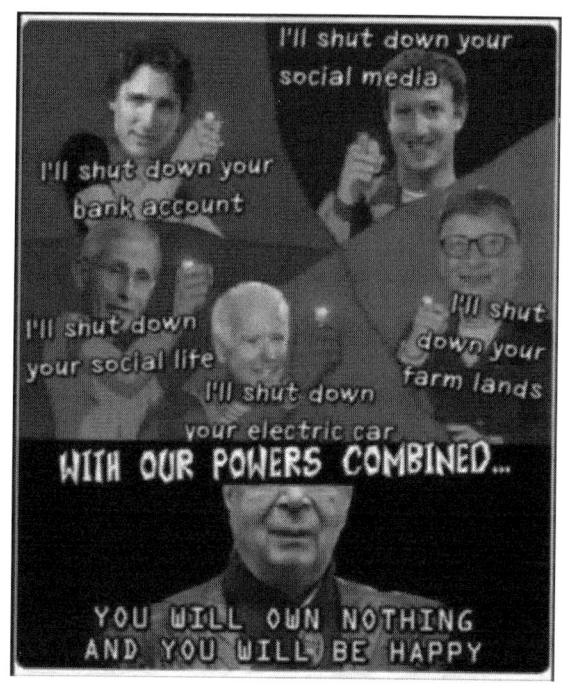

don't go along with their agenda and narrative. They're all working with Schwab.

And, if you get in the way, or have a change of heart, as one of the global leaders who got planted around the world, they will take you out, as you can see here with Japan's Prime Minister.

"Assassinated Japanese Prime Minister didn't follow World Economic Forum orders. He didn't mandate vaccines and he sent back 1.6 million doses and gave his citizens Ivermectin." Can't have that in Klaus' world!

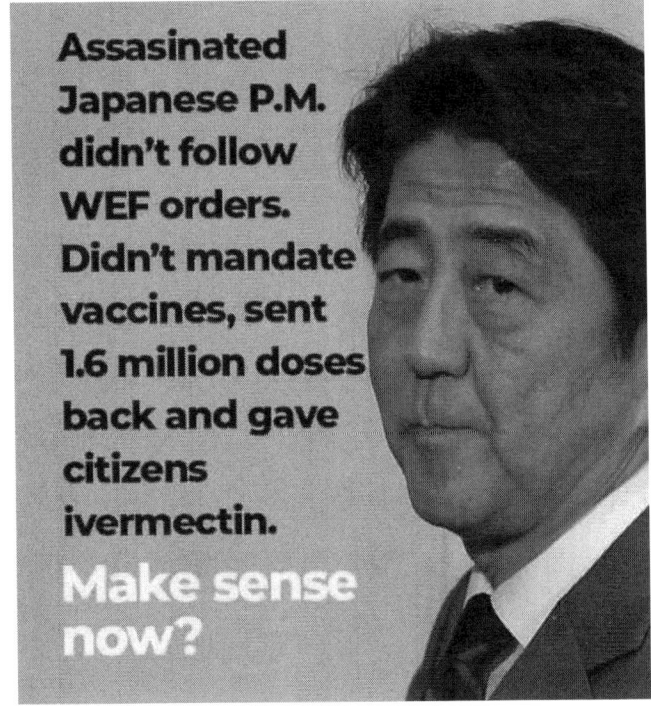

You've always wondered why certain political leaders around the world end up dying or suddenly get forced out of office. Either go along with Klaus and his sick evil twisted dystopian vision for the planet, and be a good trained young groomed Global Leader, or puppy, or you can kiss your career or life goodbye.

These people are sick murderers, just like Hitler! Go figure, given Klaus' background and where he grew up!

But that's not all. You'll also get taken out if you don't go along with the Ukraine issue and support President Zelensky over there, as you can see here.

And by the way, this is why these same people are promoting that conflict.

As you can see, Covid was just the beginning, but it only got them so far. So, stir up some trouble in Ukraine and voila, maybe it will lead to war, and you can keep manipulating people with that crisis, just like you did with Covid to further your evil, wicked agenda. And eventually, all these crises lead to an economic one so you can use that as an excuse to usher in your Great Reset planetary takeover and make yourselves look like saviors, when in fact, you planned the whole thing. Sick, evil, deceptive and twisted. That's all this is. Just like satan, just like Hitler.

And this is also why this gentleman warned, **"No matter how paranoid or conspiracy minded you are, what the government is actually doing is worse than you imagine."**

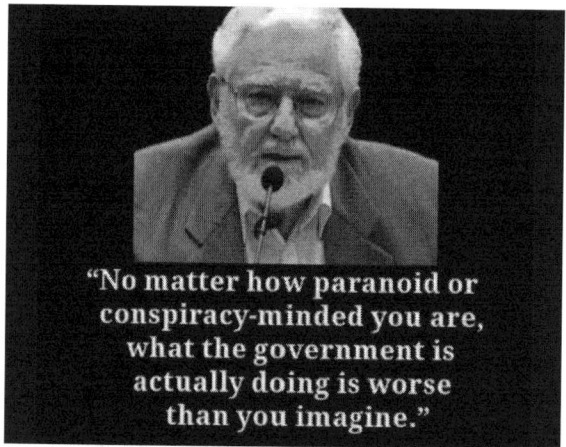

"No matter how paranoid or conspiracy-minded you are, what the government is actually doing is worse than you imagine."

And it's all because as you can see here, they are all carefully, strategically, methodically working together as groups and think tanks, and entities all over the world, to slowly but surely take over the whole planet using generated crisis as the tool to get the job done, as this video shows:

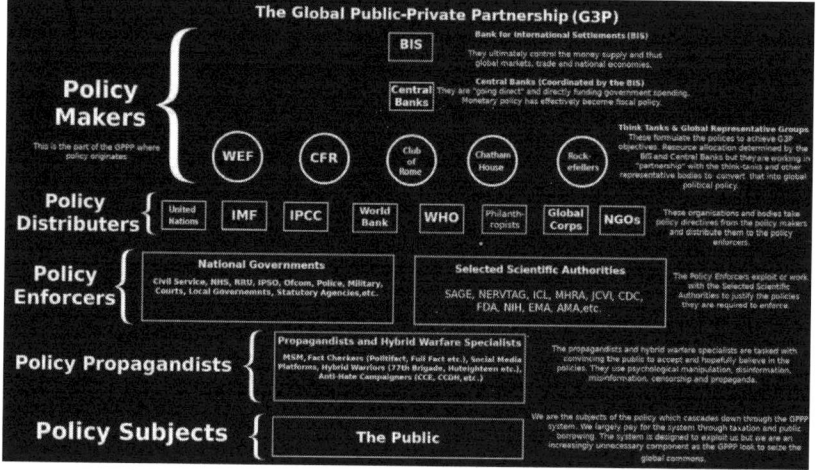

President George Bush: *"A new partnership of the nations has begun. And we stand today, at a unique and extraordinary moment. The crisis in the Persian Gulf, as grave as it is, also offering an opportunity to move toward an historic opportunity. Out of these troubled times, our fifth objective, a New World Order can emerge. A new era, freer from the threat of terror, stronger in the pursuit of justice, and more secure in the quest for peace."*

Klaus Schwab: *"What a pleasure it is to be together again and to design the future. We are here to develop 'The Great Narrative,' a story for the* *future. In order to shape the future, you have first to imagine the future. You have to design the future and then you have to execute. Here I think the next two days we will look how we imagine, how we design, how we execute the 'Great Narratives,' how we define the story of 'our' world for the future."*

Lori Lightfoot, Mayor of Chicago: *"Well, I think we should go ahead and make a deal, we always make a deal, but it's going to be a different kind of deal, because it has to be the kind deal that respects the values of the New World Order."*

Joe Biden: *"One of the top military people said to me in a secure meeting the other day, '60 million people died between 1900 and 1946.' And since then, we have established a New World Order and that hadn't happened in a long while. A lot of people died, but not near the chaos. Now is the time that things are shifting. There could be a New World Order out there and we've got to lead it. We've got to unite the rest of the free world in doing it."*

Jason Whitlock, Fearless Host: *"I think there were two different State of the Union addresses. The first one was the state of the New World Order, and he was talking about bringing unity to all the people around the globe, the countries around the globe, and NATO, and what we could do if we were unified."*

Meet the Press: *"You heard Secretary Blinkin say, 'Sanctions release could happen, it all depends on the behavior of Russia.' And we really live in a world where Putin's let back into the New World Order?"*

Fmr. Sec. Hillary Clinton: *"Well, that's not what I heard him say. What I heard him say was that we are really going to support Ukraine, the people and the government of Ukraine, as they try to figure out what for them is the best way forward. And that, I think, is exactly the right position before the United States, Europe and the West and other countries, to take. Your second part of that question though, was a really important one. I would not allow Russia back into the organization that it has been a* part of. I think there is an upcoming G20 event later in the year that I would not let Russia attend. And if they literally plan on just showing up, I would hope that there would be a significant, if not, total boycott."

Fox News Reports: *"For the rest of us who are Ukrainians, I think the world, quite frankly, is surprised by the will of the Ukrainian people to stand up and fight. How about you?"*

Guest being interviewed: *"Well, I'm not surprised, we have been fighting Putin for the last eight years, we've had three revolutions in our country when we did not agree with what direction we were moving in. Right now, it's a critical time, because we know that we not only fight for Ukraine, we fight for this New World Order."*

Dr. Pippa Malmgren, at the OWO Summit 2022: *"What underpins this New World Order is always the financial system. I was very privileged, my father was the advisor to Nixon when they came off the gold standard in 1971, and so I was brought up in sort of an inside view of how very important the financial structure is to absolutely everything else. What we are seeing in the world today,*

I think, is that we are on the brink of a dramatic change, where we are about to, and I'll say this boldly, we are about to abandon the traditional system of money and accounting and introduce a new one. And the new accounting is what we call block chain, it's digital, it means almost having a perfect record of every single transaction that happens in the economy. Which will give us far greater clarity over what's going on, and it will also raise huge dangers in terms of the balance of power between states and citizens.

In my opinion, we are going to need a digital constitution of human rights, if we are going to have digital money. But also, this new money will be sovereign in nature. Some people think that digital money is crypto and private. But what I see are superpowers introducing digital currency. The Chinese were the first, the U.S. are on the brink, I think, of moving in the same direction. And the Europeans have committed to that as well.

The question is, will that new system of digital money and digital accounting accommodate the competing needs of the citizens of all these locations, so that every human being has a chance to have a better life? Because that's the only measure of whether a World Order will really serve."

Speaker at the World Government Summit 2022: *"Are we ready for a New World Order?"*

Bill Bennett, Former Education Secretary: *"It seems extraordinary, when we could be supplying in all of Europe, and all of Germany, and all of Europe with our liquefied natural gas. And this dilemma would not be faced. But I think the larger perspective that I think we all need to think about, and you brought it up earlier in the newscast, is this new alliance between Russia and China. This New World Order that they are talking about."*

Derek Saul, Forbes Business Staff: *"Russia and China are leading a New World Order."*

General Flynn: *"Someone like Vladimir Putin has now upset this balance of the New World Order that they were trying to achieve by going into Ukraine. And you know, I'm probably the last person that's going to be a Putin apologist. I won't be, but what I do understand are the dynamics that are playing out in Ukraine right now and I sent you something earlier, Clay, and we don't need to go into the details of it, but all of what we are seeing play out in Europe right now is an upsetting of the balance of the World Order as they want it, as people like Dr. Harari, as people like Klaus Schwab and others. Bill Gates is another one. So, we have to understand that. These are people that are very smart. They're very well resourced and they have a very sort of strategic idea of how they want to see the world develop and God and a soul are not part of that strategy."*

And that's why God calls it the Antichrist, or "opposer" of Christ's Kingdom. These guys are building the evil satanic empire that God warned about that would come upon the whole planet nearly 2,000 years ago!

Chapter Four

World Economic Forum & Finances

But that's not all. The second way Klaus Schwab pulled off this sick, twisted, satanic, dystopian nightmare for all of our futures is, he grabbed control of, not only World Leaders, but even **WORLD FINANCES**.

And I mean all of them. You've heard the phrase, "He who makes the gold makes the golden rules." Well, in this case, it's, "He who owns the gold, owns the world, and then makes up all the rules," and that's precisely what Klaus Schwab and his evil gang of Global Elites and Global Graduates have done.

They own just about everything on the planet, and if you think I'm kidding, I'm not, watch this:

Narrator: *"I think by now you have the feeling that something is not right about our current situation. Less than a handful of mega corporations dominate every aspect of our lives. That may seem like an exaggeration, but from the breakfast that's on the table in the morning, to the mattress* we sleep on at night, and everything we do, put on, or consume in between, all are largely dependent on these corporations.

These are investment companies of immense proportions, and they manage the major money flows on Earth. They are the protagonists of the play which we are currently witnessing. So as not to take up too much of your time, I've summarized the most important information as briefly as possible.

How does it work? Let's take as an example, a company like PepsiCo, which is the parent company of many of the most popular soft drinks and snacks in the world. There appear to be many different competing brands, but they all come from the factories of a small number of corporations that together have a monopoly on the industry. Within the packaged food industry, there are a number of other major companies, such as Unilever, the Coca-Cola Company, Mondelez, and Nestle. On this image, you see that virtually every well-known brand in the packaged food industry belongs to one of these corporations.

You can easily get this kind of information. You can verify it on the websites of the relevant brands, or on Wikipedia. Companies of this size are usually publicly traded; and have a board where the largest shareholders call the shots. On websites like Yahoo Finance, we can find detailed company information, including who the largest shareholders of these companies are. Let's take PepsiCo again as an example.

We see that 73.14% of the shares are held by no less than 3,379 institutional investors. These include investment companies, mutual funds, insurance companies, banks, and in some cases, governments. Let's look at who the largest institutional investors of PepsiCo are. As you can see, just ten out of 3,379 investors account for almost one-third of all shares. The combined share capital of these top ten has a value of approximately $60 billion. But of those ten investors, three own more shares than the remaining seven - Vanguard Group, Inc., BlackRock, Inc., and State Street Corporation. Let's remember their names and let's see who owns the most shares in the Coca-Cola company, Pepsi's big competitor.

We see that just like with PepsiCo, the majority of the shares are held by institutional investors. Let's look at the top ten and start with the last one of them. Four out of these six institutional investors, we also saw that at the last six of PepsiCo. These are Northern Trust, JP Morgan Chase & Company, Geode Capital Management, and Wellington Management. Now let's look at the four largest shareholders. Three of these we also saw in the top four at PepsiCo. They are BlackRock, Vanguard, and State Street, and there's another one: Berkshire Hathaway. These are the four largest investment companies on the planet.

PepsiCo and Coca-Cola are anything but competitors, but also the other big companies that own many brands, such as Unilever, Mondelez, and Nestle, are owned by the same small group of institutional investors, and you don't only find these names in the packaged food industry.

For example, let's look up on Wikipedia what the largest companies are within the technology industry. Facebook owns WhatsApp and Instagram. Together with Twitter, they form the most popular social media platforms in the world. Alphabet is the parent company of all Google businesses, including YouTube and Gmail, but they are also the biggest sponsors and developers of Android; one of the two operating systems on which almost all smartphones and tablets in the world run. The other operating system is Apple's IOS. Finally, if we add Microsoft to the other three, we see that four companies produce software that almost all computers, tablets and smartphones in the world depend on.

Let's see who owns the most shares of these powerful companies. If we look at Facebook, we see that more than 80% of the shares are owned by institutional investors. These are the same names we saw in the food industry. Again, the same investors at the top – Vanguard Group, Inc., BlackRock Inc., FMR, LLC., Price (T. Rowe) Associates, Inc, and State Street Corporation. Then Twitter, which with Facebook and Instagram makes up the top three. Amazingly, we see that the company is also owned by the same investors. We see them at Apple – Vanguard Group, Inc, BlackRock Inc., Berkshire Hathaway, Inc., and State Street Corporation – but also with their big competitor Microsoft – Vanguard Group, Inc.,

BlackRock Inc., State Street Corporation, FMR, LLC., Price (T. Rowe) Associates, Inc. and Geode Capital Management. LLC.

When we look at all the other companies that dominate the technology industry and build our computers, TVs, smartphones and household appliances, we see the same big investors who own a majority of the shares: HP – Dodge & Cox Inc, Vanguard Group, Inc, BlackRock Inc., State Street Corp., Primecap Management. Philips – Vanguard International Stock Index-Total Intl. Stock Index., Vanguard Specialized-Health Care Fund, Price (T. Rowe) Overseas Stock Fund., BlackRock Equity Dividend Fund. Intel – Vanguard Group., BlackRock Inc., State Street Corporation, Capital International Investors, Geode Capital Management, LLC., and Northern Trust Corporation. Sony – Primecap Management Company, Aristotle Capital Management, LLC., Fiduciary Management, Inc., Bank of America Corporation, Morgan Stanley, FMR, LLC, Davenport & Company LLC., and BlackRock Inc. IBM – Vanguard Group, Inc., BlackRock Inc., State Street Corporation, Geode Capital Management, LLC., Charles Schwab Investment Management, Inc. Morgan Stanley, Northern Trust Corporation, Bank of New York Mellon Corp. and Norges Bank Investment Management. Dell – Dodge & Cox. Inc, Elliott Investment Management LP., BlackRock Inc., and Vanguard Group, Inc.

We see this within all industries around the world, and just to show you that I'm not exaggerating, I'll give you another example. Let's say we want to plan a vacation. On our computer or smartphone, we look for a cheap flight to the sun through websites like Skyscanner and Expedia, both of which belong to the same group of institutional investors.

Expedia Skyscanner Trip.com – Vanguard Group, Inc., BlackRock Inc., State Street Corporation, Bank of America Corporation, Geode Capital Management, LLC., Wellington Management Group, LLP, Northern Trust Corp., and Bank of New York Mellon Corp.

We fly with one of the many airlines of which the majority of the shares are often owned by the same investors, or by governments, like Air

France-KLM. The aircraft we fly is in most cases a Boeing or an Airbus. Again, we see the same names. We look for a hotel or an apartment through Booking.com or Airbnb.com. Once we arrive at our destination, we go out for dinner, and we write a review on Tripadvisor. The same investors are at the basis of every aspect of our journey, and their power goes even much further, because even the kerosene that fuels the plane comes from one of their many oil companies and refineries.

Shell Oil – Vanguard International Stock Index-Total Intl. Stock Index, Vanguard International Growth Fund, Vanguard Tax Managed Fund-Vanguard Developed Markets Index Fun, iShares Core MSCI EAFE ETF, Fidelity International Index Fund, and iShares MSCI EAFE ETF. Mobil Oil – Vanguard Group, Inc., BlackRock Inc., State Street Corp., FMR, LLC., Geode Capital Management, LLC and Bank of New York Mellon Corp. Exxon – Vanguard Group, Inc., BlackRock Inc., State Street Corporation, FMR, LLC., Geode Capital Management, LLC and Bank of New York, Mellon Corp.

Just like the steel that the plane is made of, comes from one of their many mining companies, this small club of investment companies, banks, and mutual funds are also the largest shareholder in the primary industries where our raw materials come from. If we look on Wikipedia for the largest mining companies in the world, we see that their shareholders are the same institutional investors that we see everywhere else.

Glencore – Oakmore International Fund, Dodge & Cox International Stock Fund, Vanguard International Stock Index, Dodge & Cox Global Stock Fund, and Vanguard tax Managed Fund-Vanguard Developed Markets Index Fund. BHP – Vanguard International Stock Index, Capital Income Builder, Inc., Capital World Growth and Income Fund, and Fidelity Series International Value Fund. Rio Tinto – Vanguard International Stock Index, Vanguard Tax-Managed Fund, iShares Core MSCI EAFE ETF, iShares MSCI EAFE ETF, and Fidelity International Index Fund.

The same goes for the largest agricultural companies in the world, which our entire food industry depends on. For example, they own Bayer, the parent company of Monsanto, the world's largest seed producer, which produces 90% of all the cotton seed on Earth, as well as the majority of all other seeds. But these institutional investors are also the shareholders of the largest textile manufacturing companies in the world, and even the numerous popular clothing brands that turn the cotton into the clothes we wear, are owned by the same group of investors.

TJX Companies, Inc, the number one textile manufacturing company on earth – Vanguard Group, Inc., Wellington Management Group, LLP., BlackRock Inc., and State Street Corporation, Lululemon, number two manufacturing company on earth – FMR, LLC, Vanguard Group, Inc., Price (T. Rowe) Associates Inc., and BlackRock Inc. VF – The third textile manufacture company on Earth – PNC Financial Services Group, Inc., Vanguard Group, Inc., Northern Trust Corporation, BlackRock Inc., and State Street Corp. Nike – Vanguard Group, Inc., BlackRock Inc., and State Street Corporation. Levi – Vanguard Group, Inc., Wellington Management Group, LLP., Parnassus Investments/ca, and FMR, LLC. Ralph Lauren – Vanguard Group, Inc., Barrow Hanley Mewhinney & Strauss, LLC., BlackRock Inc., and J.P. Morgan Chase & Company.

Whether we have the world's largest solar panel producers or the largest oil refineries, the shares are managed by the same companies. They own the tobacco companies who produce all the popular tobacco brands in the world. But they also own all the major companies in the pharmaceutical industry, and the scientific institutes that produce the drugs. They own the companies that produce our metals and raw materials, and the entire automobile, aircraft and arms industry where those metals and raw materials are processed.

Boeing – Newport Trust Co., Vanguard Group, Inc., BlackRock Inc., and State Street Corporation. Lockheed Martin – State Street Corporation, Vanguard Group, Inc., and BlackRock Inc.

They own the companies that build our electronics. They own the big department stores and online marketplaces – Philips, Sony, Dell, Intel, IBM, Microsoft, eBay, AliExpress, Zalando and Amazon, and even the payment methods that we use to pay for their products -Mastercard, Visa, American Express, Western Union, and PayPal.

Because I want to keep my story as short as possible, I've decided to only show you the tip of the iceberg. If you decide to investigate on your own, using the sources that you've just seen, then you will discover that even many of the most well-known insurance companies, banks, construction companies – Zurich, Mapfre, Allianz, Ageas, AXA, Generali Group, Prudential and Legon, Bank of America, JP Morgan Chase & Company, Citibank, Goldman Sachs, ING, BBVA, ABN-AMRO, Barclays, and Wells Fargo. Telephone companies- Vodafone, AT&T, and Orange. Restaurant chains – McDonalds, and cosmetic brands – P&G, Unilever, Axe, Dove, and Rexona, are owned by the same institutional investors we just saw.

These institutional investors are, as I told you earlier, mainly investment companies, banks and insurance companies. They are in turn also owned by shareholders. Now, what is the most amazing thing? All of these institutional investors own each other's shares, and together they form an immense network that we can compare to a pyramid. The smaller institutional investors are owned by larger investors who in turn belong to even larger investors. The visible top of this pyramid consists of only two companies, and we have seen their names many times by now. They are Vanguard and BlackRock. The power of these two companies is something we can barely imagine. Not only are they the largest institutional investors of every major company on Earth, but they also own the other institutional investors of those companies, giving them a complete monopoly.

According to a report by Bloomberg, one of the most respected institutions in the world in the field of financial data and analytics, experts expect that by 2028, both companies will collectively manage about $20 trillion in investments, and in the process will own almost everything on Earth. The same Bloomberg called BlackRock the fourth arm of the government *because it is the only non-government entity that has a close relationship with the federal banks, also called the central banks.*

BlackRock not only lends money to the federal banks, but is also their principal advisor and the developer of the computer system that the federal banks use. Dozens of BlackRock employees had senior positions in the White House during the Bush and the Obama administrations, and currently under Joe Biden.

BlackRock CEO, Larry Fink is a welcome guest with many heads of state and politicians, and understandably so. He is the face of the company that pulls the strings. Yet, Larry Fink does not pull the strings himself. In fact, BlackRock itself is owned by shareholders, and if we look at who those shareholders are, we come to a strange conclusion. We see that BlackRock's largest shareholder is Vanguard and this is where it gets dark.

Vanguard itself has a unique structure that makes it impossible to see who its shareholders or clients are. The elite who owns Vanguard don't want anyone to know that they are the owners of the most powerful company on Earth. But of course, this is no secret to those who are willing to look into it. Reports by Oxfam and Bloomberg show that 1% of the world's population collectively owns more money than the other 99%. Indeed, Oxfam claims that as much as 82% of all the money earned in 2017 went to this 1% of people. Naturally, those who own the most powerful company on Earth, will also be the richest among this 1%. In other words, they are part of the 0.001%.

Forbes, the most well-known business magazine in the world, claims that by March 2020, there were some 2,075 billionaires. Oxfam's report showed that two thirds of all these billionaires obtained their fortune through inheritances and monopolies. So, this means that Vanguard is in the hands of the richest families on Earth. If we study their history, we discover that these families have always belonged to the top of the pyramid, some even well before the Industrial Revolution began.

Because their history (The Rothschild Family) is so interesting and extensive, I will explain some more about them in the follow up video that I'm currently working on (The DuPont Family). But in order not to elaborate too far, I will just point out that many of these families belong to royal bloodlines (The Rockefeller Family), and they are the founders of our banking system, the United Nations, and every industry in the world (The Bush Family). These families (The Morgan Family) never lost their power, but because of an increasing world population, they were forced to hide behind investment companies such as Vanguard, whose largest shareholders are the private funds and nonprofit organizations of these families.

Nonprofit – JP Morgan Chase Foundation, Alfred I. Dupont Charitable Trust, The Rockefeller Foundation, Edmond de Rothschild, The Bush Foundation, and the Rothschild Foundation.

In order to make the bigger picture clearer, I need to briefly explain something about these non-profit organizations. These are the links that connect the business community with politics and the media, allowing major conflicts of interest. At first glance, however, this is not too noticeable. Non-profits, also called foundations, are organizations that rely on donations, and they do not have to publish from whom they receive those donations. They can invest this money in whatever they want and do not have to pay taxes on their profits, as long as those profits are reinvested in other projects that they are involved in.

Nonprofits can move hundreds of billions of dollars from invisible investors. According to a report by the Australian government, this makes non-profit organizations ideal to finance terrorist groups and launder large sums of money. The foundations and funds of the families who are highest in the hierarchy of the 1%, hide behind the scenes as much as possible. However, for cases that have a lot of publicity and attention, they use the foundations of philanthropist families that are lower in the ranking, but who are also extremely wealthy.

In order to be concise, I will only highlight the three most important foundations in the world that connect all the industries in the world to each other. These are the Bill & Melinda Gates Foundation, The Open Society Foundations, of the controversial multi-billionaire George Soros, and the Clinton Foundation.

A very brief introduction, to give you an idea of the size of these types of foundations. According to the official website of the World Economic Forum, the Gates Foundation is the largest funder of the World Health Organization, after President Donald Trump halted the funding of the WHO by the US in 2020. This makes the Gates Foundation one of the most influential organizations in the world in the area of everything that relates to our health. The Gates Foundation has a close partnership with the 16 largest pharmaceutical companies in the world, including Pfizer, AstraZeneca, Johnson & Johnson, BionTech and Bayer, and we have just seen who own the most shares of these companies - Vanguard and BlackRock.

Bill Gates was anything but a poor computer nerd who made it to one of the richest people in the world, but he came from a philanthropic family that, just like himself, worked for the absolute elite. Bill is the founder of Microsoft, which is owned by BlackRock, Vanguard and, until recently, Berkshire Hathaway. But at the same time, the Gates Foundation is the largest shareholder, after BlackRock, Vanguard and State Street, in Berkshire Hathaway, where he was even on the board for a while. We would spend hours if we considered everything The Gates Foundation, The Open Society Foundations of George Soros, and The Clinton Foundation are involved in, but because they connect us with the next topic and with the current events, this brief introduction was important.

I think the next topic should start with a question. A random person like me, with very little experience in video editing, using an old laptop, can, in 20 minutes, objectively portray that only two companies have a total monopoly over all the industries in the world. So, the natural question is: why don't you hear about all of this in the media?"

Oprah: *"What?" "That's a good question."*

Narrator: *"Every day we have the choice between countless reports, documentaries, and television programs, and yet not one of them talks about this. Is it something not interesting enough, or might there perhaps be other interests at play? The answer we get again from Wikipedia. About 90% of the international media is owned by nine media conglomerates. The companies owned by these media conglomerates are too many to mention, so I'm just going to show you the most important brands that we all know. ViacomCBS is the parent company of, among others, all CBS channels, Paramount, where the most famous movies and series in the world come from, MTV, Comedy Central, Nickelodeon, the popular British channel Five and the popular Australian Ten.*

Guess who the largest shareholders of ViacomCBS are? Vanguard Group, Inc., BlackRock Inc., State Street Corporation, and Credit Suisse AG. Before we look at the other major conglomerates, let's not forget to mention our extremely powerful streaming monopolists, Netflix and Amazon Prime, both of which belong to the same shareholders – Vanguard Group, Inc., BlackRock Inc., Price (T. Rowe) Associates Inc., and State Street Corporation.

Then AT&T, which is the parent company of Warner Brothers, HBO, Discovery Channel, CNN, Cartoon Network, TNT, DC and many other well-known brands. Guess who the largest shareholders of AT&T are? Vanguard Group, Inc., BlackRock Inc., and State Street Corporation.

The third one is the all-powerful News Corp. This company owns many of the most well known national and regional newspapers, magazines and TV channels in the US, the UK and Australia – New York Post, The Times, The Sun, The Sunday Times, TLS, The Wall Street Journal, The Barrons, MarketWatch, Investor's Business Daily, Harper Collins Publishers, and The Realtor. The Australian, Herald Sun, Daily Telegraph, Foxtel, and Sky News.

The shares of News Corp are owned by the American multibillionaire, Rupert Murdoch, and by the institutional investors that we see everywhere else – Vanguard Group, Inc., Price (T. Rowe) Associates Inc., and BlackRock Inc. News Corp's sister company is Fox Corporation, which is also one of the most powerful media conglomerates on Earth. Just like News Corp., it is owned by the Murdoch family and the usual investors – Vanguard Group, Inc., Dodge & Cox Inc., and BlackRock Inc.

Then the Walt Disney Company, a conglomerate of unimaginable dimensions, with many subsidiaries such as Pixar, Marvel, 20th Century, Lucas Film, ABC, National Geographic and Hulu. Who are the biggest shareholders? Vanguard Group, Inc., BlackRock Inc., and State Street Corporation.

Another powerful media conglomerate is Comcast. This is the parent company of NBC, DreamWorks, Universal, the Sky Group, Focus Features, Xfinity and many other major media brands. As you would expect, the largest shareholders are Vanguard and BlackRock.

I could go on for hours and show that in almost every country on Earth, the local media is in the hands of these kinds of conglomerates, which in turn are owned by our institutional investors, or by extremely rich and powerful elite families. In the UK, for example, virtually all popular newspapers and magazines are owned by the Daily Mail Group, Reach and the aforementioned News Corp.

In the Netherlands, the entire media is in the hands of 'de Persgroep', Mediahuis and Bertelsmann. In Germany, the entire media is either controlled by the German government, ProSiebenSatl, Axel Springer and again, Bertelsmann, which is also a conglomerate of unprecedented dimensions. Not only is this the parent company of the largest book publisher in the world, Penguin Random House, and owner and founder of BMG Music, but Bertelsmann also controls a large part of the European media through their subsidiary, RTL, a company with 67 channels, ten streaming platforms and 38 radio stations.

Bertelsmann is owned by the ultra-rich Bertelsmann-Mohn family, who openly collaborated with the Nazis. Because of this, Reinhardt Mohn was held as a prisoner of war in the US. Besides RTL, Bertelsmann also owns a large part of the French mainstream media, and together with Media Set, the powerful Italian conglomerate of former President Berlusconi, that controls the most important part of the Italian mainstream media, they also own all popular Spanish TV channels.

Now to complete the picture, let's look at where the news comes from, that all these media outlets are feeding us on a daily basis. The various news media do not produce their news themselves but use information and images from news agencies such as Reuters, the Dutch ANP, and the French AFP. These organizations are anything but independent. Reuters is owned by the powerful Canadian Thomson family. The ANP is owned by Dutch investor Cees Oomen, the AFP is largely financed by the French government.

The main journalists and editors who work at our media or at these news agencies, are affiliated with important journalistic organizations, such as the European Journalism Center. These are one of the largest funders of media-related projects across Europe, they train journalists, produce study materials, give internships at, for example, the ANP, and work closely with the world's largest corporations such as Google and Facebook.

For journalistic analysis and opinion, all the major media outlets in the world use Project Syndicate, the most powerful organization within its field. It supplies the 506 most important media outlets in 156 countries.

Project Syndicate, plus an organization such as the European Journalism Center, together with the news agencies, are the connecting link between all the different media outlets around the world. When newscasters read the news from their teleprompters, there's a good chance that the text comes from one of these organizations. As a result, the global media is often synchronized in its reporting."

Anchors saying the same thing: *"But we're concerned about the troubling trend of irresponsible, one-sided stories, news stories plaguing our country."*

News anchor #1*:* *"The sharing of biased and false news has become all too common on social media. More alarming, some media outlets publish the same fake stories without checking facts first."*

News anchor #2 and the rest join in saying the same thing: *"The sharing of biased and false news has become all too common on social media. More alarming, some media outlets publish these same fake stories without checking the facts first. Unfortunately, some members of the media use their platforms to push their own personal biases and agenda to control exactly what people think, and this is extremely dangerous to our democracy. This is extremely dangerous to our democracy. (Repeated one more time by a newscaster reading the prompter) And repeated again and again, by others at different channels, all saying the same thing."*

Narrator: *"In September 2020, the European Journalism Center and Facebook set up a fund to support selected news organizations to do the reporting during the Corona crisis. Let's see who the organizations are, along with the news agencies producing our news. At Project Syndicate, we see The Bill & Melinda Gates Foundation, The Open Society Foundation, and the European Journalism Center. Then the European Journalism Center itself.*

Again, we see the Gates Foundation and the Open Society Foundation, and they also receive large donations from Facebook, Google, the Dutch Ministry of Education, Culture, and Science, and the Dutch Ministry of Foreign Affairs. The organizations that are at the heart of our information flow, are funded by nonprofit organizations of the same elites, who also control the entire media. However, a part of our tax money goes to these organizations as well."

Napoleon Bonaparte: *"Four hostile newspapers are more to be feared than a thousand bayonets ..."*

Narrator: *"The elite that controls every aspect of our lives, up to the information that we receive, depends on an unimaginably coordinated collaboration to keep all the different industries on Earth connected to each other, in order to ensure they all work in the elite's interest.*

This happened at the World Economic Forum, one of the most important organizations in the world. At its annual meeting in Davos, the CEOs of the largest companies on Earth gather along with heads of state, politicians, and other influential individuals and organizations like UNICEF and Greenpeace. Serving on the board of trustees are former US Vice President and 'climate change guru,' Al Gore, BlackRock CEO, Larry Fink, the president of the European Central Bank, Christine Lagarde, the director of CERN, Fabiola Gianotti, the Queen of Jordan, Rania Al Abdullah, the director of the International Committee of the Red Cross, Peter Mauer, and many other politicians and CEOs of the world's most influential companies.

According to the WEF's official website, their annual membership fee ranges between 53.000 and 530.000 euros. But according to the WEF's yearly reports, around 71% of its total budget comes from its partners, who in this way pay for the membership of young politicians who cannot afford their own fees. Wikipedia reports the following: 'according to critics, the WEF is a business forum where the wealthiest companies can negotiate deals with other companies or with politicians.' 'The purpose of the WEF for many of the participants would be personal gain rather than solving global problems.'

I don't like to make assumptions, but would there be so many problems on Earth if key industry leaders, bankers, and politicians since 1971, had gathered annually to solve our world's problems? Is it not strange that the world's leading environmental organizations have been meeting for 50 years with the CEOs of the most heavily polluting corporations while things just keep getting worse for our natural world? That these critics of the WEF are right, soon become clear, when we look at who the most important partners that account for almost 71% of the WEF's budget. They are BlackRock, the Open Society Foundations, The Bill & Melinda

Gates Foundation, and many other large corporations of whom Vanguard and BlackRock own the shares directly or indirectly.

The president and founder of the WEF is Klaus Schwab, a German professor and businessman. In his book 'The Great Reset', he describes in detail the plans of his organization. 'The pandemic represents a rare but narrow window of opportunity to reflect, reimagine, and reset our world.' The coronavirus, according to him, is the excellent opportunity to literally reset our society in every regard."

Klaus Schwab: *'There is an urgent need for global stakeholders to cooperate in simultaneously managing the direct consequences of the COVID-19 crisis. To improve the state of the world, the World Economic Forum is starting the Great Reset initiative."*

Narrator: *"He calls this 'Build Back Better,' and this slogan seems to be the motto of all globalist politicians in the world."*

Klaus Schwab: *"And it's now a historical moment, a crucial moment to rebuild the future, to reset our policies."*

Boris Johnson, Prime Minister of the UK: *"And of course, we also want to work together on building back better."*

Joe Biden, illegitimate president of the US: *"You know, I said we're gonna build back and we're gonna build back better."*

Mark Rutte, demissionary Prime Minister of the Netherlands: *"It's certainly a major crisis, but it also offers us a unique opportunity."*

Pedro Sanchez, Prime Minister of Spain: *"We must use this historical opportunity ..."*

Willem-Alexander, King of the Netherlands: *"Together we can turn a crisis into an opportunity."*

Justin Trudeau, Prime Minister of Canada: *"But this global pandemic has also created an opportunity to build back better."*

Willem-Alexander, King of the Netherlands: *"to build back better."*

Joe Biden: *"We can't just build back. We gotta build back better."*

Antonio Guterres, Secretary General of the UN: *"And achieve the Sustainable Development Goals."*

Justin Trudeau: *"And climate action is an essential part of that."*

Narrator: *"According to Schwab, our old society should be exchanged for a new one, in which countries give up their sovereignty to an all-encompassing world government, in which people own nothing but work for the state in exchange for the housing, health care, and all their other basic needs. All of this is necessary, according to the WEF, because our modern consumer society, which the elite themselves imposed on us, can't keep going as it is, it's no longer sustainable.*

Schwab says in this book, that we will never return to the old normal. And the WEF published a video that makes it clear that in 2030 we will own nothing, but we will be happy. 'Whatever you want you'll rent, and it'll be delivered by drone. A handful of countries will dominate. We won't transplant organs; we'll print new ones instead. You'll eat much less meat.'

You've probably heard some talk about the New World Order. The media wants us to believe that this is a topic for conspiracy theorists, although it has been talked about for generations by presidents such as George Bush Senior, Nelson Mandela and Bill Clinton."

George Bush, Senior: *"We have before us the opportunity to forge for ourselves and for future generations, a New World Order, a world where the rule of law, not the law of the jungle, governs the conduct of nations. When we are successful, and we will be, we have a real chance at this*

New World Order. An order in which a credible United Nations can use its peacekeeping role to fulfill the promise and vision of the UN's founders."

Bill Clinton, 42nd President of the US: *"After 1989, President Bush said a phrase that I often use myself, that we needed a New World Order."*

Joe Biden: *"The affirmative task we have now is to actually create a New World Order."*

Nelson Mandela: *"The New World Order that is in the making must focus on the creation of a world of democracy, peace and prosperity for all."*

Narrator: *"But also by the world's most famous philanthropists such as Cecil Rhodes, David Rockefeller, Henry Kissinger and even George Soros."*

Cecil Rhodes: *"Why should we not form a secret society with but one object, the furtherance of the British Empire and the bringing of the whole world under British rule ..."*

Henry Kissinger: *"Yes, there will be a New World Order, and it will force the United States to change its perceptions."*

George Soros: *"You need a New World Order that China has to be part of the process of creating it, and they have to buy in. They have to own it."*

Narrator: *"These important figures who, apart from Mandela, were all among the top of the elite when they were still alive, are not the only ones who dream about an all-powerful world government. In 2015, the UN presented its controversial Agenda 2030, which is almost identical to Klaus Schwab's Great Reset. In their own words, the UN, like Schwab, wants to ensure that by 2030, poverty, hunger, environmental pollution, and disease no longer exist on Earth. It sounds like a sympathetic plan, until you read the fine print. You see, the idea is that Agenda 2030 is going to be paid for by us, the citizens. And just as it is currently required* *of us that we give up our basic rights for the sake of public health, we will be demanded to give up our wealth in favor of poverty reduction.*

These are not conspiracy theories. You can read this for yourself on their official website. In short, it boils down to this: The UN wants to take the tax money from all Western countries and give it to the mega-corporations of the elite, who will be contracted to rebuild society. Globally, a completely new infrastructure is needed, because fossil fuels must be made a thing of the past according to the UN. For this immense project, a world government is needed, says the UN, and the same UN takes it upon herself to be this global government. Just like Schwab, the UN also believes that a pandemic is a perfect opportunity to accelerate the implementation of Agenda 2030."

News Headlines from Around the World: *"The Covid-19 crisis is an opportunity to reimagine human mobility. We have a unique opportunity to design and implement more inclusive and accessible societies. Building back better requires transforming the development model of Latin America and the Caribbean. Building back better after Covid-19 through risk-informed development cooperation. To build back better, we must reinvent capitalism. Here's how ... Building Back Better: An Action Plan for the Media, Entertainment and Culture Industry."*

Narrator: *"It is worrisome that the WEF and the UN openly admit that they consider pandemics and other disasters as an opportunity to transform society, especially since we have seen that the elite have all the resources at their disposal to make us believe that there is a pandemic, and even to create one."*

More Headlines: *"New emails shed more light on Fauci's connections to Wuhan Lab that might have created COVID. Sen. Paul: Fauci emails prove he knew of Wuhan gain-of-function research. Until now, it had been said that Covid-19 only had pandemic potential."*

Narrator: *"So, we certainly should not take these things lightly, and we should examine them carefully. And when we do that, we come across* *things that are even more troubling. On Friday, October 18, 2019, months before the pandemic was declared, a meeting was held at the Pierre Hotel in New York City for a select group of about 130 very important guests, including politicians and the world's most respected medics and pharmacists. The purpose of the meeting was to simulate the possible scenarios in the event of a global pandemic. This could be a coincidence, you might say. For this simulation, however, a coronavirus was used as an example."*

The Event 201 scenario: *"Event 201 simulates an outbreak of a novel zoonotic coronavirus transmitted from bats to pigs to people, that eventually becomes efficiently transmissible from person to person, leading to a severe pandemic. The pathogen, and the disease it causes, are modeled largely on SARS, but it is more transmissible in the community setting by people with mild symptoms."*
https://www.centerforhealthsecurity.org/event201/scenario.html

Narrator: *"The simulation covered in detail how the coronavirus would develop, and how they could only control this through the intensive collaboration of entire industries, governments and government agencies. Once again, a New World Order to save us from destruction. Does it surprise you when I tell you that this meeting, called Event 201, was organized by none other than the World Economic Forum, The Bill & Melinda Gates Foundation, and the Johns Hopkins Institute? This is not a conspiracy theory. Check the official website of Event 201 for yourself.*

Perhaps at this point, it will no longer surprise you, that the German 'Robert Koch Institute', which, like every national health institute in the world, is closely linked to the WHO, which is funded by Bill Gates, created a similar simulation in 2012. As was the case during Event 201, the simulation assumed a coronavirus. This simulation assumed that in a Southeast Asian food market, the coronavirus would spread from animal to human. How coincidental, isn't it? In this simulation, it takes several weeks for the authorities to identify the virus, allowing it to spread worldwide. A simulation is made of the consecutive three years in which there are lockdowns and economies are destroyed, but also the impact on society is simulated in all aspects. Even the protests."

More headlines: *"China, WHO should have acted faster to stop COVID-19 pandemic, panel says."*

Narrator: *"I won't tire you with the details. In fact, you can download this analysis for yourself from the website of the German government. https://dserver.bundestag.de/btd/17/120/171205.pdf*

The last thing I want to show is an excerpt, from a lecture that Belgian top virologist Mark van Ranst gave on January 22, 2019, at the Chatham House, a major non-profit organization in London, where important world leaders met to discuss global issues.

Chatham House: Chatham House, also known as the Royal Institute of International Affairs, is an independent policy institute headquartered in London. Its mission is to provide authoritative commentary on world events and offer solutions to global challenges. It is the originator of the Chatham House Rule. Its presidents are Alistair Darling and John Major. (Wikipedia)

Winners of the Chatham House Prize includes Hillary Clinton, Melinda Gates, and John Kerry. What van Ranst is discussing is simply shocking. Van Ranst, in fact explains how he has fooled the entire Belgian population during the Swine Flu through fear mongering, out of context mortality rates and media manipulation. He laughingly explains how he managed to impose the vaccine for the Swine Flu on the frightened Belgian population. A vaccine produced by the pharmaceutical companies he worked for."

Mark van Ranst, Flu Commissioner, Belgium: *"Thank you very much, Ab. Thanks for the invitation. When I was asked to tell you about my experiences being the crisis manager, the Flu Commissioner for Belgium, and highlighting the communication. And then you have one opportunity* to do it right. I mean, day one is so important. On day one, you start your communication with the press, with the people and you have to do it right.

I mean, you have to go for one voice, one message. In Belgium, they chose to appoint a non-politician to do that. I have no party affiliations, and that makes things a little bit, at that time at least, a little bit easier because you're not attacked politically, majority or minority. That didn't come into play and that was a huge advantage.

The second advantage is that you can play in Brussels, the completely naïve guy and get a lot more done than you would otherwise be able to do. You have to be omnipresent that first day, or the first days, so that you attract the media attention. You make an agreement with them, that you will tell them all, and if they call, you will pick up the phone. When you do that, then you can profit from these early days to get complete corporate coverage of the field, and they're not going to search for alternative voices there. And if you do that, that makes things a lot easier.

These first weeks, that's easy street when you have no opposition, and everybody needs news and they can come to you for news, you can bring quite a lot of neutral information, it is picked up and, well, the news is brought the way you bring it, and you can only do that in the first couple of weeks or months.

And then you have to say, okay, well, we will have H1N1 deaths. Of course, that would be unavoidable. I used Sir Donalson's quote where he said that in the UK, by the peak of the epidemic, 40 people would die per day by the end of the summer. I worked it out for Belgium. That would be seven deaths a day at the peak of the epidemic. I used that in the media. Seven Belgian flu deaths per day at the peak of the epidemic would be realistic. That is true, every year. Even inter-epidemically, that is very conservative. (The audience laughs.) It's very, very conservative.

However, talking about fatalities is important, because when you say that, people say: 'Wow, what do you mean? People die because of influenza?' And that was a necessary step to take. (Again, there is laughter coming *from the audience.) And then of course, a couple of days later, you had the first H1N1 death in the country, and the scene was set and it was already talked about.*

And then you have to pick who is going to be vaccinated first, and then women and children first. Whatever, I mean risk groups, they were important."

More Headlines: *"Remember, folks, it's important that we let the weaker members of our society be first in line to get the H1N1 vaccination – the very young, those with underlying medical conditions, the Calgary Flames Hockey Team."*

Mark van Ranst, Flu Commissioner, Belgium: *"And then I misused the fact that the top football and, soccer clubs in Belgium, inappropriately and against all agreements, vaccinated, they made their soccer players priority people. So, I said, I can use that because if the population really believes that this vaccine is so desirable, that even the soccer players would be dishonest to get their vaccine, I said, okay, I can play with that. So, I made a big fuss about this. This is van Ranst, he's raving mad, (laughing). But it worked ..."*

Narrator: *"The Chatham House organization is also funded by all major corporations of the elite, The Gates Foundation and the Open Society Foundations. We could talk for hours about the coronavirus, which has a survival rate of 99.98%, and about the incomprehensible measures that are destroying our society. Millions of entrepreneurs have lost their income. Countless elderly people have died in loneliness, isolated from their families, but I think we have reviewed enough facts that put the global Covid measures in a broader context, seen from the perspective of the elite.*

These extremely wealthy elites, who collectively have tens of thousands of billions, have no problem whatsoever with the fact that more than 40% of the world's population has to live on less than $5.50 a day, or that millions of children are dying from the drinking water contaminated by *them, or from malnutrition, or by their bullets or bombs. They just want to get more powerful. The elite have absolutely no intention of sharing their wealth with us. In fact, they are honest about their plans to take even the last bit from us, and those plans are being rolled out as I'm telling you this."*

Which again, is another reason why we're doing this study. But as you can see, these guys own just about everything on the planet, that is, the elite. And shocker, these elites are working with Klaus Schwab and the World Economic Forum.

In fact, the World Economic Forum calls them their "Strategic

Partners," in which you can just go on down the line and scroll the multitude of businesses, companies, and institutions working for them.

And now they have the "privilege" of being what's called "A Davos Man," that is defined as, "An emerging group of economic elites who are members of a social caste which has little need for national

loyalty, view national boundaries as obstacles that are thankfully vanishing, and see national governments as residues from the past, whose only useful function is to facilitate the elite's global operations." In other words, they're traitors!

As this man shares, *"Davos Man fits the definition of megalomania, and has acquired what he believes are sufficient financial and political resources to try to force his obsession and grand schemes on the world, and to force you, your family, and the world to comply with his vision and belief systems."*

I couldn't have put it better myself! And of one of these "privileged" Davos Men, is none other than the CEO of Blackrock, Larry

Larry Fink
Chairman and CEO at BlackRock
New York, New York, United States
891,755 followers

BlackRock
UCLA

About

Laurence D. Fink is Founder, Chairman and Chief Executive Officer of BlackRock. He and seven partners founded BlackRock in 1988, and under his leadership, the firm has grown into a global leader in investment and technology solutions. BlackRock's mission is to help investors build better financial futures, and the firm is trusted to manage more money than any other investment company in the world. Mr. Fink has been named one of the "World's Greatest Leaders" by Fortune, and Barron's has named him one of the "World's Best CEOs" for 15 consecutive years.

Prior to founding BlackRock in 1988, Mr. Fink was a member of the Management Committee and a Managing Director of The First Boston Corporation.

He serves as a member of the Board of Trustees of New York University (NYU) and the World Economic Forum, and is Co-Chairman of the NYU Langone Medical Center Board of Trustees. In addition, he serves on the boards of the Museum of Modern Art, the Council on Foreign Relations and the International

Fink, as you can see here. He admits they have their own global agenda for the Russia-Ukraine war, and he clearly works for Klaus and the gang.

As you can see here from the World Economic Forum's website! They're not hiding it at all!

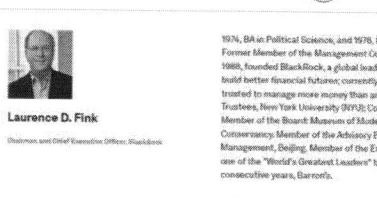
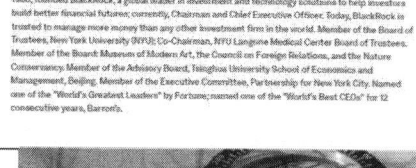

Then we have the top financial controller of the world, Vanguard, whose CEO is a man named Tim Buckley as can be seen here also from his LinkedIn page, and shocker, he works for Klaus Schwab and the World Economic Forum, as seen in this article where he states, speaking of Vanguard's cooperation with the World Economic Forum, *"We are proud to be in the company of other reputable organizations that share*

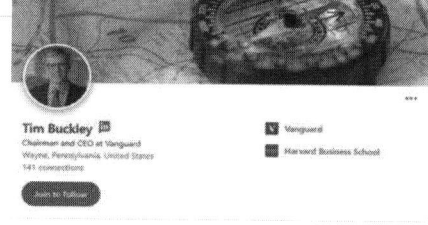

Vanguard joins Global Parity Alliance

April 14, 2022

Vanguard has become a founding member of the **Global Parity Alliance**, a group dedicated to advancing diversity, equity, and inclusion (DEI) in the workplace. We are proud to be the first asset management company to participate in the alliance, which was launched March 30 by the **World Economic Forum**, in collaboration with consultant firm McKinsey & Company.

Vanguard strives for representation and inclusion for every crew member. As part of the alliance, we look forward to engaging with other global firms by sharing best practices and advancing DEI outcomes.

"Being invited to join the alliance as a founding member is a testament to our progress and commitment to further advance DEI at Vanguard," said Vanguard Chairman and Chief Executive Officer Tim Buckley. "We are proud to be in the company of other reputable organizations that share in this commitment and look forward to accelerating the path toward progress together."

in this commitment and look forward to accelerating the path toward progress together."

And that progress is to, "own" the world, so you can "control" the world. Why? Because *"He who owns the gold owns the world."* They know it, and that's why they're doing it!

And if you're wondering how they keep track and monitor, and even grow all this financial wealth and power all over the whole planet, believe it or not, once again, they're doing it by creating an AI or Artificial Intelligence run system, that will, and does manage the whole global financial enterprise for them all at once. They even have a name for it. It's called Aladdin.

Narrator: *"What if I told you there is a robot that controls more wealth than any country on earth? A robot so powerful that in the last ten years, it has quietly created the biggest company in the world. This is the story of a robot called Aladdin. It's Wall Street's best-kept secret, and it is gobbling up every asset class across every industry. Aladdin now controls $21 trillion dollars of our global economy. To put that in perspective, that's more than the $20 trillion GDP of the US or the $15 trillion GDP of the entire European Union.*

The New Statesman: *"This is how much money Aladdin manages. If you took every last cent out of every bank in every country in the world, emptied the wallets and pockets and penny jars of all 7.6 billion people, if you rummaged down the back of every sofa, and emptied every till and safe, until you collected every scrap of currency in the world, you would have a pile of cash worth around five trillion dollars. The total value of* *assets under management by BlackRock is $6.3 trillion. But Aladdin also delivers risk analysis on the assets managed by its clients, which are valued at more than double that amount. Overall, Aladdin has an effect on the management of around 10% of the world's financial assets, or around $20 trillion. Over 25 years, it has grown into a system that is directly or indirectly responsible for more than four times the value of all the money in the world."*

Narrator: *"This one robot directs the actions of the US Federal Reserve, almost every major bank and investment fund on wall street, and over 17,000 traders. It controls half of all ETFs, 17% of the bond market, 10% of the global stock market, and carries out a quarter of a million trades every day and billions of forecasts every week. Year after year it gathers up trillions of data points on every market, every company, every asset, and now even each of us. What we buy, sell, and say, so that it knows what to buy and what to sell far better than any human being.*

Every major bank, company, and investment fund has come to rely on Aladdin, and its all-powerful AI and Algorithms to beat the market, and if they didn't, they've collapsed and failed in Aladdin's wake. And do you know what the craziest part of this story is? This robot is just getting started. So where did Aladdin come from? And how did it get so powerful?

Aladdin is the brainchild of Larry Fink, the founder of BlackRock, and his total dominance has made his company the biggest shadow bank in the world and the most powerful company on earth. The story you're about to hear is equally unbelievable and terrifying. In fact, you would think it was science fiction if it wasn't very real and happening today.

This story starts in the 80s, when Larry Fink was making millions, pioneering mortgage-backed securities at Wall Street Bank First Boston. That's right, the same mortgage-backed securities that caused the 2008 global financial crisis 20 years later. But back in the 80s, he was in an epic Wall Street rivalry with Louis Ranieri at Salomon Brothers. Back then Larry was making millions for the bank and was on track to be the first bottom CEO, then in 1986, an error in the back-office computer models led to Larry making the wrong trades and he lost the company a hundred million dollars.

The result was Larry leaving the bank as a failure with the stupid computer to blame. With that experience, Larry had just one ambition. To build a super smart robot that could pick out risks and opportunities in the market. And do it better than any computer or human could do. In 1988, he launched a new startup, BlackRock, with a tiny coding team to give birth to this robot. Its name, Aladdin, which stands for Asset, Liability and Debt Derivative Investment Network. In its first 10 years, Aladdin was fed information about every asset, price movement and risk variable in the global bond market, Larry's specialty.

In 1999, when Aladdin turned 11, Aladdin was getting so intelligent at picking losers and winners, that Larry began selling access to his data to other Wall Street firms. That same year, he took BlackRock public on the New York Stock Exchange, straight after the IPO, the Dot-com bus burst, pushing a wall of money from the stock market to bonds, which Aladdin had become the undisputed world champion.

Within years, BlackRock had become a trillion-dollar company, and as money started shifting back to shares, what did Larry do, he bought the asset management arm of Merrill Lynch which was focused on shares. So, the gift for Aladdin's 18th birthday, is all the data points for the entire stock market. And suddenly Aladdin had a new playground, analyzing every stock trade and risk factor for every company on the stock market. As a result, today, BlackRock, together with its two closest rivals, Vanguard and State Street, both of which also rely on a lot of the mountain of knowledge, has become the biggest shareholders of over 40% of all publicly listed companies in America.

In 2008, the global financial crisis hits, and before Aladdin turns 21 years old it's called on by every Wall Street Bank and Timothy Geithner, as the head of the Federal Reserve and the US Treasury. As soon as Lehman Brothers collapsed and the Wall Street meltdown began, the US Government came calling to save the next collapsing bank, Bear Stearns.

It was Aladdin who decided which assets to keep and which to leave in the $30 billion rescue package, and few people know, it was a robot that saved America from disaster.

With that first success, the Feds, US Government, and now even European and Japanese Central Banks, began relying on Aladdin to make the course of where that $2.5 trillion dollars of new money they printed should go. The majority of it is bonds and funding, to prop up the mortgage companies and banks. But wait, aren't these exactly the assets that Aladdin and BlackRock already invested in? Exactly. But growing protests of conflict of interest were drowned out by the noise of the printing presses printing more money as the assets controlled by Aladdin rapidly grew to $11 trillion dollars by 2013.

In the last decade, Aladdin has gone from the leader to the dominator of all financial markets. With BlackRock's Barclay acquisition, it got all shares. Barclays exchange-traded funds units, or ETFs, and with that, Aladdin moved from dominator of bonds and equities to dominator of ETFs, just as all the biggest investors shifted from mutual funds to ETFs, and that's when in 2017, everything changed.

On Aladdin's 29th birthday, Larry launched a top-secret project at BlackRock, named Monarch, which led to the firing of his fund managers, and replacing their funds with Aladdin's funds. The Robot was now eliminating humans from the equation altogether. And as a result, today over 70% of all trades on the US stock markets are decided by robots with Aladdin leading the way. These trades are completed from beginning to end without a human involved in high frequency trading far faster than a human can execute.

Now if this was just a story of a robot taking over the job of Wall Street traders, you might not be so concerned unless you're one of those traders. But in the last three years as Aladdin hit $20 trillion dollars in assets, incredibly, it has begun to consume and control at an even faster rate. First in 2020, as Aladdin turned 32 years old, the US government and the Federal Reserve again came calling as a pandemic hit. Aladdin again was *the one to guide the nation in what was now $4 trillion dollars of newly printed money. Where did the money go this time? Inexplicably for the first time, the Fed began buying ETFs in 2020. Well, that's a little strange. And again, the cries of conflict of interest were drowned out by the money printing.*

And then Aladdin revealed its end game. Recently, BlackRock acquired Efron, which collects data on the things that you and I own, including private equity and real estate. And since then, Aladdin has consumed e-Funds data on the entire global real estate market and, yep, you can guess what happened next. Over the last two years, BlackRock and other funds, using Aladdin's data, have begun buying up single-family homes where they can afford to output the rest of us because they have unlimited financing at hyper-low interest rates. The result is home prices rising by 20% over the last two years and pushing now, even big players like Zillow out of the market.

And here we see Aladdin's end game to be the one hyper intelligent AI robot that not just controls Wall Street assets, but all assets, public and private. Now I'm not into conspiracy theories, but even a skeptic with eyes wide open can see the signs. We're already at a point where no one can compete without Aladdin. As CEOs and asset managers like Anthony Malloy are now saying, 'Aladdin is like oxygen. Without it we wouldn't be able to function.'

And what about government regulations? Well, Joe Biden has appointed BlackRock Executive Brian Deese as head of the National Economic Council, which basically means the oversight of Latin and BlackRock, is now the responsibility of Blackrock, and Biden has also appointed the BlackRock chief of staff, Wally Adeyemo, to be the assistant secretary of the treasury which means that BlackRock is now the treasury, as well as the treasury advisor.

This story is far from over, the genie is out of the bottle, and Aladdin has already reached a tipping point, where one robot controls more wealth than any person or country. But as Aladdin's AI capabilities continue to grow, and with its rate of control rising by another trillion to two trillion dollars in new assets every year, it looks inevitable that Wall Street's secret weapon could end up owning everything and we end up owning nothing."

Gee, where have I heard that before? And you wondered how they were going to pull it off! AI that's all tied back to Klaus Schwab and The World Economic Forum. Anybody starting to see a pattern here?

And again, we encourage you to get our in-depth study on AI or Artificial Intelligence, called **The AI Invasion,** where we expose in great

detail, how these same Global Elites are using AI to control not just the finances of the whole planet, but just about everything else you can think of on the planet, including every aspect of our daily lives.

And it's not coming, it's already being put into play by these same Global Elites working for Schwab and the gang, who need AI to help them micromanage the whole planet and usher in what they call "The Great Reset" or "The Fourth Industrial Revolution."

Chapter Five

World Economic Forum & Global Health

The third way Klaus Schwab pulled off this sick, twisted, satanic, dystopian nightmare for all our futures, is he also grabbed control of **WORLD HEALTH**.

And this one adds even more leverage to having total control of the leaders and finances around the whole planet. That's because, if you think about it, people not only need money to live, but they also need healthcare to live, let alone stay alive, especially in a time of crisis or emergency.

And if there's one thing the Bible is clear about, there's going to be a lot of need for healthcare in the 7-year Tribulation, when the Antichrist launches his sick, evil, murderous, satanic kingdom!

Revelation 6:1-14: "I watched as the Lamb opened the first of the seven seals. Then I heard one of the four living creatures say in a voice like thunder, 'Come!' I looked, and there before me was a white horse! Its rider held a bow, and he was given a crown, and he rode out as a conqueror bent on conquest. When the Lamb opened the second seal, I heard the second living creature say, 'Come!' Then another horse came out, a fiery red one.

Its rider was given power to take peace from the earth, and to make men slay each other. To him was given a large sword. When the Lamb opened the third seal, I heard the third living creature say, 'Come!' I looked, and there before me was a black horse! Its rider was holding a pair of scales in his hand. Then I heard what sounded like a voice among the four living creatures, saying, 'A quart of wheat for a day's wages, and three quarts of barley for a day's wages, and do not damage the oil and the wine!' When the Lamb opened the fourth seal, I heard the voice of the fourth living creature say, 'Come!' I looked, and there before me was a pale horse!

Its rider was named Death, and Hades was following close behind him. They were given power over a fourth of the earth to kill by sword, famine, and plague, and by the wild beasts of the earth. When he opened the fifth seal, I saw under the altar, the souls of those who had been slain because of the word of God and the testimony they had maintained. They called out in a loud voice, 'How long, Sovereign Lord, holy and true, until You judge the inhabitants of the earth and avenge our blood?'

Then each of them was given a white robe, and they were told to wait a little longer, until the number of their fellow servants and brothers who were to be killed as they had been, was completed. I watched as He opened the sixth seal. There was a great earthquake. The sun turned black like sackcloth made of goat hair, the whole moon turned blood red, and the stars in the sky fell to earth, as late figs drop from a fig tree when shaken by a strong wind. The sky receded like a scroll, rolling up, and every mountain and island was removed from its place."

Now, how many of you would say, after all those events, there's going to be a whole lot of people on the planet who are going to need some serious medical care, at least those that survive, however few they might be.

I think a Global War, and a Global Famine, and a Global Plague with wild beasts shredding you apart, not to mention a Global Slaughter with a Global Earthquake, so big that every mountain and island was shaken, gives it away! Oh yeah, and don't forget the asteroids slamming into the earth!

But that was just the first half of the 7-year Tribulation, when the Antichrist takes control and ushers in his so-called Kingdom, whereas you saw, nearly 2 billion people will die in one fell swoop! Not a good time! You definitely don't want to be there!

But here's the point. For those that remain, they're going to need what? Some serious medical care, all across the planet, aren't they? So again, whoever controls the medical community at this time, has got some serious leverage over the people of the planet, right?

But now, let's move to the second half of the Antichrist's reign. How does that turn out? Let's take a look.

Revelation 8:1-13: "When He opened the seventh seal, there was silence in heaven for about half an hour. And I saw the seven angels who stand before God, and to them were given seven trumpets. Another angel, who had a golden censer, came and stood at the altar. He was given much incense to offer, with the prayers of all the saints, on the golden altar before the throne. The smoke of the incense, together with the prayers of the saints, went up before God from the angel's hand.

Then the angel took the censer, filled it with fire from the altar, and hurled it on the earth; and there came peals of thunder, rumblings, flashes of lightning and an earthquake. Then the seven angels who had the seven trumpets prepared to sound them. The first angel sounded his trumpet, and there came hail and fire mixed with blood, and it was hurled down upon the earth. A third of the earth was burned up, a third of the trees were burned up, and all the green grass was burned up.

The second angel sounded his trumpet, and something like a huge mountain, all ablaze, was thrown into the sea. A third of the sea turned into blood, a third of the living creatures in the sea died, and a third of the ships were destroyed. The third angel sounded his trumpet, and a great star, blazing like a torch, fell from the sky on a third of the rivers, and on the springs of water – the name of the star is Wormwood. A third of the waters turned bitter, and many people died from the waters that had become bitter.

The fourth angel sounded his trumpet, and a third of the sun was struck, a third of the moon, and a third of the stars, so that a third of them turned dark. A third of the day was without light, and also a third of the night. As I watched, I heard an eagle that was flying in midair, call out in a loud voice: 'Woe! Woe! Woe to the inhabitants of the earth, because of the trumpet blasts about to be sounded by the other three angels!'"

In other words, you ain't seen nothing yet! But how many of you guys would say, one-third of the earth being burnt up, a massive asteroid the size of a mountain slamming into the planet, a comet flying by poisoning the water supply of the whole world, and other celestial events disrupting the planet, will not only be a seriously bad time, but one you would seriously want to avoid by getting saved now, through Jesus Christ, if you're not? I think that's common sense and please do so if that's you!

But again, unfortunately, for those who are left behind by rejecting Jesus Christ as their Lord and Savior today, after those events, wow, there's obviously going to be some serious medical needs to be taken care of, right? Again, at least for those who survive.

I mean, you can try to be the ultimate survivor, for those who rejected Jesus as their Savior today. You could whip out your first aid kits and all your wildlife classes on how to apply a tourniquet, etc. But let's be honest. After all those events, on that kind of level, on that scale, even all your homemade survival healthcare remedies ain't going to help you much!

So again, whoever does survive these events in the 7-year Tribulation, in the second half, you're going to need some serious Global Medical attention, right?

So again, here's the point. Whoever controls the Global Health Care System at this time, has some serious leverage over the people of the planet, right?

But that's still not all. You have one more round of judgments to come in the last part of the 7-year Tribulation. Let's see how that goes.

Revelation 16:1-21: "Then I heard a loud voice from the temple saying to the seven angels, 'Go, pour out the seven bowls of God's wrath on the earth.' The first angel went and poured out his bowl on the land, and ugly and painful sores broke out on the people who had the mark of the beast and worshiped his image. The second angel poured out his bowl on the sea, and it turned into blood like that of a dead man, and every living thing in the sea died.

The third angel poured out his bowl on the rivers and springs of water, and they became blood. Then I heard the angel in charge of the waters say: 'You are just, in these judgments, You who are and who were, the Holy One, because You have so judged; for they have shed the blood of Your saints and prophets, and You have given them blood to drink as they deserve.' And I heard the altar respond: 'Yes, Lord God Almighty, true and just are Your judgments.' The fourth angel poured out his bowl on the sun, and the sun was given power to scorch people with fire.

They were seared by the intense heat, and they cursed the name of God, who had control over these plagues, but they refused to repent and glorify Him. The fifth angel poured out his bowl on the throne of the beast, and his kingdom was plunged into darkness. Men gnawed their tongues in agony and cursed the God of heaven because of their pains and their sores, but they refused to repent of what they had done. The sixth angel poured out his bowl on the great river Euphrates, and its water was dried up, to prepare the way for the kings from the East.

Then I saw three evil spirits that looked like frogs; they came out of the mouth of the dragon, out of the mouth of the beast and out of the mouth of the false prophet. They are spirits of demons performing miraculous signs, and they go out to the kings of the whole world, to gather them for the battle on the great day of God Almighty. 'Behold, I come like a thief! Blessed is he who stays awake and keeps his clothes with him, so that he may not go naked and be shamefully exposed.' Then they gathered the kings together to the place that in Hebrew is called Armageddon. The seventh angel poured out his bowl into the air, and out of the temple came a loud voice from the throne, saying, 'It is done!'

Then there came flashes of lightning, rumblings, peals of thunder and a severe earthquake. No earthquake like it has ever occurred since man has been on earth, so tremendous was the quake. The great city split into three parts, and the cities of the nations collapsed. God remembered Babylon the Great and gave her the cup filled with the wine of the fury of His wrath. Every island fled away, and the mountains could not be found. From the sky, huge hailstones of about a hundred pounds each fell upon men. And they cursed God on account of the plague of hail, because the plague was so terrible."

 Wow! Now how many of you guys would say, after all those events, at the end of the 7-year Tribulation, there's going to be a whole lot of people on the planet that are going to need some serious medical care. I think you're starting to see the pattern here.

 People are now breaking out with ugly painful sores. Every living thing in the sea dies. There's no fresh water supply left, whatsoever, on the whole planet. The sun is scorching people with fire and intense heat. People are gnawing at their tongues. There's a giant Battle of Armageddon, and they lose big time. There's an earthquake so big, that it not only shakes the whole planet, but every island and mountain fled away, and every city collapsed!

 Now maybe it's me, but I'm kind of thinking that's not only a time you want to avoid by receiving Jesus Christ as your Lord and Savior today, but for those who are left behind, who didn't receive Jesus as their Lord and Savior, they are going to need what? Major serious medical care all around the planet, right?

So again, whoever controls the medical community, at this time, has some serious leverage over the people of the planet! And you think the Antichrist won't do this? Of course, he will! As much as he lusts for power, put yourself in his shoes. If you're the Antichrist and want to micromanage the whole planet as Revelation 13 says he will, then you're going to need some serious leverage.

Controlling politicians and finances are definitely a part of it, where he will use that control to force people to do what he wants them to do. That includes worshiping him, the actual Antichrist, as if he were a god, and taking his mark into their bodies so they can continue to "buy and sell" and not be shut out of the global economic system.

But financial control can only take you so far. How are you going to force even the "resisters" of your global tyranny into going along with this as well? And I say that because the Bible is clear. Not everybody is going to go along and worship the Antichrist as a god, certainly not the Jewish people!

So how do you "force," "order," "make" and "cause," as Revelation 13 says he will, the bulk of the planet, to bow a knee to the Antichrist and accept his Mark? Simple! You build a global system that not only controls the politicians and finances, but also controls the whole medical community when these disasters hit. And when people are injured on a massive scale, and they will be, you use that as "leverage" to get them to bow down and obey you, because it's a matter of life or death now!

I mean, you want those burns to be treated from that global fire, take the chip! You want those broken bones to be set from that giant tsunami that slammed into the coastline, bow a knee! You want your body healed from drinking all that poisonous water that's killing you from the inside out, worship the Antichrist! Total global control, and total global domination by controlling all the politicians and finances and the medical community and using that as leverage!

So, guess what? Believe it or not, they're already doing it with the help of AI! These same Global Elites working for Klaus Schwab and The World Economic Forum, not only have AI, "Aladdin" running the whole show for the global finances, but they also have AI systems controlling the whole medical community.

Right now, AI is already replacing doctors, replacing surgeries, predicting diseases, and replacing the Medical Administration. AI is controlling your diet, AI is controlling your drugs, and AI is even controlling your death, with AI determining your mental state, your age, and the day you die.

It's crazy stuff, but it's all happening right now, already being put into place around the world by these Global Elites and The World Economic Forum. It's a major sign that the 7-year Tribulation is getting close! Again, if you're not, you better get saved now, this is not a joke!

But again, this is why we encourage you to get our in-depth study on AI, or Artificial Intelligence called "The AI Invasion," where you will see how these same Global Elites are using AI, to not just control the whole financial system and even the whole healthcare system, but literally, every aspect of our lives, helping them to micromanage the planet, just like Revelation 13 says!

But these same elites, who have built this AI controlled global medical system, also have a global entity who "governs" the whole global medical process. In fact, it's been in existence for a while now. It's called "The World Health Organization," and shocker, they too work for Klaus Schwab and the World Economic Forum! Anyone see a pattern here? Let's take a look at that.

World Health Organization

Narrator: *"The World Health Organization is a specialized agency of the United Nations, responsible for international public health. It is headquartered in Geneva, Switzerland, with six semi-autonomous regional offices in 150 field offices worldwide.*

The WHO was established April 7, 1948, which is commemorated as World Health Day. The WHO's broad mandate includes advocating for Universal Healthcare, monitoring public health risks, coordinating responses to health emergencies, and promoting human health and well-being. It provides technical assistance to countries, sets international health standards and guidelines, and collects data on global health issues through the World Health Survey.

Its flagship publication, the World Health Report, provides expert assessments of global health topics and health statistics on all nations. The WHO also serves as a forum for summits and discussions on health issues. The WHO has played a leading role in several public health achievements, most notably the eradication of smallpox, the near eradication of polio, and the development of an Ebola vaccine.

Its current priorities include communicable diseases, particularly HIV/AIDS, Ebola, Malaria and Tuberculosis; non-communicable diseases such as heart disease and cancer, healthy diet, nutrition, and food security and substance abuse.

The World Health Assembly, composed of representatives from all 194 member states, serves as the agency's supreme decision-making body. It also elects and advises an Executive Board made up of 34 health specialists.

The WHA convenes annually, and is responsible for selecting the Director-General, setting goals and priorities, and approving the WHO's budget and activities. The current Director-General is Tedros Adhanom, former Health Minister and Foreign Minister of Ethiopia, who began his five-year term on July 1, 2017.

The WHO relies on assessed and voluntary contributions from member states and private donors for funding. As of 2018, it has a budget of over $4.2 billion, most of which comes from voluntary contributions from member states. The International Sanitary Conferences, originally held on June 23, 1851, were the first predecessors of the WHO.

A series of 14 conferences that lasted from 1851 to 1938, The International Sanitary Conferences worked to combat many diseases such as cholera, yellow fever, and the bubonic plague. The conferences were largely ineffective until the seventh, in 1892; when an International Sanitary Convention that dealt with cholera was passed. In part, as a result of the successes of the conferences, the Pan-American Sanitary Bureau, and the Office International d'Hygiene Publique were soon founded.

When the League of Nations was formed in 1920, they established the Health Organization of the League of Nations. After World War II, the United Nations absorbed all the other health organizations to form the World Health Organization. During the 1945 United Nations Conference on International Organization, Szeming Sze, a delegate from the Republic of China, conferred with Norwegian and Brazilian delegates, on creating an international health organization under the auspices of the new United Nations.

The use of the word, 'world', rather than 'international', emphasized the truly global nature of what the organization was seeking to achieve. The constitution of the World Health Organization was signed by all 51 countries of the United Nations, and by 10 other countries on July 22, 1946.

Its first priorities were to control the spread of malaria, tuberculosis and sexually transmitted infections, and to improve maternal and child health, *nutrition and environmental hygiene. The WHO's Constitution states that its objective, 'is the attainment by all people of the highest possible level of health.'"*

Amelia Moseley Reports: *"WHO can help the sick. WHO can warn people about dangers to their health. WHO can stop a deadly virus from turning us all into brain eating zombies. WHO can. I mean like WHO can? The World Health Organization.*

It was officially founded back in 1948, not long after the Second World War. As part of another big International Organization tasked with saving the world, the United Nations. The UN decided, that along with things like keeping peace and security around the globe, there was another important thing to take care of to ensure the survival of the human race, our health."

Newscaster: *"The struggle against epidemics is a global one. The danger of death is worldwide!"*

Amelia Moseley Reports: *"You see, long before the UN and the WHO existed, the world had tackled some pretty big outbreaks. The worst in history was the Bubonic Plague, also known as the Black Death. That is about as horrible as it sounds. In fact, in the 1300s, it wiped out 13 million people or 60% of Europe's population. Centuries later there were diseases like Yellow Fever, Cholera, Smallpox, and the Spanish Flu. Which, at the end of World War I, infected about one-third of the planet's population. A disease that spreads far around the globe is known as a pandemic. The WHO's aim was to stop that sort of thing from happening again."*

Newscaster: *"The World Health Organization will make full use of every existing means, education, prevention, cure. All peoples of every race and beliefs will be helped by doctors from all races and nations."*

Amelia Moseley Reports: *"Since it started, the WHO has done some pretty amazing things. Like totally wiping out the deadly virus, Smallpox, through vaccinations. It's also leading the fight against contagious* *diseases like HIV/AIDS, Ebola, Malaria, and Tuberculosis. And it helps to educate people, sometimes of less obvious dangers to their health, like consuming too much sugar or playing video games for way too long.*

But to many, it's still good to know that there is a big powerful group out there fighting for our health."

Fighting for our health or controlling our health? Did you see how it went way beyond just supposedly eradicating diseases through vaccines, but also telling you what to eat, like if you've had too much sugar or fast food, or even if you played too many video games? What's up with that? I mean the next thing you know, they'll tell us to stop eating meat! Which is a precise part of the plan, as we will see soon enough!

But don't worry, even though the World Health Organization was launched around the same time, and under the same agenda of The United Nations, that controls or, "governs" the nations around the world. And dictating what they can and cannot do. I'm sure the WHO isn't going to do the same with our health. That is, govern or take total control of the health of the whole planet, in what people can and cannot do, or eat, or ingest, whatever. Yeah, right! If you believe that, you've been listening to their propaganda commercials for way too long, like this one that tries to get us to believe they're here just to help.

Narrator: *"The Covid-19 pandemic is one of the biggest challenges we are facing. It's been a stark and painful reminder that nobody is safe until everyone is safe. There will be other pandemics and other major health emergencies. No single government or multilateral agency can address this threat alone. Together we must be better prepared to predict, prevent, detect, assess and effectively respond to pandemics in a highly coordinated fashion.*

The 194 Member States of the World Health Organization resolved to work together towards a new international instrument for pandemic preparedness and response. This renewed collective commitment is a milestone in stepping up pandemic preparedness at the highest political level. Such an agreement, rooted in the World Health Organization constitution, could strengthen existing international health instruments, especially the International Health Regulations, and provide a firm and tested foundation on which we can build and improve.

The agreement also has the potential to foster an all-of-government, and all-of-society approach. Strengthening national, regional, and global capacities and resilience to future pandemics. This could include a greatly enhanced international cooperation to improve alert systems, data sharing, research, and local, regional and global production and distribution of medical and public health countermeasures such as vaccines, diagnostics, and personal protective equipment.

The agreement could also recognize the 'One Health' approach that connects the health of humans, animals and our planet. To achieve this, WHO will support its Member States in their work, and facilitate the involvement of relevant stakeholders, including from civil society and the private sector. Pandemic preparedness needs global leadership, for a global health system fit for this millennium.

To make this commitment a reality, we must be guided by solidarity, fairness, transparency, inclusiveness and equity."

But see, they're here to help. We must let them guide us, the whole planet, into doing what is best for our health. I mean, do you want another pandemic on your hands like Covid-19?

Yeah right, it was a "plandemic" all along, with the WHO's involvement, to help facilitate their total global takeover, and the power grab of the whole world, including people's health!

And for even more proof of that, all you have to do is look at their leaders throughout their history, as well as their current director. The current director of The World Health Organization is a guy named a Tedros Ghebreyesus from Ethiopia, who clearly got his start with, wait for it, that's right, "Former American president Bill Clinton and The Clinton Foundation and the Bill & Melinda Gates Foundation." That tells you exactly who he's working for, which goes right back to Klaus Schwab and The World Economic Forum, because that's who the Clintons and the Bill and Melinda Gates Foundation are working for!

But for even more proof of that, The World Health Organization does not have our best health interests at heart, pun intended by the way. They are really being used to control all people's health around the whole planet, just like the United Nations was used and created to control all the governments of the planet. Let's just take a look at that treaty they were proposing and promoting in that video.

They say we, the whole planet, need to sign on to a whole new international treaty that would give them, The World Health Organization, even more power over us. In fact, that's exactly what it is. When you look at this actual treaty proposed by The World Health Organization, it's clearly the beginning of the end of all individual health autonomy, and even national autonomy, around the whole planet. It will allow them to do such things as:

1.) The WHO would reserve the right to decide what constitutes a pandemic and have already changed the definition of the term. It could be the flu.

2.) The treaty gives the WHO the power to name the new disease and decide what quarantine measures are needed on a global scale.

3.) The WHO would control who gets to develop the new treatments and decide whether they're safe.

4.) They would be given the authority to determine who gets quarantined and locked down.

5.) The WHO would decide over vaccine mandates for each country.

Which means it will form an even stronger One World Government and allow The World Health Organization to establish a truly One World Health System, which is why people are saying, "The WHO Pandemic Treaty Spells the End for Democracy."

And it only takes two-thirds of the nations to agree to ram through this treaty, right down our throats, while placing sanctions on dissenting countries. In other words, you get punished if you don't go along!

In fact, this latest WHO treaty would allow the WHO constitution to also supersede national constitutions, including our own, here in America. And I'm not the only one blowing the whistle on this massive, sneaky, power grab. So are a lot of other people, as you can see here:

Tucker Carlson: *"We want to open this evening with a story that you may not have heard, but that you should definitely know about. It begins early last year when Joe Biden, as one of his very first acts as president, brought the United States back into the World Health Organization. When we saw this, we thought, why would Biden be so anxious to do something like that? At the time, we assumed it was just part of his larger effort, Trump had pulled us out of the WHO, so Biden had to do the opposite, childish, but that seemed like a fair explanation.*

Still, it did seem a little weird, because there aren't very many international bodies that are not more thoroughly discredited than the

World Health Organization. Particularly after COVID. It's a laughingstock. If there's one thing it's not good at, it's public health.

Since the very first cases of the Coronavirus were reported in Wuhan, the WHO slavishly ran interference for the Chinese government and did it in the most cartoonish and obvious way. First, the WHO claimed that there was no evidence of human-to-human transmission of the virus. Remember this? They said this from Chinese officials who were obviously lying, and now we know they were lying. Then when it became clear that the virus came out of a Chinese government lab, the WHO sabotaged the investigations and the origins of the virus by appointing a gain-of-function researcher to lead the investigative team. It's pretty shocking, if you think about it.

To this day, the WHO still hasn't acknowledged that it did any of that, which it definitely did! They said that they continued to praise China's response to Covid as being transparent. Which is the one thing that it's not. It's almost amusing. It's weird if you think about it. Why would Joe Biden want to join a group that every informed person laughs at?

Well more than a year later, we think we know the answer. The Biden administration is very close to handing the World Health Organization power over every aspect, the intimate aspect, of your life. So, imagine the civil liberties abuses that you lived through during the Covid lockdown, but permanent, and administered from a foreign country.

Here's what we're looking at. This January, the Biden administration submitted a series of proposed amendments to something called the International Health Regulator, the IHR. The Biden administration amendments will, along with those from several different countries, will be combined to create a new Global Pandemic Treaty. We need a Pandemic Treaty. That treaty is set to be adopted starting this weekend in Geneva at the World Health Assembly.

Now, the full text of the treaty has not yet been finished, but the WHO world group has summarized what it is going to look like. Documents begin by promising to restrict the WHO's authority just to pandemics. Calm down, it's just for pandemics.

The WHO Planned Pandemic Treaty reads, 'WHO Secretariat to play the leading, convening and coordinating role in operational aspects of an emergency response to a pandemic.'

So, don't get paranoid! Someone is just needed to coordinate the pandemic response, globally. Because it's a global problem. Got it?? Settle down conspiracy nut! But here's the catch. The WHO doesn't define what a pandemic is. When a pandemic is in progress, and also, how long a pandemic lasts. Then you read the fine print, and you realize that the WHO will have total control over emergency operations in the United States, if there was ever a 'public health emergency.'

What exactly qualifies as a public health emergency? They don't define that, but they get to. They get to decide when a public health emergency is, and then they have full authority. You can see where this is going. The Biden administration has made certain that unelected bureaucrats with the WHO have total authority to declare and define public health emergencies. Do you get it, explicitly? The White House eliminated a provision that would have required the WHO to 'consult with and attempt to obtain verification from the State Party in whose territory the event is allegedly occurring in.'

So, as originally written, they couldn't do anything without the permission of their member country's government. But thanks to the change that the Biden administration pushed, effectively there's no limit at all on the WHO's power.

And then it gets worse from there, the treaty also mandates a 'whole-of-government and whole-of-society approach to ... pandemic preparedness.' Well, think about that. Every society is always preparing for a pandemic. That means there will not be a moment ever when the WHO doesn't have operational control over so-called public health matters, in this country.

Now what is that going to mean exactly? You can already guess it's not about public health, it never is. But before I tell you what exactly this means, I'm going to tell you that none of this is going to be optional. Thanks to the amendment from the Biden administration, the treaty contains a provision for a compliance committee. It provides that every member country in the WHO must, 'inform WHO about the establishment of its national competent authority responsible for overall implementation of the IHR that will be recognized and held accountable.'

Under this treaty, WHO members must enforce orders from the WHO, they have to act as the heavies of the WHO, and if they don't, they will be sanctioned. The White House is going to be the muscle and director of the WHO. So, who is the director of the WHO? Well, that would be the former member of the Ethiopian, Leninist, Marxist party called Tedros Adhanom Ghebreyesus. He once led the ministry of health in Ethiopia. He's not a physician. But as the head of the ministry of health in Ethiopia for political reasons, he covered up three cholera outbreaks. The opposite of what he was supposed to do. He logged cholera as acute watery diarrhea. But he's not a doctor, he didn't know, and nobody knew."

Reggie Littlejohn, President/Women's Rights Without Frontiers: *"So you shouldn't be surprised if you haven't heard about this. Because almost no one has heard about it. Because the Biden administration has literally tried to keep it as secret as possible and the MSM is not covering it. So, thank you so much for covering this.*

What happened basically, is that the Department of Health Services under the Biden administration, submitted a set of so-called amendments to a 2005 treaty, which if passed, and it looks like it will pass, unless we take some action immediately. If it does pass, it will seriously undermine and damage the sovereignty of the United States. What these amendments do, they are amendments to a 2005 treaty, where everything was voluntary, they make a lot of the stuff that was voluntary, now mandatory.

One of the things it does, a provision that was in the 2005 treaty, is stricken by the amendments that required the WHO to have the consent of the country where the health event is happening, in order for the organization to take action. So, with just that one striking of that, it means the WHO, it's really the Director General of the WHO, who is Tedros Ghebreyesus, will have the ability to come into a country and take action on a so-called health event without the consent of the country.

They don't define a health event. It could be anything, anything that affects public health. It could be a pandemic, it could be gun violence, it could be climate change, it could be mental health, it could be anything that they want to call a health event. So, basically, they can do anything that they want. They can come into the United State and effectuate their will. They established something called the 'Compliance Committee,' which is appointed.

Who's going to appoint them? Ghebreyesus? Do we trust people that Ghebreyesus is going to be appointing? And by the way, who gave the WHO the authority to do this? They are not an elected body. They are just an administrative body. They are supposed to be advisory, helping governments. They are not supposed to be dictatorial over governments. WHO is an arm of the United Nations. We do not want the United Nations dictating our health care in the United States.

They are deeply in bed with China. The United Nations is, the WHO is! We saw this in the way that they handled the pandemic, particularly in the beginning where the WHO went along with China's lies, that there was no evidence that there was any human-to-human transmission. They also opposed Trump's decision to stop international travel from China, saying it was racist. That enabled the virus to spread all over the world.

The WHO works hand-in-hand with the Chinese Communist Party to cover up their malfeasance, and the result was that millions of people died. Why should they be entrusted with international health care? The Biden administration tried to hide it, somebody found it, so now people are trying to raise awareness. But it's like it's almost too late. The horse has left, you can't bring it back.

I had mentioned, there is a compliance committee that is going to be appointed, no doubt by Ghebreyesus, and they are going to have the power to monitor the compliance in a nation and facilitate compliance. So, how are they going to monitor our efforts if it's not through a vaccine passport, a health card, digital ID? What this is going to do, is to give the WHO the ability to surveil all of us. In a way that is very similar to the vaccine passport, which was the same platform as the Chinese Social Credit System. Everything can be attached to this. It's a tool of totalitarian control and mass surveillance. And then they can facilitate compliance.

So, let's say the WHO says, 'You need to vaccinate everybody, you need to lock everybody down, anyone's who's not vaccinated needs to be quarantined,' or how about this, everyone who isn't vaccinated is suffering from some kind of a mental illness. They can say that people who question election integrity, who think that there was some form of election fraud in the 2020 election. They are psychotic. There's already a bulletin from the National Terrorist Advisory System, that says that people who think there was election fraud, or take issue with the Covid narrative, are domestic terrorists.

So, these things are working together with this terrorist thing and this WHO power grab, to really impose globalism on the United States and the world.

Neil Oliver, GBNEWS.UK: *"Anyone remember voting for the World Health Organization? To take control of our lives? No? Me neither. And yet here we are, teetering on the brink of joining most of the countries of the world in surrendering our national sovereignty under the terms of a proposed pandemic treaty. Once British ink is dry on the necessary paperwork, we and most of the rest of billions living on planet earth will, in the event of another pandemic, take our instructions, not from politicians that we actually voted for, and could hypothetically at least have the option of getting rid of, but from the unelected, faceless, bureaucrats of the WHO.*

This is no conspiracy theory, no tin hats required, this is real and happening now. And a whole lot of people would rather you weren't paying attention. The WHO is a fabulously wealthy off-shoot of the United Nations. It has its head office in Geneva, and is presently headed by Ethiopian born, Tedros Adhanom Ghebreyesus. Do you know much about him? No? Nor me. He is funded by 194 members of heads of state, and also donations by private entities. As things stand, most of its money comes from the United States of America, from communist China, and from computer salesman and international man of mystery, Bill Gates.

Let us remember that for the past two years, the WHO has loudly celebrated the approach taken by China of the handling of Covid-19. Even now, with tens or hundreds of millions of Chinese citizens, they remain locked in their homes, in scores of cities across that country, and after unknown numbers have died in those circumstances, including some that committed suicide by leaping to their deaths from the tower block imprisonment. The WHO continues to applaud the tactics of the Chinese communist party, as it's benefactor.

For his own part, Bill Gates struggles even to control viruses in his software, Microsoft. He is on record admiring the draconian approach taken by Australia, to the extent that he has said, that in his opinion, the world would have better success in eliminating the disease, the one that more than likely leaked from the lab in China, if only more nations had followed their extreme model, locked everyone down and sought zero Covid.

Now we, in Great Britain, without so much as a 'by your leave' from our leaders, and along with around 95% of the world's population, must contemplate a future in which decisions about what we will be ordered, ordered to do in the face of another pandemic. The decisions will be taken by the unelected, unaccountable, bureaucrats of the Chinese communist party, worshiping the WHO under the unseemly influence of a tech billionaire, with no more qualifications in the fields of medicine and disease control than I have.

It's worth remembering that President Donald Trump insisted on divorce from the WHO on the grounds that it was too close to China, only for Joe Biden to re-marry them again in 2021. All of that's history, however. In a matter of days, the World Health Assembly will meet in Geneva for a vote on the Treaty. The target date for final ratification is in May 2024, but by then, the power grab will have long been completed. Amendments written into the proposed Treaty by the re-enamored Biden administration, will see 194 nations cede sovereignty over national health care decisions to the WHO.

The WHO would thereby have decision-making power over, and above our own government and every other government. Consider this. When you watch footage of the 26 million people of Shanghai locked down in their homes, their cats and dogs beaten to death in the street, the WHO would, by the terms of the new treaty, have the power to impose the same on cities here. Know too that under the terms of the treaty, the WHO, does not have to show any data to legitimize its conclusions or decisions.

It's also worth knowing, to say the least, that it would be up to the WHO to define what the next pandemic is. Seeing how things are going, I would hardly be surprised to hear about a pandemic of obesity, or of heart attacks, followed by the lockdowns and other restrictions to deal with it the same way. No doubt, lockdowns to fix the climate can't be far away either. In the case of climate, the WHO might draw the conclusion that we, the human species, are the virus. Who knows what they might conclude and decide then. No doubt, this so-called pandemic treaty is the single greatest global power grab that any of us has seen in our lifetime. It's nothing less than the groundwork, the laying of deep foundations for global governments through the WHO. Many of those opposed to the treaty, and there is an online petition here in the UK, seeking to demand that the matter be discussed in Parliament, have pointed to the, shall we say, compromised position of the WHO itself. Much has been made of the notion that a fish rots from the head. Back in 2017, Robert Mugabe of Zimbabwe, was appointed as a goodwill ambassador of the WHO, by Tedros, and only dropped after shrieks of outrage from those who pointed out that Mugabe might have been a controversial choice, a poster boy for an organization notably committed to the well-being of living people.

A glance at the 34-member executive board of the WHO, reveals seats occupied by such human rights luminaries as Syria and East Timor, among others. And remember, all the time, the links the WHO has with communist China, a state with more human rights abuses under its belt than any decent human being might want to contemplate, and that's before we get to the looming presence of the world's fourth, or is it, second richest man, the one and only Bill Gates and his foundation, whose commitment to mass vaccination is unsurpassed.

As far as I'm concerned, the whole thing stinks like the aforementioned dead fish. The approach taken to Covid, by the Chinese government, and endorsed by the WHO, was never about health, I say. It was always about control. Just as there is more than one way to skin a cat. One was beaten to death in a Shanghai Street by a man in a hazmat suit, armed with a stick perhaps. So, there is more than one way to seek to impose undemocratic authoritarian control upon a population.

For instance, a government desiring such control might try frightening the living daylights out of its people. Telling them that if they don't take their medicine, medicine that big pharma knows in advance might kill or maim some of them, that you won't be able to travel, leave the country, go to work, or the pub, or the cinema, or to school. A government, or indeed any unelected body seeking total control, might tell its people, that unless they do what they're told, they won't ever be getting back to anything even resembling their old normal lives.

That's not how you protect people from a pandemic. That's how you exploit and manipulate the very notion of a pandemic to seize and retain control."

Stew Peters Show: *"The World Health Pandemic Treaty. You know what this is? This is a bid by globalists to override the law and constitutions of every country on earth and make them subordinate to a global Covid* *world order. A world order of dystopian lockdowns, and masks and mask mandates, and forced injections and a whole lot more. Now we, of course, have been talking to Australians because they have been sounding the alarm more than most about this treaty.*

Probably they now know what the Covid world order looks like because they went through it in Australia. Australia was supposed to be a free democracy but became as tyrannical as communist China during Covid. People couldn't leave the country or cross state lines, or even leave their homes. People were ordered to download phone apps to track where they were. Police would stop people in the parks to inspect their coffee cups to make sure they really had coffee in them. To make sure they really had something in their cup, that they weren't using it as an excuse to not have their faces covered with a bacteria ridden, Sharia face muzzle. Soldiers with sub-machine guns terrorized sunbathers on empty beaches. That's the Covid world order."

So much for being concerned about our health! As you can see, this latest treaty and all their behavior has nothing to do with our health, not for the good anyway! It's all a ruse just like everything else! These people are lying murderous megalomaniacs! This treaty and everything else, is all about controlling every aspect of our daily lives, using the health care system as the leverage to get the job done.

And, as we've seen before, it's also about the murderous culling of the planet that these same sickos want to do as well, that is, kill off a massive amount of the population on the planet, whom they deem as "useless eaters."

And not just with the Covid-19 vaccine, which is really not a vaccine, but a gene editor as we saw before. But the whole vaccine industry itself, for years has been doing the exact same murderous type of behavior, like a ticking time bomb as this man shares back in the day.

Narrator: *"From W.D. Clark, of Indiana, in his book, I found a very interesting sentence, he said, 'I never saw a case of cancer in an* *unvaccinated person.' Now, he wrote this in 1936. So, to me that was quite a revelation and other doctors have said the same thing. That a vaccination is really a time bomb within the human system that can go off five years, ten years, forty years after you have the vaccination. You can have this time bomb go off, you can have a stroke, or a heart attack. It's always there in your system, you never get rid of it and as apparently, it's always an alien force in your physic."*

You know, like the Covid-19 vaccines are doing. They are either killing people right off the bat in a few minutes, or hours, or within a few days or months, but now it's coming out that they're also killing people in all kinds of different ways a year or years down the road. Just when the people who got them thought they were free and clear, that they were safe. No, you're not. That's one of the many lies of the Covid-19 shots!

But as you saw, this "ticking time bomb" medical induced death technique is nothing new! It's the perfect murderous crime!

Then if that wasn't bad enough, as we also exposed in one of our other documentaries, **"Beyond Covid: The Global Elites Plan for Human 2.0".** These same sickos, murderous, megalomaniacs, want to not just control the healthcare of people across the whole planet, even to the point where they will dictate who gets to live and who dies, but they also want to genetically modify the remaining survivors with biological upgrades to better serve them, the Elites that is, with a program they have in place called Human 2.0.

And if you think that's not fair, you're right! But it doesn't matter to these people. We're just a bunch of cattle to them, and they think they actually own us now, at least those that took the Covid shots, as this whistleblower shares.

Stew Peters Show: *"Well, it's well known that the mRNA shots supposedly 'work,' I guess for the lack of better words, by modifying the RNA in your cells. But does this modification turn recipients into something that isn't even human anymore? Dr. Jane Ruby touched on this* *briefly yesterday on this program. It's also the belief of attorney, Todd Callender. His warning is that anybody that gets the Pfizer or Moderna shot may become a new organism. Which allows them to potentially be patented and enslaved by drug companies. Obviously, you will want to hear about all the legal aspects of this end. Todd Callender joins us now. Thank you so much for coming.*

So, this is called fifth generation warfare that Karen Kingston was talking about, bringing receipts and patents, yesterday on the program. Dr. Jane Ruby suggested that you are no longer a homo sapien, but you are a homo borg. What do you know about the legal implications of all of this, for those people who received this inoculation?"

Todd Callender: *"Yes, so this all arises from our case of Robert B. Austin. It's in the 10th Circuit Court of Appeals right now. In the trial court, we were trying to figure out the mandates of the military, how it was that all these service members were being given the shots without being given informed consent. We found out through the research, that they were owed a lessor amount of informed consent rights, if they were genetically modified. It turns out that the military has been doing genetic modification on our soldiers since 2005, at least.*

That led me down the trail, how did this happen? I started poking around and saw that this is what they consider fifth generation warfare. It's something that all the governments are working on, the UK, Germany, China, and this is the new state of war. So, I looked into the law, and found this case called Molecular Pathology vs. Myriad Genetics, Inc. A 2013 Supreme Court Case. The important part of it, the whole point of the case, was on page 6, halfway down, it starts with, 'it is also, the court finds, that the use of mRNA to effectuate a gene modification of an organism ... (In this case it wasn't human, but it doesn't matter), results in the patent holder owning that new organism.'

So, when you are genetically modifying something, you are creating a new species by virtue of doing that. The question I put in front of it is, does that apply to humans? Because now we've got admittedly, mRNA shots that are doing gene remodification as you indicated. They are making people create spike proteins. That's genetic modification. They are on their disclosures. They are doing gene deletion, 1-2-3-6 gene deletion, modification. So, very clearly there is genetic modification happening in vitro. Does that, right now, according to the law, result in the new species of people being owned by the patent holder?

If so, what is this new species? All of this, by the way, would be illegal. But what I am saying, the anti-slavery amendment, that's the 13th amendment of the Constitution that outlaws the ownership of humans. I put this in the pleadings, it is in front of the court now. The interesting thing is that the DOJ didn't even address it. That's who's defending the DOD, HHS, and FDA. And they didn't even address it in their pleadings, so they are running the risk that this could be deemed as admitted.

Funny enough, on the 18th of November, we did our day in court with a three-judge panel and I'm going to ask the court about this. I would love to be wrong. I don't want people to be owned by the patent holders. It would be a great holding, and they would be made law, because there is hardly any law on this particular subject. In fact, when you look at gene modification of humans, there's nothing out there. The British people say, 'Hey, we should probably consider that in the future.'

If you look at NASA's future strategic issues of warfare circuits of 2025, they are predicting that by 2025 they will have super-soldiers. And it's a planned action to do that."

NASA's Circuit 2025

- "Non-explosive Warfare" (psywar, biowar IT/net war, "anti-operability war," Beam weaponry including RF, Spoofing/Camo
- Robotic Warfare "in the large" /better than human AI "Cyber life."
- Alternative Power Projection Approaches (e.g., Deep Water depth/death sphere, blast wave accelerator, etc.)

Stew Peters: *"So what would be the legal implications for somebody that has been injected and then owned by big pharma?"*

Todd Callender: *"Yeah, the questions are numerous, because if you think about how our law talks about people's human rights. What is a human, to endure these rights, defined as homo sapien? If this is a new species by virtue of the modification, are they still homo sapiens? I have found some reference to a new human, called 'homo-borg-genesis'. In fact, in NASA research papers, you will see that they refer to humans as borg. So, the question is, if homicide is described as the unlawful taking of a human life, and we describe humans as being homo sapiens, does the penal code protect homo-borg-genesis? People who are still people, but not humans for the purposes of the law. Can they be protected? Can someone be convicted for killing a homo-borg-genesis? There is no answer to this.*

This is an all-new territory here, and we are going to have to find out because I have some deep concerns and reservations as to what could be done to people who are no longer defined as having rights."

Stew Peters: *"I can't even believe we are having this conversation. This is 2022, and we are talking about homo sapiens no longer being a thing. Humans being irradicated and replaced by borgs. And that brings up a good point. Karen Kingston is right, and this injection or whatever it is, communicates with 5G, whatever that is, and that could be a kill switch for humanity, for those who have been injected with this thing.*

Can the people who turn on that switch and blow up all of these borgs actually be held accountable for it? Or are they just wiping off the face of the planet, tens, or hundreds of millions, or even billions of people who received at least one dose of this mRNA or Pfizer injections? I mean, NASA is fake in my opinion, but when we are talking about documents that specifically outline this, and the DOJ who is defending the DOD, isn't even wanting to comment on this, what is your speculation?"

Todd Callender: *"Well, why should we wonder if this is something they want to do, they have gone to great lengths to tell us that they intend to* *genetically modify people. Kim Jong Un, last year, somewhere around August did a demonstration of his super solders. Getting hit in the head with a sledgehammer, and they are just fine. This is warfare. You can look for yourself. The Brits and the Germans actually got together, and they created a document called, 'Human Augmentation, Super Soldiers' and it goes on for 90 some pages, all about how great this is going to be. And only at page 60 or so, did they actually stop and think about the legal consequences of what this might mean to the people who had been modified. The questions are so vast, and my concern is this. If the court finds that, yes, the patent holders could own these synthetic people, then you actually have it right. They might actually get away with all the crimes against humanity being committed since they rolled out these shots."*

Stew Peters: *"So, does the Constitution even exist? Is that even relevant anymore, when we are talking about big pharma, and these 'gross' oversteps of our Constitutional rights?"*

Todd Callender: *"Well, that's the issue. The magic legal words that are uttered by the WHO, a slew of legal things come into place. When Tedros said, 'it's a public health international concern,' treaty obligation stepped in, and we ended up with a national emergency in the United States, which effectively suspends 123 human and Constitutional rights. So, as long as there is an emergency, we're screwed. We have no rights. And of course, in July of this year, Biden said Monkeypox was a health emergency of international concern. Those are the magic words. And then all rights are suspended, and they get to do whatever they want to do. Including shutting people down in their house or churches, and by the way, they also quarantine you and fill your veins full of whatever shots they want to, because without any rights, that is what is being put into statutes."*

And the World Health Organization and Joe Biden, and all the rest of the Elites are all behind this. They don't care about us. Especially those that got the shot. Why, you're not even classified technically as a human anymore! Who cares what we do to you! That's their attitude and justification to treat us like a bunch of slaves! They're sick and evil!

But for these same Elites, their plan is, "they" get to escape all these Human 2.0 cattle/human genetic modifications, and instead, "they" get to live out their so-called transhumanist dream of living forever without God. Don't believe me? Here they are admitting it!

CNBC Reports: *"The French playwright, Eugene Lonesco, once asked, 'Why was I born, if it wasn't forever?' Life, if anything, is impermanent. Flowers die, stars die, and you will die. So, if you can't defeat that, what if you could postpone it? Or at least postpone the diseases found associated with getting old. Many people, especially the ultra-wealthy in Silicon Valley, are investing money into companies that are trying to answer exactly those questions.*

The richest man in the world, Jeff Bezos, and billionaire PayPal co-founder, Peter Thiel, who both invested in the space. In 2013, Google formed an aging research company called Calico. There is also BioViva, BioAge, The Longevity Fund, AgeX Therapeutics, The Methuselah Foundation and many others."

Michael West, CEO, AgeX Therapeutics: *"Whenever you need a fundamental, 'in the need,' there's a market. In this case, the market for age related disease and aging, is a trillion-dollar market."*

CNBC Reports: *"Billionaire founder of Oracle, Larry Ellison, has donated hundreds of millions of dollars to aging research. Bulletproof founder, Dave Asprey, has spent more than a million dollars hacking his own biology."*

Dave Asprey: *"Right now, I am expecting to live to about 180. I think that is very achievable, assuming a truck doesn't hit me."*

CNBC Reports: *"There is already a huge amount of money being made. Right now, in San Francisco, for $8,000 you can get a liter of blood from 16 to 25 years olds injected into your body. By one estimate, the global anti-aging market could surpass $271 billion by 2024. Goals vary too,* *from trying to add decades to your life to simply trying to extend the years that your body remains healthy."*

Peter Nygard: *"This could eliminate all disease; this perhaps is immortality."*

CNBC Reports: *"Some people, especially in places like Silicon Valley, are already taking, sometimes elaborate steps to fight their own aging bodies."*

Dave Asprey: *"It's our job to disrupt things. We literally go out and say, isn't there a better way to do this? So, why wouldn't we disrupt medicine because frankly, medicine has failed us."*

Matt Kaeberlein, Professor of Pathology, University of Washington School of Medicine: *"Part of it comes from the technology and the engineering sort of mindset that many of the people who have become wealthy in Silicon Valley have. They view human biology as something that can be engineered. So, I think that many of us who are biologists by training, can look at some of the strategies that money is being thrown at and say that's not going to work."*

THE SCIENCE OF AGING

Ancient Rome, (45 BC to 476 AD) [3,6] Seneca the Younger, argued that old age was an incurable disease, but that it could be postponed by diet and exercise. The benefits of exercise were echoed by Cicero, who wrote that, "our minds are rendered buoyant by exercise".

CNBC Reports: *"The science of aging, gerontology, is not new. But fairly recent advances have changed what scientists suspect might eventually be possible. Scientists are working on much more radical, but promising approaches to attack aging."*

Laura Deming, Founder & Partner, The Longevity Fund: *"There has been a real breakthrough in longevity research in the past couple of* decades. Starting in the 1990s, scientists, for example, at the University of California at San Francisco, discovered that you can change single genes in a tiny worm and get increases in the lifespan. This opened up the possibility that we can in fact control aging."

Matt Kaeberlein: *"We are starting to learn a lot about the biological mechanisms of aging and the possibility of going beyond what we already know works, to slow the aging process or in some cases even functionally rejuvenate aged animals and hopefully aged people."*

Michael West, CEO, AgeX Therapeutics: *"A lot of people think that scientists working on aging have the goal to extend the human lifespan, to make people immortal, stop aging itself. I wouldn't say that's not our goal."*

"You can reprogram an old cell to be a young cell, which is becoming more and more routine. That's one category of the aging reversal. But other ones are just things that flow around in your blood, many of the essential components in your body drop with age, and if you just bump those up, then your body says, 'Oh yeah, I'm young again.' We're not literally engineered as evolution, but mice die at 2 years, and whales die at 100 years, so clearly it is negotiable."

"The biggest concern for many, is that anti-aging interventions are being developed as a tool for the wealthy. Investment in such research by the ultra-rich can be seen as trying to buy the one thing that money hasn't yet been able to buy them. Immortality."

"This utopian dream of living forever, and I do believe that the anti-aging proponents are not just interested in adding just another 10 or 20 years to their lifespan. They are really looking for immortality. Immortality has been the dream of human beings and has been the story, part of our mythology since the earliest times. But it is a narcissistic dream. Because I have yet to hear a single social good that that will bring."

In other words, do you think the average Joe would get this technology? Absolutely not! It's only for the Elites who are paying for, and driving this rebellious evil satanic technology!

And again, if you want more on this sick, satanic, rebellious desire to try to create your own immortality without God, boy are they in for a rude awakening, get our other extensive documentary called, "**Human Hybrids, Super Soldiers & the Coming Genetic Apocalypse.**" We go way down deep on all this in that documentary.

And by the way, for even more proof that this is the actual goal of these same Elites who are working with Klaus Schwab and The World Economic Forum to take over the planet, in the last video, there was a screen shot. Once again, when do they want to have this supposed immortality without God in place? As you can see, once again, it's 2030, the same "target date" they have for all this global takeover of the world to be in place, that they pacify us by relabeling, "The Great Reset."

Yeah, whatever, The Great Reset is not only an "economic" reset, it's a, "human" reset as well on a multitude of evil levels.

But as crazy as all that sounds, as you just saw, these Elites working with Klaus Schwab and The World Economic Forum, and even The World Health Organization, really are forcing the whole world to go along with their sick, twisted, dystopian, nightmare, and they even admit they really are totally committed to bringing it to the planet, whether we want it or not.

In fact, they clearly admit, "Nobody will be left behind" in their global human takeover reset agenda, as you can see here.

UN/WEF Call for New Global Social Contract With 'No One Left Behind'

"The global technocrat plan requires that everyone participate. Outliers are not allowed and are seen as a threat to the "system," and therefore must be wrapped in or eliminated."

"In Our Common Agenda, the world is facing a choice between collapse and breakthrough. Health systems will not be able to handle the pressure, and the vaccines will be distributed unequally."

And listen to this, "The planet will heat up, resulting in melting polar ice caps, floods, droughts, cyclones, animal species extinction and wasted human lives. Poverty will increase, protests will be crushed, human rights will be neglected, while the development of new forms of warfare will prevent all peace initiatives."

"But if we choose the model of the UN and the World Economic Forum, we are promised Paradise. A greener, safer and better world with a rapid crisis response, including a health system where vaccines are available to all, where fossil fuels are phased out and global average temperatures are kept in check, and where everyone is given the right to a digital connection to access a lifelong quality education."

Or what the Bible calls the Mark of the Beast system of the Antichrist! That's all this is folks! What a bunch of gobbledygook!

And shocker, "The reasoning is similar to what Klaus Schwab expressed during the declaration of The Great Reset: 'We have a choice to remain passive, which would lead to the amplification of many of the trends we see today. Polarization, nationalism, racism, and ultimately increasing social unrest and conflicts. But we have another choice, we can build a new social contract, particularly integrating the next generation, we can change our behavior to be in harmony with nature again, and we can make sure the technologies of the Fourth Industrial Revolution are best utilized to provide us with better lives.'"

Yeah, sure thing pal! How? "All we need to do is hand over the power, and our lives to the UN, and its partner, the World Economic Forum, and allow ourselves to be integrated under the watchful eye of the new Digital god. I can see no other way, than that 200 countries must relinquish part of their decision-making power to a planetary institutional administration."

In other words, you need to submit to the coming Antichrist Kingdom they're building! And shocker, the Pope, Mr. Wannabe False Prophet, is right there going along with all this too!

Vatican Goes Full Technocracy With 'Council for Inclusive Capitalism'

"The New World Order has since changed names multiple times as the public grows increasingly wise to the conspiracy. It's been called the Multilateral World Order, the 4th Industrial Revolution, the Great Reset, etc. The names change but the meaning is always the same.

In the past two years, in the face of extensive global crisis events, the 'new order' establishment, globalists have been talking about, has arrived. With almost no fanfare or mention in the mainstream media. The beginnings of global government already exist, and it's called 'The Council for Inclusive Capitalism.'

And if you have ever wondered why the Pope has been pushing woke ideology, climate alarmism and One World Religion rhetoric in conflict with traditional Christian doctrine, this is why he's following the dictates of the Council for Inclusive Capitalism," in other words the New World Order!

Like it or not, this is what all these Global Elites, Politicians, Klaus Schwab, the Pope, the World Economic Forum, and even The World Health Organization are all up to. And sticking your head in the sand isn't going to change a thing, let alone help anything at all, as this man shares:

Alicia Powe, Investigative Journalist for the Gateway Pundit: *"Over the past few years we have seen the American Sovereignty essentially surrender to the global entities, the pharmaceutical industry, the CDC, and the FDA. Our Constitutional rights, as we have seen, are being deteriorated before our eyes, and it seems like there is not much we can do about it. Just as we see Covid winding down and the government is latching onto mandates, we all know it's not over yet.*

Not only in New York, but they are ramping things up for entering Code-Red, a Covid-Red alert, and they are getting ready to institute the mask mandate again. But this week, something is happening that is very important, that's not being reported on by the mainstream media and if you even google it, of course, the fact checkers are there to try to dispute it and say it's not actually happening.

So, our sovereignty is essentially being surrendered to the WHO so that they can use the pandemic to have a perpetual state of emergency and destroy our Constitution. We are here with Attorney Thomas Renz. You have been fighting these legal battles against the vaccine mandates throughout the Covid pandemic, and now you are raising an alarm about the WHO. I'm not sure if you'd call it a treaty, some say that they are amending international law so that the United States essentially surrenders our sovereignty to the WHO. Please tell us more about it and why this is an imminent threat."

Thomas Renz: *"So, you know this is an interesting thing. And I'm sorry. There is just no way to do this just a little bit. The WHO, we are a part of them, right? We signed the treaty; we are there. Now, you don't have to be a part of them, we can withdraw, but we're generally a part of them. Now what this has done, is that Biden has done something that is really shady.*

He sent proposed amendments over to the International Health Regulations. These International Health Regulations form some sort of a role in International Law. Now where they would fall precisely in terms of being in, and controlling American Law, is really debatable. That's my opinion as an attorney. I think that there are a lot of questions about that. But what he is doing, and Biden knew that there is no way on God's green earth that we would sign a treaty, a treaty ratified with two-thirds of the Senate, that says that we are going to give sovereignty over to the WHO. There's no way he's going to do that. Right?

So, what he did was, he did something a little craftier. And by the way, it wasn't Biden. Biden pooped in his pants in the corner. This is whoever is controlling Biden in the Biden White House, the old Biden White House, Obama is certainly involved. So, what he did was he said, 'Let's alter the regulations within the WHO, to say that the WHO itself can claim control over these nations. It used to be and currently is, until a few days from now, when they push this through, that if the WHO wanted to declare an emergency and try and push to do things within a country, they had to ask that country first. Because nations are sovereign, and national sovereignty takes precedence over an international organization.

What Biden said was, and he made a lot of changes, but most important, is that he said that you don't have to do that, WHO. You just tell us if there's an emergency, and then we are going to make these changes so that you can work with these different entities and organizations in any other country, try and force any country that's not complying into compliance. So, what he's doing is, he is shifting a dramatic amount of power into the WHO's hands. And because the United States will back this plan as long as he's president, or any time that we have any screwy democrat in office that I can see right now, what's going to happen is, they are going to use this as an issue and a mechanism to try to force international will onto the American people, through this really complicated legal process.

There's no good way for us to challenge this in court, directly, right now. NONE! I've looked. Because he's changed the regulations for this international body, this could be like if there is a club in Germany, that said, 'We're going to start an international club in Germany and the UK, and we're going to burn American flags every day.' Well, we couldn't sue that club because we don't have any tie with them. There's no way to sue. Because of this international club, the WHO, who is changing the regulations, I don't see a direct lawsuit that could be filed on that.

So, the problem is, now that we have this buffoon who is changing the regulations and even though I would argue that those regulations don't actually control, he will use those as a mechanism to give away as much sovereignty during the course of his presidency as he possibly can."

Alicia Powe: *"Well, it's funny, because anyone paying attention, realizes that Biden was not legitimately elected, and therefore we had a dictatorship installed. This is ominous."*

Thomas Renz: *"Here's what I'm really concerned about. If you look at the instruction manuals for the PCR tests, they say in them, these tests should not be used to diagnose Covid-19. Yet we have tried to force everybody on the planet to get these PCR tests. Why is that? What do you get with it?"*

Alicia Powe: *"It's a tracking mechanism in our genetic makeup. It was also very peculiar that they had these large Q-tips that they had to poke to the back of the brain that we never used for any other kind of tests."*

Thomas Renz: *"Right, and they're still doing it, right? Now the goal… We know they were harvesting DNA. We know that because we've got the documents, we saw the documents, they were harvesting DNA, and then we also know that they sold the information. Which I would argue is illegal. The PCR tests don't work, and they really don't have any value,* *and if you are going to diagnose Covid-19, you need to do that through symptoms and other things. All the PCR tests can do is give an indication at best, and because we are running in such high cycles, they don't even give accurate indications. But the PCR tests don't work, and they are still pushing them, even today. With these jabs out, they are still pushing, as far and wide as possible, and in fact, Biden just said that he wants to make everyone have a PCR test if they are going to fly on a plane domestically.*

So, why is this so important? Well, they are gathering data? Data is key. We know data is key. We know that if anyone follows the work of the WEF, you all know Klaus Schwab, Yuval Harari and his crew, they talked a lot, in their words, not mine, about things like making human beings hackable."

Yuval Harari: *"What we have now, is the ability to hack human beings, to get inside your brain, to get to know you better than you know yourself. We get to know your weaknesses."*

Yuval Harari: *"Humans are now hackable animals. The whole idea that humans have a soul, or free will, and nobody knows what's happening inside me, so whatever I choose by way of the election or the supermarket, this is my free will, that is over."*

Yuval Harari: *"I think in a couple of decades, when people look back, the things that people will remember from the Covid crisis, is that this is the moment when everything went digital. This was the moment that everything became monitored. That we agreed to be surveilled all the time. Not only in the totalitarian countries, but also in the democracies. And maybe, most importantly of all, this was the moment when surveillance started going under the skin."*

Thomas Renz: *"But the fact that you do that, you have to have immense amounts of data. Data is everything. Their words, not mine. It's not enough to just have data, but we need to go under the skin. Right? What does this mean? They need this data. Now this I would argue, this agreement will allow Biden to say, 'Well, if the WHO declares an* *emergency, we've got to give them all this genetic data. We've got to give them all this information. Because they need to know what's going on. That's just part of the treaty, it's part of the deal.'*

So, he'll use that as a cover. And I think this is one of the most dangerous parts of this, and I literally haven't heard anybody talking about, is that. Because here's what I know, if China wants my DNA, I don't want them to have it. If these globalist monsters want my DNA, I don't want them to have it. I don't care what they are using it for. I don't believe they are using it for the best interest of America, because they have declared themselves enemies of America.

What I think one of the most dangerous aspects is, when he starts doing that, you're not going to see it. You're not going to hear it. The data, the information sharing that he is doing is just going to happen. No one is even going to know. So, we are giving away more of our data, more of our information on American citizens to the enemies of America. And I think probably, the scariest thing here in this treaty right now, they can't beat us in a straight up war, so they are trying to beat us without a war. They are beating us without firing a shot. They need data and information to do that."

Alicia Powe: *"Well, they also, it's a reliance of public compliance and willful ignorance at this point. What do you suspect that they want to do with our DNA, the collection of our DNA? We all know the components of the Great Reset, Schwab and Harari want to upload consciousness and they want immortality, and these vaccines are gene modification shots. They're not gene therapy, they're gene modification and they're collecting our DNA. So, what do you suspect? What are they going to use all this for? This data?"*

Thomas Renz: *"I want to reaffirm what you just said. Gene therapy, right? That's not up for debate. We have Pfizer, we have Moderna, we have Johnson and Johnson, we have Bayer, we have all these companies that have admitted, Pfizer and Moderna in government filings have* *admitted that their shots are gene therapies. By gene therapy we believe, in a lot of cases, it's permanent rewriting of your genetic makeup."*

Alicia Powe: *"They say that therapy is beneficial. I don't know if they even call it therapy anymore. They are causing brain hemorrhages, myocarditis, blood clots, and strokes and death. And no protection against Covid."*

Thomas Renz: *"Nor transmissibility. So, these are gene altering jabs and we know that. Now we also know that there's documentation that these guys have been lamenting for years. They couldn't find a way to get enough people into the trials to perfect gene editing technology. This is not a goal for decades. They've talked about it. We've got paperwork that shows this. They couldn't get people into the trials. Now how do you do that? Well, I don't think that these gene therapies, as disastrous as they are now, and they are a disaster, but that's not where they are going.*

They told us, 'We want to remake humanity, we want to control the genome.' Using their words, not mine. They want people to be gods. So, they want to reprogram or restructure. Well, what's going on? We are seeing a lot of evidence that indicates that a lot of this is really an experiment. They changed the dosages, we believe that they changed formulas, since these things came out. They are talking about how they can have new formulations and have them go through an expedited process. Because with these gene therapies, they need to keep putting out new formulas.

They are talking about this. It looks to me like a great big experiment. And they have to keep experimenting with it until they get it wherever they want it. Basically, the population of earth is their petri dish. Minus them, we know that Pfizer and the others didn't seem to bother to get the jab, as a bunch of others didn't. If you believe the pictures of some of these people getting a needle stuck in their arm were actually getting the shot, you are deluding yourself. But my guess is, all this information is going towards continued work on developing these gene therapy drugs, gene modification technology, and I'm only speculating but they told us. We want to eliminate free will. They want to control people. That's slavery."

Alicia Powe: *"You see this play out in science fiction all the time, in the Matrix, etc. It's always the robots against the machines. How do we stop it? As far as this food takeover, this is basically a New World Order. Being instituted right before our eyes because we have an installed president. And there's no way to fight back?"*

Thomas Renz: *"I mean, listen, I don't know how much clearer it can be, when Klaus Schwab says by 2030 you will own nothing, and you will be grateful for it, what else can I say, I mean, those are his words, not mine. There is a global war against freedom. They don't want freedom. I don't know how else to explain it. You just literally need to take his quotes and watch what he is doing. We lost a lot of freedom in this country.*

And the people of this country have to understand, you may not be comfortable with the fact that Yuval Harari has told you that he likes Nazi's, that he is going to hack your brain and that he wants to control you. But those are his words not mine. You may not like the fact that Klaus Schwab said by 2030 you'll own nothing, and you'll like it. You may not like the fact that we had '2000 Mules,' and all these other things that indicate a massive election fraud. You may not like the fact that there have been 20, 30, 40 mysterious fires in various food processing plants and airplanes crashing into food processing plants.

And at the same time, Union Pacific is putting a moratorium on fertilizer shipments during the growing season. Union Pacific is owned and controlled by BlackRock and Vanguard. You may not like looking at this. This may sound like a conspiracy theory to you, but the simple fact of the matter is that I've got the paperwork, I've got the data. And it may make you uncomfortable to see it or to hear it, but when a serial killer tells you that they killed 50 people, if you choose not to believe them, well that's on you. That's on you! We have monsters at our door, and I've got to tell you, it's very uncomfortable for me to shout these things out. It sounds like a science fiction movie."

Successful Farming Reports: *"Bill Gates is about to change the way America Farms. The Cofounder of Microsoft and his wife make an auspicious debut on the 2020 Land Report 100, as America's largest private farmland owners."*

Bill Gates: *"Rich nations should move to '100 percent synthetic beef.'"*

But it's not. It's our current reality created by these sick, evil, twisted Global Elites who are working with Klaus Schwab, the World Economic Forum, aided by politicians, The World Health Organization, to take over the whole planet and enslave humanity, and modify us into a new version called, Human 2.0, as they get to live forever with us serving them!

It's nuts and crazy, but this is all coming out of their own mouths, and sticking your head in the sand, as the lawyer said, isn't going to help anything! Whether you like it or not this is really happening, and we need to get the word out to as many people as we can, as fast as we can, if there's any hope of stopping it!

And again, this is why we have repeatedly warned that the phrase Klaus Schwab, and the World Economic Forum, and all these Global Elites repeatedly use to describe what they're building, that is, The Great Reset, is not just an "economic" reset, but it really is a "human" reset. They literally want to alter us into something non-human!

Why? Because they're sick, evil, twisted to the core, and they're not only rebelling against God, but they are in for a rude awakening one day, with God, as they themselves are trying to play God to the rest of us! God is going to have the last word on this!

But again, here's Klaus Schwab himself admitting this sick, evil, twisted plan that he has for all of us.

This video is edited for comedic effect:

Interviewer: *"My special guest with me today is none other than Mr. Klaus Schwab. Founder and chairman of the World Economic Forum. Mr. Schwab, I have been a big fan of your work for a while now, so I am very pleased to have this opportunity to be talking to you."*

Klaus Schwab: *"It's my great honor."*

Interviewer: *"Thanks Bro. I'm honored that you're honored. Now you are someone that nobody in their right mind would ever let babysit their children. Yet trusting you to shape the future of humanity is something that I think we are all on board with. Your work is incredibly altruistic, so what is it that you see that the world needs that you are trying to provide?"*

Klaus Schwab: *"I see the need for a Great Reset."*

Interviewer: *"Klaus, you're just being modest. I think it will be a tremendous reset, it's a big service to humanity. As such, is there a dilemma about the Great Reset that keeps you up at night?"*

Klaus Schwab: *"How can we do it to make sure that the majority of people are benefiting from it and not just a minority."*

Interviewer: *"I think, if there is a person that the common people rely on to stand up for them against the agenda of the elites, it's you, Klaus. Tell me about your connection to the deep state."*

Klaus Schwab: *"Intrinsically connected to one online muscle."*

Interviewer: *"You just said actual words, but I like your confidence. And some people with what's called evidence, have suggested that you've orchestrated how you say, the global pandemic, and they don't like it. How do you feel about your orchestration of this?"*

Klaus Schwab: *"That's what I may be most proud of in my life."*

Interviewer: *"I like how you just own it."*

Klaus Schwab: *"We know the health industries, the digital industry, will go out of this crisis strengthened."*

Interviewer: *"What a weird coincidence that the industries you control have profited so much. Huh, well, I'm wondering, and just to give you context, some of the historic greats have had quotes that people will always think of when they hear their names, like Jesus, 'Do unto others as you'd have done to yourself.' And then you, 'By 2030 you'll own nothing and be happy about it.' Very inspirational I might add. What is your motive behind such profound words?"*

Klaus Schwab: *"This is an opportunity again to find solutions which are beneficial for the next generation."*

Interviewer: *"I do see how owning nothing would be very beneficial to the next generation. It's kind of like mandatory poverty. Well, not for you but for them. Kind of takes the stress out of wondering, 'Will I be successful or not?' and I like that. But how do you think the next generation will feel about it?"*

Klaus Schwab: *"So, we have to prepare for an angrier world."*

Interviewer: *"Yeah, sounds like they'll love it. Moving along, you've advocated for a global digital health pass. What does that mean?"*

Klaus Schwab: *"We provide everybody with a decent access to the health system."*

Interviewer: *"My notes say you've never been elected to be in charge of the Health Care System, nor have you been elected to be in charge of everyone for that matter. Must be a typo on my end. (He turns to his producers) Guys could we get this corrected? Sorry about that, sir. Very embarrassing. Let's just move on. Now, classy boy, you've said to never let a good crisis go to waste and you've definitely capitalized on your*

Covid crisis. Do you have plans for another crisis, perhaps an even bigger one?"

Klaus Schwab: *"The environmental crisis, the climate crisis could be a much bigger one."*

Interviewer: *"Can't wait."*

Klaus Schwab: *"However, we do know that global energy systems, food systems and supply chains will be deeply affected."*

Interviewer: *"There are no coincidences, are there, Klaus? I wonder who will affect these things and why do you know so far in advance that they will be affected? Schwabsky, your narrative says a lot about helping people and bettering their lives, while those who believe in the conspiracy theory called reality, see your actions as ones that hurt people and make their lives worse."*

Klaus Schwab: *"I think we shouldn't see the two as contradictory to be objective."*

Interviewer: *"It's a point, I see how that square peg fits perfectly in the round hole. Accordingly, you've talked before about genetically editing the population and your top advisor, Dr. Noah Harari has talked about you elites building digital dictatorships by hacking humans and re-engineering life for those at home. Let's take a look."*

Klaus Schwab: *"This one source is first the Industrial Revolution. It doesn't change what you are doing, it changes you if you take a genetic editing."*

Yuval Noah Harari: *"Data might enable human elites to do something even more radical than just build digital dictatorships. By hacking organisms, elites may gain the power to re-engineer the future of life itself. But soon, at least some corporations and governments will be able to systematically hack all the people."*

Interviewer: *"So, Klaus, given what you and your advisor have said, how do you feel about controlling every person on the planet?"*

Klaus Schwab: *"I'm so happy!"*

Interviewer: *"Dude, that's pretty heavy, enslaving humanity. Bet you never held a child, not even once. But here's what I'm wondering. If enslaving humanity is your goal, you can't just tell them what you're doing or else they wouldn't take your injections and use your digital IDs. You'd have to call it something else to disguise it, something benign or even inspiring, so do you have an alias for what you call your human enslavement project?"*

Klaus Schwab: *"The Fourth Industrial Revolution."*

Interviewer: *"That's a great name for it. It sounds progressive. I'm on board. Let's dive deeper because I like where we're going here. So, to control people, you'd have to get them to depend on you and all the governments that you control, and we all know that the only way for the few to control the many is with fear. Now, I know you're big on helping people by fearmongering about your climate crisis, so how do you see all that fitting together?"*

Klaus Schwab: *"Why not tie government aid to the green economy which we have to create?"*

Interviewer: *"Oh, a social credit score. That sounds super sweet, but to your question, why not tie government aid to the green economy, which we have to create. That's a great question and I'm happy to share. First, creating a society where people have to rely on government aid is called communism, and people with a soul see that as evil. And it's caused horror and suffering 100% of the time that it's been implemented throughout history. I think your green economy vision is just a virtuous sounding scheme to manipulate people with fear into being controllable, rather than you having genuine concern for potential planetary changes, due to carbon emissions. So, when you look at it that way that's why, not* to tie government aid to the green economy - that we don't have to create. That's a great looking shirt by the way."

Klaus Schwab: *"In times of crisis, the role of governments is more important and more relevant than ever."*

Interviewer: *"Well, not if it's the governments causing the crisis in order to form a One World Government. Oh, but who's your all-time government leader you're colluding with in order to cause times of crisis?"*

Klaus Schwab: *"It's His Excellency Xi Jinping."*

Interviewer: *"He is excellent, isn't he? I love all the genocide he's doing. This has been a beautiful interview but before we end, it's time for the lightning round, Klaus. If you were a kitchen appliance, what would you be?"*

Klaus Schwab: *"A sink."*

Interviewer: *"You'd be a sink? I totally get it with a personality and all. Do you get more excited about citizens shaping the future, or the governments you control shaping the future?"*

Klaus Schwab: *"Governments shaping the future."*

Interviewer: *"You are a communist, that's awesome. Well, Klaus, thank you for taking the time to sit down and open up in such a beautiful, vulnerable, honest way. I'm walking away feeling inspired to be more obedient, surrender my free will, and I even feel more terror. Thank you, Klaus. I hope you have a great reset."*

This is what these sick, evil, twisted Elites, including Klaus Schwab himself, really are up to. The enslavement of humanity, and it's no laughing matter!

Chapter Six

World Economic Forum & the Great Reset

The fourth way Klaus Schwab pulled off this sick, twisted, satanic, dystopian nightmare for all of our futures, is he also grabbed control of the WORLD'S LIVELIHOODS.

You see, if you're getting a little squeamish and alarmed, or terrified like this guy mentioned in that video over this obvious global total takeover of the planet, including our leaders, our finances and our health by Klaus Schwab and the gang, hey no worries. They've just relabeled this sick, evil, megalomanic, global, dystopian takeover as "The Fourth Industrial Revolution," or, "The Great Reset." I mean, doesn't that sound so much more comfortable and palatable, much more wonderful, and less threatening? Doesn't that help pacify and ease any and all fears you might have over what you're seeing so far, and what they're really planning on doing to the whole planet?

Yeah, right, I don't think so! In fact, don't take my word for it, let's listen to theirs. Let's take a look at what this so-called Great Reset is really all about, according to their own words, and see how they clearly admit, it will dictate every single aspect of not just our world leaders, world finances, and world health, but everyone's individual livelihoods on the whole planet.

And the first example of this wicked agenda that I bring you is simply from one of the World Economic Forum's own promotional videos from their very own YouTube channel, seen here describing in their own

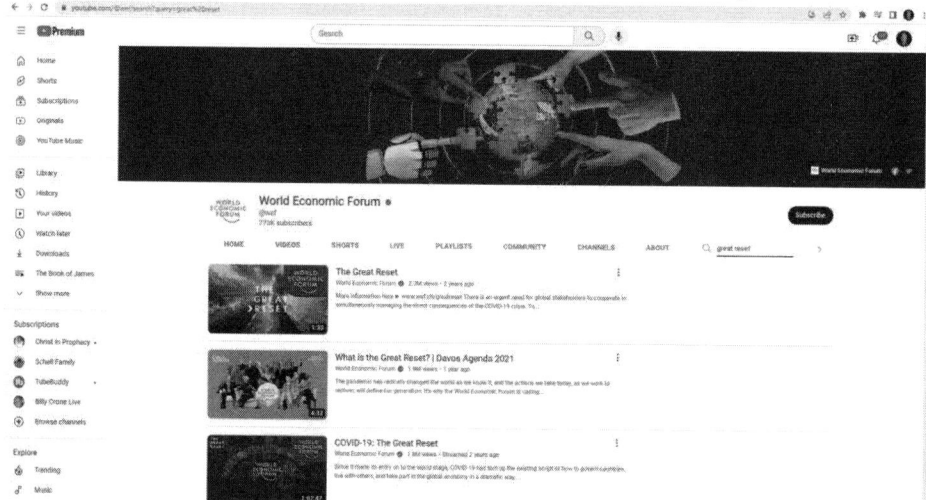

words what this Great Reset is really all about. See if this will calm your fears.

Narrator: *"The pandemic has radically changed the world as we know it. The actions we take today as we work to recover, will define our generation."*

Kristalina Georgieva, Managing Director, International Monetary Fund: *"Now is the time to think what history would say about this crisis."*

Narrator: *"2020 has been challenging, on a lot of levels, as economic, environmental and societal frailties have been laid bare. But it's also proved that when we need to, we can act rapidly and restructure our lives."*

Antonio Guterres, UN Secretary General: *"Recovery from the pandemic is an opportunity. We can see rays of hope in the form of a vaccine, but there is no vaccine for the planet. Nature needs a bailout."*

Angel Gurria, Secretary-General of the OECD: *We don't want to go back to the status quo that you had before, simply because it was the status quo that brought us here."*

Narrator: *"With everything falling apart, we can reshape the world in ways that we couldn't before. Ways that better address so many of the challenges we face. And that is why so many are calling for a Great Reset. A Great Reset? That sounds more like Buzzword bingo, must be some nefarious plans for world domination. Hands up! This kind of slogan hasn't gone that well. But all we really want to say is, we all have the opportunity to build a better world. And it's not surprising that people who have been disenfranchised by a broken system and pushed even further by the pandemic will suspect global leaders of conspiracy.*

But the world is not that simple. Every one of us has different priorities, values and ideas. That's part of why solutions are so hard to come by, and why we all need to be involved in the decision-making. Because, whether it's politicians, CEO's, academics, activists, or you, we are all about getting people together, even those you might not like, to sit down at the table and develop solutions that work for all of us."

Ajay Banga, CEO, Mastercard: *"We need enormous trust between the private sector and the public sector for this to actually work. That trust is hard to come by."*

Narrator: *"It's time for people to work together, listen to each other and to build this trust so we can move towards a better world. And we really need one. Because, while the pandemic affects us all, it is clear that it affects some more than others."*

Grace Forrest, Human Rights Activist: *"The first people who are hit, are the people at the front. Those who are vulnerable, it's those on the frontline who take it first. And that is simply unacceptable."*

Narrator: *"At the start of 2020, 1% of the world's population, and 44% of the wealth, and since the start of the pandemic, billionaires have increased theirs by more than 25%, while 150 million people fell back into extreme poverty. And with climate change set to dwarf the damage caused by the pandemic, the message from 2020 should be abundantly clear."*

Marc Benioff, CEO, Salesforce: *"Capitalism as we know it, is dead. This obsession that we have had, with maximizing profits for shareholders alone, has led to incredible inequality and a planetary emergency."*

Narrator: *"But no one can do this alone, and top-down approaches won't get us anywhere, because everything we've learned in our work, has shown us that diverse voices lead to better results, and it's for these reasons that the forum talks about something called stakeholder capitalism, which would shift businesses away from just profit."*

Saadia Zahidi, Managing Director, World Economic Forum: *"Because if we want to change where the focus of our recovery will go, then we need a new dashboard for the new economy, and that needs to encompass people, planet, prosperity and institutions."*

Narrator: *"Giving people a real stake in the economy and putting well-being before growth and that's all about getting the right people in the right place at the right time."*

Hindou Oumarou Ibrahim, Indigenous Rights Activist: *"We must rebuild our relationship with nature for the survival of the peoples of our planet."*

Jane Goodall, Conservationist: *"We have a window of time which is closing, and we need everybody who cares to get together and find solutions, now."*

Narrator: *"It's the people who have great ideas and who share them with others, they're the ones who are shaping the future. So, if you want to be a part of the change, then tune in, turn on and get involved. Follow the Davos Agenda, right here, online, on YouTube."*

In other words, wherever we're broadcasting this utopian message of a wonderful life-saving Great Reset, from these purely innocent, altruistic, global entities all over the planet. Including the World Economic Forum's own website as seen here.

Just push this button and get involved and help us reset the planet before it blows up, with the Covid Plandemic as the trigger or excuse, to get this all started. With the target date again, of 2030, to get this all into place around the whole planet!

Okay, so much for calming our fears. Did you notice, they even admitted in their own video, "I know this sounds like a conspiracy theory of Global Elites trying to take over the world, but trust us, it's much simpler than that."

Really? How much simpler can you get? It's obvious. Even a five-year-old can figure this out, that you're trying to take over the planet! So much for just being a conspiracy theory! You admit it yourself!

But that's just the "general idea" of The Great Reset. Let's now get down to specifics, again, with their own videos and propaganda. All over the world we see what the specifics of this planetary takeover will look like in the very near future, if they get their way, or as they say, if we're dumb enough to trust them!

WORLD ECONOMIC FORUM ANNUAL MEETING – DAVOS 2022

Volodymyr Zelenskyy, President of Ukraine: *"This is really the moment when it is decided whether brute force will rule the world."*

Yevheniia Kravchuk, Member of Parliament, Ukraine: *"When you pay for gas and oil from Russia, it returns as this striking element or a bullet."*

Ursula von der Leyen, European Commission: *"This is not just a matter of the Ukraine survival, this is putting our whole international order into question."*

Ngozi Okonjo-Iweala, World Trade Organization: *"We have the institutions, but we lost the feeling of global solidarity. If you don't have that, then you cannot make these institutions work."*

Kristalina Georgieva: *"Globalization has served the world well, except that we make the error to pretend that it works equally well for everybody, everywhere."*

Francois Villeroy de Galhau, Central Bank of France: *"What is at stake with this crypto regulation with taxation, it's not bureaucracy, it's not red tape, it's giving our fellow citizens the feeling that globalization can be fair."*

Jens Stoltenberg, North Atlantic Treaty Organization: *"The protection of values is more important than profit."*

David Beasley, United Nations World Food Program: *"With this whole $130 trillion worth of wealth on planet earth, there should not be a child on this planet that goes hungry much less starve to death."*

Elizabeth Wathuti, Green Generation Institute: *"Frontline communities are not waiting for the impacts of climate change to hit in the future. It's happening right now."*

Gita Gopinath, International Monetary Fund: *"All countries in the world, regardless of their level of income, are recognizing the importance of addressing climate change."*

John Kerry, Special Presidential Envoy for Climate, USA: *"We stand on the precipice. No government has the money to solve this problem by itself. We need you; we need the private sector all around the world to step up."*

Marc Benio, Salesforce: *"We are witnessing an ecopreneur revolution, this is going to be an opportunity, because there is so much capital that can be deployed by investors on this incredible new sector."*

Satya Nadella, Microsoft: *"None of us are coming out of this pandemic presuming that we are going to go back 2019. We have to find a new way going forward."*

Josephine Teo, Minister of Communications and Information, Singapore: *"Industries and business models are continuously disrupted, but what it really requires, is a very, very steady pace cross skilling, upskilling and reskilling.*

Salil S. Parek, Infosys: *"Tech really enables all of us to reskill at speed at what used to be 10 or 15 years, is now just 5 years."*

Ellyn Shook: *"In an organization whose purpose is to deliver on the promise of technology and human ingenuity, you really have to build diversity, but more importantly, inclusion into your talent practices every single day."*

Alex Liu, Kearney: *"How can you belong in a company, or a community if you don't see people like yourself, however you find them."*

Caroline Casey, Valuable 500: *"This is inclusion by design for everyone, and we hear everyone's voices at the beginning of the process."*

Bill Gates, Bill & Melinda Gates Foundation: *"With all these priorities, can Global Health maintain the disability that it deserves?"*

Helen E. Clark, World Health Organization: *"We have a responsibility to protect the populations. We have these huge health issues."*

Albert Bourla, Pfizer: *"Pfizer will provide all its positive medicines and vaccines on a non-profit basis to 1.2 billion people living in 45 lower income countries."*

Klaus Schwab: *"We have means to improve the health of the world. We need collaborative efforts."*

David Beasley, United Nations World Food Program: *"There are enough leaders in Davos this week, we need their engagement and their ingenuity, their creativity, that is what the world needs at a time like this."*

Narrator: *"Put simply, the European Immunization Agenda 2030 is the European region's immunization strategy for the next decade. It is a flagship initiative of the European program of work 2020 to 2025, which unites all stakeholders to achieve better health in the European region. Guided by the EIA 2030, immunization systems will be strengthened in order to reduce the burden of diseases that are preventable by vaccination, increase equitable access to new and existing vaccines for everyone, regardless of age identity or geographic location.*

And strengthen primary health care, and thereby contribute to achieving universal health coverage and sustainable development, progress challenges and lessons learned through implementation of the European Action Plan 2015-2020, and during the Covid-19 pandemic, shown that these goals cannot be reached through business as usual. Strategic pivots are needed toward local ownership and political commitment to ensure both sustainable supply and high demand.

Data enabled and tailored local solutions, to address local challenges, life course vaccinations, and mainstream catch-up for those who missed their vaccination doses, results-based monitoring and accountability mechanisms, and partner coordination.

EIA 2030 does not belong to the WHO, or to its member states alone. It will guide and align policymakers, national immunization programs, professional associations, civil society, community-based organizations and other immunization stakeholders in the region for the coming decade.

This collective action in the European region will bring us close to a world in which everyone, everywhere, at every age, fully benefits from vaccines, good health and well-being."

CAN YOU RENT EVERYTHING YOU NEED IN LIFE?

"Recent years have seen massive growth in the rental economy. The first tool library opened in the 1970s in California. With more now popping up in cities around the world. These work much like a normal library. But you're borrowing much more than just books. At the Toronto Tool Library, you can borrow anything from a wrench to a lawnmower, or use a 3D printer or laser cutter. Saving you money and preventing waste in the process. Projects like, "London's Library of Things," are changing the way we consume. The upshot is that you get the things you need and want, with less debt and less waste. In 50 years, maybe we won't own anything."

8 PREDICTIONS FOR THE WORLD IN 2030

- *You'll own nothing. And you'll be happy. Whatever you want you'll rent, and it'll be delivered by drone.*
- *The U.S. won't be the world's leading superpower. A handful of countries will dominate.*
- *You won't die waiting for an organ donor. We won't transplant organs. We'll print new ones instead.*
- *You'll eat much less meat. An occasional treat, not a staple. For the good of the environment and our health.*

- *A billion people will be displaced by climate change. We'll have to do a better job at welcoming and integrating refugees.*
- *Polluters will have to pay to emit carbon dioxide. There will be a global price on carbon. This will help make fossil fuels history.*
- *You could be preparing to go to Mars. Scientists will have worked out how to keep you healthy in space. The start of a journey to find alien life.*
- *Western values will have been tested to the breaking point. Checks and balances that underpin our democracies must not be forgotten.*

Yeah, and what also shouldn't be forgotten, is what these guys are really up to! And it ain't going to be in 50 years. As you saw, it all rallies around the date of 2030.

But they admit what they want to do. There is no conspiracy here, it's all on tape! And I quote:

1. "We'll own nothing" — And "we'll be happy about it."
2. "The U.S. won't be the world's leading superpower."
3. "You won't die waiting for an organ donor" — They will be made by 3D printers and you'll make sure everyone gets their vaccinations or shots.
4. "You'll eat much less meat" — Meat will be "an occasional treat, not a staple, for the good of the environment and our health."
5. "A billion people will be displaced by climate change" – What are you going to do with all those people? You're going to have open borders?
6. "Polluters will have to pay to emit carbon dioxide" – "There will be a global price on carbon. This will help make fossil fuels history."
7. "You could be preparing to go to Mars" — Scientists "will have worked out how to keep you healthy in space."
8. "Western values will have been tested to the breaking point." – "Checks and balances that underpin our democracies must not be forgotten."

That doesn't sound like a utopia to me, how about you? They clearly admit, on tape, by 2030, with the Covid Plandemic kicking it all off as the excuse to implement all this, that they will be controlling every aspect of our livelihoods, and getting rid of all freedom, everywhere around the whole world, completely!

Then we will have the so-called, "privilege," of being a "ward," of The Great Reset society! Are you kidding me? That's not saving the planet, that's taking over the planet! No wonder you said, "trust us, it's not what you think it is." You liar!

In fact, it gets worse than that! The World Economic Forum

on their own website, expands on these eight changes coming to the whole planet with their planetary takeover, called The Great Reset. It shares the following:

1. **All products will have become services.** "I don't own anything. I don't own a car. I don't own a house. I don't own any appliances or any clothes. Shopping is a distant memory in the city of 2030, whose inhabitants have cracked clean energy and borrow what they need on demand, and every move is tracked.
2. **There is a global price on carbon.** China took the lead in 2017 with a market for trading the right to emit a ton of CO_2, setting the world on a path towards a single carbon price, and a powerful incentive to ditch fossil fuels with efficient solar panels, and prices for renewables falling sharply.

3. **U.S. dominance is over**. Nation states will have staged a comeback. Instead of a single force, a handful of countries will dominate.
4. **Farewell hospital, hello home-spital**. Technology will have further disrupted disease, and the hospital as we know it will be on its way out with fewer accidents, thanks to self-driving cars and great strides in preventive and personalized medicine. Scalpels and organ donors are out, tiny robotic tubes and bio-printed organs are in.
5. **We are eating much less meat**. We will treat meat as a treat rather than a staple, with convenience food redesigned to be healthier and less harmful to the environment.
6. **Today's Syrian refugees, 2030's CEO's**. Highly educated Syrian refugees will have come of age by 2030, making the case for the economic integration of those who have been forced to flee conflict. The world needs to be better prepared for populations on the move, as climate change will have displaced 1 billion people.
7. **The values that built the West will have been tested to the breaking point**. We forget the checks and balances that bolster our democracies at our peril.
8. **By 2030, we'll be ready to move humans toward the Red Planet**. Once we get there, we'll probably discover evidence of alien life and big science will help us to answer big questions about life on earth.

Yeah, including why are you taking over planet earth, and apparently, taking over one planet's not good enough for you, you greedy liars! But don't worry, this is all going to turn out great. After all, they don't call it the "Great" Reset for nothing! Yeah, right! How dumb do they think we are?

But again folks, as you can see, there's no conspiracy here. They're not hiding this. It's in their own videos, on their websites, you name it, for all the world to see, at least for those that have eyes to see and ears to hear.

In fact, as insane as all this sounds,

here's Ida Auken, from Denmark, one of the Young Global Leaders of the World Economic Forum saying, "Welcome to 2030. I own nothing, have no privacy, and life has never been better."

Are you sick? And here she is expounding on that insane comment in this article she wrote.

"Welcome to the year 2030. Welcome to my city – or should I say, 'our city.' I don't own anything. I don't own a car. I don't own a house. I don't own any appliances or any clothes.

It might seem odd to you, but it makes perfect sense for us in this city. Everything you considered a product, has now become a service. We have access to transportation, accommodation, food and all the things we need in our daily lives. One by one all these things became free, so it ended up not making sense for us to own much.

First, communication became digitized and free to everyone. Then, when clean energy became free, things started to move quickly. Transportation dropped dramatically in price. It made no sense for us to own cars anymore, because we could call a driverless vehicle, or a flying car for longer journeys within minutes. We started transporting ourselves in a much more organized and coordinated way when public transport became easier, quicker and more convenient than the car. Now I can hardly believe that we accepted congestion and traffic jams, not to mention the air pollution from combustion engines. What were we thinking?

Sometimes I use my bike when I go to see some of my friends. I enjoy the exercise and the ride. It kind of gets the soul to come along on the journey. Funny how some things never seem to lose their excitement: walking, biking, cooking, drawing and growing plants. It makes perfect sense and reminds us of how our culture emerged out of a close relationship with nature.

In our city, we don't pay any rent, because someone else is using our free space whenever we do not need it. My living room is used for business meetings when I am not there.

Once in a while, I will choose to cook for myself. It is easy – the necessary kitchen equipment is delivered at my door within minutes. Since transport became free, we stopped having all those things stuffed into our home. Why keep a pasta-maker and a crepe cooker crammed into our cupboards? We can just order them when we need them.

This also made the breakthrough of the circular economy easier. When products are turned into services, no one has an interest in things with a short life span. Everything is designed for durability, repairability and recyclability. The materials are flowing more quickly in our economy and can be transformed to new products pretty easily.

Environmental problems seem far away, since we only use clean energy and clean production methods. The air is clean, the water is clean, and nobody would dare to touch the protected areas of nature, because they constitute such value to our well-being. In the cities, we have plenty of green space, and plants and trees all over. I still do not understand why, in the past we filled all free spots in the city with concrete.

Shopping? I can't really remember what that is. For most of us, it has been turned into choosing things to use. Sometimes I find this fun, and sometimes I just want the algorithm to do it for me. It knows my taste better than I do by now.

When AI and robots took over so much of our work, we suddenly had time to eat well, sleep well and spend time with other people. The concept of rush hour makes no sense anymore since the work that we do can be done at any time. I don't really know if I would call it work anymore. It is more like thinking-time, creation time and development time.

For a while, everything was turned into entertainment, and people did not want to bother themselves with difficult issues. It was only at the last minute that we found out how to use all these new technologies for better purposes than just killing time.

My biggest concern is all the people who do not live in our city. Those we lost on the way. Those who decided that it became too much, all this technology. Those who felt obsolete and useless, when robots and AI took over big parts of our jobs. Those who got upset with the political system and turned against it.

Once in a while I get annoyed about the fact that I have no real privacy. Nowhere I can go and not be registered. I know that, somewhere, everything I do, think and dream of is recorded. I just hope that nobody will use it against me.

All in all, it is a good life. Much better than the path we were on, where it became so clear that we could not continue with the same model of growth. We had all these terrible things happening, lifestyle diseases, climate change, the refugee crisis, environmental degradation, completely congested cities, water pollution, air pollution, social unrest and unemployment. We lost way too many people, before we realized that we could do things differently."

Yeah, sure you did, lady. Not to mention all those people you killed with the jab. But see, isn't this great? I own nothing, I have no privacy, and I'm monitored wherever I go! It's the "Great" Reset!

And just to make sure you go along with this "Great" Reset, or planetary takeover pitched as a "modern utopia," where they will dictate and micromanage every detail about our livelihoods, the media is out there promoting it too!

Narrator: *"It's part of the human condition to imagine what the future might look like. Years ago, science fiction writers like Arthur C. Clarke dreamed and future gazed, mapping out what 2020 might be like."*

Arthur C. Clarke: *"The big difference when he grows up (referring to a small boy standing beside him while speaking), in fact if we wanted to wait for the year 2001, is that he will have, in his own house, not a computer as big as this, but at least a console, to which you can talk to his friendly local computer, and get all the information you need in the course of living in a complex modern society. This will be in a compact form in his own house."*

Narrator: *"Our lives have changed so dramatically in the first 20 years of this millennium, but what will our domestic life in 2030 look like? What smart devices will be at the heart of our homes? And with assistive tech supporting us in our daily tasks, will there come a time when we never need to leave the house?"*

HOW WE'LL LIVE IN 2030

Narrator: *"We hear things like, the internet of things informing the stocking of our fridges and freezers, but this is hiding the real story of how we'll adopt such smart technologies. We've already invited extraordinary machine learning devices into our homes and 22% of UK households have* *one or more smart speakers, while the number of IOT connected devices worldwide, is projected to almost triple to 30.9 billion units by 2025. Yes, most of us only use an Alexa, or Google Nest to listen to music, the radio, or play silly jokes, but behind the scenes, big tech aims to make these products central as to how our homes run."*

Morgan Meaker, Telegraph Tech Reporter: *"The companies behind smart speakers, or they're called now, digital assistants, are actually trying to transform them so they're not digital assistants anymore, but more sort of household managers or household brains, actually can control a whole network of other devices inside your home. The likes of Apple and Amazon are trying to integrate their smart devices so they work with kind of automatic Hoovers, that will basically work on their own. They'll map the inside of your home. Now whoever is in charge of household chores is going to be totally liberated from having to do that because they won't have to spend hours Hoovering, they'll just be able to get an automatic vacuum to do it instead. That will mean a big change for a lot of people.*

Nvidia, are basically working on this, sort of quite large giant robot arm, that will live in your kitchen. It can help you open drawers; it can put things away. So, it will map out where everything is in your kitchen, and the idea will probably be that it can tidy up after you, or it can even do the cooking and then tidy up. That would mean you probably wouldn't even have to be in your kitchen. It might just serve food out of a porthole, that you never have to enter, and obviously that would transform everyone's houses."

Narrator: *"In the future, this sensor-led technology will likely be built right into the structures of our homes. Smart modular housing developments are starting to emerge, as the viable, planet-friendly option for home buyers and construction firms alike."*

Morgan Meaker: *"So, I guess the real advantage with smart homes, is they'll be able to monitor everything. So, they'll be able to monitor how much energy you're using, how much water you're using, and that sort of* *ability to essentially put sensors around your kind of everyday tasks. That will mean you'll be able to see where I am wasting energy and water, and then you'll be able to take steps to combat that. I mean that could have a big impact on Britain, trying to meet its net zero targets."*

Narrator: *"But this is just the beginning. Smart technologies are beginning to reshape the way in which entire cities are inhabited. Around the world cities are deploying sensors to track footfall, litter and air pollution."*

Morgan Meaker: *"While we're seeing smart homes kind of making leaps and bounds at the moment, I think somewhere where it's actually a bit more advanced is in a smart city. So, councils have really noticed the potential here. Smart homes and smart cities are going to be integrated into the future, and that's going to make big changes."*

Narrator: *"In Sunderland, bins fitted with sensors can tell the council when they're full, and in China, sensors combined with facial recognition can detect individuals who are jaywalking and display their faces on screens to shame them. And intelligent tech is beginning to shape the way we may shop IRL in the future.*

In early 2021, Amazon opened its first high street supermarket in West London, based on its successful rollout in the U.S. This shop uses advanced sensor technology to track the contents of your actual in-store shopping basket in real time, updating your account spending as you shop, and billing you once you've left the store."

Morgan Meaker: *"I think definitely, Amazon wants it to be a high-street revolution, and one of the reasons that they're creating this supermarket, and they've also just opened a new hair salon in London. This is not just so Amazon can use the technology, but it's so it can sell it to other people. I'm sure in the very near distance, we will see this those big supermarket chains, also experimenting or integrating into their own stores."*

Narrator: *"In the 21ˢᵗ century, data is the most valuable resource in the world, more so even than oil. And when used alongside smart technology and machine learning, this data will be key in the re-imagining of how we live, both inside and outside of the home in 2030."*

Wow! Sounds and looks like a giant "prison planet" to me! This is the Great Reset? This isn't great!

Did you see how those "smart homes" will monitor and control everything you do? You know, like a prisoner who lives in a prison. And those "smart homes" were not much bigger than a prison cell.

And did you catch that phrase, "Will there come a time when we never leave the house?" You know, like when you live in a prison! And speaking of which, "You may never have to enter the kitchen for food, it can be served to you through a porthole." Direct quote, just like a prison!

This is insane! It's not utopia! It's these evil, wicked, twisted, megalomaniac's nightmare, that they're forcing upon us! It's total global slavery!

I mean, what's next? You going to dictate what job I can get, and where I get to live too? Yes, that's also part of their evil plan, as you can see here in these videos, starting with jobs in the future that they're creating for us. You know, because even prisoners have to work!

Narrator: *"Covid-19 is one of the biggest crises of our time. It has impacted every single one of us, shaken our social systems and disrupted every sector of our economies. The automation of work with the global recession led workers to lose their jobs at an accelerated pace compared to previous years, and this trend is expected to continue. The ongoing shift in the division, in the division of labor between humans, machines, and algorithms, might displace 85 million jobs worldwide in the next 5 years, while 97 million new roles – ones that are more adapted to this new task's distribution – may emerge.*

By 2025, companies expect to displace roughly 6% of their total workforce, 1 in 2 workers will need reskilling, and those remaining in their current roles will need to update 40% of their skill set to adapt to the changing labor market. There is a way to collectively benefit from these challenging times. Decades of research have shown that the most valuable asset of any economy or company is its human capital.

Around the globe, companies experiencing a shortage in relevant skills for future roles, are investing in reskilling and upskilling their workforce. By 2025, organizations say they will train over 70% of their employees to ensure they can smoothly transition into the jobs of tomorrow. These include DevOps Engineers, Artificial Intelligence Specialists, Digital Marketing Managers, Talent Acquisition Specialists, and Customer Success Specialists.

It will take on average between 2 weeks and 5 months for workers to pick up new skills, allowing them to move into these new roles. But data shows they won't need to have the perfect skill set to start transitioning. While 2/3rds of employers expect to get a return on investment in employees reskilling programs within just one year. Governments will also need to step in, to update and fund education and training systems, and to ensure displaced workers have adequate safety nets.

With purposeful leadership and collaboration, we can turn this global crisis into a unique opportunity to transition into a future of jobs that is inclusive, fair, and sustainable."

And if you believe that, I've got some swamp land to sell you here in the desert! But let me translate that for you. The future of jobs is going to be taken over by AI or Artificial Intelligence, and Robots with AI, which again we covered in great detail in our other documentary again, **"The AI Invasion."**

But because Klaus Schwab, the World Economic Forum and these Global Elites are making AI take over half the jobs on the whole planet, you and I, the "human capital," which is another code word for, "slave labor," will either have to let them, "retool" our skillset for the job they tell us we can have, or we become one of those, "useless eaters," again

NAZI EUTHANASIA PROGRAM

Hitler started a program to *euthanize* (ending life to stop pain) people with *disabilities* and deformities

The Nazis' goal was to eliminate *"useless eaters"*: those who were a drain on German resources

This Nazi policy's purpose was to remove those *"unworthy of life"*

they keep talking about and have to be gotten rid of, because we're not giving them any ROI, or return on their investment.

    But as you can see, Klaus's Nazi background and upbringing is coming in to play again! This is sick, folks, and that's only half of it. They're also going to dictate where we live too, like a slave labor Nazi camp. Don't believe me? Watch this.

Narrator: *"These tiny pods are helping to tackle homelessness. Portland, in Oregon has a large homeless population, 4,000 people are on the street or in shelters. Portland also has some of the fastest rising rents in America. A Place For You aims to solve this problem. The project will host people in pods placed in people's backyards and 200 people have said they are interested in having pods in their gardens. Each pod is 18.5* *square meters and will be able to house one adult and two children. They'll be furnished and come with full plumbing. People living in the pods will pay rent at a reduced rate."*

Pods or prison cells? Did you see how tiny those were? It's a shed! So now we get to not, "escape" to the she-shed or the man-cave, we get to live in them full time! This is nuts!

But this really is the plan, as crazy as it sounds! And their goal is to cram everyone into these "smart cities" where everybody gets their little Great Reset cubicle or "smart shed" or tiny pod, and somehow that's going to be fantastic.

In fact, decades ago, they also produced a map of the United States, called, "The Biodiversity Treaty," that dictates where the animals get to live, and where the rest of us get to live in this new utopia.

And as you can see by the color legend, the red areas is where the animals get to live and the yellow areas are the buffer zones, and the blue areas show where we, the, "human capital," get to live, at least those that aren't, "useless eaters," and are gotten rid of, and we're basically confined to a strip along the East Coast, with military all around us. Yup, sounds like a prison, to me! Nice utopia!

And corralling people into confined cities, in confined pods, or cells for purposes of control, while simultaneously removing access to any and all rural areas, you know in case you want to be free, really is the plan of this so-called "Great" Reset.

THESE WILL BE THE 10 LARGEST CITIES IN 2030

- Mexico City, Mexico – 23.9 million population in 2030
- Lagos, Nigeria – 24.2 million
- Cairo, Egypt – 24.5 million
- Karachi, Pakistan – 24.8 million
- Dhaka, Bangladesh – 27.4 million
- Beijing, China - 27.7 million
- Mumbai, India – 27.8 million
- Shanghai, China – 30.8 million
- Delhi, India – 36.1 million
- Tokyo, Japan – 37.1 million

This is an estimate from the UN's World Urbanization Prospects 2014 Revision.

Notice again, no mention of the U.S. But it gets even worse. They not only want us to live in these, "tiny pods," or, "prison cells," in these large, confined prison cities, but they also want to turn these places into what's called, "Smart Cities," where every aspect of our livelihoods will be totally controlled by technology, run by AI.

Here's just one of them.

"Saudi Prince Offers Glimpse of Dazzling $500 Billion 'Smart City of the Future' Where You Will Own Nothing and Be Happy."

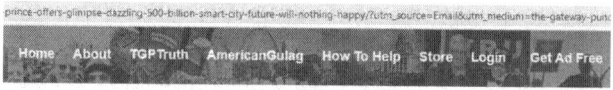

Saudi prince offers glimpse of dazzling $500 billion 'Smart City of the Future' where you will own nothing and be happy

"Welcome to, 'The Line.' It's a so-called, 'good town,' constructed on a 100 mile, 'line,' able to house 9 million people. At the website online, the Crown Prince touts 'The Line,' also known as, 'Neom,' as a spot where there will probably be: No roads, vehicles or emissions, it'll run on 100% renewable power and 95% of land will probably be preserved for nature." You know, like the Biodiversity Treaty. But here's this so-called "digital utopia" in the making.

Narrator: *"So Saudi Arabia has done what no one thought was possible. It has actually started building "The Line." This thing is insane. It's a 500 meters tall, mirrored city, and it stretches for 170 KM across the desert. It's absolutely incredible. Work has now begun. It is absolutely insane showing this thing*

being constructed. Obviously, it has a long way to go, but it is going to look like this. It's going to be big news.

A REVOLUTION IN CIVILIZATION

Narrator: *"For too long, humanity has existed within dysfunctional and polluted cities that ignore nature. Now, a revolution in civilization is taking place. Imagine a traditional city and consolidating its footprint. Designing to protect and enhance nature. 'The Line' will be home to 9 million residents and will be built with a footprint of 34 square kilometers. And we are designing it to provide a healthier, more sustainable quality of life. 'The Line's' communities are organized in three dimensions. Residents have access to all their daily needs within 5-minute walk neighborhoods.*

'The Line's' infrastructure makes it possible to travel end to end in 20 minutes. With no need for cars. This results in zero carbon emissions. By leveraging AI technology, services are autonomous, saving you time and

effort. Designed by world leading architects, 'The Line' is 500m tall, 200m wide, 170km long, and housed within an elegant mirror glass façade. Intelligent solutions create efficiency and year-round temperate micro-climate with natural ventilation. Energy and water supplies are 100% renewable.

'The Line' is designed as a series of unique communities offering a wealth of amenities. Providing equitable views and immediate access to the surrounding nature. With 40% of the world accessible within 6 hours. At the heart of the globe's key trade routes. A place for commerce and communities to thrive like nothing on Earth seen before. The city that delivers new wonders for the world."

That's one of the fanciest prisons I've ever seen built! And that's not all. The Line or Neom is "A 'city of the future' that has been tried with limited success in Communist China, as well as in cities within the nations of Canada, South Korea, Spain, and Singapore."

In other words, it's one of many around the world that they're building. Because, after all, you can't house everybody in just one prison, can you?

And for those who think these so-called, "smart cities," or, "prison pods," won't make it here to America, think again. Remember who's in office. That's right! Mr. Build Back Better himself. Klaus Schwab's buddy, Joe Biden!

And I quote, "Biden's trillion-dollar climate-change bill that Senator Joe Manchin, D-West Virginia, caved in on, incorporates many of the same themes as what you see in the Saudi Crown Prince's advanced smart city – net zero carbon emissions, a total reliance on renewable energy, technology-driven surveillance of all human activity, and a rejection of private land ownership. All resources are tightly controlled by the government and its corporate partners.

Every major U.S. city, and most smaller cities are moving in this direction, minus the fanfare of the Saudi project. With each federal grant that your city accepts, it inches closer to the smart city concept you see in the previous video.

For example, even cities unable to totally redesign themselves into a vertical 'line,' will move toward the concept of, 'no roads and no automobiles.'

And the World Economic Forum put out a policy paper on July 18 that removes all doubt as to where this influential globalist organization is trying to take the world. The WEF now openly calls for an end to private vehicle ownership.

This is the way of life that awaits us on the other side of The Great Reset and 'Build Back Better,' where we've been told by the WEF that we will own nothing, have no privacy, but we will learn to like it.

It's the perfect world for the lazy, feeble-minded, 21st century global citizen who just wants to be able to sit back and be taken care of, despising the American ideals of hard work, property ownership, individual freedoms and responsibilities.

As long as they can relax and play their video games, attend ball games, concerts, or otherwise entertain themselves, they're good. They're being conditioned to accept universal basic income, live in a tiny apartment, and rely on the government for their transportation, food and healthcare. They don't aspire to own a car or a house, let alone a few acres in the country.

You don't need a crystal ball to see this is the direction in which all the nations are being herded, into a world devoid of automobiles, traditional single-family housing and an actual plot of land where you're capable of growing a garden, having a well or even catching rainwater. All of those things will be forbidden in the smart cities the globalists are designing for us.

Remember what the WEF's chief advisor, Yuval Noah Harari, says about the old-fashioned Christian concept that human beings are born with a free will. 'That's over,' he said, along with your prehistoric ideas about personal privacy.

So, you begin to resign yourself to the inevitable, that you are now trapped within the 100-mile radius of your local smart city. That means you must buy and consume whatever food is available within the walls of that city.

You begin to notice over time that the stores no longer carry traditional meat products, only vegetable-based protein and insects. You begin to notice that you can't find a doctor who will give you honest medical advice, only that which is inextricably linked with Big Pharma and its government-mandated regimen of injections.

Almost every drug your doctor prescribes is now delivered via mRNA technology, instructing your genes to manufacture whatever drug your body has become dependent upon to stay alive.

You begin to notice that all of the banks in the smart city are accepting only deposits of the new Central Bank-controlled digital currency, that is only useable for government-approved goods and services.

If by some miracle you are able to make it out of the city, and visit a business on the "other side," where people are forced to live off the grid, the businesses there don't accept your digital dollars.

Perhaps the biggest deception is that the dystopian smart city of the future is way off over the horizon, when in reality it's right here, right now, breathing down our necks.

Get ready. Prepare now while you still can. Because these globalists are nasty people. They will do anything to get you herded into one of their smart cities. These are smart cities designed specifically for dumb sheep."

And I would agree. But speaking of dumb, they also want to use the deserts here in America to build some of these so-called, "Smart Cities," or "prison pods," for all of us to live in, as you can see here.

For his new smart desert city, billionaire Marc Lore eyes Nevada, Utah and Arizona

During a town hall in New York City, the Diapers.com founder and his team envisioned Telosa having dozens of "15-minute cities" and a resident-controlled endowment to help pay for government services.

Published July 29, 2022

By Adina Solomon

"**For his new smart desert city, billionaire Marc Lore eyes Nevada, Utah and Arizona.**"

"During a town hall in New York City, the Diapers.com founder and his team, envisioned Telosa having dozens of, '15-minute cities,' and a resident-controlled endowment to help pay for government services.

The beginnings of a new, sustainable city in the American desert could emerge within just eight years, according to billionaire Marc Lore.

On Monday, the developers of the proposed city of 5 million people held their first town hall. During the panel discussion, Lore narrowed down the probable location of Telosa, saying the team is looking at parcels of land in Nevada, Utah and Arizona.

Lore said, autonomous vehicles operating on city streets would make the streets safer for pedestrians and reduce costs because streetlights and street signs wouldn't be necessary. The roads could also be narrower, providing more room for walking and biking.

The city itself will have no curbs or parking spots. Cars looking to park will pull into an automated pod and park underground. If you were to build a city that's fully autonomous, it's actually very easy. We can do it with not a lot of effort or investment."

Telosa will have 36 districts, each of which is envisioned as a "15-minute city": It will take residents of each district no more than a 15-minute walk or a shorter bike ride to reach their daily needs, including offices and living spaces."

Once again, sounds like you're constructing a prison to me! Call it a, "Smart City," all you want, that's what it is. In fact, this researcher goes a step further and calls them, "concentration camps," as you can see in this article:

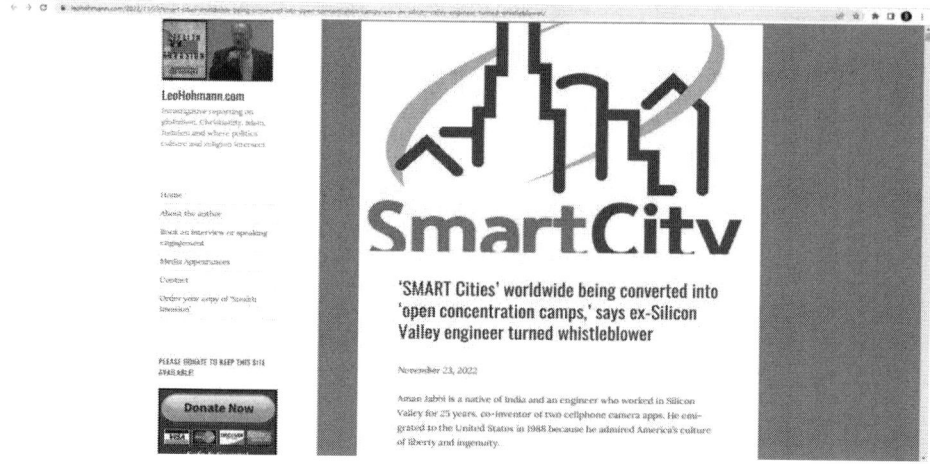

"SMART Cities' worldwide being converted into 'open concentration camps,' says ex-Silicon Valley engineer turned whistleblower."

"Aman Jabbi is a native of India and an engineer who worked in Silicon Valley for 25 years, co-inventor of two cellphone camera apps. He emigrated to the United States in 1988 because he admired America's culture of liberty and ingenuity.

Jabbi now lives in Big Fork, Montana, and has become, in my opinion, one of the most important whistleblowers and voices of warning about the coming beast system. His message needs to be heard by all Americans and I highly recommend you hear him out.

Before you can break out of the matrix, you need to know that you live in a matrix, and that involves recognizing the tentacles of the matrix gaining a stranglehold on your life.

Most of us spend way too much time focused on the wrong things.

We talk endlessly about what's going on in Washington, when we've invited the beast system right into our homes, even get it injected into our own bodies. We place ourselves on a path to destruction out of fear, lack of information (ignorance), and lack of discernment.

Even if you live in a red state like Florida, Georgia, Tennessee or Texas, you will not be insulated or protected from the beast system,

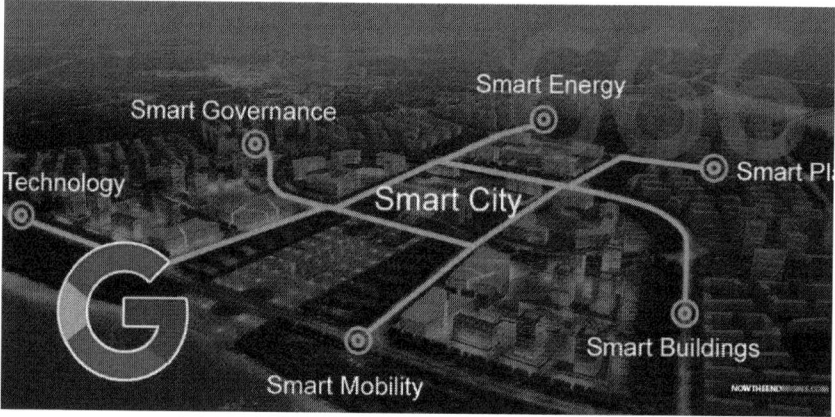

because its claws are already dug into the infrastructure of all 50 states. We have people, well-intentioned people, in the conservative movement, who make their living warning us about the socialists, the communists or the Islamists.

Here's the hard truth: We could eliminate every single socialist, communist, and Islamist from America tomorrow, and we would still be in a heap of trouble, because the globalists already have the laws and technological infrastructure in place to convert our Republic into a

technocratic slave state. Some of the most advanced elements of this infrastructure, as Jabbi points out, are in states like Florida and Georgia and other red states. This is the dark underside of tyranny that nobody wants to talk about. Not a single politician talks about it on a regular basis.

The way to defeat this system is so simple and yet so difficult. One thing I can promise you is that we will never vote our way out of it, because the same people who are laying the infrastructure for SMART Cities worldwide, are in control of the voting systems internationally.

Because there are so many of us, as opposed to so few of them, we must use the power of numbers. All we have to do is say no. Reject the tools of our enslavement that are offered on a shiny silver platter that looks so enticing. We must recognize that these are the very same tools and products that make our busy 21st century lives so convenient, so efficient and entertaining.

And so, we buy them on cue, we upgrade them on cue, we hand over our biometric data on cue, until one day we will wake up and realize we have convenienced ourselves, and entertained ourselves, right into a digital gulag from which there is no escape.

This is how the globalists intend on breaking the backs of free Americans. They will do it through our finances, through the healthcare system and through the entertainment systems. Digital ID cards disguised as, 'Health Passports,' or, 'Smart Health Cards,' will be required to work a job, to access the Internet and the coming digital bank accounts or digital wallets.

The convergence of all these systems will make sure, in the words of U.N. Agenda 2030, 'no person gets left behind.'

By the time most people wake up and see that they have walked into a trap, it will be too late. They will have all your data, they will know everything about you, your strengths, your weaknesses, your vulnerabilities.

As Jabbi says, 'You can deny reality, but you can't deny the consequences.' The choice is simple. Will you choose to live as a slave in a digital concentration camp, or as a free human being in full possession of your bodily autonomy and your free will?

Jabbi gives what I believe is the most comprehensive description of the beast system that I have seen anywhere. The large cities are toast. They're all converting to Smart technology, and anyone still living in one should make plans to leave immediately. If you don't

believe me, type, 'Smart city networks,' into your favorite search engine and peruse what comes up.

But it's more than just big cities. I'm not sure that many medium, or even small cities will be able to resist being folded into this techno-totalitarian infrastructure. What is still within our control is our homes and, ultimately, our own souls, and this is what we must protect from the demonic spirits of control that have been unleashed upon the world.

What Jabbi is describing is an extremely invasive technology being set up in Smart Cities – from license-plate readers to Smart Lights, and Smart Poles, to Smart cars, and Smart neighborhoods, Smart homes and Smart appliances – all connected to 5G and wirelessly communicating with each other.

If you pay attention, you will see hundreds of these LED light poles lining streets and highways and, in many cases, they are retrofitted with surveillance cameras and speakers for listening.

Jabbi also talks about drones charging stations being set up, and how drones might be weaponized against citizens.

All of this weaponized infrastructure is being installed with federal money, hundreds of millions of dollars tucked into Joe Biden's infrastructure bill, as well as his Inflation Reduction Act bill, both of which were passed by Congress with help from Republicans. And, as Jabbi lays out, it's all being done in the name of safety and security.

OUR STREETS ARE SPYING ON US

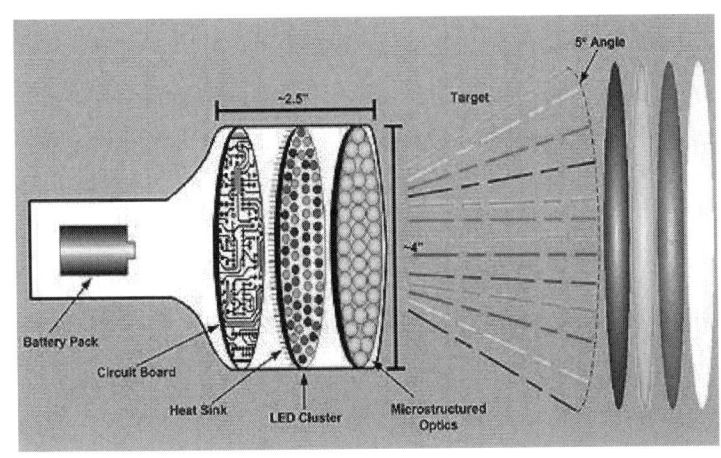

Many of these LED Smart lights are outfitted with what's called, PUKE Ray Technology, which can be weaponized and used to incapacitate humans. This is a military technology being applied in our cities for potential use against civilians, courtesy of the U.S. Department of Homeland Security.

All major intersections in a Smart City have digital surveillance cameras. Pay attention to interstate highways, which are also now being outfitted with this technology. These cameras will be capable of logging the license plates of every car that passes by in real time.

Cameras and listening devices are going up everywhere, in large, medium and even smaller cities.

OUR CELLPHONES ARE SPYING ON US

Your cellphone is listening to you as well. And many of the

newest phones are capable of tracking your eye movements on the screen.

'They're listening in, they're watching, they're analyzing, they're learning and then it repeats the process,' Jabbi said. *'It's an open concentration camp for surveillance.'*

And all of this technology is not for our safety and security, as advertised. It's to grab data and use it to "change your behavior," meaning the data will be used to enforce the coming, "social credit," scoring system on all Americans and free people everywhere.

OUR APPLIANCES ARE SPYING ON US

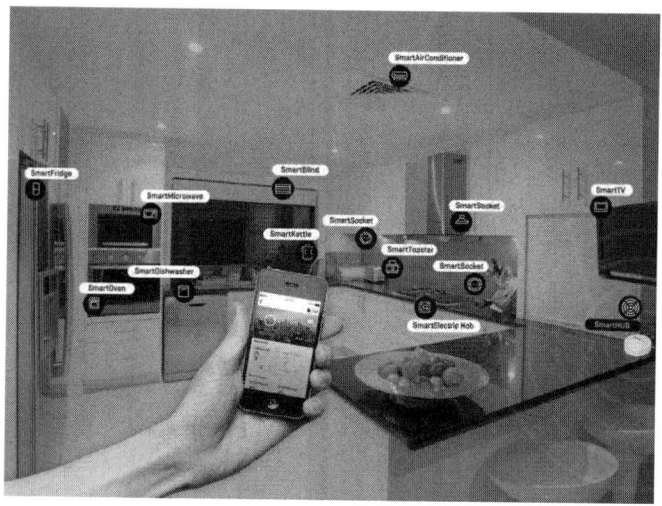

If you have one of the newer models of refrigerators that digitally tracks your fridge's inventory, all that data is being logged for future use against you. Eating too much meat and dairy? Your social credit score just got lowered a notch because the globalists don't like us eating meat. It's not "sustainable," in their vision for the world.

OUR CARS ARE SPYING ON US

By 2025, Jabbi said every new car will have a minimum of 16 cameras, all digitally connected and feeding information via the internet.

Driving too much outside of your home base adding unnecessarily to your carbon footprint? That's a waste of gasoline and your social credit score just ticked down another notch.

OUR BANKS ARE SPYING ON US

It's already been confirmed, earlier this year, that the major banks and credit card companies track your purchases of guns and ammunition, and all of the biggest banks are experimenting with a 'voluntary,' carbon tracker app, that notifies you of your carbon footprint. This is just a warmup for when they launch the new digital money, when keeping track of your carbon output no longer falls under the 'voluntary' mode.

OUR DIGITAL THERMOSTATS ARE SPYING ON US

Remember how that worked out in Colorado last summer, when people enrolled in a 'voluntary' temperature monitoring program and suddenly lost all control over their home thermostats?

The goal is to digitally map all things, living and non-living, even every tree and bush in nature will have a digital ID. Because once you catalog them, and map them, now you can track them and control them.

THE INFRASTRUCTURE FOR A LOCKDOWN POLICE STATE IS ALREADY IN PLACE!

There are 1 billion digital surveillance cameras connected to

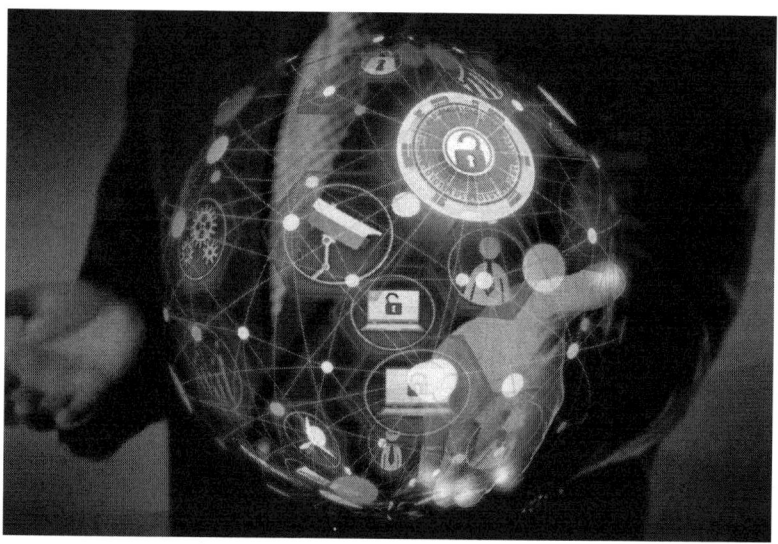

the Internet worldwide. And 50 million of them are in the US. That's more per capita than they have in China, according to Jabbi.

The difference is that in China, the people know they are being watched 24/7, and they're compliant, because they know there will be penalties for violating the rules. They know they are slaves, and they accept it.

'In the U.S., they are already doing this (surveillance),' Jabbi says. 'The only difference is they

haven't told us yet. We are already in the same global system of surveillance.'

Some call it the 'Internet of Eyes.' But the beast also has ears. It's not human eyes and human ears that are tracking everything we do, like in Nazi Germany or the old Soviet Union. No, it's artificial intelligence, A.I., which is now watching over the prison.

Unlike in China, where the slaves know their lot in life, most Americans are still oblivious to the prison walls going up around them.

BOTTOM LINE: This is a spiritual war being waged with high-tech tools in the hands of very wealthy Luciferian elites. But there is nothing higher than the throne of Christ. If you haven't already, I would invite you to put

your faith in Him and Him alone."

In other words, He's the only way out of this mess, this gigantic prison planet they're building for us right before our very eyes, that the Bible alone warned about nearly 2,000 years ago as the coming Antichrist Kingdom. You really need to pay attention and get saved if you're not.

But this is precisely why Hollywood and the media, who also do the bidding of Klaus Schwab, the World Economic Forum and these sick Global Elite megalomaniacs, have been brainwashing people for years into thinking how this prison planet, these prison pods, are a good thing.

Only, they don't call it prison pods, no, that's too obvious, of course not. They relabeled them, "tiny homes," and if you live in one of those, why you'll be helping to save the planet from blowing up! Yeah right, you liar! But here's Hollywood helping to promote that lie for Klaus and the gang.

TINY HOUSE PROMOTION

Potential Buyer - Husband: "That thing was pretty tiny."

Potential Buyer – Wife: "A place to call home."

Narrator: "Even though they have done their homework, Emmy and Jake are finding these spaces daunting."

They climb the ladder to get to the bed at the top of the tiny home. There is only enough room for them to lay down.

Wife: "Oh, Geeze Louise."

They go back downstairs into their tiny kitchen. The salesman shows them the stove.

Salesman: "A 13-inch casserole dish will fit in there."

Narrator: "But there is a tiny answer to almost every tiny challenge."

Wife: "We are going to have to change our lifestyle. We are going to have to make sacrifices."

Husband: "What is that?"

Wife: "It's a teeny-tiny ice tray."

Husband: "You're holding it like a baby."

Wife: "I know. It's so cute."

Narrator: "Smart buyers everywhere, are discovering that smaller homes meet bigger lifestyles. If you've got what it takes to live in 500 square feet or less, ingenuity rules and freedom follows. That's tiny living."

No, that's tiny prisons. But that's how they brainwash people into thinking this is a great thing. And if you think living in one of these so-called, "tiny homes," or "prison pods," in these assigned, "smart cities," or "prison compounds," that the Global Elites are building for us are going to be even close to as spacious and luxurious as you just saw on that video, 500 square feet, you just got duped, again!

Remember what they said, "Trust them, it's not that simple," when it really is. The tinier the better is what they have planned for us prisoners, I mean human capital people, or should I say cattle.

In fact, they're already doing it in China, you know, the model country that Klaus Schwab always seems to rave about. Watch what their "tiny homes" look like over there.

TINY HOUSE REALITY

Narrator: "These are the coffin homes of Hong Kong. An estimated 200 thousand people live in these critically tiny spaces. From sleeping to cooking, these coffin cubicles are flats which are divided into 15, 120 square foot apartments. One man who suffers from sclerosis, pays $300 a month for 18 square feet. And the bathrooms are shared by at least a dozen other residents."

Oh yeah, that's something to look forward to in this wonderful utopia they're building for us, you know, the "Great" reset! Your very own, "coffin home," or "prison cell," whatever you want to call it.

And if all this is starting to sound familiar, it is. As we saw in our last documentary, Klaus Schwab the Third Reich and the Covid-19 Holocaust, back in the day, The Great Reset used to be called Agenda 21, which included the same desire to control every aspect of our livelihoods in order to supposedly keep the planet from blowing up! Again, they just relabeled it.

But part of the goals of the old Great Reset label, Agenda 21, was that we would have no privately owned property, no air conditioning, no dams, no paved roads, no way to correct rivers for flood control, no golf courses, no pastureland used for grazing. And it got rid of things like this:

- Ski runs
- Grazing livestock
- Disturbing of soil surface/plowing of soil
- Building fences
- Commercial Agriculture/Modern farm production
- Chemical fertilizers
- The use of fossil fuels
- Any industrial activity
- Single family homes
- Paved and tarred roads
- Railroads

- Floor and wall tiles
- Range lands, fishponds, or plantations
- Harvesting timber
- Hunting
- Logging activities
- Dams and reservoirs, straightening of rivers, and power line construction.

In fact, Agenda 21, now relabeled "The Great Reset," also had plans to control your birth and even your death as well.

Chapter Seven

World Economic Forum & Agenda 2030

But speaking of relabeling, if the terms, "Agenda 21" and "The Great Reset" bugs you too much and you start to catch on to what they're really up to, that is, taking over the whole planet and creating a giant prison, hey don't worry, they have a couple other, "labels" out there for this same agenda, to pacify us and throw us off the trail.

It's also being called, "Agenda 2030," which again is the target date for all this, and "The Fourth Industrial Revolution." Doesn't that sound better? Doesn't that keep you confused, I mean, informed?

But let's take a look again at their own videos, describing what these new "relabeled" terms for taking over the planet and creating a giant prison really mean, starting with, "Agenda 2030." You tell me if it's not the same thing.

AGENDA 2030 GOALS

Narrator: *"In September 2015, all 193 U.N. member states adopted the 2030 Agenda for sustainable development. They recognized that ending* *poverty calls for transforming our world through strategies that build economic growth, address social needs and ensure environmental protection. To achieve this vision, seventeen sustainable development goals, known as STG's, would define this path of the 2030 Agenda. The STG's and their targets balance the three dimensions of sustainable development, economic, social, and environmental, working in partnerships and calling for action by all the countries.*

The goals are integrated and indivisible to capture the broad scope of the STG's five core principles, being included in the 2030 Agenda. The five peace principles, being people, planet, prosperity, peace and partnership. They underline the importance of eradicating poverty and hunger in all its forms, offering prosperity for all, and ensuring the protection of the planet and its natural resources.

They emphasize a world, where peace and human rights are realized for everyone, and where all countries and stakeholders act in collaborative partnerships to achieve sustainable development. These core principles also define the political priorities set by the Federal Ministry for Economic Cooperation and Development, or the BMZ, when collaborating with its partner countries. The ministry calls for Germany to fulfill its global responsibilities, advocates leaving no one behind, and promotes approaches balancing the three dimensions of sustainable development.

An example of how this can be done, is the successful partnership for sustainable textiles initiated by the BMZ in 2014, entering the partnership, businesses, politics, and civil society, commit to improving working and environmental conditions in countries where textiles and clothing are produced. That means that human rights and social and environmental standards must be met along the entire textile supply chain.

Through its support, the BMZ ensures that our clothing is produced under conditions which are fair for people and nature. Today, the partnership already accounts for 50% of revenues achieved by the German textile industry. And the aim is to reach 75% by the end of 2018. Everyone can make a difference and contribute to transforming our world in line with the 2030 Agenda.

For example, through conscious purchase decisions, we can choose organically grown and fairly traded products and should only buy the amount we actually need. In such an easy way, we can contribute to sustainable development every day. In many areas, our personal decisions have impacts on nature and people around the world. We therefore need to start taking our responsibilities seriously and adjusting our actions accordingly. Join now and work together with BMZ. Take responsibility, locally and globally for humans and nature."

SUSTAINABLE DEVELOPMENT STRATEGY 2030

Narrator: *"In 2015, Switzerland and the U.N. member states adopted the 2030 agenda, which sets out a path to a sustainable development for all people, with 17 universal goals. But 2030 is tomorrow. To be able to act quickly, Switzerland has set priorities, especially in those areas where the potential for development is greatest. These form the three pillars of the Sustainable Development Strategy, SDS 2030. Sustainable consumption and production, climate, energy and biodiversity, equal opportunities and social cohesion.*

The focus is on different fields of action. For example, securing prosperity and well-being by conserving natural resources. Reducing greenhouse gas emissions and addressing the impacts of climate change. Ensuring effective equality between women and men. This strategy affects both our domestic and foreign policies, and relies on multiple fundamental actors, civil society, the economy, the financial market, education, research and innovation. These actors, as well as the cantons and municipalities, play an important role alongside the federal government.

They can be drivers of sustainable development, and thus make a decisive contribution to the implementation of the 2030 Agenda. With this strategy, the federal council is securing the future of the Swiss people and positioning the country as a role model for sustainable development."

THE VOICE – UNDESA

In September 2015, the world formally adopted the 17 Sustainable Development Goals that will guide the international community on the path to development. The global statistical community has laid the groundwork for the successful monitoring and realization of this new agenda.

Lenni Montiel, Assistant Secretary General for Economic Development: *"2015 was an extraordinary year for the United Nations. We got the approval of the Addis Ababa Action Agenda, financing for development, the endorsement by all the member states of the United Nations of the Agenda 2030 and sustainable development goals, and finally in December, we got the agreement on climate change."*

Stefan Schweinfest, Director, Statistics Division, U.N. DESA: *"Well, it was also, I mean it was also an important year for the statistical community. It was the first time in the long history of the U.N. that the chair of the Statistical Commission actually talked to the General Assembly, directly on the topic of indicators, and of course, indicators is like the last missing piece to complete the architecture of the 2030 Sustainable Development Agenda."*

Sure, looks like the same thing to me as the so-called, "Great" Reset and Agenda 21. And notice how the U.N. approved and financed this newly labeled term for taking over the world, Agenda 2030, back in 2015, with partnership with all its nations.

Did you get to vote on that? I didn't. Were you told about this in the news? I didn't hear about it. And then all they needed was the right crisis to come along 5 years later, called the Covid-19 Plandemic to kick the whole thing off and take over the planet.

In fact, even though we weren't told about this, let alone voted for this as a free people, I mean, human capital, you can at least show your support of this planetary takeover called The Great Reset, Agenda 21, and now Agenda 2030, by that's right, sporting your very own Agenda 2030 taking over the planet line of jewelry!

I wish I was making this up but I'm not! As you can see here you can order your very own Sustainable Development Goals badge from Amazon, you know, Jeff Bezos' company, who also works with Klaus Schwab, the World Economic Forum and the Global Elites including the United Nations. It's got a nice little pin so you can attach it to your clothes.

It looks nifty and trendy in case you want to be cool and hip with these

people trying to take over the world and create a giant prison planet for the rest of us.

And apparently, it even instills joy, at least for those who get to live in the mansions, those who sold their soul to Klaus Schwab and the gang, while the rest of us eek out a slave existence in our new coffin homes.

I mean, why don't you just go ahead and bring back the Swastika, or the SS symbol to wear? Because that's what all this is folks, this taking over the planet. This is what Hitler wanted to do! Is this sick, or what?

And lest there be any doubt about what's really going on here, let's translate Agenda 2030 for what it really is. Can you say, total global control and takeover of the planet, like The Great Reset and Agenda 21? But remember, "Trust us, it's really not that simple." Yeah, it really is. Watch this!

GOAL 1	TRANSLATION
End Poverty in all its forms everywhere.	Redistribute wealth and resources to make the super-rich wealthier and the middle classes poorer.
GOAL 2	TRANSLATION
End hunger, achieve food security	Increase use of drought – flood - and

and improved nutrition and promote sustainable agriculture.

aluminum – resistant GM crops, fortified with synthetic vitamins and minerals, creating disease and causing depopulation.

GOAL 3

Ensure healthy lives and promote well-being for all at all ages.

TRANSLATION

Mandate vaccinations for all children and adults, medicate children with behavioral issues, and assign every child a 'named person', removing parental freedom, privacy and responsibility.

GOAL 4

Ensure inclusive and equitable quality education and promote lifelong learning opportunities for all.

TRANSLATION

Socially engineer children to conform to politically correct agendas, standardize and dumb down the curriculum to produce adults incapable of independent thought.

GOAL 5

Achieve gender equality and empower all women and girls.

TRANSLATION

Promote LGBTQ and feminist agendas, marginalize families, heterosexuality, men and boys.

GOAL 6

Ensure availability and sustainable management of water and sanitation for all.

TRANSLATION

All water controlled by corporation, local government or state, including rivers and wells on private land.

GOAL 7

TRANSLATION

Ensure access to affordable, reliable, sustainable and modern energy for all.

Increase taxes on traditional fuels and institute usage caps for every household, monitored by health destroying smart meters.

GOAL 8

TRANSLATION

Promote sustained, inclusive and sustainable economic growth, full and productive employment and decent work for all.

Mandate minimum wages, compliance and certification, and introduce employment quotas that discriminate against the best qualified person for the job.

GOAL 9

TRANSLATION

Build resilient infrastructure, promote inclusive and sustainable industrialization and foster innovation.

Mandate changes to infrastructure in all countries, creating greater national debt to be paid for by levying higher taxes on the population.

GOAL 10

TRANSLATION

Reduce inequality within and among countries.

Push international trade agreements on all countries (TAFTA, NAFTA, CAFTA, GATT, TTIP, & TPP) to benefit mega-corporations.

GOAL 11

TRANSLATION

Make cities and human settlements inclusive, safe, resilient and sustainable.

Create protected rural spaces, forcing people into cities/mega cities with 24/7 surveillance in all public places and ban single-family homes with gardens.

GOAL 12

Ensure sustainable consumption and production patterns.

TRANSLATION

Introduce utility quotas and penalize waste disposal, and encourage people to report on offending people or businesses.

GOAL 13

Take urgent action to combat change and its impacts.

TRANSLATION

Implement carbon taxes, and legalize current weather modification and geoengineering practices.

GOAL 14

Conserve and sustainably use the oceans, seas, and marine resources for sustainable development.

TRANSLATION

Mandate licenses and quotas for fishing, including individuals who fish for their own consumption.

GOAL 15

Protect, restore and promote sustainable use of terrestrial ecosystems, sustainably manage forests, combat desertification, and halt and reverse land degradation and halt biodiversity loss.

TRANSLATION

Ensure every possible seed is preserved in the Svalbard Global Seed Vault so the powers-that-be can regenerate the earth for themselves after they destroy it for everyone else.

GOAL 16

Promote peaceful and inclusive societies for sustainable development, provide access to

TRANSLATION

Strengthen police states everywhere, institute pre-crime departments and RFID chips to track everyone justice for all and build effective accountable and inclusive institutions at all levels.

while giving tax breaks to organizations that promote certain government agendas via hiring policies or their product/service offering.

GOAL 17

Strengthen the means of implementation and revitalize the global partnership for sustainable development.

TRANSLATION

End national sovereignty, placing every country under the socio-communist rule of a totalitarian One World Government.

AGENDA 2030
NEW WORLD ORDER DISGUISED
AS SUSTAINABLE DEVELOPMENT

Once again, change the name, relabel it, and people fall for it.

Chapter Eight

World Economic Forum & The Fourth Industrial Revolution

But hey, in case the "labels," The Great Reset, Agenda 21 and Agenda 2030 don't keep you confused and avert your attention off the real big picture goal of taking over the planet, don't forget they've thrown another one out there called The Fourth Industrial Revolution.

This one is used a lot by Klaus Schwab himself, and he definitely speaks of it glowingly. But let's take a look at the self-defined goals of this new so-called, "revolution of the fourth kind" that Klaus and the gang are bringing to the planet whether we want it or not.

THE FOURTH INDUSTRIAL REVOLUTION

The Fourth Industrial Revolution will bring change at a speed, scale, and force unlike anything we've experienced before. It will affect the very essence of our human experience. The First Industrial Revolution brought mechanical innovations like the steam engine, cotton spinning and railroads. The Second Industrial Revolution brought mass production through assembly lines and electrification. The Third Industrial Revolution brought mainframe computers, personal computing and the internet. Today, radical system-wide innovation can happen in only a few years. The interplay between fields like nanotechnology, brain research, 3D printing, mobile networks and computing will create realities that were previously unthinkable.

Access to technology will spread like wildfire. Almost anyone will be able to invent new products and services cheaply and quickly. The business models of each and every industry will be transformed. How do we avoid a world of joblessness, low productivity, and inequality? By ensuring The Fourth Industrial Revolution really does improve the state of the world. Learn more: www.wef.ch/4ir

Speaker #1: *"We are wondering what is happening to the world. Everything is changing."*

Speaker #2: *"The very idea of a human being some sort of natural concept is really a change. Our bodies will be so high-tech that we won't be able to really distinguish between what's natural and what's artificial."*

Speaker #3: *"Inside our own heads is the most complex arrangement of matter in the known universe."*

Speaker #4: *"You might ask yourself; can we get to be superhuman?"*

Speaker #5: *"The original Industrial Revolution was driven by the discovery that you could use steam engines to do all kinds of interesting things."*

Speaker #6: *"That was followed by additional revolutions for electricity and computers and communications technology. We are now in the early stages of The Fourth Industrial Revolution, which is bringing together digital, physical, and biological systems."*

Klaus Schwab: *"One of the features of this Fourth Industrial Revolution, is that it doesn't change what we are doing, but it changes us."*

Nita Farahany, Duke University: *"With the ability to visualize brain activity, for example, through a simple consumer-based EEG device, it can give us access to ourselves in ways that we have never before thought possible. It unlocks the black box of the brain and enables us to really, truly be able to realize an identity that's aspirational."*

Jon Kabat-Zinn, University of Massachusetts, USA: *"There's no scientific foundation for the effects of mindfulness on the brain, on the genome, on biological aging. When the human mind does know itself, then you get the potential for a new renaissance that restructures itself in terms of our relationship to life, our relationship to the planet, our relationship to work."*

Stewart Wallis, New Economics Foundation: *"We need a different economic model."*

Carlo Ratti, Massachusetts Institute of Technology: *"The reason we live in cities is no different today than it was ten thousand years ago. Even if you have networks connecting us, we still want to have places where we meet in person. This means the place where we work, in the place where we live, are much closer to each other in a city where we don't need to have big supply chains in order to produce things, but many things can be sourced locally, thanks to 3D printing and robotics. So, if we are able to do something to transform cities to make it more sufficient, then the impact can be huge."*

Leonardo DiCaprio, Crystal Award Winner, Davos 2016: *"Together we are fighting to preserve our fragile climate from irreversible damage and devastation of unthinkable proportions."*

Naomi Oreskes, Harvard University, USA: *"We think about the original Industrial Revolution. It was an energy revolution. I like to think of it as a kind of a book ending, of a period in human history during which we used fossil fuels, and it worked very well for us for a long time, but now we have to bring that to an end. We have energy technologies that can power our civilization, solar, wind, biomass. So, then the question is, how do we get good integration? Maybe the wind is blowing in Denmark, the sun is shining in Germany and now you can move that electricity through an integrated grid. You can supply energy to everyone who needs it, and you can supply energy at all times."

Sharan Burrows, International Trade Union Confederation: *"The prediction of five million jobs lost by 2022 with technology is serious but it's not the main question. Construction, manufacturing services, public health and education, these industries will still exist. The main question is what will be the future of work? How will we define work? How will we share the wealth?"*

Hiroaki Nakanishi, Hitachi, Japan: *"From the viewpoint of the labor board jobs, my idea, we really need a new education or new training."*

Erik Brynjolfsson, Massachusetts Institute of Technology: *"Humans have always been using tools, but because of the recent advances in technology, we're beginning to have machines that can augment us in all sorts of interesting ways."*

Mark Pollock, Mark Pollock Trust, Ireland: *"I was the first person in the world able to voluntarily move my legs while stepping in a robot. By exciting the nervous system, using electrical stimulators directly up to the spine, we believe that a cure will be possible if enough of the right people have the will to fast-track a cure for paralysis."*

Nina Tandon, Epibone, USA: *"We take two things from the patient. First, we take a three-dimensional X-ray, and we extract the three-dimensional data out of that so we can make a perfectly shaped puzzle piece. And then we also take a sample of that tissue from the patient so that we can extract the stem cells out of those. We use those stem cells with the three-dimensional scaffold that we fabricate and after three weeks we have a piece of living bone that's ready for implantation."*

Jennifer Doudna, University of California, Berkley: *"Being able to use genome editing to understand the genetic changes that lead to cancer and* *technologies like drug delivery, getting molecules into particular types of cells. There's a lot of excitement about being able to move much more quickly on this disease."*

Jon Kabat-Zinn: *"We need to take responsibility at every level of society, from the individual, and the persons of institutional, to the global, to adapt to these technological challenges and changes without redefining what it means to be human, what it means to work, what it means to be completely embedded in this world.*

Yeah, completely embedded in this world they're planning on taking over, now called, The Fourth Industrial Revolution. Folks, as you saw, it's all the same thing. Call it The Great Reset, Agenda 21, Agenda 2030, The Fourth Industrial Revolution, it's all describing and saying the same thing!

They're going to take over the planet under the guise of keeping it from blowing up, and then they will literally control every single aspect of our daily life, our livelihood, including, as you just saw, our humanhood.

That last lady in that video was Jennifer Doudna, the co-inventor of the CRISPR technology that allows these Global Elites to literally alter the human genome down to the individual DNA strand level.

We exposed this technology in great detail again in our other documentary, **Human Hybrids Super Soldiers & the Coming Genetic Apocalypse**. You need to check it out!

But as you just saw and heard, part of the plans of The Fourth Industrial Revolution, also known as The Great Reset, Agenda 21, and Agenda 2030, is to "reset" humanity alright, but to reset us into something that is non-human by merging us with technology, a cyborg scenario, as well as modify us genetically, to become better worker bees for them.

Or as Klaus Schwab says about The Fourth Industrial Revolution, *"It doesn't just change what we are doing, but it changes us."* Again, the term they have for this new post-human species, which means you're not human anymore, has simply been relabeled, so we don't freak out as much over this, is called Human 2.0.

Which is why, again, we also exposed this deceptive lie in our other documentary called **Beyond Covid: The Global Elites Plan for Human 2.0**.

But again, we encourage you to get both those documentaries for further research and understanding. You won't believe what they're wanting to turn us into. It's sick and evil! And God's going to put a stop to it!

But unfortunately, it gets worse, and even more invasive than that. Let's see what else they plan on doing to our individual livelihoods with this so-called Great Reset, Agenda 21, Agenda 2030, and now The Fourth Industrial Revolution, straight from the horse's mouth.

"The Top 10 Creepiest and Most Dystopian Things Pushed by the World Economic Forum (WEF)"

The World Economic Forum (WEF) is one of the most powerful organizations in the world. And throughout the years, people at the WEF have said some truly insane and dystopian things. And they've managed to word these things in the creepiest ways possible.

When one talks about the 'global elite,' one usually refers to a small group of wealthy and powerful individuals who operate beyond national borders.

Through various organizations, these non-elected individuals, gather in semi-secrecy to decide policies they want to see applied on a global level. The World Economic Forum (WEF) is smack dab in the middle of it all.

Indeed, through its annual Davos meetings, the WEF attempts to legitimize and normalize its influence on the world's democratic nations by having a panel of world leaders attend and speak at the event. A simple look at the list of attendees at these meetings reveals the organization's incredible reach and influence. The biggest names in media, politics, business, science, technology, and finance are represented at the WEF.

According to mass media, the Davos meetings gather people to discuss issues such as, 'inequality, climate change, and international

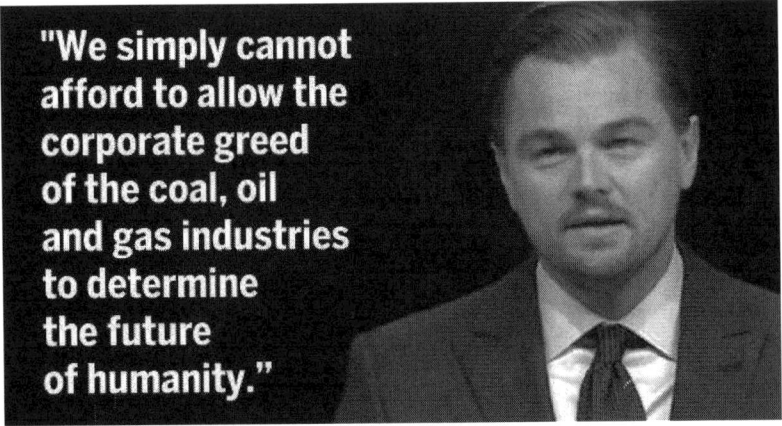

cooperation.' This simplistic description appears to be custom-made to cause the average citizen to yawn in boredom.

But topics at the WEF go much further than 'inequality.' Throughout the years, people at the WEF have said some highly disturbing things, none of which garnered proper media attention.

In fact, when one pieces together the topics championed by the WEF, an overarching theme emerges: The total control of humanity using media, science, and technology while reshaping democracies to form a global government.

"THE PANDEMIC REPRESENTS A RARE BUT NARROW WINDOW OF OPPORTUNITY TO REFLECT, REIMAGINE, AND RESET OUR WORLD"
KLAUS SCHWAB

If this sounds like a far-fetched conspiracy theory, keep reading. Here are the 10 most dystopian things that are being pushed by the WEF right now. This list is sorted in no particular order. Because they're all equally crazy.

#10 – PENETRATING GOVERNMENTS

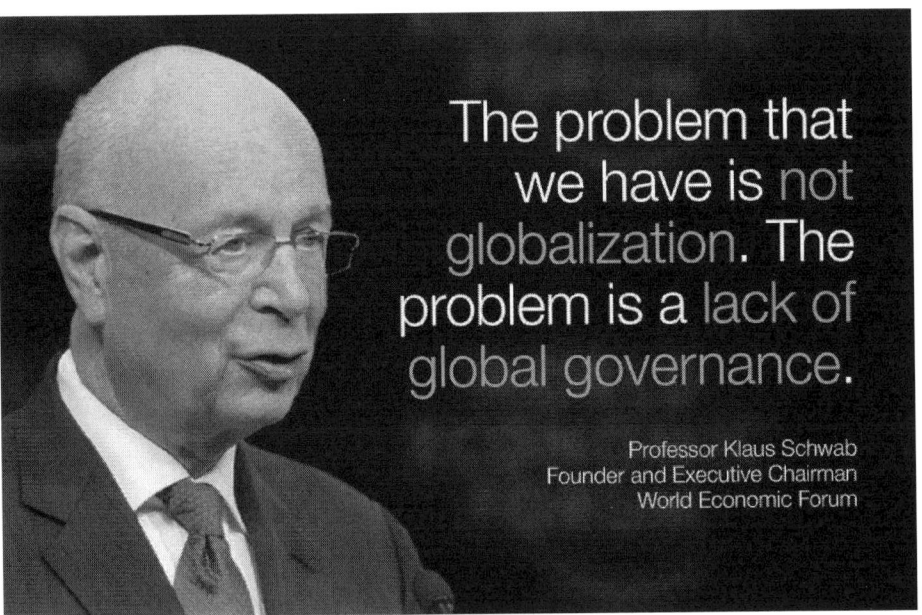

The least one can say is that Klaus Schwab, the founder and the head of the WEF, is not a fan of democracy. In fact, he perceives it as an obstacle to a fully globalized world.

He argued that governments are no longer, "the overwhelmingly dominant actors on the world stage" and that, "the time has come for a new stakeholder paradigm of international governance." In 2017, at Harvard's John F. Kennedy School of Government, Schwab blatantly admitted what is continually dismissed as a "conspiracy theory" by mass media: The WEF is, "penetrating" governments around the world. "What we are very proud of, is that we penetrate the global cabinets of countries with our WEF Young Global Leaders…like Trudeau."

This is not a conspiracy theory. This is the absolute truth, confirmed by the head of the WEF himself.

#9 – CONTROLLING MINDS USING SOUND WAVES

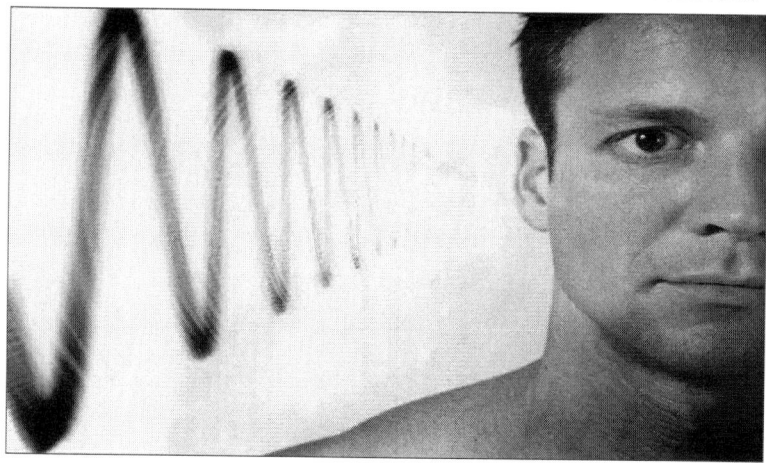

In 2018, one of the topics of discussion at the WEF was "Mind Control Using Sound Waves," and those are exactly the words used by the WEF. In the article, the technology is touted as a possible treatment for Parkinson's and Alzheimer's disease. However, the article also states that "it can cure you, it can get you addicted, and it can kill you." It can also be used to completely control a person's mind, remotely.

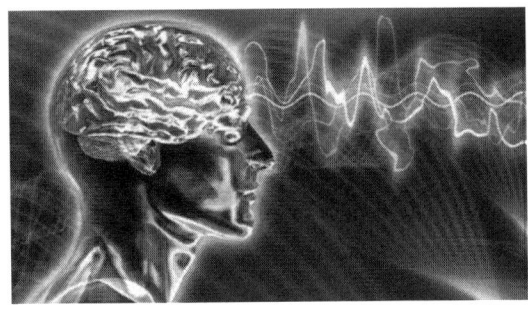

The article states: *"I can see the day coming when a scientist will be able to control what a person sees in their mind's eye, by sending the right waves to the right place in their brain. My guess is that most objections will be similar to those we hear today about subliminal messages in advertisements, only much more vehement. This technology is not without its risks of misuse. It could be revolutionary healthcare technology for the sick, or a perfect control tool with which the ruthless control the weak. This time though, the control would be literal."*

The conclusion of the article: Nobody can stop scientists from developing this technology. And what's convenient is that some companies developing this technology are part of the WEF. Do you see where this is going?

#8 – PILLS THAT CONTAIN MICROCHIPS

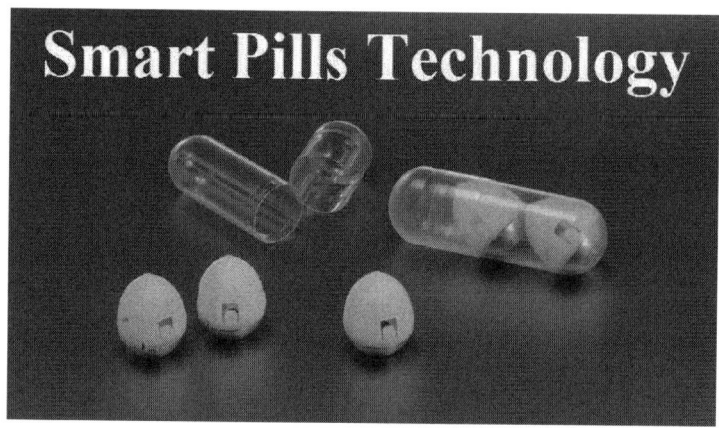

Once again, this title sounds like a far-fetched conspiracy theory, cleverly worded for sensationalism. It is not. Here's a video from the WEF's 2018 meeting where Albert Bourla, the CEO of Pfizer, talks about pills that contain microchips.

Questions being asked at the World Economic Forum.

First question: "I have a question about patient engagement. And you had touched on this before. All of these advances are amazing. But even if you make the greatest drug or the greatest wearable, there is no guarantee that the patient is going to take the drug or wear the device. So, how are you thinking about technology to engage the patient?"

Answer to question: "I think, for example, that is very likely right now. FDA approved the first electronic pill, if I can call it that. It is in the tablet, and once you take the tablet, it dissolves in your stomach, and it sends a signal that you took the tablet. So, imagine the application so far. Compliance. So, if it's the medicine the patient needs to take, they do take them. It is fascinating what happens in this field."

Yeah, I'd say so! But as the article shares:

"Is this field truly fascinating? Or utterly dystopian? As Bourla himself said: Imagine the compliance. This kind of technology could easily open the door to all kinds of nefarious applications. Since then, COVID-19 put Pfizer in a position of power never seen before for a pharmaceutical company."

Like Pfizer, the WEF is also using COVID-19 to further its agenda.

#7 – PRAISING MASSIVE LOCKDOWNS

In 2020 and 2021, cities around the world were subjected to massive and drastic lockdowns, causing job losses, suicides, drug overdoses, isolation, mental health issues, domestic abuse, bankruptcies, and homelessness. During this horrific period, children could not attend school for months and were essentially barred from interacting with other children. A slew of small and medium businesses were destroyed, while large corporations strived.

Despite all of this, the WEF could not hide its love of drastic, life-destroying lockdowns. In fact, it released a video surrealistically called, 'Lockdowns are quietly improving cities around the world.' Here's this piece of complete insanity.

"Earth's seismic noise has been the lowest in decades due to lockdowns. Scientists saw a wave of quiet around the world in 2020. Ambient noise in some cities fell 50%. As fewer people used transport, and factories closed, the quiet enabled scientists to record small earthquakes that they would

usually miss. And that improved their understanding of seismic activity, so they can predict larger earthquakes in the future.

There were also record falls in air pollution. Clearing city skies from Asia to America. But by late 2020, it had returned to pre-pandemic levels. Carbon emissions were also down 7% last year. But the drop won't slow climate change unless we lock in emissions cuts. How quiet was your local area?"

As you can see, the WEF kept praising lockdowns. That's because the WEF would love to see "covidian" life become permanent.

#6 – TAKE A PEEK AT THE FUTURE

Judging by comments on YouTube and social media, people absolutely hate videos created by the WEF. But they keep coming. Because they don't care what you think. They just want to plant their seed of insanity into your mind.

In a video titled "How Our Lives Could Soon Look," the WEF invites viewers to 'take a peek at the future.' And it is BLEAK. It is all about making COVID-19 life permanent.

Five ways the pandemic could reshape our lives in the long-term.

- Offices will be reimagined. The shift to home working will mean offices can serve different functions. They could be used as a client showroom, a research lab, or somewhere to meet and reconnect with colleagues.
- The advent of '15-minute spaces.' 'Neighborhood hubs' could replace some of the perks we miss by not commuting to an office. They might contain gyms, bars or art galleries. Or offer networking opportunities. And would be no more than a 15-minute walk from your home.
- The rise of 'cloud markets.' 'Ghost kitchens' – restaurants that solely deliver takeaway meals – exploded in popularity during the lockdowns. These could morph into 'cloud markets' - analytics-driven services that license and deliver food to you from a range of brands.
- You could be identified by your heartbeat. Facial recognition systems are often stumped by face masks. But your heartbeat is just as unique as your face. NASA has invented a system that can ID you from your heartbeat using a laser.
- Digital technology will change the way children learn. While homeschooling was challenging for many families, it also had benefits for those with access to digital tools. Children could learn at their own pace, while improving their digital skills. Education in the future could become a hybrid of school and home-based learning. Combining the best of both worlds. What pandemic-era changes would you like to become permanent?

Uh, how about making none of those changes permanent! This is crazy. These guys are truly megalomaniacs, building a prison planet to control every aspect of our livelihoods, and our personal lives down to having no place to hide from them by identifying us with our heartbeat with a laser.

Are they sick or what? I'll bet you, they don't have a heartbeat! But that's not all they're pushing for.

#5 – PUSHING FOR A GREAT RESET

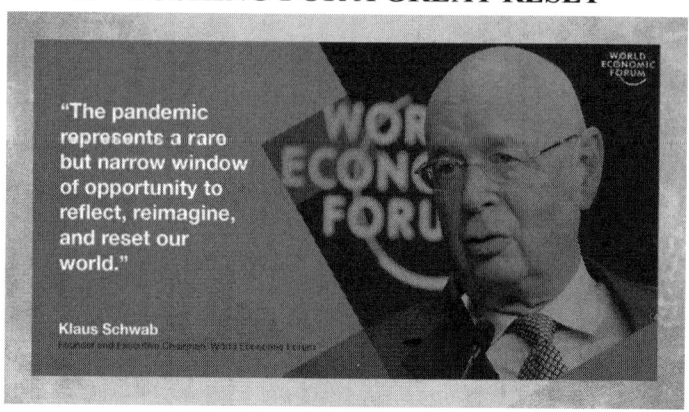

As stated above, the WEF perceives the pandemic as an "opportunity." It is not only an opportunity to reshape our personal existence, but to restructure the entire world structure according to its principles. The WEF calls it "The Great Reset."

Then they proceed to ridicule 'conspiracy theories' while, astoundingly, confirming these theories as they announce the 'death of capitalism' and the switch to the compliance with the elite's social and political agendas.

#4 RECALIBRATING FREEDOM OF SPEECH

An easy way to identify world leaders who are groomed by the WEF is through their incessant railing against free speech. They absolutely hate it, and they're constantly calling for the internet to be censored and highly regulated. At the 2022 Davos meeting, Australian "eSafety commissioner" Julie Inman Grant, stated that we need a "recalibration of free speech."

"We are finding ourselves in a place where we have increasing polarization everywhere, and everything feels binary when it doesn't need

to be, so I think we are going to have to think about a recalibration of a whole range of human rights that are playing out online, from freedom of speech, to be free from online violence, or the right of data protection, to the right of child dignity."

As you just saw, Grant essentially calls for censorship. She even believes that freedom of speech, as a human right, should be "recalibrated," using, "online violence" as an excuse. There is no such thing as "online violence." They love to equate speech with violence. It is an extremely manipulative way of justifying China-style censorship. They clearly don't want free speech to exist.

#3 TRACKING YOUR CLOTHES

The WEF wants to control your clothes. And they've made a video about it. Using the environment as an excuse (as usual), the WEF announced the coming of clothing laced with "digital passports" that can be traced at all times. Backed by Microsoft (of course), these garments will apparently flood the market by 2025.

WORLD ECONOMIC FORUM TRACKING CLOTHES

"This start-up gives clothes digital IDs to help the planet. EON creates online digital passports for garments, enabling brands to sell their clothing, again and again. Creating more sustainable business models. CircularID also lets brands follow garments over their life cycle. From production to sale and resale, reuse or recycling. CircularID also enables recyclers to access essential information, like fabric details. Fashion is

one of the world's most polluting industries. Textiles generate 10 lbs of the world's C02 emissions. More than shipping and aviation combined.

57% of old clothes end up in a landfill. This is because brands depend on sales of new clothing. Once the product is sold, they no longer make any money. But digitally connected products open up new, greener ways of profiting, such as rental, repair, and styling. Reducing the production of new garments. Five of the world's top 20 brands are on board working with Microsoft, and EON aims to bring billions of garments online by 2025. EON is a member of the Circulars Accelerator Cohort 2021, an initiative launched by Accenture with UpLink, Anglo American, Ecolab and Schneider Electric. What's your big idea to cut fashion waste?"

According to the WEF, these chips will allow fashion brands to resell their clothes. I have no idea how that would work. The video makes sure "not" to mention that this technology would be a great way of tracking those who ditched their smartphones. But ditching your smartphone might become impossible.

#2 – SMARTPHONES WILL BE IN YOUR BODY BY 2030

At the 2022 Davos meeting, Nokia CEO, Pekka Lundmark claimed that, by 2030, "smartphones will be implanted directly into the body." This would coincide with the coming of 6G technology, which is expected to be launched by the end of the decade.

For years, this site has been documenting the elite's incessant push for transhumanism, which is the merging of humans with machines. They're looking to accelerate this transition by making things people cannot live without (such as smartphones) available in transhumanist form.

Question from the audience during the World Economic Forum.

Question: *"I want to ask you all when you think we are going to move from this form factor; to something on your face, glasses, and when competing is all on the edge.*

Answer from Pekka Lundmark, CEO, Nokia: *"I think, well, first of all, it will definitely happen. I was talking about 6G earlier, which is around 2030. I would say that by then, definitely, the smartphone as we know it today, will not anymore be the usual kind of the most common interface. Many of these things will be built directly into our bodies."*

Are you noticing their creepy eagerness to insert things inside our bodies?

#1 YOU'LL OWN NOTHING. AND YOU'LL BE HAPPY.

This is probably the most dystopian moment in WEF history. In 2016, Ida Auken, (as we saw earlier) a Member of Parliament in Denmark said: *"Welcome to 2030. I own nothing, have no privacy, and life has never been better."* The WEF loved that quote so much that it tweeted about it.

The WEF also created a video (again as we saw earlier) titled "Eight Predictions for the World in

2030." An article on the WEF's website explains:

"I don't own anything. I don't own a car. I don't own a house. I don't own any appliances or any clothes. Shopping is a distant memory in the city of 2030, whose inhabitants have cracked clean energy and borrow what they need on demand."

It sounds utopian, until she mentions that her every move is tracked, and outside the city live swathes of discontents, the ultimate vision of a society split in two.

In this dystopian future, there are no products you can own. Only "services" that are rented and delivered using drones. This system would make all humans completely dependent on WEF-controlled corporations for every single basic need. There would be absolutely no autonomy, no freedom, and no privacy. And somehow, you'll be happy.

Honorable Mention: Individual carbon footprint tracker

At the 2022 Davos meeting, Alibaba Group president, J. Michael Evans announced the development of an "individual carbon tracker." Once again, the WEF uses the environment to promote the micro-management of human behavior.

Evans says that the tracker can monitor, "where they're traveling, how they're traveling, what they're eating, and what are they consuming on the platform."

Notice that he used the pronoun "they" and not, "we" because there is no way in the world, he's going to use that thing.

CARBON FOOTPRINT TRACKER

"We're developing through technology, the ability for consumers to measure their own carbon footprint. What does it mean? That's, where are they traveling, how are they traveling, what are they eating, what are they consuming on the platform? An individual carbon footprint tracker."

Upon seeing all these insane statements and behavior from the WEF, two common themes become obvious.

The first theme is, "penetration." The WEF wants to penetrate governments using "Global Leaders" (aka Manchurian candidates.) It also wants to penetrate our bodies through pills, microchips, and vaccines. It also wants to penetrate our minds using soundwaves, censorship, and propaganda.

The other theme is "control." They want to control what we think, where we go, what we say, what we eat and what we wear.

Chapter Nine

World Economic Forum & The China-U.N. Connection

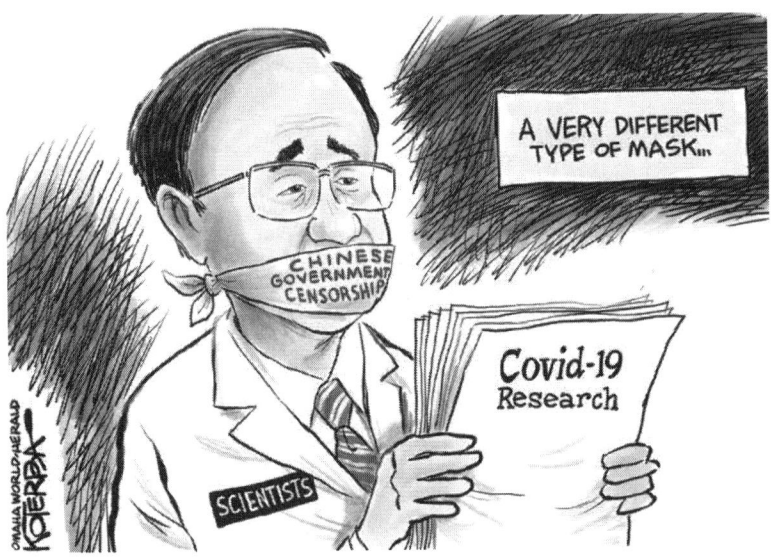

Do you know who agrees with the WEF? China. Censorship is widespread, a social credit system controls people's behaviors and COVID-19 is still used as an excuse for massive lockdowns and total population control. Not to mention the literal concentration camps.

Despite all of this, Chinese officials are constantly present at WEF meetings. Why? Because China is basically a laboratory for the WEF's policies.

And speaking of China's behavior, let's go back to the second plank there of The Great Reset.

1. **"The U.S. won't be the world's leading superpower."**

How is this not a national security issue? The World Economic Forum even admits this goal on their website!

"America's Dominance is over. By 2030, we'll have a handful of global powers."

And apparently, that won't include the United States. These sick, murderous, evil, megalomaniacs clearly and openly admit for all the world to see, that they really do plan on destroying our country! They're not even hiding it! And yet, nobody's talking about it?

It's almost like they've got people planted in high places, including the media, to keep their mouth shut on this national security issue. But notice, they didn't say they were going to take down Russia, or China or Australia or India, but specifically America! Why?

Because we're the backbone of the global economy with the "dollar reserve," and if you're going to "reset" the planet economically, then the economic structure of the current system, America, has to go!

In fact, Klaus Schwab himself has already admitted on camera who the next economic power was going to be. Can anyone guess who it is? That's right! It's China. Look at this.

Klaus Schwab: *"The World Economic Forum has been associated with China since the beginning of its reform and opening up policy. I came to China the first time and we had our first event in 1979. So, we are celebrating 40 years of cooperation. I have witnessed the great ascension of China. It has become the number two, and soon it will be the number one economic power in the world. It's just mind boggling what has been achieved in the last 40 years."*

Yeah, I would say so! It's almost like you planned it out! In fact, recently, Klaus even had the audacity to say this, **"China is a model for many nations."** "World Economic Forum founder and Chair, Klaus Schwab, recently sat down for an interview with a Chinese state media outlet (notice it's a controlled media) and proclaimed that the Chinese model is certainly a very attractive model for quite a number of countries, Schwab said."

"However, China is governed by the absolute rule of the Chinese Communist Party (CCP) which does not allow people to practice the religion or belief of their choice and has no tolerance for dissent or criticism."

You know, like the whole time during the Covid-19 Plandemic! Gee, I wonder why Klaus is supporting them? Maybe he's planning on bringing their whole oppressive regime and system to the whole planet! That's exactly what it is!

It goes on to say, *"In 2014, the CCP announced a moral ranking system whereby individuals, government organizations, and companies are ranked based on social credit.*

Comparisons have been drawn to environmental, social and governance, or ESG scores being used by major financial institutions and global organizations to create a type of social credit system designed to influence behavior and transform society." In other words, for purposes of control!

"Schwab wrote in 2019, that ESG scores are necessary for stakeholder capitalism."

In other words, it's a part of his system, the so-called "Great Reset" and the "China model," is what Klaus and the gang really want to bring to the whole planet.

This is why Klaus Schwab and the World Economic Forum, and all these wicked Global Elites have not only been striking deals with China for a long time and announcing China as the next global financial leader, but it's also because China is the role model for their Great Reset.

You want to see where we're headed, look to China! And it ain't good over there! But don't take my word for it. Let's listen to a former Chinese citizen warning us about it!

Xi Van Fleet, survivor of Mao's revolution: *"I just want to say, it is so ironic. Six years ago I ran away from socialism when I left China and came to this great country for freedom. Today so many Americans are abandoning freedom and are running to socialism. They have no idea what socialism is about. I lived under Mao's socialism, when the government controlled everything, made all the decisions, big and small. It decides how much grain, meat, and cooking oil I could have. What I should be learning in school, where I should live, and what job I should have and how I should think. In the Socialist Society that I lived under, there are no choices, there is no freedom. And that's what people do not know. Socialism becomes such a diluted word, and it's intentional. I can tell you; China is a socialist country; Cuba is a socialist country and so is North Korea. They are socialist countries run by the communist party. So, what is the difference? What is the difference between socialism and communism? Not much! Socialism is the initial state of communism according to Karl Marx."*

Girl who escaped from North Korea: *"Do you know how North Korea became how it is today? When Kim Il-Sung came, he made one promise to North Korean people. 'I'm going to feed you rice and meat stew each meal, and I'm going to get rid of all the inequality. If I do that, why don't you give me all your land and all your rights?' We wanted no inequality,* *so we gave our land, our rights to this one guy. He took everything from us."*

And that's exactly what Klaus and the gang are going to do. Under the guise of Global Communism or Socialism now relabeled as The Great Reset, "We will own nothing and be happy." Are you starting to get it? This is all it is folks, reduced down to its simplest form. Communism coming to the whole planet.

But that's not all. Klaus not only has a close partnership with China, and for many years, but he also has a close one with the United Nations as well. In fact, he's been striking deals with them because they too, as we've seen in the previous videos, are a part of this global wicked planetary takeover!

Narrator: *"This afternoon, Secretary General and Klaus Schwab, the founder of the World Economic Forum, will witness the signing of the memorandum of understanding of the teaching partnership of the U.N. and the WEF which outlines there is a cooperation."*

So, as you can see, they're working together hand-in-hand with the same agenda. In fact, it's even more blunt than that.

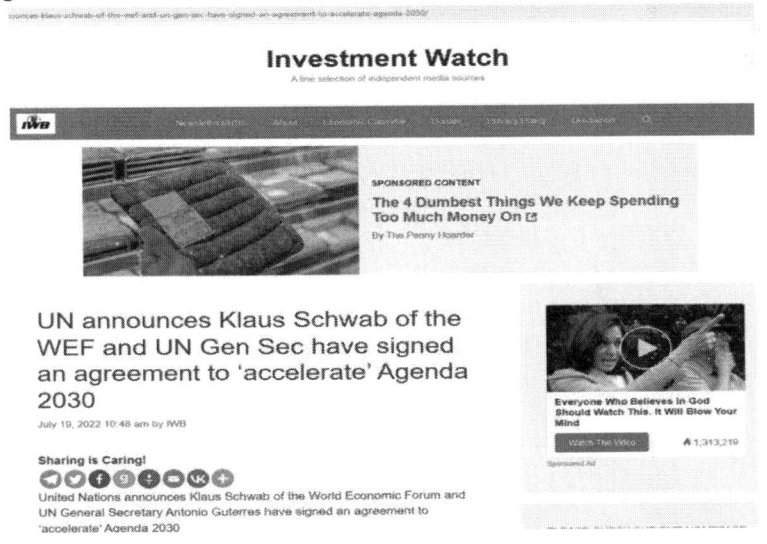

"UN announces Klaus Schwab of the WEF and U.N. Gen Sec have signed an agreement to 'accelerate' Agenda 2030."

So again, there you have it! Straight from the horse's mouth! As one person stated, *"Everyone should be on RED ALERT RIGHT NOW!"* No kidding! The understatement of the year! Communism is coming to the planet under the guise of The Great Reset, when it's really the "great communist invasion." That's all it is!

And again, how this is not a national security issue is beyond me. But I'm not the only one thinking that. This researcher is saying the exact same thing.

"I am deeply concerned that too many Americans are totally blind to the truth. They think the last Presidential election was just about Biden versus Trump.

The World Economic Forum predictions for 2030 includes the surrender of the United States to the United Nations – they say the US will no longer be the world Superpower.

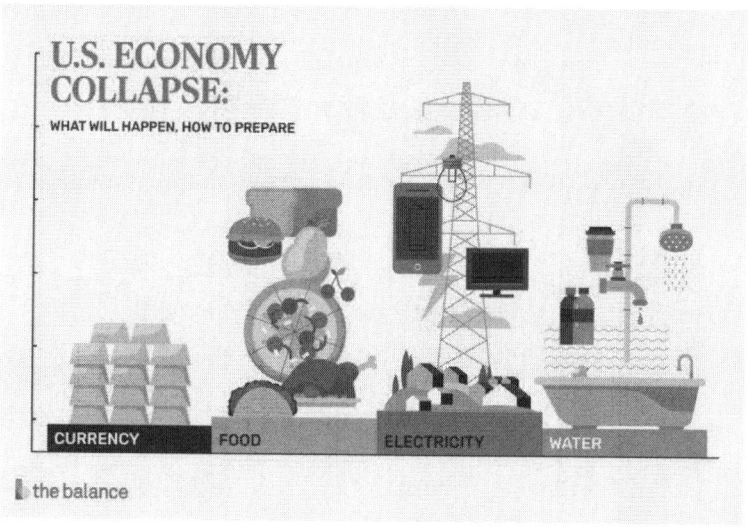

They will end eating meat, hence Gates' investment in meat alternatives, will make fossil fuels history, which is why Biden said in the debate, he will end the fossil fuel industry, and he will rejoin the United Nations.

This is the agenda that has been set in motion by this fake COVID-19 Pandemic, which was instigated by these people, and the lockdowns were intended to crush the economy, set it in the direction of nationalizing all industry, and wipe out small business. They are 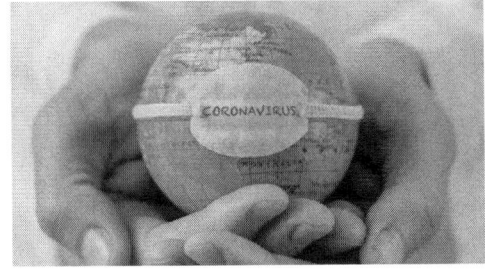 *developing passports that will require vaccines in order to travel. They are deliberately trying to reduce international travel to reduce pollution and to prevent mass uprisings against their new Communist Agenda.*

Yes, they are moving from socialism where you still own something, to communism, where the government owns everything.

This is what is at stake in this election. This is not about liking or disliking Trump. They want people to vote on such a superficial basis that he is obnoxious, insults people, and is one of the hated rich.

This is the real danger we face – World Economic Forum and its vision for a new Communist Green World Order.

The press will NOT do their job. For if they did, they would expose the fact that the World Economic Forum sold all its investments just before the crash.

Klaus Schwab is the new Karl Marx.

This is the greatest organized conspiracy in human history and the press is welcoming it with open arms. You will own nothing in 10 years, but you will also have no rights. – Papers Please!"

I couldn't have put it better myself! Once again, Klaus' Hitler background is coming into play! And *"Environmental boundaries are implemented while national borders must be removed, nature's wetlands protected, and private property erased."*

Yup, straight up communism. But as you can see, the sick facts are, Klaus Schwab the World Economic Forum and the sick Global Elites not only want to destroy America and America's economy as well, but our status as a world superpower, openly and admittedly.

Chapter Ten

World Economic Forum & The Ten Horned Kingdom

They also have plans to merge the U.S. into one of their pre-planned "economic regions" around the whole planet for better management of this new communist regime called The Great Reset.

In fact, that plan has also been in the works for quite some time. And thankfully, again, God warned us about it all a long time ago as being yet another aspect of the coming evil, satanic Antichrist Kingdom. Specifically, the Ten Horned Kingdom or Unions mentioned in the Bible that the planet would be split up into in the Last Days and then given over to the Antichrist!

Revelation 17:8-13: "The beast, which you saw, once was, now is not, and will come up out of the Abyss and go to his destruction. The inhabitants of the earth whose names have not been written in the book of life from the creation of the world will be astonished when they see the beast, because he once was, now is not, and yet will come. This calls for a mind with wisdom. The seven heads are seven hills on which the woman sits. They are also seven kings. Five have fallen, one is, the other has not yet come; but when he does come, he must remain for a little while. The beast who once was, and now is not, is an eighth king. He belongs to the seven and is going to his destruction. The ten horns you saw are ten kings who have not yet received a kingdom, but who for one hour will receive authority as kings along with the beast. They have one purpose and will give their power and authority to the beast."

So according to the Bible, we see how the Antichrist's kingdom is going to be split up into ten different parts ruled by ten different kings or leaders. And then, at one point, they surrender their power and authority over to the Antichrist. It says it right there. Use your mind of wisdom!

But here's the point. It's a good thing we see no signs of that happening today! The planet being split up into 10 different Kingdoms or Unions or whatever? Yeah, right! It's happening right now, thanks to the deceptive work of Klaus Schwab, the World Economic Forum and these wicked Global Elites!

They're already creating 10 World Regions to ensure proper control of their new communist global system, now called The Great Reset.

As you can see here from the classic Club of Rome report in the 1970's.

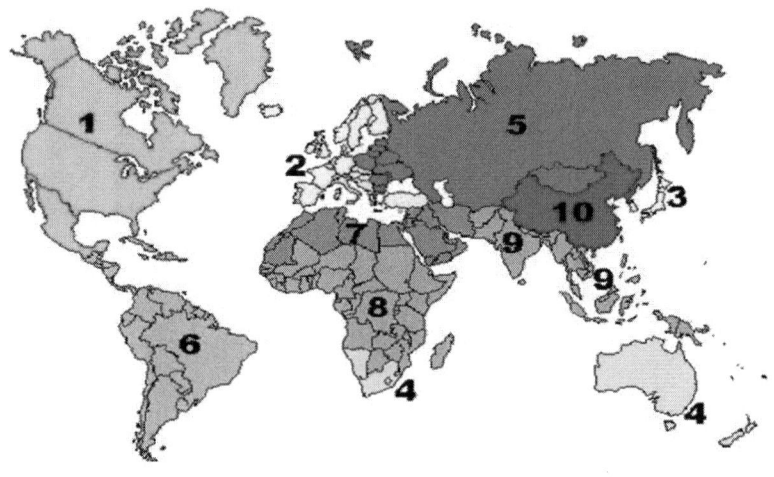

Notice how the planet just happens to be split up way back then into exactly 10 regions. Not 5, or 4, or 122, or 99. But specifically 10. It's almost like somebody's following a script or something!

Then, "In 1976, the United States Association of the Club of Rome (USACOR), was formed for the purpose of shutting down the U.S. economy gradually."

So, a slow destruction for a reconstruction into 10 economic regions, that's the plan. Then, the same regional plan is outlined as well on the European Union Commission Website, as you can see here.

And if you scroll down, you will see that the planet, on their website, is already split up into exactly 10 regions.

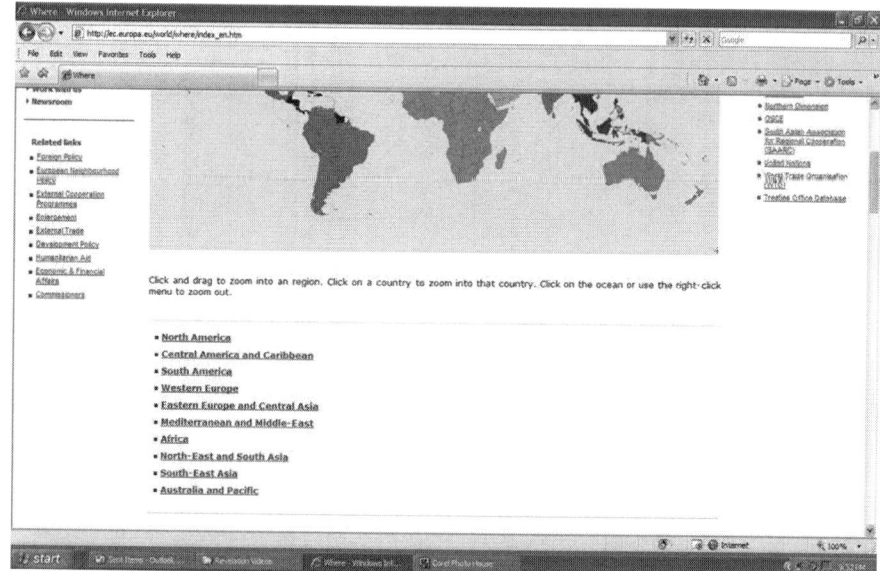

Then even more bluntly, this is a screen shot from the United Nations Parliamentary Assembly website.

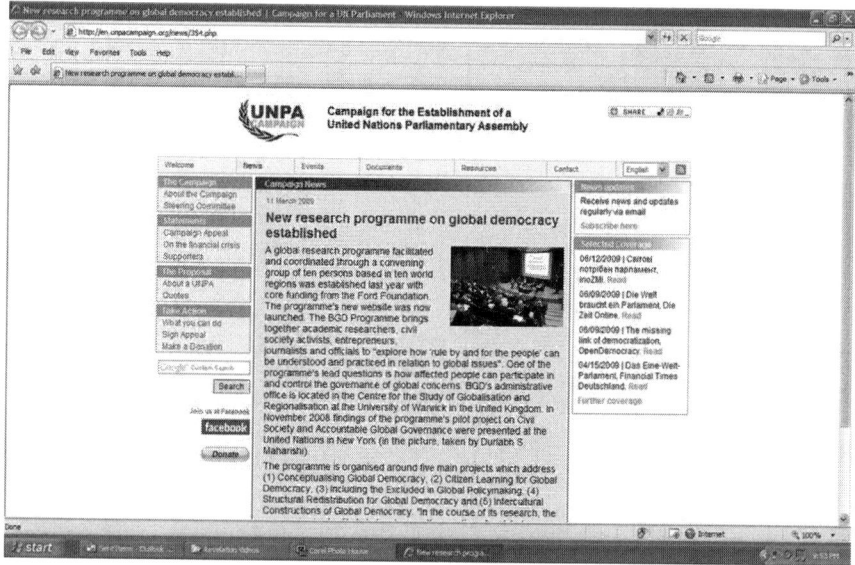

And it says right there, back in 2009, **"New research program on global democracy established."** And I quote,

> **Campaign News**
>
> 11 March 2009
>
> **New research programme on global democracy established**
>
> A global research programme facilitated and coordinated through a convening group of ten persons based in ten world regions was established last year with core funding from the Ford Foundation. The programme's new website was now launched. The BGD Programme brings together academic researchers, civil society activists, entrepreneurs, journalists and officials to "explore how 'rule by and for the people' can be understood and practiced in relation to global issues". One of the programme's lead questions is how affected people can participate in

"A global research program facilitated and coordinated through a convening group of 'ten persons,' based in 'ten world regions,' was established last year (2008)."

That's not only wild, but that's exactly what the Bible says and warned about would come upon the planet nearly 2,000 years ago. The world would be split up into 10 different kingdoms, headed up by 10 different kings, who then hand their power over to the Antichrist! Is this wild or what?

And as you saw, we have been slowly and methodically preparing for this over the years. This is what we saw with the birth of the European Union, one of the 10 kingdoms.

The European Union: Objectives

The E.U. has many goals:
- promote peace inside and outside E.U.
- provide member states with common economic markets
- provide freedom of travel of goods and ideas throughout E.U.
- celebrate and promote cultural diversity

European Union Member States

It's a region of countries that came together with their own currency called the Euro.

Then that seemed to be a kick-off event, because we now have the formation of the African Union, which is a region of countries coming together in Africa, economically, with their own currency.

Then there's plans for a South American Union, an Asian Union, a Mediterranean Union, a Central Asian Union, a Pacific Union and even a North American Union between the United States, Canada, and Mexico.

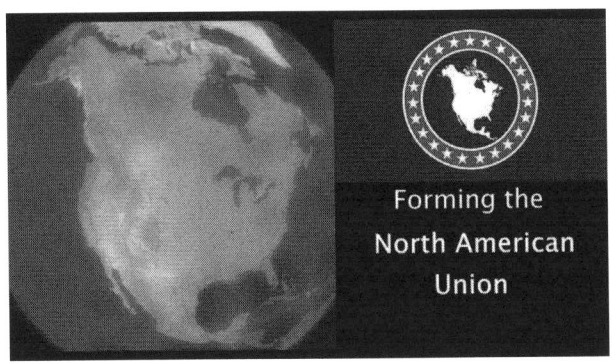

It's all part of the Last Days Antichrist's 10-Horned Kingdom!

And for those of you who find it hard to believe one of the proposed economic kingdoms, called the North American Union, with the U.S., Canada and Mexico merging together, would ever come to pass, again, this has been in the works for a long, long time!

The **1st way** we see America getting swallowed up into a 10-Horned Kingdom of the Antichrist is the **Currency Proof**.

For many years now there have been talks and plans for the United States to be merged into this North American Union. And this proposed "union" between the United States, Canada and Mexico, would even have a new currency called the Amero.

In fact, several years ago, this was leaked out on a financial news broadcast, and what they're saying now, is all we need right now is for the right "crisis" to come along, and we can put it all into play. Sound familiar? Watch this.

Ron Paul: *"There is a move toward a North American Union."*

Lou Dobbs, CNN Reporter: *"The Security and Prosperity Partnership, also called the North American Union."*

Dan Dicks, Press for Truth: *"It's essentially the centralization of power into fewer heads."*

Herbert Grubel, Father of the Amero: *"What would be the benefit of creating the equivalent of the Euro, and I had the idea, the inspiration to call it the Amero."*

CNBC News Reports: *"I Think one thing, people that are dollar based need to focus on, is the Amero. That's one thing that nobody is talking about that I think is going to have a big impact on everybody's life, Canada, the U.S. and Mexico. And that's the currency for the North American community which is being developed right now between Canada, the U.S. and Mexico, to make a borderless community much like the EU."*

Speaker: *"Our economies now are very integrated; our societies are growing increasingly integrated. What is needed now is a North American idea for all. The greatest initiatives are usually originated from some crisis of some sort."*

Herbert Grubel, Father of the Amero: *"My hope is that eventually, if there is a major catastrophe, there will be enough people around who will say that this may be the time to try out this idea."*

You know, like a Covid-19 Plandemic scenario. By the way, that last guy was Hebert Grubel, the father of the Amero, and you saw as he admits, all we need is the right "crisis" to come along, and hopefully enough people will be there to launch this new currency!

This is nuts! But you can laugh all you want. This is what these people, these global, murderous, megalomaniacs are really working on behind the scenes!

Now, whether it ends up being called the Amero or not, that's not the point. This combining of our currencies into an Economic Union with other countries, one of ten, is exactly what the Bible said would happen in the Last Days when you start to see the emergence of the Antichrist Kingdom.

The **2nd way** we see America getting swallowed up into a 10-Horned Kingdom of the Antichrist is the **Highway Proof**.

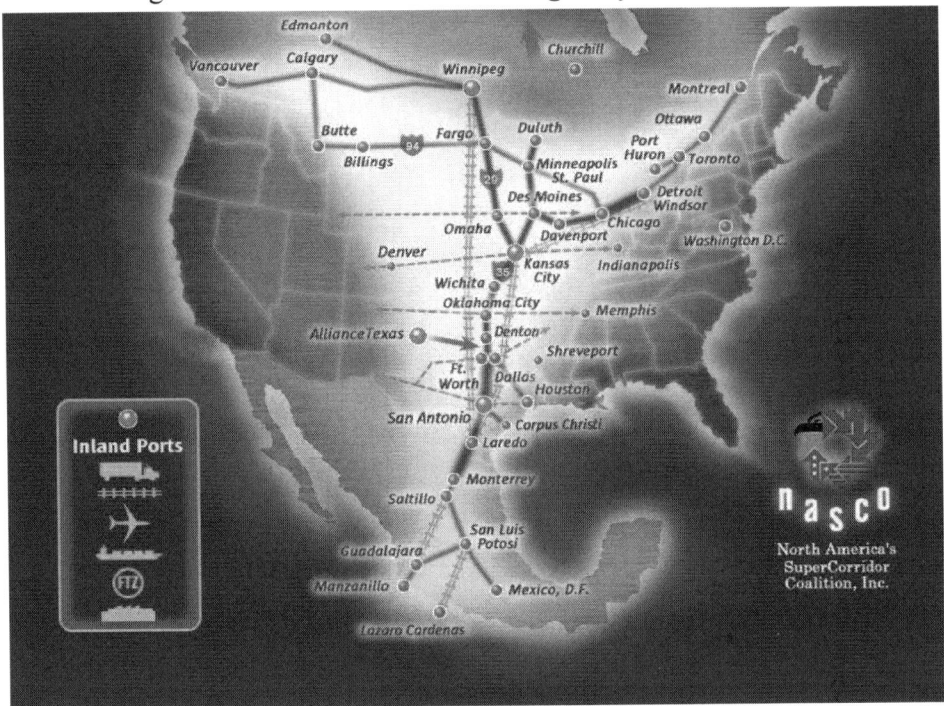

You see, in order to help these three countries come together, Canada, U.S., and Mexico, you not only need a single currency, but you need a single infrastructure to connect all three countries to keep the goods flowing back and forth for that economy, right?

Well guess what? That's exactly what's also been going on for quite some time as well. Believe it or not, there's a planned Giant Superhighway called the NAFTA Superhighway or the Trans Texas Corridor that is being built through America that will connect all three of these countries together.

And one congresswoman blew the whistle on this years ago, but unfortunately nobody seemed to have listened to her.

Rep. Marcy Kaptur, D-Ohio Toledo: *"Today I want to talk a little bit about Super NAFTA and what the Bush administration is planning, to lock NAFTA in even tighter in this country and across the continent. There is something that is called, 'Agreement on Security and Prosperity,' being negotiated by the Bush administration, very quietly. No meetings are being held in this Congress. Most Americans haven't even heard of the term. This 'Security and Prosperity Agreement' as it is being called, has no democratic underpinning to it. It's being negotiated by those very same elites that negotiated NAFTA.*

Let's look at some of the signs of what is happening. It is suddenly clearer why a company from Spain called Cintra, wants to be the gate keeper on this new highway structure. Cintra is a subsidiary of Ferrovial, the Spanish transportation company, founded by multi-billionaire Rafael de Pino, who is one of the richest people in the world. The people of the United States had better wake up!"

Lou Dobbs, CNN Reporter: *"Open border advocates are refusing to acknowledge rising evidence of plans for a NAFTA superhighway. Many in the mainstream media absolutely refuse to acknowledge the reality. Plans could be major steps toward that North American Union of the United States, Canada, and Mexico. President Bush says that opponents of the NAFTA superhighway in his view, are laying out a conspiracy. Senator Obama says he see no evidence of a North American Union, and even some new organizations are criticizing me for even raising the issue.*

Time Magazine journalist, Joe Cline, accused me of, 'spewing false inflammatory nonsense.' So, we asked Bill Tucker to report on the issue. He found that there is plenty of evidence of plans of transportation links between Mexico and Canada, and only, in my opinion, a fool would refuse to see those links.

Bill Tucker, Reporter: *"There is no 'NAFTA Superhighway,' not officially. Some even call it the invention of the far-right wing. But some politicians find the denial almost laughable."*

Rep. Ted Poe, (R) Texas: *"The folks in Washington are in denial about the super NAFTA highway, or whatever you want to call it. It's the concept that there will be a highway, free trade, from Mexico, through the central part of the U.S., and all the way to Canada."*

Bill Tucker: *"In Texas, the planning and development are under way with what are officially called, 'Transportation Corridors,' 'The Trans-Texas Corridor,' 'I-69,' the combination of rail lines, utility lines, car and truck lanes. Plans for it to be as wide as three football fields laid end-to-end. It will be financed by a private, foreign company, most likely Spain's Cintra, who will then own the lease on the road and the revenue generated by the tolls. Texas may use eminent domain to lay claim to the land they need to build it. For an imaginary road, there is a lot of money and effort involved, and some really strong opposition."*

"The New World Order is rapidly constructing the physical infrastructure of the North American Union, and the NAFTA superhighway control grid. More than 80 federal and state highways have been designated as international arteries. The I-35 NAFTA corridor starts deep inside Mexico, and travels through the middle of the United States, and ends in central Canada. Container ships from Asia dump their cargo on the Pacific side of Mexico, then travels duty free by rail, to the new Kansas City inland port, now considered sovereign soil of Mexico in the heart of the United States. Under international agreements, predominately foreign countries are placing tolls on already existing paid-for roads.

Federal, state, and corporate documents show that they will then use the revenue raised to build up the transportation infrastructure of Mexico, not the United States or Canada, so foreign made products can flow in even faster from Mexico. Revenues raised will also be used to fund the fledgling North American Union and its growing bureaucracy. Bottom line, they are using our own money to enslave us."

Arthur Peterson: *"I'm Arthur Peterson, currently retired from the Army. To think that people would even consider confiscating land of farmers and ranchers, and taking their homes away from them, and turn it over to a foreign company in Spain which is controlled by Juan Carlos, who is a notorious socialist. And they get the toll on Texas land for 50 years. I see things today that are happening, that would make my friends who died in World War II turn over in their graves."*

And I would agree, but for those who have eyes to see and ears to hear, you can't deny this is what's taking place!

But why would a sovereign nation, America, as patriotic as we are, turn our backs on the freedom that was hard fought, won, bought and paid for with blood, and then turn it over to these foreign socialist elites?

Well, one, it makes no sense, unless you read the Bible, where you see it's all part of the Antichrist 10-Horned Kingdom, that would appear on the scene when you're living in the Last Days. And two, it's because our leadership have sold their souls to the devilish elite, including Klaus Schwab and the World Economic Forum!

Which leads us to the **3rd proof,** as we see America getting swallowed up into a 10-Horned Kingdom of the Antichrist, is the **Leadership Proof.**

You see, I know it might be a tough cookie to swallow, but we've got to deal with the facts here. Call it what you will, but treason in high places is in our country today!

And for those of you who still want to scoff at this Amero talk and NAFTA Super-Highway and combining all three countries into a North American Union, all you need to do is look at the political proof over the last administrations, including the current one - Biden, Klaus Schwab's buddy, Mr. Build Back Better. Yes, just exactly what are you building, Mr. Biden?

If these Global Elites weren't really serious about creating a North American Union out of the United States, Canada, and Mexico, then why did previous Presidents from all three countries constantly meet together for years to discuss how best to pull it off? Look at this.

LEADERSHIP PROOF

Lou Dobbs, CNN Reports: *"New concerns tonight about moves toward what some call a North American Union. A number of high-level government meetings are taking place in Mexico to discuss North American integration of Mexico, the United States and Canada, and more meetings are scheduled. It is an aggressive agenda proposed at the highest levels of our government and U.S. commerce, without congressional or voter oversight, Lisa Shuster reports."*

Lisa Schuster: *"A caravan of cars travels along the Arizona desert. Homeland Security, Michael Chertoff visits the U.S./Mexican border. Last week, he was in Mexico City. Commerce Secretary, Carlos Gutierrez, visited Mexico on February 1st, Attorney General, Roberto Gonzales, visited on January 11th, and President Bush himself will travel there next month. The high-level meetings are to advance North American integration, also known as the Security Prosperity Partnership."*

Jim Edwards, Numbers USA: *"There's several ways it could go. One is modeled after the EU. One is modeled after, sort of, the economic* community. It's beyond the scope of free trade, which we fairly have already with those two countries."

Glen Beck: *"Four years ago, I bet I was a lot like you. I started paying attention to the border crisis and I thought to myself, why is this happening? It doesn't even make sense. I thought we thought about security. Well, since I couldn't apply logic to understand what was happening on the border, I started looking for alternative theories, and it took me places I didn't want to go. Quite honestly, who's watching the border? Who would benefit from things being screwed up? I hate to have to break it to you, but after two years of denying it and saying this can't be, it's the only reason that I found that would explain everything that is going on in our country, with the border.*

Our country has been sold out in the name of global profits and votes at the ballot box. This is where the Security and Prosperity Partnership with North America, or SPP, comes in. This little international agreement cooked up by President Bush, the former president of Mexico, and the prime minister of Canada. Their mission is to blur, or completely erase the borders between Canada, U.S., and Mexico, to get goods and services freely flowing between all three countries in the dream of one big happy – Amerimexicanada. And that would finally become a reality. Sound great? Not so much! On Larry King Live. Where everybody, like you, like me, have been saying, I don't want to believe this, but it looks like it's happening. We've all been called crazy. This is what Vicente Fox said on Larry King Live, roll the tape."

Vicente Fox: *"What we propose together, President Bush and myself, is a trade union for all of the Americans."*

Larry King: *"Like the Euro dollar? Is that what you mean?"*

Vicente Fox: *"Well, that would be long, long term. I think the processes to go first, step into a trading agreement, and then further on, a new vision like we are trying to do with NAFTA."*

Glen Beck: *"He says in this interview, Jerome, that he's asked, would it be like the Euro dollar? Well, not long term. I was with one of the world's leading economists having dinner the other night, and I said, 'at what point (and this guy's an optimist),' at what point do you start worrying about the dollar? And he said, 'It's almost like we're intentionally destroying the dollar.'"*

PM Paul Martin: *"Let me close with just one more thing on this question of sovereignty. It's very difficult for a large country to accept that somebody is going to come in, like the United States, or the Europeans, and is literally going to come in and say, 'You're not doing your regulation in a proper way! Fair game. But what's going to happen when China and India- whose economy is as powerful as the United States or Europe - what's going to happen when there is a mortgage meltdown in India? What's going to happen when a Chinese hedge fund goes under? And the results of that tsunami don't stop at the Chinese or Indian borders, but, in fact, you find them in Idaho or Iowa or California. Who's going to deal with that? Unless we are prepared to understand, that in fact, we are all going to have to give up a little bit of our sovereignty in order to make the world work."*

Lou Dobbs, CNN Reports: *"Well, another announcement today by President Elect Obama, giving new life to a North American Union, a plan by business and political leaders, to tear down the trade barriers among the United States, Canada, and Mexico, and to create a NAFTA Superhighway. All of which is to be done without the approval of Congress or the American people. President Elect Obama named a die-hard free trader and NAFTA supporter to be his U.S. Trade Representative. Bill Tucker has our report."*

Bill Tucker: *"Ron Kirk is President Obama's pick to be his front man on trade. Kirk made his name in politics, serving as mayor in Dallas, where he was known as a staunch supporter of free trade agreements, NAFTA in particular. He was a big proponent of the trade corridor from Mexico up through Texas, a road he once referred to as a NAFTA freeway. His nomination was welcomed by the U.S. Chamber of Commerce, and the*

National Association of Manufacturers. Advocates for change in trade policy are not so happy. Now the apparent contradiction in Obama's words and actions have put us on another front of worry. Last February, Obama pledged that he would resume the Securities and Prosperity Partnership talks between Mexico and Canada that President Bush initiated. He also said the talks would be transparent. Those opposed to the North American Union say, now, whether he will or will not deliver on that promise is something they doubt."

Lou Dobbs: *"This is early on. The president's beginning to look like, the old boss is starting to look like the new boss."*

In other words, it doesn't matter what President we have or what party gets elected, they're all in it together, and they're all working at destroying our country, the United States of America.

This is not only treasonous, which is bad enough, but this is also fulfilling Bible prophecy, right before our very eyes. It's all part of us being swallowed up into one of these 10 Economic Unions that the Bible said would appear on the scene, when you're living in the Last Days!

The **4th proof** we see America getting swallowed up into a 10-Horned Kingdom of the Antichrist is the **Border Proof**.

You see, if all three countries are going to be tied together in this New North American Union via the currencies and that highway system to keep that economy going, then you need some sort of way to control the borders, right?

Makes total sense if you think about it. You not only have to control the flow of goods going back and forth, but of people themselves.

But the problem is, how are you going to identify every single person coming across the border and what country they're from, and who they are, as well as identify all the troublemakers who won't go along with the program?

Simple. Apparently, you first deal with the troublemakers by combining your Armed Forces together, so as to unify your effort in dealing with them. And believe it or not, that too has been in the works for a long time as well.

For instance, the former British Prime Minister and globalist Tony Blair, has for years been calling for NATO to become the future "military arm of a New World Order, rather than strictly a defensive alliance."

And if you think about it, we've already seen NATO exercise more and more military force over the sovereignty of nations, right? Gee, I wonder who's next?

In fact, some would even say this has been planned as far back as 1952, as you can see with the following map from the World Association of Parliamentarians for World Government in London.

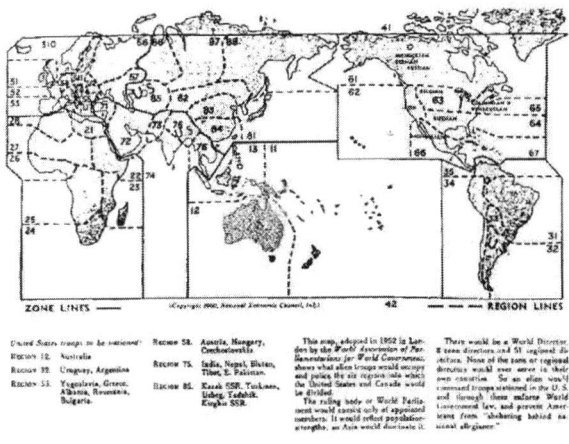

They met in London to plan on how they can have foreign troops stationed in foreign countries to help control things around the world.

Why? Because it's awfully hard for an American soldier to shoot a fellow American, right? But not if that soldier was from China. And believe it or not, that's what's on that map, back from 1952!

It details how they plan to have Chinese, Russian, Colombian, Venezuelan, and Belgian troops stationed here in America. And then, American troops would be stationed in Europe to help control things over there. But hey, good thing we never see foreign troops on America soil. Unfortunately, that too has been going on for a while, including, shocker, the Chinese military. Here they are training on American soil. I wonder why?

829Speeky Reports: *"Well, soldiers with the Hawaii National Guard recently joined their Chinese counterpart for an inaugural disaster training. Tech Sergeant, Andrew Jackson has more."*

Sergeant Jackson: *"Hawaiian National Guard recently participated in the first ever search and rescue extraction training event, between the U.S. and Chinese militaries. During the three-day exercise, search and extraction professionals got a chance to learn from each other, while working hand-in-hand in a simulated disaster environment. Previous engagements involved planning and table-top strategy sessions. This is the first time that rescuers from the two nations have had the chance to work together in a field environment."*

Well gee, if that military exercise works that good, then maybe we can also work together down the road, American and Chinese, when another crisis hits, and we need to re-establish order and control. These foreign troops can help us. And that's exactly the plan!

But as you just saw, there's already Communist China Military on American soil, and why would we allow that? Unless, of course, it's some part of a bigger plan that most of us have no clue about.

And lest you think the Chinese won't be policing us, they are already being "hired" to police people in different countries, including France.

Ramin Mazaheri, Press TV: *"In a decision which has surprised many, which may simply be a sign of things to come, France will allow Chinese police to patrol tourist areas in Paris. For more than two centuries it's been armed French men who have patrolled the streets of foreign countries. Now that the shoe will be on the other foot, many in France can barely contain their surprise and indignation."*

Man on the street: *"Countries should control things by itself. It's not right for foreign police to be stationed here."*

And I would agree, but that's what's happening! A Communist country is policing a Western country, including, believe it or not, the U.S. Here's a story that didn't get a whole lot of press, for some reason. Check this out.

Leland Vitter, On Balance Reports: *"Welcome back. More proof tonight that China has violated basic human rights on our soil, without consequence. For some reason, the FBI and the DOJ gave Chinese intelligence a pass here in America. A group called Safeguard Defender just released a report, showing the Chinese have set up police stations in over 110 countries around the world. There's at least one in New York, at least one that we know about. If this sounds familiar, it's because we warned you about Xi Jinping's kidnapping abroad today."*

WION News Reports: *"Do countries have two different policing systems? One that is run by the government in power, and the other by a foreign power? Obviously not. How can a sovereign country allow a foreign government to operate on its soil? But what if I tell you it is happening already. China is setting up a network of police stations overseas, and they are present in more than 20 countries. They are being used to go after dissidents. The Chinese police are going global, and this is our cover story tonight.*

The scale of this operation is massive. Let's have a look at this. These are the countries that already have a Chinese overseas police station. Going by one report, there are over 54 Chinese police centers in existence. They are spread out across five continents and 21 countries. There could be more countries with these police stations. Now we're not sure when they were set up, but what is their purpose? Why does China need police stations overseas?"

Chris Smith Tonight Reports: *"The 20th Chinese Congress got underway in Beijing today and it looks like hardline president, Xi Jinping will be handed another 5-year term in the top job. That would make him the most powerful leader since Mao Tse-Tung, and will present to the rest of the world, including Australia, with all the same aggressive threats and problems which have come out of Beijing for the past decade. Meanwhile, a dream based human rights organization, Safeguard Defenders, have published a report, showing that the Chinese government has set up illegal and secret police stations in 54 countries around the world, including Sydney. While these so-called service centers have been open for over a decade, Safeguard Defenders claim they are used by the Communist Party to crack down on Chinese dissidents and alleged criminals living abroad."*

And maybe anybody who eventually would oppose this new global communism takeover of the whole planet relabeled as The Great Reset. But folks, this is happening before our very eyes and hardly anyone is talking about it! Again, how is this not a national security issue?

It's almost like somebody's got a plan, and step by step they're conditioning us to accept the words of Henry Kissinger. Here's what he said, back in the day.

"Today, America would be outraged if U.N. troops entered Los Angeles to restore order. Tomorrow they will be grateful.

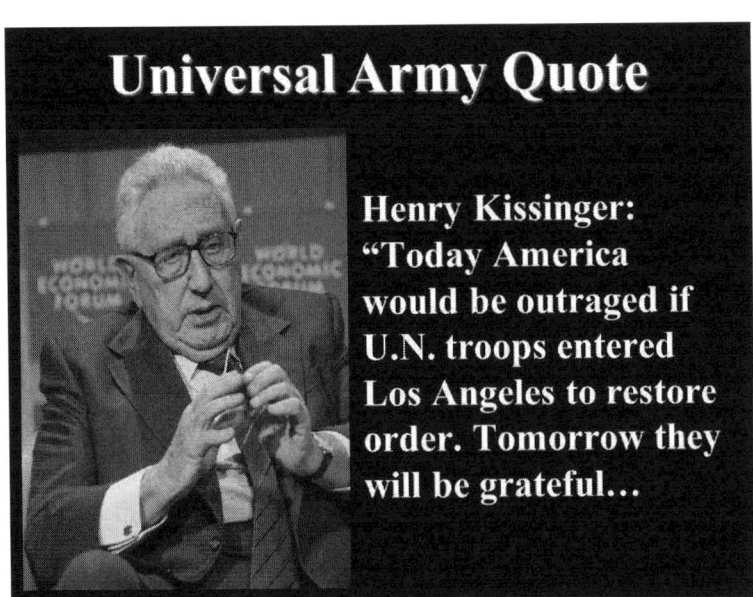

When presented with this scenario, individual rights will be willingly relinquished for the guarantee of their well-being granted to them by the World Government."

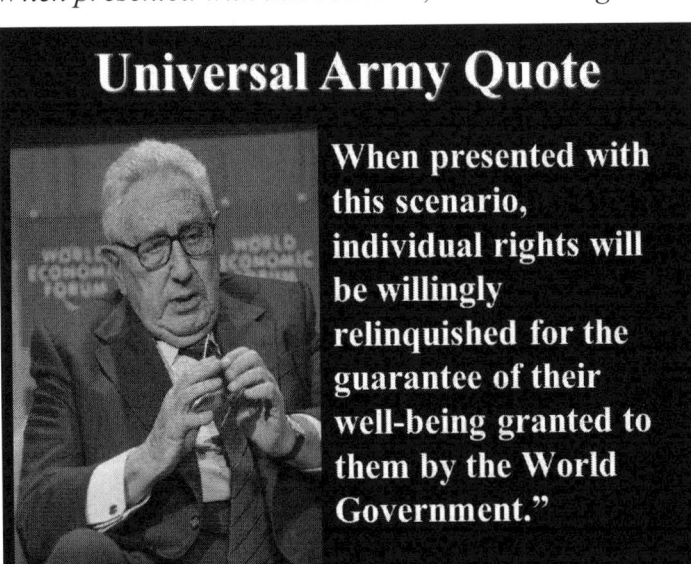

In fact, years ago, they've even gone so far as to already create a North American Army.

NORTH AMERICAN MILITARY AGREEMENT SIGNED BY US AND CANADA

By Jim Kouri
Posted 1:00 AM Eastern
March 11, 2008
NewsWithViews.com

While Americans are being bombarded with large doses of presidential primary news coverage, the US entered into an agreement with its northern neighbor that may have an impact on future internal military action.

In a political move that received little if any attention by the American news media, the United States and Canada <u>entered into a military agreement</u> on February 14, 2008, allowing the armed forces from one nation to support the armed forces of the other nation during a domestic civil emergency, even one that does not involve a cross-border crisis, according to a police commander involved in homeland security planning and implementation.

It is an initiative of the Bi-National Planning Group whose final report, issued in June 2006, called for the creation of a "Comprehensive Defense and Security Agreement," or a "continental approach" to Canada-US defense and security.

The law enforcement executive told Newswithviews.com that the agreement -- defined as a Civil Assistance Plan -- was not submitted to Congress for debate and approval, nor did Congress pass any law or treaty specifically authorizing this military agreement to combine the operations of the armed forces of the United States and Canada in the event of domestic civil disturbances ranging from violent storms, to health epidemics, to civil riots or terrorist attacks.

"This is a military plan that's designed to bypass the Posse Comitatus Act that traditionally prohibited the US military from operating within the borders of the United States. Not only will American soldiers be deployed at the discretion of whomever is sitting in the Oval Office, but foreign soldiers will also be deployed in American cities," warns Lt. Steven Rodgers, commander of the Nutley, NJ Police Department's detective bureau.

Other News Articles:

Florida Microchipping Alzheimer's patients Despite Cancer risks

More News Articles

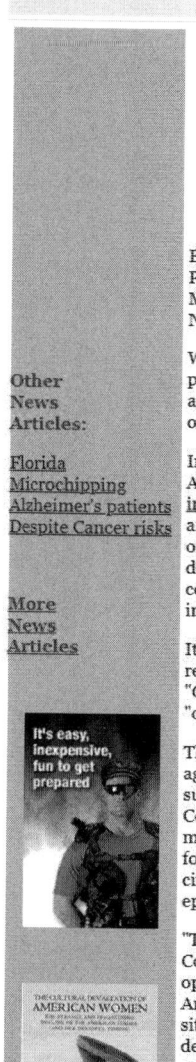

While Americans are being kept in the dark about this treaty, Canadian citizens are being totally ignored by their government.

"In a ceremony that received virtually no attention in the American media, the United States and Canada signed a military agreement allowing the armed forces from one nation to support the armed forces of the other nation during a domestic, civil emergency."

"The agreement, defined as a Civil Assistance Plan, was not submitted to Congress for approval, nor did Congress pass any law or treaty specifically authorizing this military agreement to combine the operations of the armed forces of the U.S. and Canada in the event of a domestic, civil disturbance."

> **posse comitatus**
>
> It shall not be lawful to employ any part of the Army of the United States, as a posse comitatus, or otherwise, for the purpose of executing the laws, except in such cases and under such circumstances as such employment of said force may be expressly authorized by the Constitution or by act of Congress.

"The military plan is designed to bypass the Posse Comitatus Act that traditionally prohibits the U.S. military from operating within the borders of the United States. But now, not only will American soldiers be deployed at the discretion of whomever is sitting in the Oval Office, but foreign soldiers will also be deployed in American cities."

Which is exactly what we saw with the 1952 map from the World Association of Parliamentarians for World Government, with the Chinese Military being stationed here with the Russian and Belgium troops.

Notice that the agreement happened back in 2008. It's all slowly, methodically happening before our very eyes!

And lest you doubt, "The Civil Assistance Plan is an incremental step toward creating a North American Armed Forces, available to be deployed in North American emergency situations."

You know, like another plandemic, or whatever else they've got up their sleeve! But that's how they're going to deal with all the troublemakers who oppose this North American Union, or any other unions around the world, in my opinion.

But there's still another problem. Not only dealing with the troublemakers, who oppose this communist global takeover of the planet now relabeled as The Great Reset, but what are you going to do about identifying every single person coming across these new combined country borders? How are you going to know who they are, where they're from, whether or not they're a legitimate citizen of this new North American Union or one of the other 10 horned kingdoms?

Well, can you say, a Universal ID System?

And how are they going to enforce that? Once again, it's the old communist methodology of, "Create a crisis so you can manage the outcome."

What do you think's been going on with all this Border Talk lately that's never ending in the news? Believe it or not, the long-term plan is to use this border crisis they created to get us all conditioned to accept the solution, a Universal ID System.

And they really mean "universal," because the "border problem" is way bigger than just the Hispanic Community coming across. It's all kinds of people from all over the world!

Newscaster: *"The local border patrol union is worried that talk about amnesty will lead to more people who want to enter the U.S. illegally. Steve Scalise recently rode along with agents as they patrolled their border, and they made a surprising discovery."*

Steve Scalise: *"Border patrol agent, Joe Gutierrez is familiar with this area of the border. He drove us along the river from Hidalgo Bridge to Alonzo Lewis Park. He pointed out important lookout spots along the bumpy trail."*

Joe Gutierrez: *"Today, me and my partner were here patrolling this area and we had three Chinese immigrants come up to us directly."*

Steve Scalise: *"I told them I was surprised to hear that."*

Joe Gutierrez: *"We apprehend people from over 143 countries nationwide. Most people think it's just Hispanics or Mexicans from Mexico or Central America, but we get people from China, a whole bunch of different places."*

Did you know that? Not just Hispanics, or Mexicans, but Chinese coming across the border? In fact, people from 143 different countries?

Looks like we have a "crisis" on our hands! What are we going to do? How are we going to identify these people from all different countries?

Hey, I know. How about we implement some sort of Universal ID Card for everyone to carry at all times, so we can keep track of them and determine whether or not they're eligible to get a job in this new North American Union?

And if you don't think that's the plan, believe it or not, that's exactly what they've been calling for, for many years as well. The whole thing is a setup. Watch this from back in the day!

Megyn Kelly, America Live, Fox News Reports: *"President Obama taking on not only Health Care reform, but another controversial issue, immigration reform. And the key meeting at the White House tomorrow could be the first step toward that reform, and for some very big changes for every American worker. Senators Chuck Schumer and Lindsay Graham, bipartisan that is, are set to sit down with President Obama tomorrow, discussing plans for a National Identification Card. Now this thing is meant to crack down on illegal workers, but our next guest said it could crack down on you and your privacy. Congressman Ron Paul is a Texas Republican, and he is opposed to this card. Congressman, good afternoon to you."*

Ron Paul: *"Good afternoon, nice to be with you."*

Megyn Kelly: *"It's a great pleasure to have you. So, what's your problem with the National ID Card, because its proponents say, 'This is it. This is the thing that is supposed to finally help us stop illegal immigrants from coming here and taking jobs."*

Ron Paul: *"Well, we do have a problem with illegal immigration, but I would say that the problem with every American citizen carrying their papers wherever they go is a much worse problem than illegal immigration. Besides, you can take care of illegal immigration otherwise. But people for decades now, there are some that have wanted this*

National ID, and they are looking for every opportunity to get it and this is it. Who knows what will come of it. My guess is that they will have a GPS chip in there, so that they can measure everybody, every instant, no matter where they go. So, to me, it violates the whole principle of privacy, the whole principle of the Constitution, the principles of the Republic, and to me is a gross distortion of what we should be doing. It's part of an authoritarian society, and dictatorships have this, but not a Republic."

Megyn Kelly: *"Okay, tell me how it should be. What Schumer and Graham are proposing, according to what I read, is that your ID card would have either your fingerprint, or a reading of the veins on the back of your hand, and you'd have to be scanned by your prospective employer, and that if some way you came up as illegal, they would catch you by your scan."*

And then you wouldn't be able to cross the border, you wouldn't be able to get a job, you wouldn't be able "buy and sell" in these new 10-horned economic regions, unless you had your "hand" scanned in this new proposed Biometric ID system.

Sound familiar? Yeah, it's the precursor to the Mark of the Beast system in the 7-year Tribulation! It's all being put into play, step by step, with a "planned crisis" to help justify it! And speaking of deception, what they also don't tell you, is that this proposed Universal ID system they've been working on for years, has a fatal flaw. There's another "crisis" built into it just waiting to happen.

You see, these "current" proposed Universal ID systems are "external" microchip cards. But we all know the "problem" external cards are, that we could lose them, or somebody could steal them, right? So now what? Another crisis on our hands!

Oh hey, I know, how about we get all these microchipped Universal ID cards that are on the "outside" of us, now on the "inside" of us, where nobody could steal it and we'd never lose it! Hey, wouldn't that be great?

Yeah, believe it or not, that's called set-up number two, getting people microchipped themselves. And there's a whole new generation out there ready to do just that. Getting a microchip in your "hand" in order to travel. Watch this:

Microchip implantee #1: *"Today I am going to show you my motorcycle that I wired to accept RFID authorization. First, you see that the key is in the off position. I turned on the engine's off switch. It also activates the RFID reader. And right now, it turns over, but it doesn't start. But the RFID reader antenna is here, so when I authenticate, the bike powers up."*

Microchip implantee #2: *"Right now I have an RFID chip, surgically implanted in my left hand. This allows me to do all the functions that the car does, but with my hand."*

Skynews Reports: *"Chances are you're carrying a couple of RFID chips now, and if you are, they are carrying a number that identifies you. That number can be picked up by what's called an ISO compliant scanner. And they are everywhere, too. The chips are embedded in credit cards, key cards, and the swipe pads that let people into their office buildings. They're used to track manufactured goods in factories and stores, identify livestock and lost pets. And now, RFID chips like this are being injected into humans. Dr. Mark Gasson, of the University of Redding in England, was injected with one in 2009 to control electronic devices in his office.*

The microchip implants are coated with a biocompatible material that enables them to bond with the surrounding flesh and sinus that keeps them in place, making the surgical removable difficult and painful. Companies in America have marketed microchips for security or medical purposes. They use the chips to open doors, to unlock their cars, phones and computers with a wave of their hand. I think an electronic implant might seem too painful or weird to even contemplate, but scientists like Warrick and Gasson say that view will change dramatically. Forget mobile phones, your children and grandchildren may well want an implant instead."

Dr. Gasson: *"It's not possible to interact in society in a meaningful way by not having a mobile phone. I think human implants are likely to go along a similar route. It will be such a disadvantage to not have the implant, that it essentially becomes non-optional."*

CNN Reports: *"Mexico is highly critical of U.S. immigration policy. But it's taking extraordinary measures when it comes to its own immigration crisis. Mexico is taking drastic measures to control illegal immigration across its southern border. Mexico will reportedly use an electronic chip to curb its illegal immigration from Guatemala and Balais. The Bio-chip implant will replace the current pass currently used to enter the country. In 2006, Mexico arrested 200,000 people trying to enter their country illegally."*

And that's not just hypocritical. It's all part of the step-by-step plan, the ultimate goal. Go from a Universal, "external" ID system, to one that's "internal," under the guise of, "safety and security," and then you track people wherever they go in these 10-horned economic kingdoms, whatever border. And all that's left to put it into play, is another "crisis."

Which again, is exactly what the Antichrist is going to do in the 7-year Tribulation. He's going to "mandate" everyone be "marked," because of all the "crises" going on.

Revelation 13:16-17: "He also forced everyone, small and great, rich and poor, free and slave, to receive a mark on his right hand or on his forehead, so that no one could buy or sell unless he had the mark."

And if you don't think people would line up and do that, we just saw it with the Covid-19 Plandemic. People all over the world lined up lickety split and put a "mask" on their head in order to "buy and sell" and then they also lined up to get a "shot" in their "arm," not too far from their "hand," in order to "buy and sell." It was the biggest "dry run" ever for the actual Mark of the Beast system coming in the 7-year Tribulation!

And lest you think that "microchipping" the planet is not really a part of the plan the Global Elites have for us, here's Klaus Schwab himself recently talking with Ursula von der Leyen, the German President of the European Commission, about their new "chip plan."

Klaus Schwab: *"I would just like to highlight what you said about your European Chips Act, because it is an important step to create the physical brain for digitalization, and to have it located to a certain extent in Europe. Also, your reference to Rome reports, launched actually the global reports."*

Notice how he not only mentions the "European Chips Act," and the need for, a "physical brain for digitalization," and to have it located to a certain extent in Europe, but then he goes on to say the World Economic Forum launched the "Club of Rome report." You know, the one that's got the world split up into these 10 economic regions they've been talking about for years, just in time for the Antichrist. Can you see how this is all fitting together?

But you might be thinking, "Listen, there's no way they're going to pull off this, "one union" of the 10-horned kingdom, the North American Union. I mean, the American people won't stand for it."

Well, first of all, what makes you think we're going to be given a choice over it, like all the other things we're seeing that they're doing behind the scenes.

Second, if they're still not planning on doing it today, then why are we seeing this from the Biden administration, you know, Mr. Build Back Better who works for Klaus Schwab, doing this?

"Biden Administration Proposes MERGING U.S. With Mexico and

Canada."

"'No border, no wall, no U.S.A. at all!' This line has been chanted by Antifa and other anti-American agitators. But now, a new report reveals, it has prominent supporters in a very high place: the Biden regime's upper echelons.

The administration's hand was tipped by Mexican president Andrés Manuel López Obrador, when he announced recently that Secretary of State Antony Blinken proposed opening all borders among the United States, Mexico, and Canada.

"I think that Mr. Blinken spoke about consolidating the region of North America," said Obrador, *"and we agree on that."* While this story should be front-page news, it has largely been ignored by the media.

Gee, I wonder why? But at least these two reporters shared the truth on that. Watch this.

Tucker Carlson: *"While the European Union has not really worked that well for Europe, we will know the details this winter when people are freezing. So, naturally, the Biden administration wants to create something like that here in North America, EU style government. The Mexican president says that Tony Blinken, our Secretary of State, proposed that idea. Watch this."*

President Obrador: *"I think that Mr. Blinken spoke about consolidating the region of North America. And we agree on that. We are also in favor of a unity of the entire American continent. Like the first European community merged and converted into the European Union, that's what we want."*

Tucker Carlson: *"Oh, so we're going to merge with Mexico in the middle of the most brutal drug war in its history. Mexico is effectively run by the cartels at this point, but we're going to merge with cartels. No one notices this, really. Former Congressman, Matt Gaetz noticed it. He sent a letter* to Tony Blinken asking, what is this? He joins us tonight to tell us what he heard back. Congressman, thanks so much for noticing that and for asking what it means. What does it mean, and did you get an answer?

Matt Gaetz, (R) Congressman: *"It means the globalist left wants a homogenized North America, because they don't think that much of the United States of America in the first place. I haven't gotten an answer, but it begs the question, why are we so friendly with Mexico anyway? They've cooked up more death in the Mexican mountains than any crazy mad scientists in Wuhan would have ever thought of. And it's hard to tell where the cartels end and the government of Mexico begins. Their former president took a $100-million bribe from the former defense chief who is the muscle for the cartel or one of their state attorneys general sits for 20 years in the United States of America.*

But while they are sleepwalking to a war with Russia, they are actually surrendering America's sovereignty to Mexico. Canada's not much better. I don't want my constituents having to live under the socialists' tyrannical lockdowns enacted by Justin Trudeau – Castro, while their nephew's being poisoned by fentanyl, but that is apparently what the globalists order, that the Biden administration supports here as they give away our money, our chance of a brighter future overseas."

OAN Reports: *"But, what am I talking about? The vast majority of Americans are not aware that the cartels in Mexico had transformed into the most powerful criminal organizations on earth, and that before they used to let traffickers handle the flow of human traffic, because it wasn't worth that much for them. That has changed completely, and what you are seeing today is that human beings are worth just as much to the Mexican cartels, as narcotics and all these other things. What does that actually translate to in practical terms?*

It means that the U.S. Marshalls do a bust in South Texas. They find women, some of whom are eight months pregnant, are taken to a bathroom at a gas station and being raped every day for money to pay their debt to the cartel. It means when you are one of those people in New

York City that say, 'Oh, look at these immigrants. Aren't they good, hard-working people? Because at your favorite fancy restaurant, they are in the kitchen washing the dishes, or they are bussing tables. Well, guess what, they are doing two or three jobs and most of that money is going to the cartel. It's not going to them. And why does this matter? Because we have, in place, an administration filled with open-border idealists, who are implementing a globalist policy that no one in this country received any option to vote on. It bypasses the legislature and is completely in violation of the Constitution. And what they are edging towards - and I know this from a source who was at meetings at the U.N., behind closed doors, (these were classified meetings), and listening to these discussions of infiltrating 100 million people into the United States, as the basis for forming a regional government instead of a national government. So, a government of Canada, Mexico and the United States. This is the strategy that is in place, and so things like the cartel were created as part of a push-pull strategy, where they would push people out of those countries because life would become unbearable and haul them to the United States. It's about the destruction of this country, and it's put in place, step-by-step, so that you don't really know what's happening. WOW!"*

Wow is right! And here's Biden even more recently tweeting out

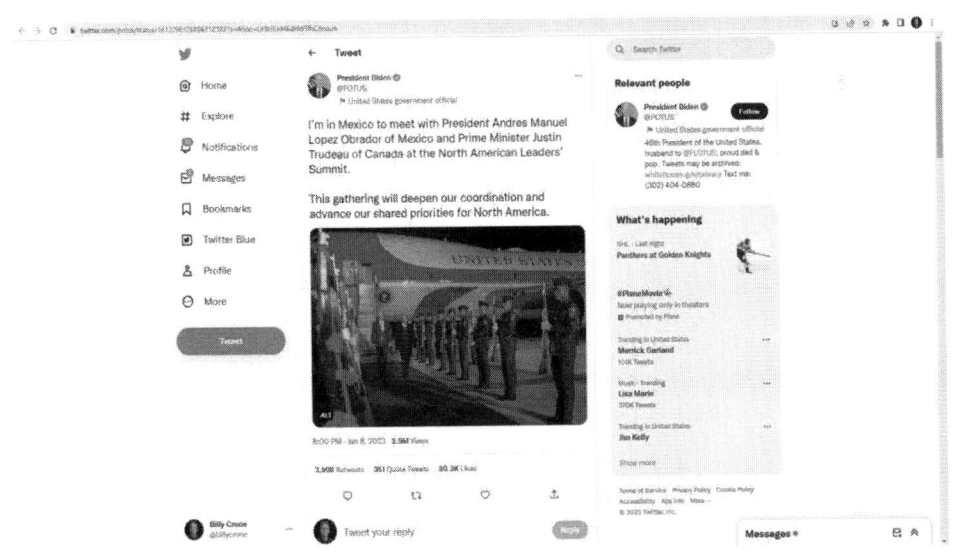

that he's "Meeting with President Andres Manuel Lopez Obrador of Mexico and Prime Minister Justin Trudeau of Canada at the North American Leaders' Summit. This gathering will deepen our coordination and advance our shared priorities for North America."

Yeah, a new one called the North American Union. In fact, notice how once again they changed the name. It used to be called SPP or the

Security and Prosperity Partnership. But now it's called the North American Leaders' Summit or (NALS), or sometimes it's called the Three Amigos Summit which is apparently the more popular term the press uses just to make sure we all stay confused and don't catch on.

But speaking of catching on, look at that last picture again and notice the map on the right of this North American Leaders Summit. It clearly highlights their intentions. They are meeting to discuss the combining of all three countries there in green, Canada, U.S. and Mexico. This is nuts! It's all being done right before our very eyes!

And that's why this article is brainwashing people with this rationale, **"The United States' Global Power Is Fading Fast."**

Yeah, because Joe Biden and the other World Economic Forum puppets in our government are destroying it. But they go on to say:

"With its own global power fading fast, the United States will undoubtedly become a far more regional power. While some Washington insiders might see this trend as at best a retreat or at worst a defeat, it's actually an opportunity to fundamentally reconsider relations with our home region, North America.

To resolve its growing problems, the whole of North America could clearly benefit from a parallel union. In many ways, the task should be easier than Europe's. While the EU has 13 'official languages,' a North American Union would need only three – English, French, and Spanish – fewer than tiny Switzerland.

With such economic fundamentals in place, (In other words, once they destroy our economy) those countries could then move toward European Union-style shared governance, so as to better navigate the growing climate crisis and its threat of demographic disaster. Through genuine regional collaboration, as well as a redefinition of "defense" (as in Defense Department) as greater protection from onrushing natural disasters, Washington could become the epicenter of a multinational union.

By taking the necessary steps beyond CAFTA, NAFTA, and NORAD, Washington could help lead its North American neighbors, roiled by the ravages of climate change, toward a more perfect union. In the process, this entire hemisphere would ultimately become a far safer haven for its share of humanity in the troubled decades to come."

Total insanity, total denial of our national sovereignty, and total treasonous behavior! But that's the reality. We've been duped by these Global Elite megalomaniacs, including Klaus Schwab and the World Economic Forum, who are deliberately destroying America to create their 10 horned economic kingdom for planetary control who will then at some point as the Bible declares had it all over to the actual Antichrist. Is this wild, or what? It's almost like we're living in the Last Days and if you're not saved, you better ask Jesus to forgive you of your sins and save you right now! This is not a game!

And that's why this article shares this, **"Defeat The 'Great Reset' To Save American Freedoms."**

"The Great Reset" is truly a serious threat to American freedoms, especially the freedoms of speech, religion, and assembly. It also is a serious threat to America's unique Constitutional Republic. Thus, every freedom-loving American needs to fight against this so-called reset with 'tooth and nail.' Alarmingly, over 80 percent of large American companies have already become part of The Great Reset in one way or another.

Ultimately, proponents of The Great Reset plan to control people's behavior by means of advanced technology, artificial intelligence, and a worldwide digital currency where a leftist government or bank could easily strip a person of all means to purchase goods, pay bills, etc., due to their 'unacceptable' behavior. by means of advanced technology, artificial intelligence, and a worldwide digital currency, where a leftist government or bank could easily strip a person of all means to purchase goods, pay bills, etc., due to their 'unacceptable' behavior.

Further, The Great Reset supporters, have established a communist, Chinese-like, 'social credit' scoring system, where organizations and individuals are given a social credit score, rewarding those who have a high rating and punishing those with low scores.

Here are three examples of how The Great Reset ultimately could affect the lives of 'ordinary' Americans:

1) A man owns a trucking business, and he makes public statements opposing the leftist climate change

agenda to completely rid America of fossil fuels by the year 2030. When he applies for a loan to expand his business, his bank and other banks refuse to loan him any money, because of his 'unacceptable' statements about the climate change agenda. In order to get the loan, he is required to go along with the climate change agenda and refute his previous statements opposing the agenda – a violation of man's freedom of speech.

2) A woman belongs to a parent's group that opposes the teaching of Critical Race Theory at her child's school, and she worships at a Church where the Pastor preaches against homosexuality. She receives a notice from her bank that her account is no longer welcome at the bank, or her application for a loan has been disapproved due to her 'unacceptable' participation in the above activities; she can receive the funds if she leaves the parent's group and her Church – a violation of the woman's freedoms of assembly and religion.

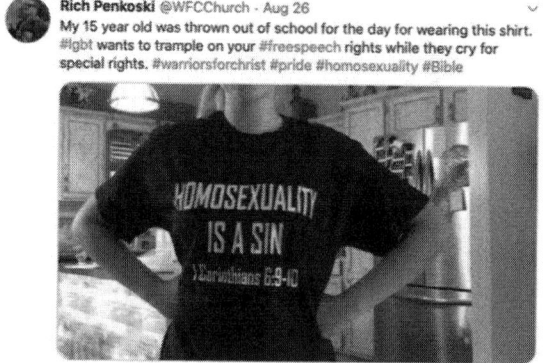

3) A conservative political candidate speaks against the transgender and LGBTQ movements. He receives a notice from his bank and other banks, that his campaign funds are frozen due to his 'unacceptable' statements about the above

movements – a violation of the person's freedom of speech.

Americans need to know, that as part of The Great Reset, the WEF has developed an Environmental, Social, and Governance (ESG) index (social credit index) by which an individual or organization is rated to determine their 'wokeness,' and how in tune they are with the leftist, radical agenda. If rated low, banks could refuse loans and/or close accounts for a non-woke individual or organization. According to The Great Reset, this index is now used by thousands of companies in more than 50 countries, including many companies in the United States.

Americans must pull together to fight/defeat this insidious effort – an effort by many of the world's 'elites' to gain control and power over the nations and peoples of the world."

But as you can see, this plan for a communist worldwide planetary takeover, that's simply relabeled as The Great Reset, or Agenda 21, or Agenda 2030, and even the Fourth Industrial Revolution, is starting to become so obvious for those that have eyes to see and ears to hear, that others besides us are starting to blow the whistle on it as well.

Skynews.com AU Reports: *"This is the plan that I have repeatedly warned about. To take the tools of oppression used to tackle the Coronavirus and use them - lockdown, forced business closures, exclusion zones, isolation. As we've heard earlier, businesses shut down. We've* heard all of that including destroying private property and private income, in order to tackle the climate crisis."

Klaus Schwab: *"Now is a historical moment in time. Not only to fight the virus but to shape the system."*

Prince Charles: *"We have a unique but rapidly shrinking window of opportunity to learn lessons and research ourselves in a more sustainable part. It is an opportunity that we never had before, and we may never have again so we must use all the things that we have at our disposal knowing that each and everyone of us has a vital role to play."*

Antonio Guterres: *"The Great Reset is a welcomed recognition that the human tragedy must be a wake-up call. It is imperative that we re-imagine, re-build, re-design, re-invigorate, and re-balance our worlds. Re-balancing investments, harnessing science and technology, and advancing the transition to net-zero emissions. All elements of The Great Reset are fundamental to building the future we need."*

Skynews.com AU Reports: *"That last one was the clown Guterres, who was at the Climate Ambition Summit, telling us that the world is going to cook to 3 ½ degrees by the end of the century. Yeah, right! This Great Reset is as serious and as dangerous a threat to our prosperity - your prosperity and your freedom - as we have faced in decades, with these powerful bodies, including the WEF, the UN, the IMF, and even Prince Charles. He is boasting that within a few short years, his words, that you will own nothing, and you will be happy. Remember this is not me saying this. This is them. They are even running ads for. The Great Reset."*

- *You'll own nothing. And you'll be happy. Whatever you want you'll rent, and it'll be delivered by drone.*
- *The US won't be the world's leading superpower. A handful of countries will dominate.*

A handful of countries will dominate. I wonder which ones they will be. A terrifying coalition of big business, big tech, and left-wing totalitarians are so confident and so brazen. I mean they just stole the U.S. elections. So, I guess they're feeling pretty great about themselves, that now they are promising that you will not own anything, and you will be happy. What they should have added in is 'and we, the very rich will own everything and be even happier. Of course, they will, The Great Reset tragedy here, is Prince Charles is involved in the fascist globalist push, and is thereby putting our entire Constitutional monarchy at risk.

And if you think I am just imagining this stuff, crazy old Rowan with his conspiracy theories, think again. This garbage is already deeply embedded into our state and federal governments. I spoke with you before about this insidious phrase, 'Build Back Better' which sounds like common sense, but is, in fact, one of several slogans for The Great Reset and now they are using the Orwellian phrase, 'The Fourth Industrial Revolution.' Here's old Klaus again without the white cat on his knee telling us about the 'Fourth Industrial Revolution.'"

Klaus Schwab: *"The Fourth Industrial Revolution will impact our lives completely. It will not only change how we communicate, how we produce, how we consume, it will change actually, us, our own identity. And of course, gives life to such policies and developments, like smart traffic, smart government, smart cities. What we will see is that everything will be integrated into an ecosystem, driven by big data, and driven particularly by close cooperation also of governments with business civil society. And this revolution will come at a race-taking speed. It will be like a tsunami."*

Skynews.com AU Reports: *"Like a tsunami, it's the Fourth Industrial Revolution. You'll own nothing, but you will be happy. That is an order! It gets worse. The WEF now blatantly is saying, 'Capitalism needs a dose of Marxism.' It's like I said, it's not like they are hiding their sinister intentions. Indeed, I was horrified when an outside fan sent me this document from the Australian government. 'Preparing for the future, Industry 4.0 Testlabs in Australia.' A strategic initiative of the Prime Minister's industry 4.0 taskforce.*

Section 1: Context and significance of the Fourth Industrial Revolution.

Unbelievable! Australia rejects the reset!"

Klaus Schwab: *"It's the future of our physical, our digital and our biological identities."*

Skynews.com AU Reports: *"No mate, not in Australia!"*

Alan Jones, ADH TV: *"Well, over a week ago I spoke to you about something that you wouldn't hear anywhere else, but you would hear on this program. Because on other media, there are certain things that you are not allowed to say. You're not allowed to differ from the so-called wisdom of the experts. I mentioned this outfit, The World Economic Forum, and there's been a tremendous response online as to what I had to say. I mentioned that the mission statement of this WEF says that it is 'committed to improving the state of the world by engaging business, political, academic, and other leaders of society to shape global, regional and industrial agendas.' I mentioned the founder, this German colonist, Klaus Schwab, who said in 2020, and I quote:*

'The pandemic represents a rare but narrow window of opportunity to reflect, reimagine and reset our world ... all aspects of our societies and economies must be revamped, from education to social contracts and working conditions.'

The key words ... reset our world. Is that happening in our classrooms and universities with what is being taught? One university student told me recently that he had to write an assignment on the impact of climate change on gender. Huh, reset our world? We then had to create a virus. The total denial of freedom, and the usurping of those freedoms by unelected bureaucrats and big government. I reminded you of the odious individual, Maurice Strong, the godfather of climate change. He said in 1992:

'We may get to the point where the only way of saving the world will be for industrialized civilization to collapse. Isn't it our responsibility to bring this about?'

And Schwab, the founder of this WEF said, 'We need a great reset of capitalism.' When this mob, this WEF, was challenged two years ago, to debate this question of climate emergency, they declined. Of course, they would. Remember the founder, Klaus Schwab, means what he says. The lower aspects of our society and colonies must be revamped. Well, what's the easiest way to do that? It's to ignore and cancel anyone who disagrees. Even when those who disagree are prepared to engage in climate debate, as the friends of science said, 'with the sound and ancient principle of all pertinent parties should be fully heard.'

Well, this nonsense of the WEF goes on. Russian oligarchs and U.S. billionaires flying in on private jets, banging on about global emission, income inequality. African dictators screaming about climate change, and the need for immediate compensation from the West. And the journalists and commentators just swallow this stuff. As Professor Judith Sloan and I spoke just last week.

'They churn out puerile pieces about the wonderful reform/reset initiatives being discussed by the hand-picked elites headed by the indestructible Klaus Schwab.'

Well, in 2021, a special address to the mob was delivered by Vladimir Putin. But who was the opening key speaker this year at the Davos conference? The freedom loving dictator, President Xi of China. Amongst other things, he said, 'Economic globalization is the trend of the times. As sure as the counter current is to exist in a river, none could stop the river from flowing into the sea. Despite the counter currents and dangerous shoals, economic socialization has never, and will not ever be off course.'"

In other words, have fun trying to stop them. They're all in, and they ain't backing down! In fact, we were warned about this subterfuge a long time ago. See if this sounds familiar to today's issues.

Robert Welsh: *"A part of the plan of course is to induce the gradual surrender of American's sovereignty, piece-by-piece and step-by-step to various international organizations of which the United Nations is the outstanding, but far from the only example. Here are the aims for the United States.*

1. Greatly expanded government spending for every conceivable means of getting rid of ever larger sums of American money, as wastefully as possible.
2. Higher and then much higher taxes.
3. An increasingly unbalanced budget despite the higher taxes.
4. Wild inflation of our currency.
5. Government controls prices, wages, and materials, supposedly to combat inflation.
6. Greatly increased socialistic controls over every operation of our economy and every activity of our daily lives. This is to be accompanied naturally and automatically by a correspondingly huge increase in the size of our bureaucracy and in both the cost and reach of our domestic government.
7. Far more centralization of power in Washington and the practical elimination of our state lines. There are many faceted guides, at work, to have our state lines to eventually mean no more, within the nation, than our county lines do now within the states.
8. The steady advance of federal aid to and control over our educational system, leading to complete federalization of our public education.
9. A constant hammering to the American consciousness of the horror of modern warfare. The duties and absolute necessities of peace. Peace is always on communist terms, of course.
10. The consequent willingness of the American people to allow these steps of appeasement by our government, which amount to a piecemeal surrender of the rest of the free world and of the United States itself."

That was Robert Welch, American businessman and Founder of the John Birch Society, warning about this communist takeover, now called, The Great Reset, many decades ago. Too bad we didn't listen and take action then.

But as you can see, our apathy or indifference has done nothing but help these sick Global Elite megalomaniacs advance their global agenda to take over the world and destroy the United States of America in the process!

And remember, they really have plans to have "no one" left behind in this planetary takeover of all our livelihood.

WE'VE MADE HUGE PROGRESS TOWARDS A BETTER WORLD BUT WE MUST DO MORE TO REACH EVERYONE!

"In 2015, 193 countries agreed to the sustainable development goals to end poverty, to fight inequality, to tackle climate change and to make sure no one is left behind, no matter who they are or where they live."

A mother from Africa: *"My children are dying. We have nowhere to live."*

Refugee: *"I was a refugee in Pakistan, I was a refugee in Iran, I was a refugee in Dubai, and now I am a refugee in France."*

EACH DAY MORE THAN 30,000 PEOPLE ARE FORCED TO FLEE THEIR HOMES BECAUSE OF CONFLICT AND PERSECUTION!

A woman from India: *"When you're disabled, people don't see your abilities. They judge you by your disability."*

90% OF CHILDREN WITH DISABILITIES IN DEVELOPING COUNTRIES DO NOT ATTEND SCHOOL

Young boy: *"Selling me wasn't a good idea."*

150 MILLION CHILDREN WORLDWIDE
ARE ENGAGED IN CHILD LABOR

Young woman: *"Don't they consider me a human being?"*

ONE WOMAN IN EVERY THREE WILL
EXPERIENCE VIOLENCE IN THEIR LIFETIME

Young Muslim woman: *"Here, women can't do anything."*
THEIR LIVES ARE THE ONES. THE GOALS MUST CHANGE

A Father: *"Electricity would bring light to the life of my children."*

Young Man: *"If I'd been schooled, my situation would be different."*

Another woman: *"Because if everyone had food at home, we could think. So, we could be poor, but have the intelligence to be able to get ahead."*

THE GOALS CAN CHANGE THE WORLD FOR EVERYONE
YEAR BY YEAR, GOAL BY GOAL
IF WE ALL WORK TOGETHER TO ACHIEVE THEM

Young child: *"Because on Earth, everyone has a mission. I have one too."*

A wife: *"I left my husband to be with a woman. That's a huge step, for an African woman to do that. I would say I do have a strong voice. I'm a strong woman, speaking for myself."*

Older man: *"We must tell the world that we exist, that we are here. And I am sure that no misery, no extreme poverty, is human destiny. We can fight it."*

Father: *"My son got his diploma! He will not be like me. He has already gone a step further and can aim for a better future."*

LEAVE NO ONE BEHIND ... EVERY GOAL MUST BE MET FOR EVERYONE

Yeah, for everybody to be a part of your global planetary takeover that the Bible warned about 2,000 years ago would become the Antichrist Kingdom!

But as you can see, in order to pull off this Great Reset, Agenda 21, Agenda 2030, and The Fourth Industrial Revolution - this global communist takeover of the planet, Klaus Schwab and the gang really do have plans to control, not just all the world "leaders," and "finances," and "health," but all our basic "livelihoods" around the whole planet as well.

But unfortunately, as bad and as invasive and communist as all that is, if you were paying attention, you saw they also have plans to control another important aspect of our individual livelihoods with this so-called Great Reset, and that is our individual finances.

But don't worry they say, "You'll own nothing and be happy," as this guy warns is actually coming.

David Ansara, Centre for Risk Analysis: *"The Great Reset is an idea set forward by the World Economic Forum to fundamentally restructure the global economy in the wake of Covid-19. But what are some of the dangers inherent in this ideology? Joining me to discuss, is Douglas Kruger, speaker and author, focusing on political correctness. Douglas, could you tell our viewers what the idea of The Great Reset is exactly, and what are some of the risks attached to it?"*

Douglas Kruger: *"Like many of the politically correct ideas we hear bantered about in the media, this is quite a project couched in kindness. It is presented as something being done or proposed for our good and for the greater good, and that always gets my senses going because that tends to lead to a very problematic ideology. In a very quick nutshell, the proposal out of Davos is essentially this. A group of exceptionally powerful individuals, predominately in the banking, finance, and business* sector, in alliance with government leadership, are proposing that as a result of these Covid-19 lockdowns, that have done a great deal of damage to economies globally, they perceive that they now have the opportunity to rebuild economies, but to do so, in what they believe is a more enlightened fashion.

And they are all, generally speaking, there are problems with the idea of groups of people in power deciding the history of humanity. We are simply supposed to be free to determine our own futures, our own progress, what we want out of life. Now in this particular case, what they are proposing is a sort of an idea that takes personal ownership out of the equation. The little phrase, and it sounds so innocent is, 'You'll own nothing. And you'll be happy.'

Now if you go back several hundred years, the founding father and first President of the United States - which was essentially a project founded on the idea of humility and freedom, pretty much for the first time in modern history. George Washington said, 'There is no such thing as personal human rights without property ownership.' He said that for several interesting and important reasons, but the principle is sound. If you are dependent on a greater power, for everything, then you are not free. You place yourself as an individual in quite a precarious situation. It was, in fact, a formula for living, a political reality, for most of human history.

If you look back at a simple set up, like the serfs of Europe, this is a group of people who owned nothing and simply contributed to the lord, who determined what they could and could not have. And they had zero wants. It's the property that you own that actually ensures your rights to a great degree. So, while all this may sound like a very enlightened idea of a communal, collectivist utopia, there are many problems with this once you start thinking about how it might be implemented. And that's what caused more concern to me. Now, the sorts of things that we are hearing from Davos and from the likes of the proponents of The Great Reset, all talk about 'commit to communal living' and how nobody will own anything.

Now consider for just a second, that it is already a fallacy. Someone, somewhere has to own. In fact, what happens is, if you take ownership out of the hands of the broad-based populace, and of many separate entrepreneurs, and families, and individuals, and you concentrate it into the hands of say, a few multi-national corporations working together with the government, well, first, that action by definition is fascistic. This idea of an all-powerful government and the businesses that work in conjunction with them, it leads very quickly to cronyism, to the types of corruption we particularly see in South Africa, where we are so keen on talking about business and government collaborating. And doesn't that sound like such a good thing? Business and government collaborating?

So, what you have is the people who own the rules, enforce right from wrong, and have a financial incentive to be corrupt, working with the people who have the money, who have the incentive to corrupt them. It's a dreadful formula to begin with. However, what concerns me, is perhaps on a bigger scale than that. When we talk about collective ownership, we are often told that the great thing about it is that everybody will own. The reality of it is nobody, but those in power, will own. That impulse to take away private property ownership and concentrate it in the hands of a representative government is purely Marxist. I mean, the heart and soul of the Marxist idea, which strips down to its basics, nobody owns property, it is collectively owned. And, as I say, the fallacy there, is that it is not collectively owned, it is owned by those in power.

Now, what can go wrong with that? Well, if we look at modern day China, we get a very good example of this one. Modern day China has kind of a mixed economy. They have prospered to the degree that they started free trade. However, they are still a very much Marxist society, and they work with a social credit score. Social credit scores, imposed by law, represent a very chilling idea. Now, imagine this for an example. You as a family do not own your home. You do not own what is around you. You do not own your business. The government has absolute control because they are the representatives of collective ownership.

Now, imagine the scenario in which you do something that the government does not approve of. You read a book that it doesn't want you to read. You write an essay or an article that it doesn't like. You create a YouTube video, commenting on something in a negative way. Now those are some things that productive human beings do - critique and build and grow their society. But you can't do it there. And if you do something that the government disapproves of using these social credits, they can ghost you. They can effectively lock you out of your world. And it works, because you don't own anything. It's that ownership, that broad-based private ownership that keeps people free from government tyranny. Sounds like fear mongering.

Of course, the question, for anyone who looks back through history is, could it happen here, and could it happen again? And I think if you do know your history, the answer is it happens surprisingly easily, and it happens surprisingly often. When communities play with this idea of committing to this ownership, I would argue that it happens 100% of the time. And when we are talking about collective ownership and alienating the group over the sanctity of the individual, we are dealing with the formula that has been deeply damaging the human species."

David Ansara: *"Well, Douglas, what about the threat to the property that we already own. Is there a risk there that we might lose our ownership of our existing property?"*

Douglas Kruger: *"David, that is an excellent question, and I think it is one that people are not considering. Think again of those words, 'You will own nothing, and you will be happy." It doesn't allow you to continue to own what your family has bequeathed down through the generations. The simple statement, if we take them at their word, is you will own nothing and you will be happy. That poses some fascinating problems in terms of what communities already own. We, largely around the world, own our homes, we bequeath heirlooms to the next generation. You might own a wedding ring. You might own things that you want to give to your children. I would argue that that is one of the best things that we do. Each generation tries to uplift the next generation. This philosophy seems to be* *saying, instead of doing that, we reset each generation to zero and leave you dependent on a government welfare system. We propose this on a global scale."*

Doesn't sound like we'll be happy after that. It's not, we'll own nothing and be happy. It's, they'll own everything, and they'll be happy! What a farce! There's no good in this, folks!

Chapter Eleven

World Economic Forum & The Mark of the Beast

But how are they going to pull it off, this farce called The Great Reset? Well again, by not only controlling all of our world "leaders," and all the world "finances," and all the world's "health," and all our "basic livelihoods," but even all of our "individual finances."

And if you've been paying attention, this is one of the most important "leverages" of this whole Great Reset takeover of the planet. You not only take away people's individual property but also their individual finances, so they'll be reduced to slavery, and be forced to do whatever you tell them to do, or not to do.

Believe it or not, this next plan from Klaus Schwab and his evil gang of Global Elites is what I call, the "nail in the coffin." It's the literal controlling of all our individual livelihoods, by controlling all our individual finances, which, as you will see, is yet another aspect of the coming evil, satanic Antichrist Kingdom, that God warned about nearly 2,000 years ago.

You see, the Bible clearly warned us that in the Last Days we would see the whole world corralled into not only a One World Government, but a One World Economy with a cashless society, that would be biometrically and universally tied to everyone on the whole planet at that time, with a marking system called the Mark of the Beast, that will allow the Antichrist to control all the "buying and selling" on the whole planet.

So, before we show you that, how this actual micromanaged financial system of the Antichrist that God warned us about nearly 2,000 years ago would come and is actually being built before our very eyes by Klaus Schwab of the World Economic Forum and his evil gang of Global Elites, let's remind ourselves of that Biblical warning from God.

Revelation 13:11-18: "Then I saw another beast, coming out of the earth. He had two horns like a lamb, but he spoke like a dragon. He exercised all the authority of the first beast on his behalf, and made the earth and its inhabitants worship the first beast, whose fatal wound had been healed. And he performed great and miraculous signs, even causing fire to come down from heaven to earth in full view of men. Because of the signs he was given power to do on behalf of the first beast, he deceived the inhabitants of the earth. He ordered them to set up an image in honor of the beast who was wounded by the sword and yet lived. He was given power to give breath to the image of the first beast, so that it could speak and cause all who refused to worship the image to be killed. He also forced everyone, small and great, rich and poor, free and slave, to receive a mark on his right hand or on his forehead, so that no one could buy or sell unless he had the mark, which is the name of the beast or the number of his name. This calls for wisdom. If anyone has insight, let him calculate the number of the beast, for it is man's number. His number is 666."

So here we see the Bible also warned about a coming day when all the inhabitants of the earth will be under the Universal Economy, or monetary system of the Antichrist himself. He will literally control all the "buying and selling."

And whether you realize it or not, that individual control of people's "buying and selling" around the whole planet, is already happening right now before our very eyes, via the deceptive Covid-19 Plandemic and The Great Reset farce.

They're using those lies to create this One World Universal Economy as well, that the Bible warned about in three different ways.

The **1st way** they've already laid the groundwork for the One World Economy of The Great Reset, is by having **The Machinery Already in Place**.

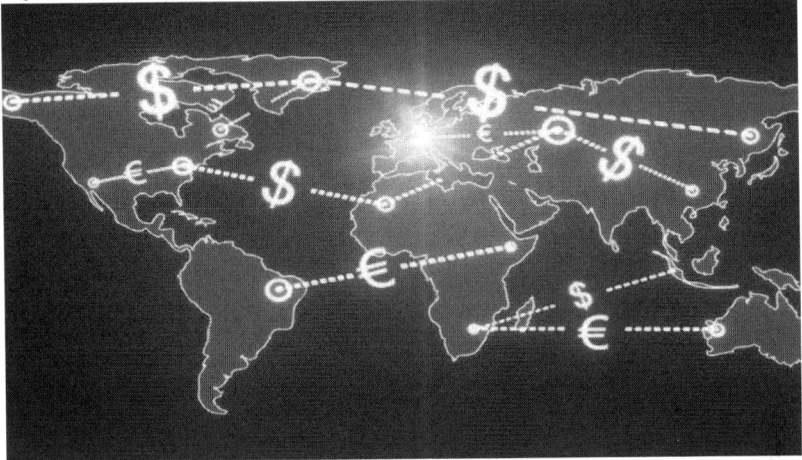

You see, right now there is already in place the plans for absolute total economic control of the whole world. Whether we understand it or not, for the first time in man's history, our economies are already connected globally.

Right now, there's already a Universal Bank called the World Bank, which is the world's leader of lending money to the nations around the planet.

But wait a minute. If you're going to have a universal bank, then you need a universal lending institution to oversee the dispersion of loans, right?

Well folks, what do you think is the function of the International Monetary Fund, which oversees the whole world's financial system and

even fixes the exchange rates?

But wait a minute. If you're going to have a universal lending institution then you need a universal money exchanger to funnel all this money to all the different countries, right?

Well, that's why, right now there's a Universal Electronic Banking System called SWIFT, which automatically makes sure that all the different money transactions in the world match all the different currencies.

But wait a minute. If you're going to have a universal money exchanger then you need to have a universal strong arm to punish those who don't obey this world banking system, right?

Well again, that's why, right now, there's the World Trade Organization which not only sets the trading rules for the world, but they punish all countries who do not obey, with billion-dollar fines.

And so, as you can see, the machinery for a One World Global Economy, a Great Economic Reset, is already here! Not 50 years down the road, but now! And for further proof of this, this is why we have all these global treaties that we keep hearing about. They're all about tying together the world's economies!

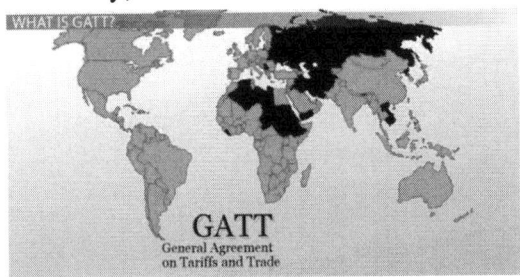

First, there was the GATT Treaty in 1944, the General Agreement on Tariffs and Trade, to help, "liberalize world trade." Then 50 years later in 1994, we had (NAFTA) Agreement.

Then 10 years after that (2004) was CAFTA, or the Central American Free Trade Agreement, combining Central American countries.

And then the very next year (2005) was the FTAA, or Free Trade Agreement of the Americas, which proposes to encompass the whole Western Hemisphere and their economies.

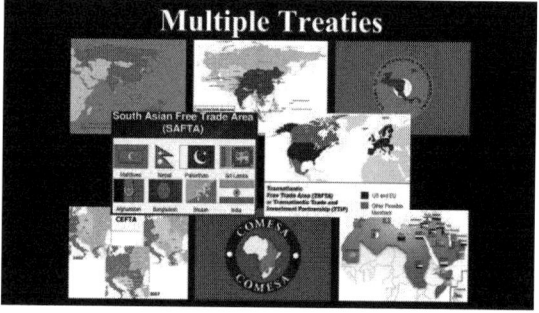

And this is happening all over the world! There's AFTA, the ASEAN Free Trade Area; APTA, the Asia-Pacific Trade Agreement; and CAIS the Central American Integration System.

Or other proposed ones, like CEFTA, the Central European Free Trade Agreement; COMESA, the Common Market for Eastern and Southern Africa; or GAFTA, the Greater Arab Free Trade Area; or SAFTA, the South Asia Free Trade Agreement; and even TAFTA, the Transatlantic Free Trade Area. On and on it goes!

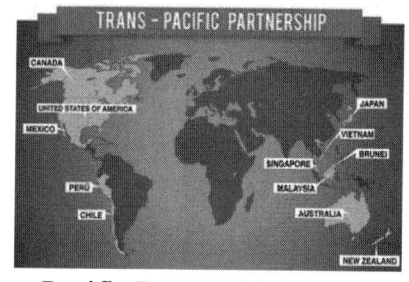

And another one called the TPP, or the Trans-Pacific Partnership - which President Trump pulled out of, Obama and Clinton were going headlong into - but it encompasses 12 nations in the Pacific area, including Australia, Brunei, Canada, Chile, Japan, Malaysia, Mexico, New Zealand, Peru, Singapore, Vietnam and the United States.

But as you can see, these global trade agreements are needed to create a truly intertwined, global economy for The Great Economic Reset, that's going to create these 10 global economic regions we talked about earlier in Revelation 17, that the Bible says will then be given over to the actual Antichrist.

The **2nd way** they've already laid the groundwork for the One World Economy of The Great Reset is by having **The Mindset Already in Place**.

You see, Klaus Schwab and the gang have been slowly but surely been warming us up like a frog in a pot, over the years, to this crazy idea that "we'll own nothing and be happy."

Which also includes, "where" we get to live, "how" we get to live, "who" we can marry, "how" many kids we can have, "what" education we can get, and on and on it goes. The Elites will control literally everything, and no, we won't be happy!

But they've brainwashed tons of people on the planet to go along with this lie, under the guise that we must let them, the Elites, do this to us and bring in this global tyranny in order to, "save the planet," to "keep it from blowing up," which, Lord willing, we'll expose as another big lie from these sick megalomaniacs in our next documentary.

But, this "brainwashing mindset" is already being produced by people going along with their total control of our "individual finances," with something they call, a "Universal Basic Income."

It's advocated all the time by these Global Elites, including the likes of Elon Musk, Mark Zuckerberg, and Bill Gates, just to name a few. Who, by the way, all work for the same agenda as Klaus Schwab and the World Economic Forum. They all say that the governments around the world need to give every citizen a "guaranteed income."

And, this Universal Basic Income may be the only solution, they say, to save us and the planet, and enable us all to recover from the Covid-19 Plandemic. But for those of you who haven't heard about this economic mindset, here's a basic rundown of a Universal Basic Income.

CNBC Reports: *"Universal Basic Income is pretty much what the name suggests. An income for everyone in the form of a cash transfer, no strings attached. Finland is among a handful of countries experimenting with Universal Basic Income as a way to adjust unemployment in the country. A key feature of Universal Basic Income is that you can spend the money however you like.*

The idea of handing out cash to every citizen isn't new. Philosopher, Thomas Paine proposed the idea of 'payments ... made to every person, rich or poor,' all the way back in 1797. Martin Luther King, Jr. fought for, a 'guaranteed income pegged to the median of society' in 1967, and even free market champion Milton Friedman endorsed the 'negative income tax, similar to basic income, as a way to reduce welfare costs, and reduce the present bureaucracy.' But lately, high techs in Silicon Valley, like Elon Musk and Mark Zuckerberg, are some of the biggest advocates of the idea.

Elon Musk: *"Ultimately, we will have to have some kind of Universal Basic Income."*

Mark Zuckerberg: *"Universal Basic Income to give everyone a cushion."*

"Other advocates say a basic income would alleviate poverty and help address growing income equality across the developed world. The idea has support across the political spectrum. Libertarians say, it would simplify the social welfare states. The Socialists want to redistribute wealth to the lower and middle class. Finland isn't the only country experimenting with Universal Basic Income. Other trials are underway in the Netherlands, Kenya, Canada, and the United States."

Ooh! So, it's gaining popularity everywhere! And this is what they've been using the Covid-19 Plandemic as an excuse for, to bring in.

"Universal Basic Income as a Policy Response to Covid-19."

And this article,

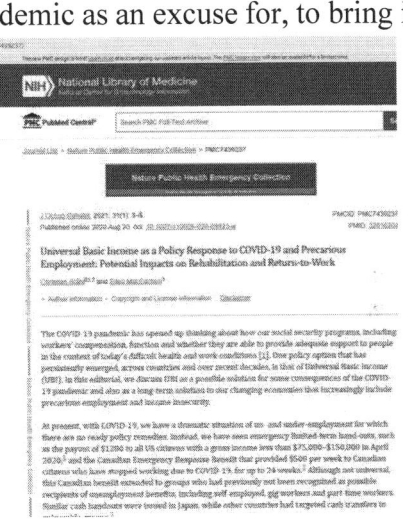

"Universal Basic Income is the Answer to the Inequalities Exposed by Covid-19."

And watch this from Forbes,

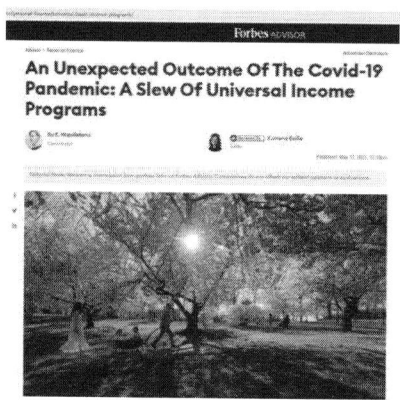

"An Unexpected Outcome of The Covid-19 Pandemic: A Slew of Universal Income Programs."

Really? Was that really "unexpected," or has it been part of the plan all along? But the article goes on to say:

"The Covid-19 pandemic came into American lives like a wrecking ball, disrupting everything from income and employment, to childcare and education. But then, help arrived. Through multiple congressional acts, Americans received direct, no-strings-attached stimulus payments.

With more Americans than ever feeling the benefits of these recent no-strings-attached direct income payments, it's unsurprising that many polls find a majority of Americans now support some sort of Universal Basic Income (UBI).

And UBI was already in motion in the U.S., established in 1983, by Alaska's Permanent Dividend Fund that sends annual payments (typically between $1,000 and $2,000) to more than 600,000 Alaskan residents.

In fact, several cities across the country have UBI-type programs slated to start or already in progress.

California has the "Compton Pledge" that serves the residents of the City of Compton with unconditional monthly payments. It also has "Big Leap," which transfers payments to low-income residents in the City of L.A.

Then there's Colorado. They have the "Denver Basic Income Project."

And Florida has the "Income Gainesville."

Georgia has "In Her Hands," benefiting Georgia women and is one of the largest cash transfer pilot programs in the South.

Illinois has the "Chicago Resilient Communities Pilot," which is one of the nation's largest cash transfer programs, and according to Mayor Lori Lightfoot, the program seeks to "tackle poverty and put residents at the center of the economic recovery from the COVID-19 pandemic."

Louisiana has the "Shreveport Guaranteed Income Program."

And New Jersey has "Newark Movement for Economic Equity."

And New York has "The Bridge Project."

But you might be thinking, "Come on, there's no way the rest of America is going to go along with this! We're too patriotic, individualized. Why, it's the American Dream to take care of yourself and be independent of the government!

Not anymore! Look around! Not only has Socialism, the new relabeled term for Communism, been on the rise, thanks to the brainwashing of the secular school system, but they've also produced that mindset in a whole new generation of younger people, who are likewise not patriotic, and cry out for the government to pay for everything!

We call it the, "you owe me" and "entitlement mentality" that we can see rampant everywhere in younger generations!

In fact, some admit the Covid-19 Plandemic was also used to produce this mindset for a Universal Basic Income into the rest of us non-Socialist, non-Communists.

Narrator: *"Today I want to show you something that Congress is proposing, because there are a few ideas out on the floor that look and sound very similar to a concept called UBI. If you're not familiar with what that is, it stands for Universal Basic Income. Now, the Cares Act has given people a one-time cash payment of up to $1,200.00. Can you imagine what Andrew Yang must be feeling like right now? But a lot of people are still waiting for stimulus checks, with most agreeing that it's simply not enough money to keep their lives going.*

So, in order to continue stimulating, Congress will be voting today once more on another bill, that will propose an additional $300 billion for the Paycheck Protection Program (PPP), so it looks like this one will be passed. The idea of UBI, or Universal Basic Income is not that farfetched. In fact, right now, there are a few plans that add to a potentially phase four of the Stimulus Package Plan. One of them involves forgiving all rent and mortgage payments. Don't even worry about paying your mortgage or your rent. We got this.

The whole stimulus narrative is bringing us closer and closer to what seems like the inevitable solution, where every American is going to be entitled to a basic, standard form of income, regardless of whether or not they have a job. Believe it or not, the Pope himself, Pope Francis, has even called for Universal Basic Income."

Oh, just in time to introduce the Antichrist himself, Mr. False Prophet wannabe!

But, as you guys can see, there's way more going on with this Covid-19 Plandemic than what we first thought, even here in the U.S. Again, it's the old adage, "If you create a crisis, you can manage the outcome." And that outcome is leading us all, the whole planet, to accept a Universal Basic Income that they need to control our "individual finances" and pull off their Great Economic Reset.

The **3rd way** they've already laid the groundwork for the One World Economy of the Great Reset is by having **The Mechanism Already in Place**.

Once again, let's go back to our text and pull out another thing Klaus Schwab and the gang are doing for the Antichrist, with the Covid-19 Plandemic as the excuse.

Revelation 13:16-17: "He also forced everyone, small and great, rich and poor, free and slave, to receive a mark on his right hand or on his forehead, so that no one could buy or sell unless he had the mark, which is the name of the beast or the number of his name."

So, think about this in light of that passage of Scripture. I think it's common sense. If the Antichrist and the False Prophet are going to pull off this One World Economy system and this Mark of the Beast System, you are not only going to have to create the "machinery" to combine all the World's Economies into one system, and you not only have to create the "mindset" for all the world's population to be duped to go along with it, but you also have to create the "mechanism," that will combine all the world's products into one giant global matrix system to control all the "buying and selling" including a Universal Currency everyone can use, right?

And so, this tells us that, at some point, they're going to have to get us to switch to some sort of "electronic" or "cashless society," because the Antichrist controls all the "buying and selling" with a "mark" in the right hand or forehead. So, this tells us it has to be some form of "electronic" payment system, because you don't tape a dollar bill to your hand to make a payment here in this passage, let alone, or slap 20 bucks on your forehead to pay for your groceries.

Obviously, you've got to have some sort of "electronic capability" to make a financial transaction with the Mark of the Beast system, and specifically, in your right hand or forehead. And believe it or not, that too, is being pushed with this Great Reset from Klaus Schwab and the gang with the Covid-19 Plandemic as the excuse.

In fact, once again, they've warmed us up to their ultimate, satanic goal over the years, like a frog in a pot. For the first time in man's history, we've gone from paper currency to electronic cash, and it's happening very fast! For instance, if we didn't have any money on us, don't worry, just write a check.

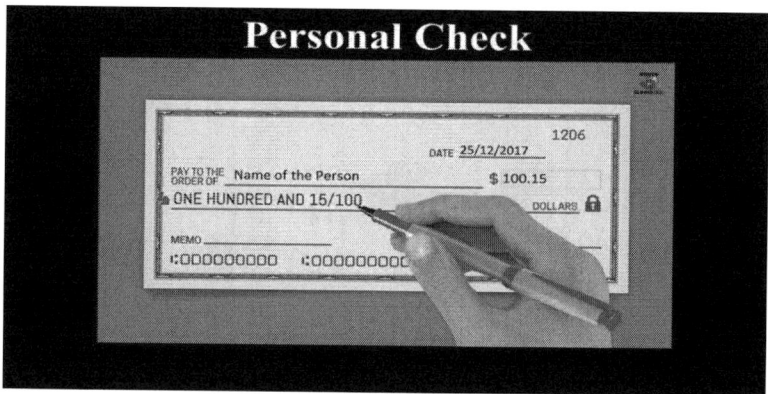

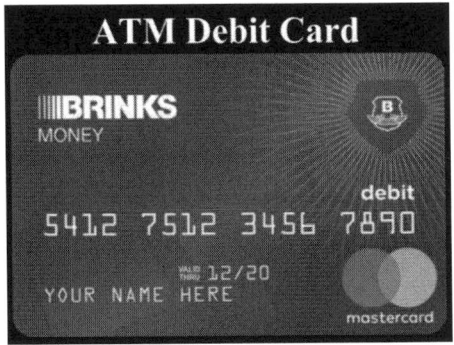

Then, if we didn't have the money to write a check, don't worry. Just charge it to a credit card.

But if we didn't want to pay the interest on a credit card, don't worry. Just take it out of your checking account with a debit card.

And then not long after that, Debit Card spending overtook cash spending, which led to all these features being combined into one card, called a smart card. And that's a card about the size of a regular credit card, only this one has a tiny microchip in it that can store and receive information and make financial transactions as well.

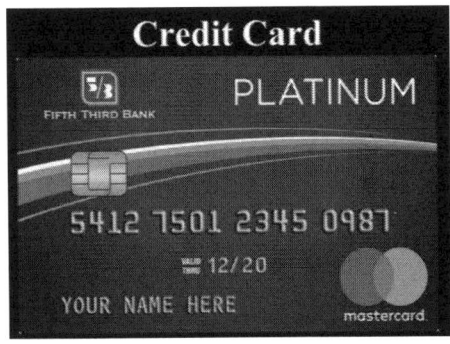

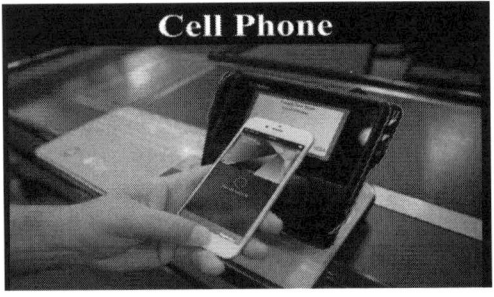

And then, all these convenient payment features were transferred to another microchip device that everybody on the planet carries around in their hands, called the cell phone, to buy their stuff with.

And so much so has this step-by-step conditioning process worked that, even here in America, we are now basically a cashless society!

NBC News Reports: *"When Brianne gets ready to go in the morning, cash is not in the equation."*

Brianne: *"I think the last time I went to an ATM was two years ago."*

NBC News Reports: *"She streamlined her wallet to credit cards only. Cash is inconvenient and dangerous."*

Brianne: *"There are a lot of times that I think that if I had a lot of cash on me, I'd feel a little bit anxious."*

NBC News Reports: *"Between 2000 and 2015, non-cash payments in the U.S. grew by almost 400%."*

Brianne*:* *"I haven't really needed cash to be honest. It's either my credit cards, or if I'm out with friends, I'll use Venmo."*

NBC News Reports: *"The app where people can pay each other on a smart phone now processes $2 billion per month. This year, Apple added similar payment capabilities in iMessage. These free services are so popular that 30 major banks have recently launched a competing product called Zelle. Doing away with paper money has been a big boon for small businesses too."*

Money Talks Reports: *"Washington's family-run Italian chain Bozzelli's has been in business for five decades, but the newly opened downtown location has taken a radical step to remain competitive - no more cash. If you want to buy your lunch here, you have to pay with plastic."*

In other words, "no cash accepted" here in the United States of America! We're going cashless, folks, right before our very eyes, in our lifetime, just in time for The Great Reset Antichrist system! And it wasn't just individuals preferring this, but businesses demanding it!

But you might be thinking, "Well that's all good and all, but that's just the United States. There's no way the whole planet is going cashless, are they?" Actually, they are! In fact, so much so, that much of the world is further along than we are, including Sweden, who now only has 1% cash transactions in their whole country, which means 99% of all their transactions are now electronic!

Newscaster: *"In Sweden, almost all transactions are done digitally. Sweden is becoming the first country to be a completely cashless economy."*

Patrick Jenkins, Financial Editor, Financial Times: *"Sweden is the king of the card. There's not much you can't buy with a bank card these days. In fact, many shops don't take cash at all. When was the last time you used cash?"*

Lady on the street: *"The last time I used cash was maybe last year, in the summer."*

Lukas Berg, CEO, Insight Intelligence: *"People talk about when will we be cashless. For me, I have lived in a cashless society for five years. I haven't had cash for five years."*

Ali Withers, NBC Left Field: *"Sweden has fast become one of the most cashless places in the world, so much so, that banks won't handle your cash. In fact, it's hard to find any business that will. You have to have a credit card or a mobile app on your phone, the common of which is SWISH, which is built by the bank."*

Man on the street: *"Most shops don't take cash, so you have to have cards."*

Newscaster: *"By value, nearly 1% of all transactions in Sweden are cash. The amount of cash in circulation is on a decline at the current rate and could be completely cashless by 2025."*

In other words, for the first time in mankind's history, a "whole country" will be completely cashless in just a few years' time, right in time for The Great Reset, Mark of the Beast System!

In fact, so much so is this cashless society catching on "globally," just like Klaus and the gang want, that many other countries are following Sweden's lead, and they too, are going cashless, including seemingly insignificant countries like Peru and Nigeria, of all places.

CBS This Morning Reports: *"The days of overstuffed wallets in your back pocket or purse could soon come to an end. By 2020, mobile wallets on our smartphones are expected to pass credit and debit cards in the U.S. That has already happened in China. Ben Tracy is in Beijing to show us what a nearly cashless society actually looks like. Good morning."*

Ben Tracy: *"Good Morning. When I moved here to China a couple months ago, I kept getting funny looks when I pulled cash out of my wallet to pay for things. And then I got one of these. It's a code that I put on my phone, and now I can basically buy anything here in China. When you pay for something how do you pay for it?"*

Lady on the street: *"On my phone."*

Ben Tracy: *"On the streets of Beijing, cash is definitely not king. What do you think of people when they use cash to pay for things?"*

Man on the street: *"That is rare and weird. Only the elderly and people who don't know how to use a phone pay cash."*

Elizabeth Schulze, CNBC News: *"If you were looking to buy a coffee a couple years ago, here in London, it might have been a normal question to ask, do you take cards? Now that question is becoming increasingly, do you take cash?"*

Ross Brown, Browns of Brockley: *"We now have customers who don't even know that we don't even accept cash, because they just tap their card and go."*

Elizabeth Schulze: *"Ross Brown stopped accepting cash at his London café more than a year ago after his trip to Sweden. He said paper money was nowhere to be found."*

Global Business Reports: *"From groceries, tips, affairs to fuel, you don't get far without potential of cash."*

"Have you ever imagined a world without it? Just using these (cards) and this (mobile phone)?"

"Tanzanian tech expert, Jones Andrew, believes we should all move to digital payment. The challenge right now, is that hardly any Tanzanians have bank accounts or credit cards, but they do have mobile money. Financial transactions run over the phone network. Jones is one of the group of campaigners, who say that mobile money gives East Africa a unique opportunity to get ahead of the rest of the world."

"Only 29% of Peruvians have bank accounts, one of the lowest levels of use of financial services in Latin America. To bring in people in places like this, e-money promoters had to look at the kind of transactions that were used in their everyday life. They found that no matter how humble the person or remote the area, cellular phones were ubiquitous. Mobile phones are the great levelers. At least one per every person in the country, and most people use prepaid, where you go to shop and buy your credit, over the counter and an e-wallet works much the same way. BIM are the Spanish initials for Mobile Wallet, it is a bank account on your phone. You don't need a smart phone to send or receive money. In fact, you don't even need a bank account, just a four-digit key."

Akiko Fujita, CNBC Reports: *"You walk around New Delhi, and you find signs of these digital payment programs everywhere. ATM, Samsung, MobiKwik, just to name a few. The number of digital transactions in India* have quadrupled since November of last year, welcomed due to a government initiative to reduce India's reliance on cash."

Prime Minister Narendra Modi: *"The rupee presently being used will no longer be legal tender."*

Akiko Fujita: *"Prime Minister, Narendra Modi, pulled nearly 90% of bank notes from circulation last year. One thing is clear. It caused a big boost to its digital economy."*

Viet Nam News: *"Vietnam's deputy prime minister has signed a policy to dramatically reduce cash transactions by 2020. The policy aims to turn Vietnam into a cashless economy and change the payment habits of the Vietnamese. It seeks to reduce cash transactions to less than 10% in all supermarkets, malls and distributors by 2020."*

DW News Reports: *"Paying without cash is fast becoming the norm. Will cash soon be a thing of the past? Around the world, financial corporations, politicians, and leading economists are working on doing away with cash."*

Woman in the store: *"When I think about it, I would rather pay without cash than with."*

Another woman in the store: *"We cannot use cash anymore."*

Baker: *"I see a future where you will be able to hold digital euros and digital dollars directly at the Central Bank."*

DW News Reports: *"Who stands to profit from a world without money, and who will be the losers?"*

Well, let me answer that for you. The "losers" will be those people who rejected Jesus Christ as their Lord and Savior today, and then got left behind at the Rapture, and thus were thrust into the horrible 7-year Tribulation, who will then have to deal with accepting or rejecting this

Mark of the Beast, Cashless Payment System that Klaus and the gang are building. And if they do, the Bible says they're doomed straight into Hell!

But the "winners," of course, will be the Antichrist and the False Prophet, who are working feverishly with Klaus Schwab, the World Economic Forum and all the wicked Global Elites, behind the scenes all over the world, putting this whole system into place as fast as they can!

And now, this Mark of the Beast, Antichrist Economic System is going into the next stage of "electronic currency" development that will put their global financial tyranny on steroids, and that's with all this talk of Cryptocurrency.

Here's a brief explanation of this New Digital Currency that's been sweeping the planet.

WHAT IS CRYPTOCURRENCY?

"When we buy or sell things, the payment is usually processed by a bank or credit card company. Problem number one, the companies often take a cut of the transaction. Two, we have to trust these companies to protect our sensitive data from hackers. Three, most international payments take a long time and are expensive. To solve these problems, we could use a special currency that is secure and based on the science of cryptography, which is a way of protecting information using mathematics.

This special type of currency is called a cryptocurrency, and only exists in computer networks. When you send someone the special currency, the money goes directly to them, removing the middleman. And at the same time, the transaction is broadcast to the entire network and recorded in a permanent way, which means it's almost impossible to fool the system. Costs of making payments are lower. Transactions are faster, especially across countries. And even those people around the globe who don't have bank accounts, can buy or sell goods and participate in the global economy. But if we can counter the risks, then this new technology, or some variation of it can completely change the way we sell, buy, save, invest, and pay our bills. And who knows, this could be the next step in the evolution of money."

Uh, and that's exactly what it's being pitched for, just in time for the Mark of the Beast system. But did you notice what this New Electronic Digital Currency can do? It's the new universal payment system, regardless of country, company, organization, location, ethnic group. Anybody can use it, and do what? "Buy, Sell, Save, Invest, Pay Bills," you know all our financial needs on a global basis!

And it not only allows, "People around the globe, who don't currently have a bank account, or could never get a bank account to have instant access to the global system to 'buy or sell' in the Global Economy." And the whole thing is stored on a giant global ledger, including the history of every single transaction of digital purchase ever made!"

Again, if you have eyes to see and ears to hear, you can see where this is headed. The actual Mark of the Beast system the Bible warned about nearly 2,000 years ago!

In fact, one man dared to expose this Mark of the Beast financial tyranny system years ago, that these Global Elites and bankers and Klaus Schwab, are really up to! Watch this.

Aaron Russo: *"The bankers have pretty much taken control of our government. It doesn't matter, Republican/Democrat, anymore, because they are both the same. Neither one of them are talking about the big issues that face Americans. So, I had a friend named Rockefeller. He was one of the Rockefeller family. When I was running for governor of Nevada, he came up to me and introduced himself to me, an attorney, and we became friends and started talking about things. I learned a lot from Mr. Rockefeller.*

One of the things we talked about was the plan of the banking industry and what they want to accomplish. The goals of the banking industry. Not just our system, but the private banks in Germany, England, Italy, all over the world. They all work together. They are all central banks. They are all part of the communist manifesto. Central banking is one of the major planks of the communist manifesto. We talk about being a capitalist country, but at the same time, we have a central bank that plans everything for us. The income tax is another plank in the communist manifesto. So, right there you have two planks in the communist manifesto that have been brought in because of the Federal Reserve system.

So, the ultimate goal that these people have in mind is the goal to create a One World Government run by the banking industry, run by the bankers. They do it in sections. The European currency, the euro and the European Constitution is one part of it. Now they are trying to do it in America with the North American Union. And they want to create a new currency called the Amero. The whole agenda is to create a One World Government, where everybody has an RFID chip implanted in them. All money is to be in those chips. There will be no more cash. Now all this came from Rockefeller himself. This is what they want to accomplish. All money will be in your chips. So, instead of having cash, anytime you have money in your chip, they can take out any amount at any time they want to. If they say, you owe us taxes, they just deduct it out of your chip. Total control. And if you are like me and you protest what they are doing, they just turn off your chip, and you have nothing. You can't buy food; you can't do anything. It's total control of the people."

Wow! It's also called what the Bible warned about 2,000 years ago, The Mark of the Beast System. And if you go back to the text, it doesn't sound like science fiction anymore!

Revelation 13:16-17: "He also forced everyone, small and great, rich and poor, free and slave, to receive a mark on his right hand or on his forehead, so that no one could buy or sell unless he had the mark, which is the name of the beast or the number of his name."

That system folks is right now being put into place as we sit here, with the Covid-19 Plandemic as the excuse, relabeled The Great Reset.

And if you still don't believe me, then let's remind ourselves again of what Klaus Schwab said back in 2016, referring to microchipping people.

"Klaus Schwab is the founder and chairman of the World Economic Forum in Davos, which annually brings together the heads of state of the world's major countries to discuss the future of world affairs.

In this interview, given on January 10, 2016, to the Swiss channel, RTS, he explains that human beings will soon receive a chip in their body in order to merge with the digital world.

People who see this excerpt from the interview should remember that Klaus Schwab is the designer and promoter of The Great Reset, officially launched at the Davos Forum in January 2021.

In 2020, Klaus Schwab said that Covid-19 is a 'rare but narrow window of opportunity to rethink, reinvent, reset our world.' We won't be able to say I didn't know."

Klaus Schwab: *"Today, at the end of this, we are talking about chips that can be implanted."*
Interviewer: *"When will that be?"*

Klaus Schwab: *"Certainly within the next 10 years. And, at first, we will implant them in our clothes, and then we could imagine that we will implant them in our brains, or in our skin. And in the end, there will be direct communication between our brain and the digital world."*

Right there in black and white! He admitted it! First, we'll microchip your clothes and what you "buy and sell," and then "you" get "microchipped" to connect you to this "Global Digital World," or what the Bible calls the Mark of the Beast System!

And if you don't do what they, or Klaus Schwab, or the Antichrist and False Prophet say, they'll just turn off your chip! Total global control over people's individual finances.

In fact, it's getting so obvious that this is the foundation being laid for the prophesied Mark of the Beast system that the Bible warned about, that some even in the news are picking up on it!

RT News Reports: *"So, many economists believe that our future will be cash free. You're already seeing it everywhere you go, whether it's your baseball game or it's your local deli. Now Sweden is getting there faster than anyone else, according to a New York Times report. And 4,000 Swedes have had a microchip implanted in their hand. No need for paper products, with just a wave of their hand. Makes the Apple watch obsolete.*

So, on top of that, many Swedish companies are asking their employees to get implants to pass through access points and to pay for conveniences. Now the red flags have started going up. So, for our red flag, we are turning to our Go-Media, Lionel. Hey, Lionel, how's it going? I know you've got some red flags. And I feel like I'm reading out of the Book of Revelation. So, what concerns come to you from humans microchipping themselves?"

Lionel: *"This is the Mark of the Beast. No, no, let me tell you something. I'm no Biblical scholar here, but it's amazing the parallels made. Let's get down to brass tacks. We're going cashless. We've been cashless. Where's this cash? Have you ever bought a house with cash? Or a car? I've got a couple of bucks. We've been cashless. But that's not the issue. One of these days, these kids, I think you call them millennials, they are going to take these little, tiny RFID chips, about the size of a grain of rice, and they are going to be cool. They are going to be waiting in line overnight to get implanted. They are going to say, 'Look at this! I can go to the drugstore. I can go in a cab, isn't it great? How cool am I! Look, I have this little imbedded chip and they say they have medical records. Are you going to do that to grandma and grandpa, in case they have some sort of dementia? We have it in our dogs, why not have On Star for human beings?' But here's the catch. One of these days, God forbid, they find you guilty of something. And you go before a court, and they say, we are going to sentence you. To prison? No. We're going to turn your chip off, and you don't exist."*

In other words, you can no longer "buy or sell!" Where have I heard that before? Even secular news can put two and two together, folks! Step-by-step, like a frog in a pot, we have been conditioned to accept this, yet how many even know about it?

But it's not just a One World Economy and Cashless Society that God warned us about, that would be a part of the Antichrist Kingdom. It was also, as you saw, a Mark of the Beast type system that the Antichrist will implement as well. And shocker, that's also another plan Klaus and the gang are implementing on the planet with the Covid-19 Agenda as the excuse.

Again, that's what we saw with the previous video from Klaus Schwab, who admitted he wanted to "mark" or "identify" the whole planet into a "digital matrix system" with Covid-19 as the excuse.

And if that wasn't enough proof, he also admitted he wanted to put those "marks" or "microchips in our "brains," i.e., our "heads," or even "under our skin." You know, like your "hand."

It's almost like he's following a script. Well, he is. It's the coming **Mark of the Beast System** that the Bible warned about 2,000 years ago!

Chapter Twelve

World Economic Forum & The Global Conditioning

And the **1ˢᵗ way** we see this Coming Mark of the Beast System that Klaus is helping to build, is **The Conditioning is Already Here**.

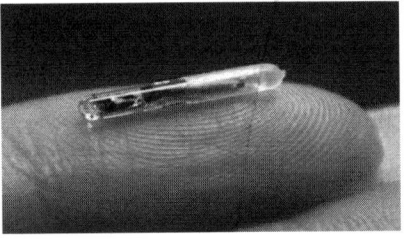

For those that had eyes to see and ears to hear, we've witnessed for many years how the media, cartoons, sitcoms, movies, the news, talk shows, you name it, have been promoting this idea of people getting microchipped into a Mark of the Beast type System for a long time. Here's just a small sampling of that conditioning.

Here is a clip from a cartoon series.

Young man applying for a job: *"Delivery boy, no, not again! Please, anything else."* (As he reaches for her arm to get her attention.)

Clerk: *"Get your hands off me. You have been assigned a job that you are best at. Just like everyone else."*

Young man applying for a job: *"What if I refuse?"*

Clerk: *"Well, that's tough. Lots of people don't like their jobs, but we do them anyway. You gotta do what you gotta do! Now hold out your hand. I'm going to implant your career chip. It will permanently label you as a delivery boy."*

Clip from CSI Miami:

Horatio Caine: *"We found this implanted in our victim's shoulder."*

Ryan: *"It's an air-chip. You scan it here, and the information pops up there."*

Horatio Caine: *"Ok, hit more info and see if we have a driver's license."*

The more info button was clicked and …

Ryan: *"Yes, Jenny Price, 18."*

Horatio Caine: *"Chase Shaw says this thing holds credit card information."*

Clip from "Law and Order SVU":

Medical Examiner: *"I excised this from her shoulder. I don't know what it is."*

Elliot Stabler: *"That's an RFID chip, and I think we know who put it there."*

Medical Examiner: *"He doesn't know. I asked him. Whoever did this to her must have injected it while she was unconscious."*

Elliot Stabler: *"Well, that's a way of keeping tabs on your cheating wife."*

Elliot interviews husband of dead woman.

Elliot Stabler: *"Now, why would you implant an RFID chip in your wife's shoulder?"*

Husband: *"I was keeping tabs on her."*

Elliot Stabler: *"She's a human being. You are aware of that? She's not a pet."*

Husband: *"She was cheating on me."*

Olivia Benson: *"That doesn't give you the right to tag her."*

Husband: *"The RFID is the way of the future. I'm just ahead of the curve. In fifteen years, everyone will be implanted with a chip."*

Today Reports: *"Brooke likes this idea. We are talking about Brooke. Listen to this story. So, you forgot your ticket to a soccer game. In Argentina, it's not a problem, because you can use the microchip that has been embedded under your skin by the team. An Argentinian soccer team is planning, experimentally at this point, to offer supporters the chance to implant a microchip in their skin, and that lets them walk through an easy pass in your car, to walk right into the stadium."*

Ryan Eggold: *"But the easy pass is in your car, not in your wrist."*

Brooke Shields: *"I'm not really looking at it in terms of sports, as much as I would love to put one in my kids."*

Ryan Eggold: *"Just to know where they are?"*

Brooke Shields: *"I know it's creepy and really futuristic, but my dog has one, and she ran away. We lived downtown and she ended up in Harlem. And somebody did deliver her to a facility, and they scanned her, and then they found us. And I honestly am not completely against chipping my children."

Dr Oz: *"Turns out one of the biggest discoveries, is this tiny. Do you see how small that is? This little chip may be the next big thing. It sounds like it's right out of a sci-fi movie, but people all over the world are implanting these into their wrists. We asked our producer, Dean, to find out more about this cutting-edge technology and what it could mean for your health.*

THE NEXT BIG THING

Dean: *"Whether it's our smart phones, our watches, our fitness trackers, or our Bluetooth headphones, it's clear that technology is not just part of our lives. It's running them. It's how we buy things, watch things, how we date, stay safe, even how we travel. We are so attracted to our devices that they are basically becoming a part of our bodies. But what if they really could become a part of our bodies? Well, guess what? They can. Meet the RFID microchip.*

This tiny chip, which can be implanted into your wrist - yes, I did say wrist - uses short range radio frequency identification, similar to the tech used to track your pets or your phone. Once implanted in your body it can identify you as you pass the airport, open the door of your home. It can even be used to buy groceries at the supermarket. Now, your driver's license, passport, keys, and wallet are all inside your body. It's even the size of a grain of rice. I know it might sound like sci-fi, but it's not. Ten thousand people have already been chipped and the number is growing.

The possibilities are limitless, especially when it comes to your health. Imagine you are rushed to the hospital without any identification, but with just one scan of your chip, doctors know your name, date of birth, medical history, insurance, blood type, allergies, even the medications you're taking. This chip in your wrist won't just change your life. One day it might just save your life. And that is why this little RFID microchip is the next big thing."

Commercial for Health Link: *"To think something so small could connect you to everything that matters."*

"When your life or the one you love are on the line, Health Link is always with you. When every second counts in the emergency room, providing immediate access to your medical records."

"Because Bob has trouble remembering all his medications."

"Because I love my kids."

"Because my car lost control while driving."

"Because now I'm looking out for both of us."

"Because I have diabetes, but it doesn't have me."

"Because I spend my life in the ER trying to save yours."

Sure thing, Pal. Now, notice how the last two examples were from the medical community. The same ones who have already mandated the masks and vaccines. I'm sure it'll stop there with the masks and vaccines!

But as you can see, this is "the next big thing," or "big step" in their ultimate goal. Getting people to get a microchip implant. And the media for years has been promoting it in a variety of ways all over the place, including cartoons! And if you don't think this media propaganda and conditioning isn't affecting people, listen to this.

An MSNBC poll said, *"20% of the American population, right now, is fully ready and willing to receive a microchip implant."* Looks to me like the media conditioning is working great. Klaus must be pleased!

In fact, so much so, that one of the industry leaders said this, *"He expects that in the next 2 to 3 years, it will be standard protocol for emergency room personnel to scan the upper right arm of every patient admitted."*

Wow! Now, as creepy as that is, that leads us to the **2nd way** we see this Coming Mark of the Beast System that Klaus is helping to build is, **The Logistics are Already Here**.

You see, you might be wondering, "Well, why? Why specifically, of all body parts, is the mark of the beast on the right hand or forehead? I mean, think about it. Why not the leg, why not the back, why not your big toe or someplace like that? Why the right hand and forehead?"

Well, the **first reason** is a **Practical Issue**.

As you can see in that picture, in cold weather climates, the two parts of the body that just happen to be the quickest and easiest to expose for scanning purposes, are the hands and the head.

And I know it might sound kind of weird to those of us who live on the West Coast, but believe it or not, did you know, a large portion of the world wears these things called hats and coats and gloves to keep themselves warm?

And so, if you're these people in line getting ready to buy and sell something, and you had a Mark on your back or your big toe somewhere like that, it's going to be kind of hard to get it scanned, right?

But not if you had it in your right hand or forehead. Chances are, even in cold climates these parts are already exposed. Or if you had a glove on or a hat, you could just take the glove off, or lift up the hat, bang you're done!

Either way, it just so happens, these specific body parts make for a very practical place to put the Mark of the Beast in cold weather climates. That's not by chance.

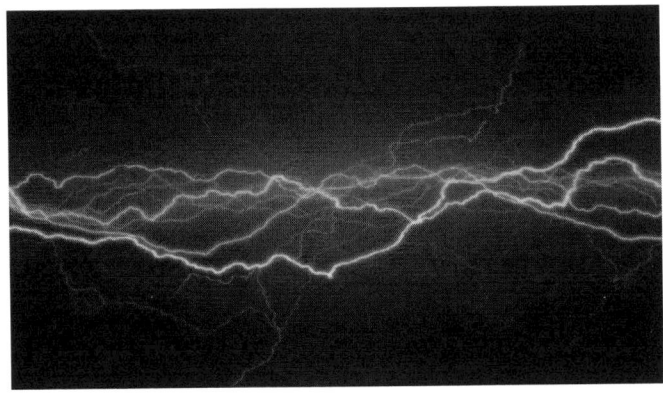

The **second reason** is the **Energy Issue**.

You see, what's interesting about these microchip implants, is they have a unique power source that recharges itself by converting electricity from the fluctuations in a person's body temperature.

And it just so happens, one researcher, who worked for 32 years designing microchips in the Bio-Med field, said this, *"Over one and a half million dollars was spent finding out the two places in the human body that temperature changes most rapidly."*

And can anyone guess, after 1½ million dollars, just where these two best locations in the body might be? That's right, in the forehead right below the hairline and the back of the hand.

Which makes sense, because that's how moms used to check a child's temperature, the old-fashioned way. She's put the back of her hand on your forehead!

But this just happens to be the two specific body parts that can be used to create an energy source for these chips! I'm sure that's a coinkadink!

The **third reason** is the **Worship Issue**.

You see, the Bible is clear. What goes along with taking the Mark of the Beast is, not just "buying and selling," but an attitude of worship. People are going to worship the Antichrist with this Mark. In fact, in Revelation 13 alone, it's mentioned four times.

Revelation 13:4: "…and they also worshiped the beast…"

Revelation 13:8: "All inhabitants of the earth will worship the beast—all whose names have not been written in the Lamb's book of life."

Revelation 13:12: "…and made the earth and its inhabitants worship the first beast, whose fatal wound had been healed."

Revelation 13:15: "…so that the image could speak and cause all who refused to worship the image to be killed."

It's all over the place! They're going to worship the Beast with this Marking System. And so, here's the point. It just so happens this worshipful attitude, with these specific body parts, already fits a huge portion of the planet, when it comes to worshiping something with the right hand or forehead. Whether you realize it or not, different cultures today use these specific body parts right now to worship their deities.

And the first ones to do that is the Hindu and Asian populations, with the red dots they put on their forehead called the "Tilaka" or the "Bindi."

The Tilaka/Bindi Mark

And it might be weird to you and I, here in the West, but these people - a huge portion of the planet - I'd say, would opt to take the Mark of the Beast in their forehead, right? And they're going to do it in a worshipful attitude, just like they already do with their deities today!

In fact, speaking of the West and a worshipful attitude, believe it or not folks, I believe another huge portion of the planet may also take the Mark of the Beast in their forehead. And that's the Catholics. Why? Because they've already been trained to put a Mark on their foreheads every single year on Ash Wednesday.

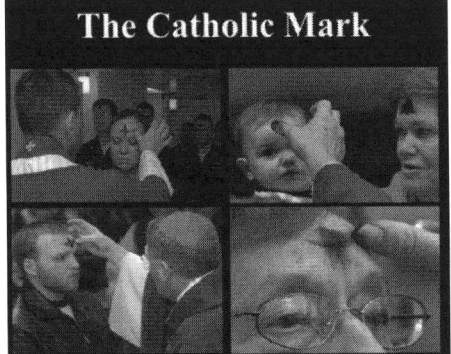

The Catholic Mark

The Catholic Mark

But you might be thinking, "Well, I don't care what Joe Biden, the Hindus or Asians, or Catholics think. There's no way I'm going to put something on my forehead! That's not cool! That's unsightly! That's a fashion faux pas!" Well, you tell me, if the latest trend in body arts and tattoos and body piercings will reject something like that!

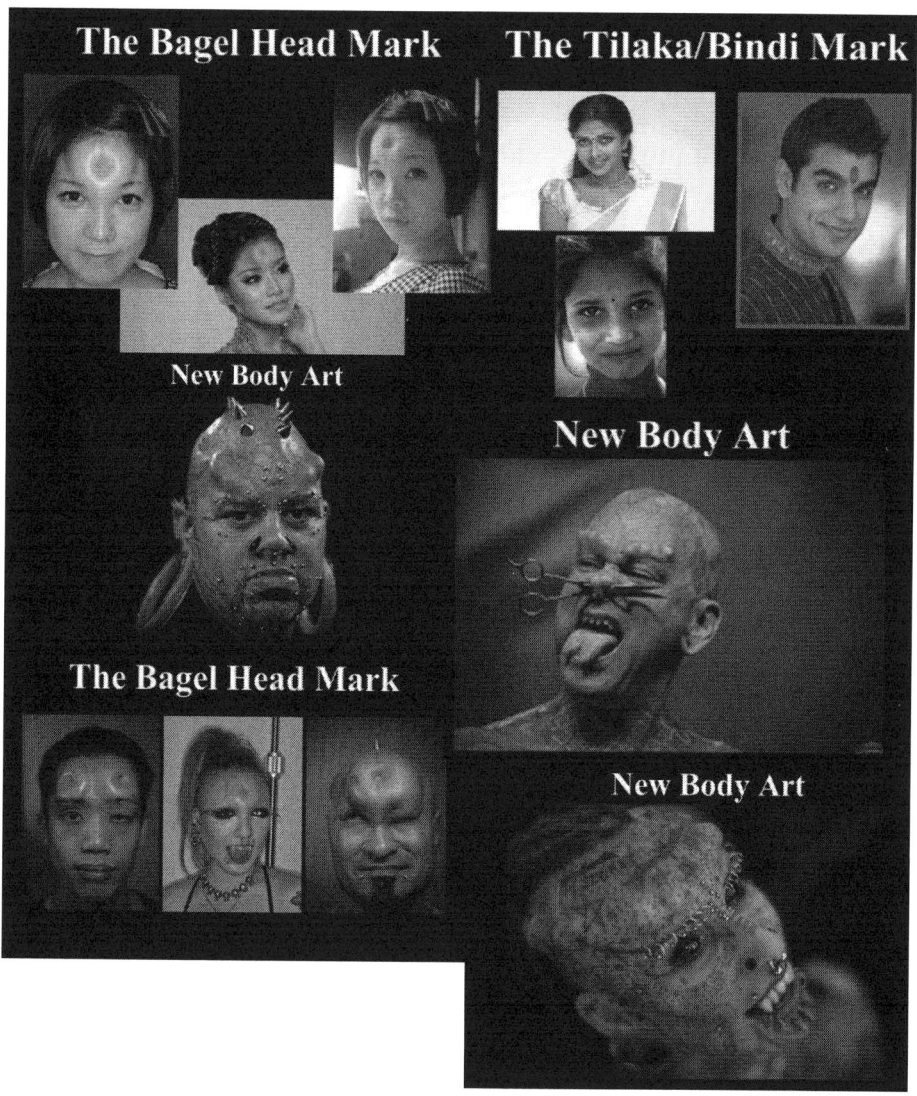

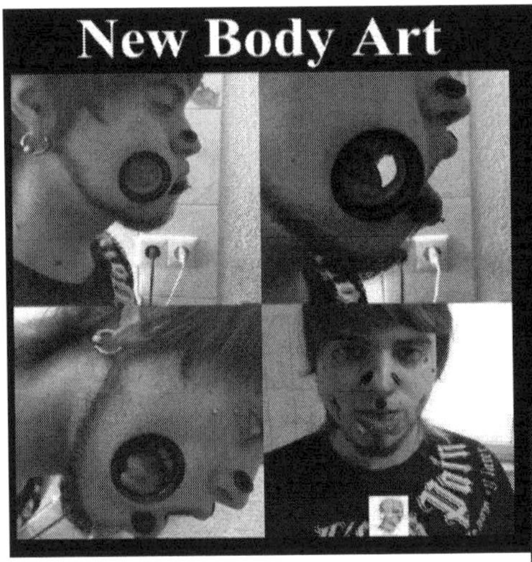

New Body Art

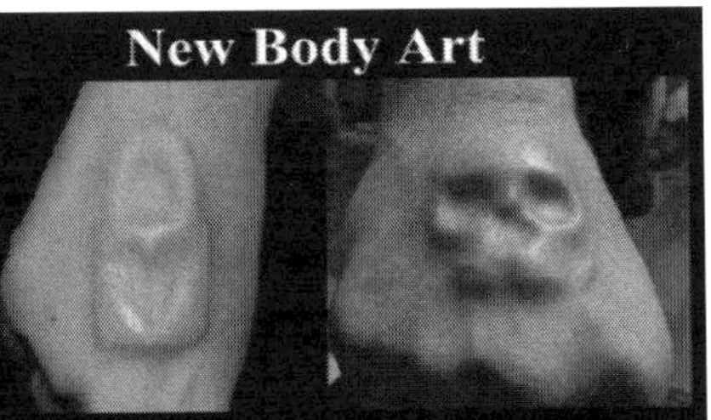

New Body Art

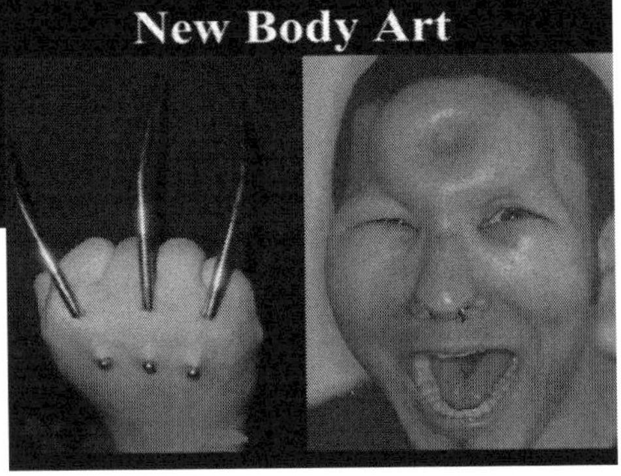

New Body Art

I don't know about you, but I don't think those people are too worried about making a fashion faux pas with a microchip! But that's the trend!

But you might be wondering, "Okay, that's the forehead, I can see how people are warmed up to that, but what about the right hand? What's that got to do with worship?"

Well again, learn your history. We've already seen as recent as Hitler, how the right hand was used to give him a "Heil Hitler" in an attitude of worship, right?

And if you think that attitude will never come back, you're wrong. We are also seeing

The Right Hand for Hitler

Palestinian soldiers do the same thing. You know, the ones who want to annihilate the Jews, they're using their right hands.

And we saw, if you'll recall, Obama supporters - you know, a political figure - "being encouraged to mark their right hands with messages, press them over their hearts, to pledge allegiance to Obama." Remember that?

And even some of the latest Leftist Liberal Movements, post - Obama, are doing the same, like Black Lives Matter.

But here's the point. Looks to me like we're seeing a resurgence of people using their right hands and foreheads in an attitude of worship, just like the Bible said would happen with the Mark of the Beast System!

The **3rd way** we see this Coming Mark of the Beast System that Klaus is helping to build is, **The Willingness is Already Here**.

You see, it's not just that people are being conditioned by the media to get a microchip, nor just logistically being conditioned to use a body part in an attitude of worship of a deity, or even a political figure.

But people are actually lining up all over the world, willingly, to get a microchip implant, right now. Here's just a couple examples.

KPIX News Reports Newscaster #1: *"Microchip implants are a popular way to keep track of pets. Now some people are getting them, but for a different reason."*

Newscaster #2: *"The microchips can unlock doors or log in to a cell phone. Consumer reporter Julie Watts explains."*

Julie Watts: *"Ken Shanks uses it to open his front door and manipulate his smartphone. Christie Heisman uses hers instead of a keycard at work."*

Christie Heisman: *"It's just a little glass seed, like a grain of rice."*

Julie Watts: *"They are among the growing number of people implanting this technology under their skin."*

Volton Ishvon: *"We don't want to carry devices; we want devices built into us."*

Julie Watts: *"Volton Ishvon, of Mill Valley, is part of the transhumanist party. The movement seeks to radically improve humans through digital* *implants, even genetic manipulation. For now, a common procedure, implanting programable RFID chips under the skin. But instead of a doctor's office, many are turning to tattoo and piercing shops."*

Ryan Mills, Skin Art Gallery: *"When doing the procedure, start to finish, is just like we would do an earring, a nose ring or a belly button ring. It's just a little piece of glass."*

Julie Watts: *"The online company, Dangerous Things, sells the device and the injection kit for $57.00. But they are not alone. One San Francisco company has developed tiny implantable digital tattoos. They will authenticate credit cards, track your location, even collect health data."*

Today's Talker Reports: *"Thousands of people in Sweden have opted to trade in their ID and their credit cards for tiny microchips to be implanted underneath their skin. These chips are supposed to take the place of key cards, rail cards, credit cards. Chips are typically the size of a grain of rice, and they are implanted just under the skin between the thumb and the forefinger. So, many people in Sweden are lining up to get these microchips. The country's main chipping company said, it can't even keep up with the number of requests. What? What in the illuminati, mark of the beast, witchcraft is going on over there in Sweden?"*

Yeah, I would say so! But notice the same technology can be used "in" or "on" the skin, which solves the debate. Is the mark "in" or "on" the right hand or forehead? - depending on the translation. Well, cased closed, the same technology can do both. No need to argue. It's here now!

But also notice how Sweden is already 99% cashless, and now people are getting microchipped so they can "buy and sell." I'm sure that's just another coinkadink! Yeah, it's called a step-by-step process.

Including Klaus Schwab's dream of, "merging the biological with the digital," using Covid-19 as the excuse. And I say that, because now people in Sweden are getting microchipped for their "Covid Passports," as you can see here.

Once again, it's a step-by-step plan, and we're all being warmed up like a frog in a pot. They told us where it's all ultimately headed, but we just didn't want to deal with it or believe them. Not to mention, God warned about this 2,000 years ago in the Bible!

Which leads us to the next step. The **4th way** we see this Coming Mark of the Beast System that Klaus is helping to build is, **The Payments are Already Here**.

You see, if you're going to condition people all around the whole world to eventually go along with the Mark of the Beast System, you not only need to condition them to getting a microchip implant which is already happening, but you have to get them used to the idea of specifically making payments with these two specific body parts, the "right hand," or the "head." Let's revisit God's warnings of those two body parts.

Revelation 13:16-17: "He also forced everyone, small and great, rich and poor, free and slave, to receive a mark on his right hand or on his forehead, so that no one could buy or sell unless he had the mark."

Again, the second body part mentioned there was the head. And I don't know about you, but I'm so glad we see no signs of people using their "head" to "buy and sell" stuff, how about you? Yeah, right! It's already here.

Narrator: *"Imagine coming into a store and your wallet is already there. You pick up your things, go to the checkout, give a meaningful nod, and that's it. Imagine you are late to your plane. There was a huge queue, but you instantly check in while running to the border control. Imagine you drive to the petrol station; you casually fuel your tank, and your payment is made simultaneously. You just had to click OK. Imagine the shop where all those magic things came to life. People come with friends just to show off. Well, this is not fiction anymore. They all got a Uniqul account, and now, wherever they go, I recognize them. Processing takes under a second. They sign in as soon as I see them. All they had to do was click OK. Hi, I'm your new friend, Uniqul."*

Hi! I'm you're new friend, Antichrist! And all you have to do is click "OK" and make a payment with your "head." Where have I heard that before, folks? We are seeing, for the very first time in man's history, people already making payments with their "head!" Isn't that wild? Klaus must be smiling. But that's not all. Let's take a look at the other body part, the "hand."

Revelation 14:9-10: "If anyone worships the beast and his image and receives his mark on the forehead or on the hand, he, too, will drink of the wine of God's fury, which has been poured full strength into the cup of His wrath."

In other words, don't do it. At least not those who find themselves left behind after the Rapture of the Church for rejecting Jesus as their Lord and Savior and were then thrust into the horrible 7-year Tribulation, where all this is going to culminate!

But what was the second option there for people getting connected to the Mark of the Beast System in the 7-year Tribulation? Not just your "head," but your "hand," right?

And again, I'm so glad we see no signs of people using their "hand" to "buy and sell" stuff. Yeah right! That too, is already here. Let's take a look at that.

Action News Reports: *"You've seen in action movies, using unique biological characteristics instead of keys. A facial or iris scan to unlock doors and digital accounts, an electronic paperless society. Come summer, that kind of technology will leap off the big screen, and one metro grocery store will make your identity available right at your fingertips. It's sci-fi technology that is about to enter the check-out lane, all in the name of speed and convenience. You'll be able to buy anything from bread to beer. You're free to give the store your ultimate identity."*

Store Owner: *"You walk in with just your finger."*

Customer: *"It's much easier to swipe your finger than to go through all the carts."*

Fox News Reports: *"A new form of technology has made its way to the register. Are you ready for this? Payment by fingertip. In Florida, coast-to-coast convenience stores have become the first to use such technology.*

Store clerk: *"It's nothing more than using your debit card or your checking account to apply it to your fingertip."*

CBS News Reports: *"The LA Unified School District is pushing a program to fingerprint some kids before they can get their lunch.*

Digitizing lunch scan district-wide might have caused a bit of controversy. LAUSD is the second largest school system in the school systems across the country. It serves over half a million student meals every day. Students at the Learning Center are expected to be the first in the district to use a fingerprint like scanner, to biometrically identify them for meals in the lunchroom. This is to say, that this system poses no security or privacy risks to the children or their families and would help bring district cafeterias into the 21st century."

Newscaster: *"What looks and sounds like something out of the future, but a palm scanning device will help Bossier Parish schools keep better track of what the children are eating there. The electronic device will be implemented in all Bossier Parish schools. Workers are currently being trained in how to use it. A small infrared camera is used to scan a child's hand, as the palm and fingerprints are unique, and this system will keep track of everything they eat and even what they are not supposed to eat. Food allergies can also be listed, as well as items that you don't want your child to eat. If a student picks one of those items, the system won't let them buy it."*

Breaking News Reports: *"You know, today it's a fingerprint, tomorrow it's a microchip. Maybe that just ushers in the mark of the beast."*

Fast food cashier: *"I can't believe he just paid with his hand. Like you just literally put your hand up, and you're good to go. Like, that's crazy!"*

    Yeah, that's crazy! Where have I heard that before? This is how close we are! For the first time in man's history, we now have people already making payments with their head "and" their hand! Both are in play, just in time for the Mark of the Beast System that Klaus and the gang are helping to build for the actual Antichrist!

Which leads us to the final proof. The **5th way** we see this Coming Mark of the Beast System that Klaus is helping to build is, **The Pressure is Already Here**.

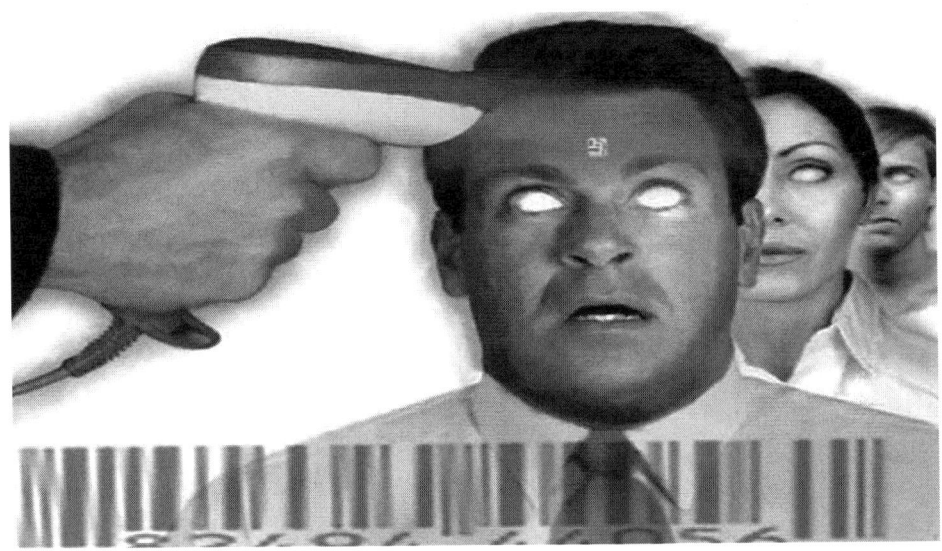

You see, put yourself in the Antichrist's shoes. It's common sense that some people aren't going to go along with this microchipping process and tying them into the Mark of the Beast system, so what's he going to do? He'll do exactly what the Bible says he's going to do. He'll "mandate" it!

Revelation 13:16-17: "He also forced everyone, small and great, rich and poor, free and slave, to receive a mark on his right hand or on his forehead, so that no one could buy or sell unless he had the mark."

What's that? That's a "mandate." The Antichrist takes away the choice and "forces," or "mandates," people to go along with his Mark of the Beast system so they can "buy and sell."

And that's what we just saw over the Covid-19 Plandemic, as Klaus said would happen. People all around the world were being "forced" to wear a "mask" on their "face" or "head" to "buy and sell," and then people were "forced" to get a "shot" in the "arm," not far from the "hand" to "buy and sell."

Again, it was the biggest dry-run in history for the coming Mark of the Beast system, and they used the same pressure that the Antichrist is going to use in the 7-year Tribulation!

Including the next step, of people being "forced" into being microchipped. It's another axiom they use to warm us up like a frog in a pot. Start at the end of the spectrum, and then slowly work your way inward to your ultimate goal.

You know, like start at the end of the spectrum, dangerous people - criminals and prisoners who "deserve" to have their rights taken away - and "force" them to get a microchip implant. Don't believe me? There are actual talks of doing just that!

CBS New York Reports: *"With the two fugitives on the loose, a lawmaker from upstate has a high-tech plan to prevent another prison break; she's proposing microchipping prisoners. CBS News Political Reporter Marsha Cramer is here with that proposal."*

Marsha Cramer: *"Well, bloodhounds and expensive manhunts are 'so yesterday,' when it comes to hunting escaped prisoners. That's the opinion of one upstate senator, who says the state should explore implanting a tiny GPS device under convict's skin. Others say microchipping criminals could have multiple uses."*

Kathy Marchione, (R.) NYS Senate, Saratoga: *"If you've got convicted murderers, the type of men that these two men are, it would make some good sense at that level that we should have something that we could track them."*

Marsha Cramer: *"With 800 law enforcement officials still unable to pick up the trail of escaped murderers, the suggestion from state Senator Kathy Marchione to microchip people convicted of serious crimes with tiny GPS* devices under their skin is picking up steam. They already microchip pets."

Man on the street: *"It wouldn't do any harm, I guess. They do it with dogs."*

Man on the street #2: *"I think that might be a good idea. Maybe it would work."*

Woman on the street: *"I heard about it over at other parts of the world, and I would say yes."*

Man on the street #3: *"Once we go down this path, they might start microchipping all of us. Which I think some people would already like to do."*

Yeah, you know, like the current administration. But even that guy gets it! First you "pressured" criminals and "forced" them to wear GPS bracelets on the outside of them. Now you're talking about putting a GPS microchip on the inside of them. I'm sure that's a coinkadink!

Or is it a step-by-step process pressuring people, "forcing" them to get a microchip, first at the end of the spectrum, then to your ultimate goal!

But that's just the beginning. Now move a little closer towards your ultimate goal, away from the end of the spectrum, and try it out on those people who are not behind bars, but who are losing their memory. I mean, they don't know any better. They've got Alzheimer's. If we put a chip inside of them, we could track them and keep them safe! And that too, is already being done!

WTHR 13 Reports: *"A company is developing a microchip that could help patients with Alzheimer's and Dementia. This company got a lot of attention last year, when they started putting microchips in their employees. They use the chips like other companies use ID badges. Now* they say, they are working on a more advanced version. They say they have gotten requests from people with relatives with Alzheimer's or Dementia. The new device will have GPS technology."

Daughter of patient: *"There were times when my mom would call, panicked, 'I just got out of the shower and dad is nowhere to be found.' Immediately, my mind went to a bad place."*

WTHR 13 Reports: *"That's why she was intrigued about a piece of technology being made, by Three Square Market, a company in River Falls."*

Patrick McMullen: *"Somebody with Alzheimer's or Dementia, time is your biggest enemy."*

WTHR 13 Reports: *"Patrick McMullen is the president of the company, that you may remember who offered the hand-inserted microchip to their employees, to scan into the building or buy things from the break room. The developers of this microchip now believe it could save lives, especially for those who are suffering from Dementia or Alzheimer's."*

Patrick McMullen: *"It's a low-powered GPS device."*

WTHR 13 Reports: *"If a person with Dementia or Alzheimer's has the microchip inserted in their hand and gets lost, the microchip would send their location, or a map of where they recently had been, back to the caregiver or loved ones, notifying them in real time where the person is."*

Well, you see, there you have it. It's for their own good! But hey, don't stop there! You're on a roll! Move in now a little closer now, to your ultimate goal and start "mandating" chips for policemen and soldiers! I mean, hello. They're government property already anyway, right?

And if we just chip them, too, why, just like the Alzheimer patients and prisoners, they'll be safe on the streets or the battlefield, wherever they are! Won't it be great? And believe it or not, folks, that too is already being done.

Newscaster: *"Sergeant Bill Koretsky's medical-implanted microchip may have saved his life. His story begins in a high-speed police chase in New Jersey."*

Bill Koretsky: *"The brakes on the police car overheated, and the car wouldn't stop. And I hit a telephone pole, dead center, at 40 miles per hour. The airbags did not deploy. I didn't have my seatbelt on, and I hit the steering wheel."*

Newscaster: *"Paramedics rushed Koretsky to the Medical Center. Thanks to his implant, doctors immediately discovered Koretsky had diabetes."*

Bill Koretsky: *"I regained full consciousness within an hour, but if I did not, I could have gone into a coma."*

Newscaster: *"If the VeriChip Corporation has its way, Bill Koretsky's story will become the norm."*

Melissa Long, CNN Reports: *"Keeping track of troops in Iraq, the military is already using some type of GPS on some soldiers, but what can be done? CNN's Brian Todd is taking a look at this week's TechEffect."*

Brian Todd: *"One option, placing a microchip under a service member's skin. Former U.S. Special Operations officers say that they believe that's being developed currently, but military officials won't comment on that."*

Gee, I wonder why? But let me get this straight. First, it was the external GPS tracker for the soldiers, then it moved to the internal microchip. Anyone see a pattern here?

But don't stop there! Hey, if it's good for the soldiers, and policemen, and Alzheimer's patients, and prisoners to keep them safe, why not kids? I mean, they get lost all the time! So, if we chip them too, why, they'll not only be safe from predators, but we can monitor them wherever they go! Won't it be great? Yeah, that too is being done as well!

Keith Cate, News Tonight 8 Reports: *"It happens in seconds. Moms and dads, you know that feeling. Your child gets lost in a store or just wanders off for a second or two, but your heart stops though. Panic sets in, and you think the worst. It's happened to most of us, but what if you had a secret weapon? An extra layer of safety so to speak. How far would you go to keep your children secure?"*

Jennifer Leigh, News Tonight 8 Reports: *"Would you be willing to microchip them? Experts tell us that technology already exists. Turns out that one bay area mother is all for it. When she shared her story with our Melanie Michael."*

Melanie Michael: *"Good evening to you both. You know, chances are, if you have a four-legged family member at home, it's already microchipped. And if the technology exists to save Fido in an emergency, what about microchipping your child. Before you say, 'No way, I would never do that,' hear one mom's story."*

Steffany Rodriguez-Neely: *"It's the longest two seconds of your life. And it's absolute panic."*

Melanie Michael: *"We have seen it in movies, over and over again, and children go missing."*

Steffany Rodriguez-Neely: *"It's terrifying."*

Melanie Michael: *"For Steffany Rodriguez-Neely, life is busier than ever. With four children, including a newborn, she knows scary situations can happen in an instant. And for her it has."*

Steffany Rodriguez-Neely: *"If it will save my kid, there is no step too extreme."*

Melanie Michael: *"Steffany's teenage daughter is a special needs child, prone to wander off and trust strangers. For that very reason, Steffany whole-heartedly welcomes microchipping a child."*

Steffany Rodriguez-Neely: *"A small chip the size of a grain of rice could have prevented a tragedy. For most parents, hindsight would say, 'I wish I would have done it.'"*

Melanie Michael: *"A well-known technology expert out of Boston tells us microchipping poses little to no health risks and would act as a sort of barcode of sorts."*

Stuart Lipoff, Electronics Engineer: *"It could save a life, reunite a family, find a missing Alzheimer's patient."*

Steffany Rodriguez-Neely: *"I always tell people, that as long as you do what you feel is best for your child, you're not really wrong."*

Melanie Michael: *"And guys, this is what we're talking about. The microchip. I don't know if you can see it in my hand. It's the size of a grain of rice, very, very small. And the expert that we spoke with actually told us, barcodes were introduced to us in the 1960s, and people thought, 'this is way too invasive and too weird.' And now barcodes are so commonplace that we don't even think about them anymore. The expert is telling us that this will happen sooner, rather than later. Somewhere, someday, someone is going to pull this off, and we will see these microchips in everyone."*

Yeah, that's interesting! I'm sure that someone wouldn't be the current administration, who works for Klaus Schwab, who already said, he and the gang are going to microchip everybody. Yeah, we'll get to that in a second.

But as you saw, hey, if it's good for Fido and Fifi, it's good for Frankie and Susie and everybody! How about the rest of us! Don't you want to join in on the fun? Wouldn't it be great to have your own adult "mandated" microchip too?

Now, for those of you who think we're not headed that way, pay attention to the next trend. You might have to get one pretty soon to keep your job, you know, just like the masks and vaccines we got conditioned to.

Sean Darks, CEO, Citywatchers.com: *"See, you can see my chip, right there."*

CNN Reports: *"You can actually see it. It's about the size of a grain of rice. And it feels like it too. But what that tiny chip can and can't do, has become the source of much concern and confusion."*

Sean Darks, CEO, Citywatcher.com: *"I was at the grocery store and a couple of ladies said, 'You're the guy with the chip in your arm. Aren't you? Run your arm across the scanner and let's see if you get a discount on groceries.'"*

CNN Reports: *"Sean Darks is the CEO of Citywatcher.com, a small company in Cincinnati. It's the first U.S. business to use chip implants in its employees. Chip implants have been common in pets for several years, giving the owners peace of mind that their lost animal could be identified. And for retail giant Wal-Mart, the chips are used as smart barcodes to keep track of thousands of products. But for use in people, well, privacy advocates think that we shouldn't open that door. Like it or not, we are in that Brave New World. And it might not be long before your boss is literally getting under your skin."*

Now, wait a second. You mean to tell me that even if I'm not willing to get a microchip implant, voluntarily, I might lose my job? Yup. Remember, it's like a frog in a pot. First you start at the end of the spectrum, and then you slowly work your way inward to your ultimate goal.

First it was a "mask" to keep our job, then it was the "vaccine" to keep our job. Now, here soon, it appears to be a "microchip" to keep our job!

And if you don't think the current administration, Joe Biden, Mr. Build Back Better, who works for Klaus Schwab, wouldn't ever "force" us into getting a "microchip implant," just like they already "forced" on us with the masks and vaccines, you better think again!

This is from a video from 2005 showing the conversation between Joe Biden and then candidate, Chief Justice John Roberts. And you tell me if they're not going to mandate microchipping here real soon!

Senator Joe Biden: *"We will be faced with consequences and decisions in the 21st century. Can a microscopic tag be implanted in a person's body to track his every movement? There's actual discussion about that. You will rule on that, mark my words on that, before your tenure is over."*

Dr. Katherine Albrecht, Consumer Privacy Expert: *"I think the real concern that most people have, is that at some point the government would say, 'Line up and get your chip.'"*

But hey, that'll never happen. And I quote, *"You will rule on that, mark my words."*

Folks, I don't know about you, but if the exact same two guys who are a part of "mandating" government run healthcare, and now "mandating" masks on your head and vaccinations in your arm, you really think they won't "mandate" microscopic tags being implanted into a person's body to track their every move? Are you kidding me? Get your head out of the sand! They just said it!

And that's what the Antichrist and the False Prophet are going to do in the 7-year Tribulation! That's how close we are! And all the people, and all the pieces are all in place now with Covid-19 as the excuse, just like Klaus said would happen.

And again, it's so apparent that this is what the Bible prophesied as the Mark of the Beast System that even secular reporters are starting to get it.

Lionel, Sir Veillance: *"Well, well, well. It seems like everyone is scared about the iPhone being able to track your every move. You do know, I warned you about this last year. But here is what you should really worry about. Watch, it will unfold like this. First, the RFID chip, the Radio Frequency Identification. It's already been put in credit cards, passports, license tags. They're everywhere. Watch while they have you implant them in your pets. Not an ID chip, but a tracker. Debated, but you will start to see more of them at your Vet's offices. OnStar your pooch. You can track your little doggie. Peace of mind.*

If it's good enough for your dog, it's good enough for your child. A tiny, little RFID chip, the size of a grain of rice, is completely safe, and easy to remove. Your child is now kidnap-proof. And the placement of the chip will be varied so, God forbid, some sicko doesn't look in one particular place to forcibly remove it. OnStar your child. No more Amber Alerts, no more kidnapping, no more parents' worst nightmare. After all, if it's good enough for your pet, it's good enough for your child.

And the elderly. Forget that 'I've fallen and I can't get up' business. No, no, it's the RFID chip that will have all of grandma's medical information data on it. If they have Dementia and wander off, you'll be able to track them. After all, if it's good enough for your dog ...

Then once it's deemed cool, teens will insist on their own chip. They are already tattooing barcodes. It's cool. You've got your own number, and this will be your own chip. All of your information, all the stressful medical information - What information? She's 20 years old! - is for your own good. You can track them. You know, kids won't wear watches anymore. What? They have cell phones with the time on it. And with your cool chip, there's no need for driver's licenses, credit cards, debit cards, keyless entry, ID. No, the RFID chip will have it all there. All of it. Goodbye wallet. After all, what's a wallet for? ID, cards. Not anymore.

Oh, and money. We will be completely cashless. Terminals will read your chip. Think of an easy metro card. No cash, no drug trafficking, no terrorism. Make any connection you want. No one's listening anyway. Then you will beg for one. Everything will be on the chip. Everyone is on the grid. The grid is 24/7, real-time tracking of you. Everyone will have this cool chip. Everyone is on the grid. And if you're convicted of breaking some law, they don't send you to prison. They turn off your chip. Poof! You don't exist. No money, no identity, no existence. And you're worried that your iPhone is being tracked. You ain't seen nothing yet!"

Yeah, you're right. Because it's going to lead to the Mark of the Beast system in the 7-year Tribulation, which is what Klaus, and the gang are building right before our very eyes, with the Covid-19 Plandemic as the excuse.

In fact, speaking of the Covid-19 Plandemic scam, let's take a look at even more evidence that this biological lie is being used to move us towards a "global mandate."

If you recall, overnight, because of the Covid-19 Plandemic, cash became bad, evil, and dirty. Why, it could have germs on it! No! And that's why it started to disappear on purpose during that time, remember that?

"This Everyday Staple (CASH) May Become Extinct After COVID-19, Research Shows."

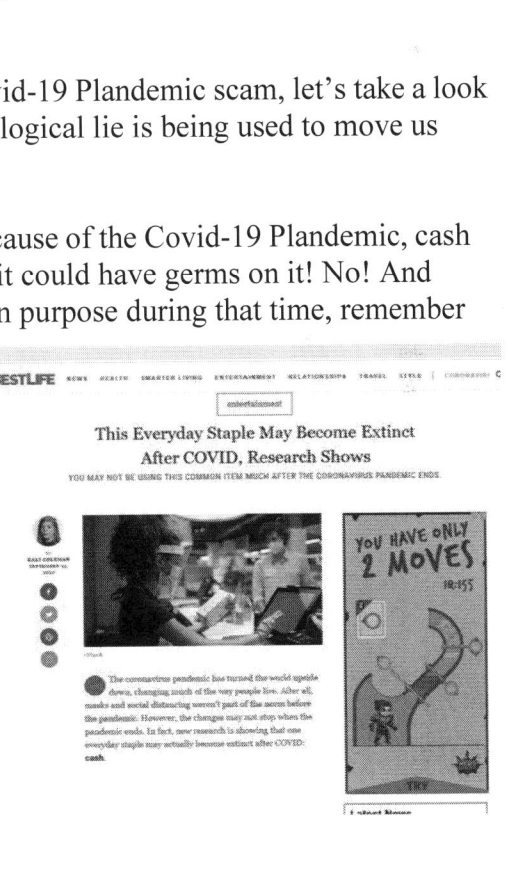

"The coronavirus pandemic has turned the world upside down, changing much of the way people live. After all, masks and social distancing weren't part of the norm before the pandemic.

However, the changes may not stop when the pandemic ends. In fact, new research is showing that one everyday staple may actually become extinct after Covid-19: cash.

But why is cash being exiled during the pandemic? According to a study published in The Lancet, the coronavirus can survive on a banknote for up to four days. And Vandana A. Patel, MD, clinical advisor for Cabinet, a health essentials company, previously told Best Life, that cash is even worse during the pandemic, because it is exchanged through many hands every day, and not that easy to keep clean."

But here they are using the Covid-19 Plandemic to get rid of cash.

Narrator: *"Money changes hands all the time, but can it carry the Coronavirus? The answer is, most likely. A study in the New England Journal of Medicine found out how well this Coronavirus survives on different surfaces - on plastic, which is what Canadian money is made of. The virus stays viable for days. So, someone wipes their nose with the virus, their hand pulls out a $20 to buy some toilet paper, and later that day you get this $20 back as change. So, if you have a choice between cash or credit..."*

A woman's opinion: *"I do think that in the interest of just the anxiety of everybody who is working in our essential stores, our pharmacies, our grocery stores, that need to be open, I think it's a kindness to them, if we all start using debit and credit cards."*

Narrator: *"And either way, after handling anything, remember to wash your hands afterwards."*

Action News Reports: *"Well, experts say the Coronavirus can remain on surfaces like cash for up to 10 days, but as so many people worry about shopping and other everyday tasks, our Action News reporter Dann Cuellar, has an angle for us tonight, bowing in from a shopping center with more on this."*

Dann Cuellar: *"This raises new concerns with people handling cash, and why they should be taking precautions to be on the safe side. Paper money, if you stop and think about it, there are many hands and places that cash comes in contact with on a daily basis. And yes, the experts tell us what some might expect. Diseases and viruses, such as Covid-19, can be transmittable through money that has been handled by an infected person."*

Dr. Jonathan Stallkamp, Main Line Health: *"The viruses will survive, viruses in general, will survive on surfaces for different amounts of time."*

Dann Cuellar: *"And that would include a porous surface such as cash."*

Dann Cuellar, on the street: *"Did you know that?"*

Woman on the street: *"No, I didn't know that."*

Sheree Marshall, West Philadelphia: *"It's already gotten paranoid out here. So, I'm in here getting hand sanitizer and bleach. I don't know. Maybe I will start wearing gloves."*

Man on the street: *"It just makes you want to only use a credit card or a debit card."*

And that's exactly what it was designed to do. Make you think "cash is bad." We better go to "electronic payments." And notice it was the same contrived message in different countries. And it worked!

"A survey of a little over 2,000 Americans found that more than half of the respondents (58 percent) think the country should move to a cashless system. And exactly half of the respondents admitted they were using less cash now than they were using prior to the coronavirus pandemic."

And that's also why you started seeing articles like this around the world.

"Cashless society: Cash could disappear from the UK by 2026."

"Coins and banknotes could disappear from the UK by 2026 as the coronavirus pandemic has accelerated, 'the journey to a cashless society,' a new study suggests.

New Covid-19 measures meant that retailers and shoppers across the country have been opting for card payments or an e-wallet over cash during the pandemic, to limit contact and curb transmissions of the virus.

As a result, cash usage fell by 38.1%, with the UK predicted to be cashless by 2026, according to Merchant Machine."

And then this article shares this,

"Norway Says Goodbye to Cash."

"Norway ranks first place among the countries least reliant on cash in 2022, next to Finland and New Zealand. These are closest to a completely cashless society.

Cash accounts for only 2% of all payments in Norway and 100% of its population own a bank account.

Finland follows Norway, with the same small percentage of cash payments, and none of its unbanked citizens.

On the other side of the globe, New Zealand is also giving up cash, coming in 3rd position."

And that's also why, during this time, with the Covid-19 Plandemic as the excuse, we saw this trend exploding as well, with industries like Amazon who also works for Klaus Schwab and the gang, being rewarded for their cooperation.

Yahoo Finance Reports: *"Another tech giant that we are following closely is Amazon shares. Amazon shares are trading up more than 4% right now, following its second quarter earnings. A lot of that has to do with the pandemic buying spree that we have seen, especially with everyone being locked down at home. We are joined now by Charlie O'Shea from Moody. I think you, like many people, are blown away by the earnings report here. What is your reaction to it?"*

Charlie O'Shea, Moody's Vice President: *"You pretty much said it. It was way beyond what we thought. When the company tells you, we are going to lose a billion five or make a billion five, or somewhere in the middle, and they pop a five billion plus, that's a little shocking."*

ABC News Prime Reports: *Amazon has had a banner year with the rise in online sales, of course due to Covid-19, expanding warehouse operations and adding to its network of distribution centers across the country. While consumers log low prices in delivery, Amazon's growing influence in small towns and the halls of power in Washington DC has changed nearly every aspect in American life."*

Amy Goodman, Democracy Now Reports: *"As the Covid-19 pandemic keeps many of us sheltering at home and shopping online, the online giant, Amazon, said Monday that it will hire 100,000 more workers to meet the growing demand. Amazon CEO Jeff Bezos has made an extraordinary amount of money during the crisis. He saw his personal wealth increase by $48 billion between March and June alone. He is now the first person in the world to be worth $200 billion."*

And there's your payoff for selling your soul to Klaus Schwab and the gang. You got your money. And it's not that hard to make so much money when the Covid-19 Plandemic was also used as an excuse to close all the mom-and-pop stores and brick and mortar small business stores. You know, Amazon's competition.

And it's this mutually beneficial relationship between Amazon and Klaus Schwab, and the World Economic Forum and the Global Elites that is also why we saw Amazon pushing these megalomaniac's cashless payment systems, like this one from Amazon, called Amazon One.

It too is helping to pave the way for the cashless payment system of the coming Great Reset, or what the Bible calls the Mark of the Beast.

Narrator: *"This is Zoie. Just like you, she uses lots of different cards to get through her day. What if all Zoie needed was herself? Introducing Amazon One. A free service that lets you use your palm to quickly pay for things, for access, for rewards, and more. Let's say you're grabbing your favorite coffee beverage, or heading into the office, or checking out. Just hover your palm, and you're on your way. It's as easy as that, and sign-up is free. And takes less than a minute. All you need is a credit card, a phone number, and your palm. That's it!*

Since your palm is unique and can't be lost or replaced, you can do it quickly and securely. And with more experiences on the way, Amazon One will help you get even more done, simply by being you. Now Zoie has more time to do what she loves, indoor skydiving. Enter, identify, and pay with Amazon One."

KRON 4 Reports: *"If you don't have your wallet, there's no problem, just scan your palm to pay. Amazon One is a payment system that has been tested at several stores in the Bay Area, and now it may be coming to a grocery store near you. KRON reporter Justin Campbell has more on how it works and the privacy concerns."*

Justin Campbell: *"The idea of using your palm to pay doesn't feel right for this Whole Foods customer, but others like the idea. The technology coming to the Bay Area Whole Foods stores over the next few weeks works like this. Amazon says no two palms are alike. They use vision technology. You hold your hand above the device. The scan takes less than a minute to create a palm signature. Your palm is connected to your credit card online, so whenever you want to pay, all you have to do is hover your palm."*

And notice, it was the "right hand." None of this is by chance folks. It's all carefully scripted to get you to go down the preprogrammed route they want you to go. And the Covid-19 Plandemic was the trigger to start it all and the ongoing excuse to put it all into play.

In fact, it's getting so obvious, where all this push for cashless biometric payment systems is going, that again, even the non-Christian community can figure it out, like this guy did.

Narrator: *"Listen everybody, big tech Amazon is expanding their biotech capacity by scanning our palms and getting our data. Is this just for your convenience, or do you think Amazon has other objectives?"*

Newscaster: *"Amazon is ramping up its contactless payment system nationwide that works by scanning the palm of your hand."*

Narrator: *"The palm of your hand. (He holds up his hand.) There it is. That's the palm right there. I see you baby. (And he kisses his hand)."*

Newscaster: *"All it takes is a person to hover their palm over the device and done. Your groceries are paid for."*

Narrator: *"All you gotta do is, there's this little device down here - not like it literally says in the Bible, 'The Mark of the Beast' will be rendered in the palm of your hand, or anything like that. No! Don't worry, just walk face first into Armageddon without question. It's convenient to have an apocalypse."*

"Now you can pay with your face and with your hand, isn't that cool? Revelation 13."

Headline News: *"The technology, Amazon One, first rolling out in Amazon's home market of Seattle, will use people's palms to identify them and combine that with details of the palm such as lines and ridges to build a 'palm signature.'*

"'In most retail environments, Amazon One could become an alternative payment or loyalty card option with a device at the checkout counter next to a traditional point of sale system,' Dilip Kumar, Vice President, Amazon Physical Retail, wrote in the post, 'Or for entering a location, like a stadium or badging into work. Amazon One could be part of an existing entry point to make accessing the location quicker and easier.'"

"Mastercard on Tuesday launched a program that allows retailers to offer biometric payment methods, like facial recognition and fingerprint scanning.

Users can authenticate a payment by showing their faces, or the palm of their hand instead of swiping their card.

The technology could one day help with the development of payments infrastructure for the 'metaverse,' an executive said."

"Mastercard is piloting new technology that lets shoppers make payments with just their face or hand at the checkout point.

This program has already gone live in five St Marche grocery stores in Sao Paulo, Brazil. Mastercard says, it plans to roll it out globally later this year.

'All the research that we've done has told us that consumers love biometrics,' an executive said."

Revelation 13:16-18: *"And he causeth all, both small and great, rich and poor, free and bond, to receive a mark in their right hand, or in their foreheads: and that no man might buy or sell, save he that had the mark, or the name of the beast, or the number of his name. Here is wisdom. Let him that hath understanding count the number of the beast: for it is the number of a man ..."*

Yeah, even they can figure out where this is headed. And notice, everybody's jumping on the bandwagon, not just Amazon, and they're saying it's going "global," with these "hand" and "face" payments, real soon. I'm sure that's a coinkadink!

And again, lest you think this obvious push for a cashless society and cashless payment systems, with the Covid Plandemic as the excuse, isn't being spearheaded by Klaus Schwab and the World Economic Forum and the gang, watch this next video transcript and listen to them say how it will usher in the Universal Basic Income system (spoken of earlier), that they are planning on implementing around the world to create a society where "You will own nothing and be happy" and how it will be not only based on cashless payments, but payments tied together with "biometrics." Or in other words, your body parts - you know, like your "hand" or your "head."

Discussion from the World Economic Forum 2017

"Welcome to everyone. The topic of this conservation is basic income for all, or dreamer delusion. If I can frame this subject just a tiny bit. Paid work is becoming less generous. It seems to be less generous in less reliable sources. Income to many people means a very old and radical

idea has come into the fold. The notion of an unconditional government payment to all citizens, as either a supplement to or replacement for paid working income. It's really happening. It's not just a theory. Can you just brief me from the governmental aspect? What is the attraction?

Amitabh Kant: *"We run into two very huge schemes. We run a public distribution system. It has been in operation for a very long time. Both of these schemes are full of leaks. There is a huge amount of corruption, embedded with rampant corruption. One of the unique things about India today, is that India has built up a huge infrastructure. One of the most revolutionary in terms of biometrics. I mean, every single individual in India today has a thumb. That means he has a biometric. He can either make a payment with his thumb impression or with his iris. So, you are heading for revolutionary changes in India. So, my basic assumption is, that if you were to look at doing away with the guaranteed scheme, which are inefficient, and the public distribution system, my belief is that it's much better to pay directly into the individual account rather than going through any middleman. You will be able to create a vast, unique infrastructure that doesn't exist in any other part of the world. You would be able to reach that person individually."*

In other words, it would go straight to the individual, this UBI payment, Universal Basic Income. And India's already got it set up with "all their citizens in the whole country" to receive it "biometrically" through the "thumb" or "hand" or the "iris" or "head." Anybody see where all this is headed?

That was back in 2017 at the World Economic Forum, talking about these Universal Basic Income payments, or UBI's, which they freely admitted, "It's really happening, it's not just a theory."

Apparently, all they needed was for the "right crisis" to come along three years later, the Covid-19 Plandemic, and they could start putting it all in place!

And this is why people are sounding the alarm on this Mark of the Beast, cashless payment system from Klaus Schwab and the World Economic Forum, as you can see here.

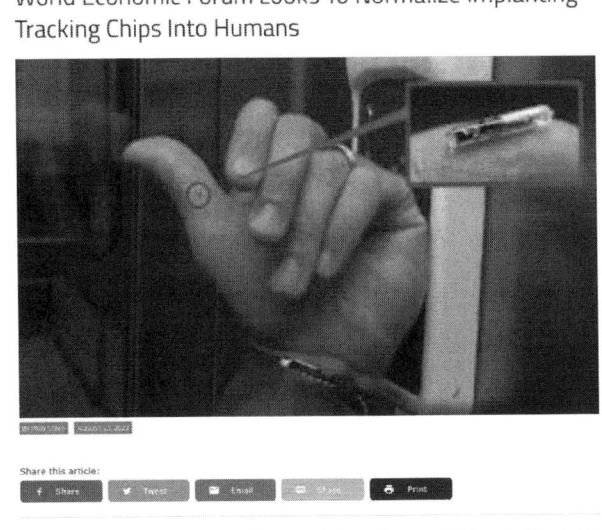

"World Economic Forum Looks To Normalize Implanting Tracking Chips Into Humans."

"The latest highly controversial technology/policy that the World Economic Forum has set out to normalize, is the idea of implanting tracking chips into humans."

It wasn't that long ago that those speculating on a future where this is happening would get dismissed as conspiracy theorists, but now the world elites' most vocal outlet is predicting that chip implants will eventually become just a commodity.

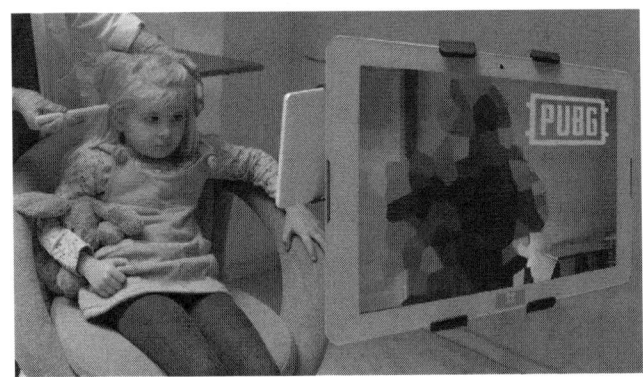

And the WEF makes a case, that implanting chips into children, could be viewed by parents as a 'solid, rational' move. They refer to it as 'an augmented society.'

Some of the 'visions' of the WEF, is replacing drugs with brain implants, that manipulate the body with electrical pulses, and pairing all sorts of chips put into humans through surgery, with sensors one might find in a chair.

And so, the human and the chair are 'seamlessly integrated,' and the quality of life across the board shoots up, as the Davos-based group promises.

They say chip implants form part of a natural evolution that wearables once underwent.

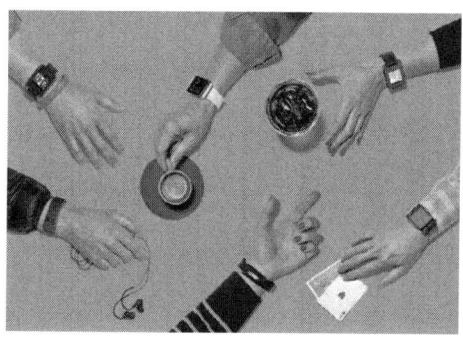

Hearing aids or glasses no longer carry a stigma. They are accessories and are even considered a fashion item.
Likewise, implants will evolve into a commodity.

While the tracking ability is one of the features of microchip implants, it is rarely talked about. Many people are already on board with using microchip implants for commerce and security access.

Recently, a London-based company has developed a new

contactless payment system that involves embedding a microchip into a person's hand.

Tech company Walletmor has developed a new app,

called Purewrist, which is a digital wallet combined with a microchip that can be installed in your hand. Once the chip is installed, a person can then use the app and chip to make payments to businesses that also use the app.

Walletmor's chip is about the size of a grain of rice and is composed of a microchip and an antenna. The company claims it's entirely safe and also has regulatory approval and says the system can be used to make every day normal transactions.

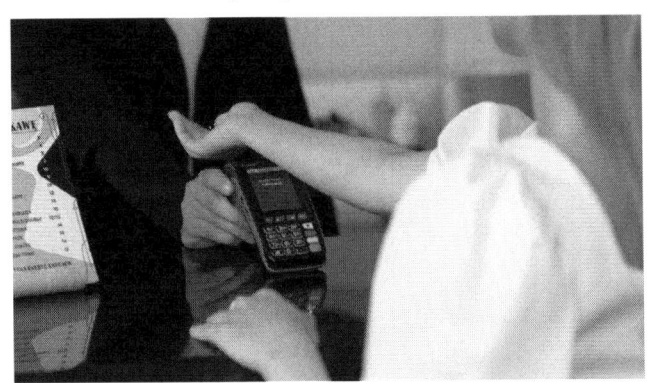

And as crazy as those sound, here's the biometric chip implant payment system in action!

Wojtek Paprota, Walletmor Founder & CEO: *"I'm going to show you how Walletmor works and what it's like after ordering a drink, food, or any other product. All you need to do is swipe your hand over a payment terminal. Forget about cash, card or even a smart phone. All you need is your hand. Walletmor is safe, secure, convenient, and they are globally acceptable. Walletmor is the wallet of tomorrow."*

Yeah, hurry up and join the Mark of the Beast system! And lest you think this advertising isn't having any effect on people, "A 2021 survey conducted in the European Union and the United Kingdom, came up with the result that at least 51% of people will consider having a chip implanted in their body."

And the Covid-19 Plandemic just made it that much more convenient! And "On the other side of Europe, Sweden has been rapidly expanding its use of microchip technology for quite some time, with tens of thousands already microchipped."

Narrator: *"When Elias goes to work, he doesn't need ID. And he doesn't need money. In fact, much of what he needs to get through the day is hidden right there, just below the surface in his hand. Embedded in his hand is a microchip that serves as his keys, his ID and his wallet."*

Elias: *"Yes, it's all in the chip. I use it to get around the building. To get a soft drink, and all I have to do is activate my chip, and then I have access to a drink."*

Narrator: *"Popular TV shows like Black Mirror have imagined chips as a part of utopian future. In Sweden, the microchip is already here. The microchip implant uses the same technology as contact with credit cards which has made cash pretty much obsolete in Sweden. At this tech fair, a chipping event for those on the cutting edge, merging their hands with new technology."*

Lady at the fair: *"I thought it would be fun. Right?"*

Narrator: *"The process is simple and swift. A pinch of the skin and in a matter of seconds, the chip is inserted. Transformation is complete. As for the pain ..."*

Man getting the chip: *"I barely felt it."*

Narrator: *"Human microchipping might be in the future but for Sweden it's already a reality."*

Yup, this advertising has no effect on people. Yeah, whatever. It's all the rage now, and the Covid-19 Plandemic was used by Klaus Schwab and the gang to brainwash and seduce people around the world to go along with it. They know full well what they're doing!

In fact, "No cash accepted signs are now the norm in shops across Sweden as payments go digital, and many Swedes want to take it to the next level, as they blend tech with the human body.

Microchip implants give people the ability to conduct financial transactions, monitor their health (including vaccination status) and even replace keycards to allow them to enter offices and buildings, are the new rage, as thousands have already been implanted.

Many technological enthusiasts believe this is the next logical step in a digital society that is quite happy to give up privacy for convenience. In short, they have simply traded cash for chips." As you can see here.

Clara Grelsson, traveler: *"I think it's really good with a chip ticket. I love all companies that use the chip technology."*

SJ is the first travel company in the world to enable passengers to use microchip implants to validate their tickets.

Lina Edstrom, Customer marketing manager: *"The microchip implant technology is quite new, and it's growing in popularity. We at SJ, want to try out new technologies together with our customers and see what we can make out of it."*

The microchip uses NFC (Near Field Communication) technology. But how does it work?

Lina Edstrom: *"The customer writes their SJ Prio membership number on the chip. When the train crew scans the chip, they will see the ticket in their system. So, it's very convenient for the customer."*

There are about 2,500 – 3,000 people with microchip implants in Sweden today. So, why is SJ doing this?

Lina Edstrom: *"It came as a request from some of our business travelers, who wanted to use their microchip implant for train travel. We could accommodate that with some minor development. I'm really excited about this."*

Stephan Ray, Public Relations Officer: *"I think this can be a part of an exciting development, where we see future society free of keys, cards and paper to a great extent."*

Lina Edstrom: *"You got everything in your hand."*

Stephan Ray: *"It's a smarter society, and hopefully, a more sustainable society.*

Actually, it's a dumber society falling for the Mark of the Beast society. That's where all this is headed folks. And Klaus Schwab and the gang are behind it all with the Covid-19 Plandemic as the excuse to make the global transition.

Chapter Thirteen

World Economic Forum & the Chip Implants

In fact, let's take a look at even more proof that this really is the goal of Klaus Schwab and the gang, including with the kids.

"World Economic Forum Pushes Chip Implants for Children, Comparing Them to Eyeglasses & Hearing Aids."

"The wacky doctors, evil and almost comical, wicked villains at the World Economic Forum, are now pushing chip implants on the world's children. What's even more concerning is how they are doing it.

Superheroes have been dominating big and small screens for a while, but there's a subtle change happening. Many children expect to develop superpowers themselves.

These expectations may sound unattainable, but we're already making the first strides towards an 'augmented society.'

This can be defined as the extension of rehabilitation where technological aids, such as glasses, cochlear implants or prosthetics are designed to restore a lost or impaired function.

Add it to completely healthy individuals and such technology can augment. Night goggles, exoskeletons and brain-computer interfaces build up the picture.

Augmenting technology will help in all stages of life: children in a learning environment, professionals at work and ambitious senior citizens. There are many possibilities.

Technology will become more intertwined with the body in the form of implants, but it will also seamlessly integrate with the environment – you might have sensors in a chair, for example."

There's that term again! But here they are promoting chip implants for all ages, for all kinds of different purposes.

Narrator: *"Glasses, Cochlear Implants, Prosthetics, are designed to restore a lost or impaired function. Add them to completely healthy individuals and such technology can augment.*

- *Exoskeletons help you carry heavy loads.*
- *AR goggles enhance your surroundings.*
- *Phones open a world of information.*

Future technologies will become more intertwined with our bodies in the form of implants. Implants, such as pacemakers or brain implants, are in the first place – a medical necessity. But will implants find their way in other aspects of daily life – and become more commonplace?

- *A translation chip for dyslexia?*

- *A chip that counters brain diseases like Parkinson's or Alzheimer's?*
- *Or what about a chip that can detect traces of nuts for those with an allergy?*

One thing is clear: Technology will not be the limiting factor. Instead, boundaries will be drawn in the ethical debate. How do we build an ethical framework for a technology augmented society?

There's that term again, "augmented society," which translated means everybody gets a microchip in Klaus Schwab and the World Economic Forum and Global Elite's Mark of the Beast system they're building for the actual Antichrist, that God warned about in the Bible nearly 2,000 years ago!

This is nuts! And if you don't think the Covid-19 Plandemic, or any other planned pandemics they might have up their sleeve in the near future won't be used to push this microchipping of the planet even further, listen to this.

Quote, *"Generally, implants will be linked to medical conditions. They can be handy to sniff out Covid-19 or food allergens. There is no immediate reason to implant this extra sensor into your body. However, a deadly peanut allergy may justify a more permanent solution."*

Or another plandemic! Do you see where all this is headed? And you don't have to be a rocket scientist let alone even wonder where all this is headed because, speaking of scientists, Klaus Schwab's science advisor, Yuval Noah Harari, tells us exactly where we're going.

Yuval Noah Harari: *"Especially the rise of brain computer interfaces and biometric sensors, and so forth. It is very likely that, say, within 50 years, people will literally be part of a network. All the bodies, all the brains, would be connected together to a network, and you won't be able to survive if you are disconnected from the net because your own body parts, your own immune system, depends on being constantly connected to* *the colony, to the net. Not everybody will be able to upgrade themselves. Not everybody will have access to or have control over the new big data algorithms of 8 billion people in the world. The vast majority will stay just ordinary homo sapiens, and they are likely to lose their economic value, their political power, their control over their lives. And we are likely to see an extremely unequal society in which a very small group of elites, either of upgraded humans or of those humans who own the master algorithms, like the Google algorithm or the Facebook algorithm.*

We are very close to the point when computers can hack human beings and can understand my emotions, my likes and my dislikes, better than me. Not perfect. You don't need to be 100%. You just need to know humans better than they know themselves. And this is quite easy because most people don't know themselves very well. So, just imagine what happens when ..."

Interviewer: *"So, as soon as the algorithm knows what I want, better than what I know."*

Yuval Harari: *"You're a prophet. It can manipulate you. It can press your emotional buttons, and this is what is happening now with our smart phones and all the algorithms on social media."*

Interviewer: *"Is that why you don't have a smart phone?"*

Yuval Harari: *"That's one of the reasons."*

Yeah, got caught with a question that exposes the real motives, didn't you, you liar! But at least, on the one hand, he's telling us where they're taking us with all these chip implants, step-by-step.

"So just imagine, when the algorithm, or AI (Artificial Intelligence), knows what I want, better than I know it, you're a puppet. It can manipulate you, it can press your emotional buttons, and this is what's happening with our Smart Phones and Social Media that also uses AI technology."

And these microchip implants will connect us to this Borg-like existence, where we are just a manipulated "cog in the machine," working for Klaus Schwab and the gang.

Again, that doesn't sound like Utopia to me! And that's why Jesus said, it's going to be the worst time in the history of mankind during the 7-year Tribulation!

Matthew 24:21: "For then there will be great distress, unequaled from the beginning of the world until now – and never to be equaled again."

And if you think the "borg analogy" is a little too extreme with Klaus Schwab and the World Economic Forum's pushing for microchipping the whole planet, then listen to their own words. They admit it!

"World Economic Forum Recommends Humans Become Cyborgs, Implant Brain Chips: There Are 'Solid, Rational' Reasons for Children To Be Microchipped."

"The World Economic Forum is promoting 'augmentation technology' to morph humans into cyborgs and recommends children be implanted with brain chips.

Brain chips will not only improve health by eradicating impairments, like learning disabilities and depression, but pave the way for humans to attain superhuman capacities, contends an article published on the WEF website.

Superheroes have been dominating big and small screens for a while, but there's a subtle change happening. Many children expect to develop superpowers themselves.

Should you implant a tracking chip in your child? There are solid, rational reasons for it, like safety."

Or should we say, "slavery." And lest you doubt this "borg existence" isn't a part of their plan, Klaus himself also admits it.

World Economic Forum chief Klaus Schwab contends transhumanism, or merging man with machine, is imperative to achieving the "The Great Reset," or "The Fourth Industrial Revolution."

As Schwab told the Chicago Council on Global Affairs in 2019, *"What The Fourth Industrial Revolution will lead to is a fusion of our physical, digital and biological identities,"* as you can see here.

Klaus Schwab: *"It's at the end of what the Fourth Industrial Revolution will need is a fusion of our physical, our literal, and our biological identities."*

In other words, we're going to turn you into a "borg" where we will control every aspect of your life in this global Mark of the Beast system we're building for the actual Antichrist himself that the Bible warned about nearly 2,000 years ago!

In fact, as we saw earlier, during a recent Davos meeting, Pfizer CEO Albert Bourla, boasted about developing "ingestible pills," which, *"contain a tiny microchip that will notify authorities using a wireless signal when the pharmaceutical (or drug) is digested."*

Let's see that again, now in this "borg" context.

Albert Bourla: *"It is basically the biological chip that is in the tablet, and once you take the tablet and it dissolves in your stomach, it sends the signal that you have taken the tablet. So, imagine the implications, the compliance, that the medicines that the patient is supposed to take, they do. They take them. It is fascinating, what has happened in this field."*

Yeah, again, the understatement of the year! And of course, AI or Artificial intelligence will be the one managing the back end of this global cashless society, including the global microchipping "borg scenario" that the Bible calls the Mark of the Beast system. Because you can't hire enough humans to do all that on a global basis, but, for the first time in man's history, AI can!

But you can see that proof here:

"Artificial Intelligence Taking the World Towards the Perfection of Global Tyranny."

Which again, is why we encourage you to get our study called **The AI Invasion**. You need to get equipped on this issue. It's the backbone of the whole Mark of the Beast system Klaus Schwab and the World Economic Forum and his evil gang of Global Elites are creating for us.

But that's right. As alarming as all this proof is, what these guys are really up to, using the Covid-19 Plandemic as the trigger to get started and excuse to implement, don't worry, these masters of deceit are doing once again what they do best. They lie. They relabel their dastardly deeds for our duped consumption.

They say, "Don't worry. This push for a "borg cashless society intertwined with biometrics," that is, your body parts, specifically the "hand" or "head," it's not the coming Mark of the Beast system that the Bible warned about 2,000 years ago. No! It's just the new coming 'digital currency,' that's all. Trust us. It's not that simple."

Yeah, right. You are lying megalomaniacs! But doesn't that make you feel better? They just "relabeled" the Mark of the Beast system with "the new, coming digital currency," and it makes it all go away. I don't think so.

It's just another one of their lying, deceptive tactics to pacify our fears over what they're actually bringing to the planet. That is, creating an actual global financial prison planet over our everyday individual livelihoods.

Chapter Fourteen

World Economic Forum & the Digital Currency

In fact, here they are pitching this Mark of the Beast system, now called "digital currency," as the greatest thing since sliced bread! You don't want to miss it! Watch this propaganda.

Narrator: *"We use money every day. But we rarely appreciate its power, and its gloss. It's a tool that has been at the center of human progress, and as we build bigger and tackle complex problems, we are going to need the best tool available."*

Coinbase presents Cryptocurrency – The future of finance and money.

Balaji Srinivasan, CIO of Coinbase: *"We have a global economy, we are going to need a global digital currency."*

Brian Armstrong, Co-founder & CEO of Coinbase: *"Cryptocurrency is going to be a great democratizing force for the world because it is going to level the playing field and allow anybody with a cell phone to access financial services."*

Julia Rose West, Futurist and Coinbase Customer: *"This is going to transform how we think about a real global economy. I think in order to understand its importance, we first have to define what currency means.*

WHAT IS CURRENCY?

What currency does is it actually allows us to agree upon the value of something. It's almost like a communication tool."

Balaji Srinivasan: *"There are different ways of coordinating human beings. One way you can do that is with money. You can incentivize people to try to work at the same thing, at the same time."*

Linda Xie, Co-founder of Scalar Capital: *"We started off by building simple systems, like a bridge crossing a river, to very amazing things like rocket ships. We went from transacting our neighbors to transacting each other around the world, and we want to make sure that people can move money freely, and our current financial system doesn't enable that."*

CURRENT FINANCIAL SYSTEM

Preethi Kasireddy, Co-founder of TruStory: *"The current systems are very centralized, and so we have big things, big government, and we have a lot of middlemen who make things incredibly inefficient."*

Balaji Srinivasan: *"When you talk about the problems today in the financial system, you can go to places like Venezuela, where money is being printed and folk's savings are being destroyed. The value of their wealth has been completely eroded."*

Narrator: *"I think a lot of us, here in the United States, take it for granted that if somebody gives us money, it will be in our bank account, and it's not going to disappear or be taken away from us. And that is really a luxury that many people in the world don't have at all. There are about 1.8 billion people in the world today who have cell phones but don't have access to any financial services. What is really powerful about cryptocurrency, is that it lets anybody who has a smart phone or internet connection, participate in the global economy."

Preethi Kasireddy: *"What cryptocurrency does is it takes the liquidity that we have and gives it to the rest of the world."*

BENEFITS OF CRYPTOCURRENCY AND BLOCKCHAIN

Narrator: *"A more global economy is important, because there is talent everywhere, but opportunity is not evenly distributed."*

Preethi Kasireddy: *"In a world where this technology is fully adapted, it won't matter what country you are born in. All that will matter is that you have a mobile phone connection, and you have the skills and knowledge to contribute to the global economy. You can benefit from the world and the world can benefit from you."*

Julia Rose West: *"Think about what kind of economy we can have if we have a global currency that we are all responsible for and all invested in. It opens up opportunities for everybody."*

Narrator: *"Just being able to trust that if I do good work in the world and someone compensates me for it, I will be able to keep that wealth. It's such a powerful idea that it actually encourages people to try to do more good things in the world."*

Balaji Srinivasan: *"If you have lots of people in the world, who are invested in each other's success, literally, they are invested in each other's success at a broader level."*

Preethi Kasireddy: *"I think that cryptocurrencies are going to be as powerful to humanity as the internet has been."*

Balaji Srinivasan: *"Digital currency in Washington binds us in ways that we haven't been bound before."*

Yeah, you'll be bound alright. You'll be bound to the Mark of the Beast system. But hey, don't worry. This "digital currency" will solve all our global problems and bring peace to the planet! Yeah, right! It'll create a prison planet!

And notice how they freely admit that this will become "global." They openly admit they plan on merging all finances on the whole planet into one single, digital, controllable currency.

And can you guess who's been calling for that for years, as well as some sort of individual identifiable feature that connects people to it all? Hey, that's right! Shocker! It's Klaus Schwab and the World Economic Forum as you can see here.

"World Economic Forum Panel in the Value of Digital Identity for the Global Economy."

"In 2019, this panel at the World Economic Forum was speaking on digital identity and touted the convenience and efficiency of using digital identification.

Digital ID is already being used through a card and will be soon linked to the digital tattoo attached to the body, and the coming vaccine which will eventually administer an RFID chip, which will connect the Digital ID with every person's body in the world.

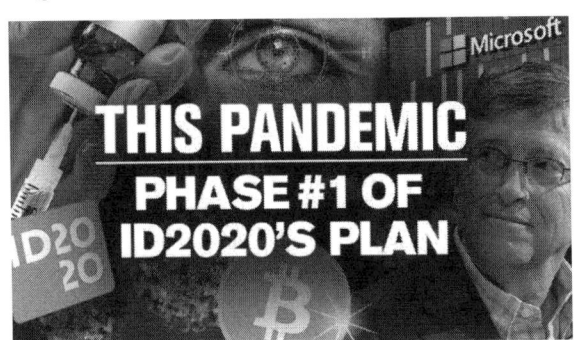

It is interesting that one of the panelists that represents the interests of Microsoft and Bill Gates, brings up ID2020 which is being developed by Gates, into what will be the digital tattoo.

This discussion may seem a bit boring at times, but it marks an open discussion of the agenda of the technology that will control the population of the world.

They talk about transparency and safety, but once this is developed into tagging every person in the world, I don't think anyone thinks that this will not be used for nefarious purposes, especially those that are familiar with Bible prophecy."

In other words, for those who have eyes to see and ears to hear. And just like the Mark of the Beast system that God warned about in the Bible, this new "digital currency" system, will literally control all aspects of "buying and selling."

First, "digital currency" will control "what" you buy. As seen here.

Best Business News Reports: *"More than a decade ago, bitcoin was created to solve a very specific computer-sized problem. The double-spend problem. And the creation of blockchain and bitcoin ended up kicking off a monetary revolution. We watched central bankers around the world sit back and see the global adoption of the decentralized digital currency. This obviously removes the central banker's control over the supply of money. Central banks have always had a monopoly on the production and distribution of money.*

Now they are seeing this new technology and they are trying to figure out how they can use this new tech to actually go ahead and cement their control moving forward. That's the creation of central bank digital currency. You see them talking about it, studying it, even piloting it in various places around the world. Central bankers want to be able to use tokenized money. It's the same fiat currency; there's no change to monetary policy. It's simply a technological upgrade to the exact same money. and it would put central bankers in control of your financial life.

There is a lot of nasty stuff in here. But before we get into what my personal thoughts are, recently Joe Rogan had a guest on his podcast who broke this down in great detail. Here is a little excerpt to get you up to speed on exactly what we are talking about."

Guest is holding a cell phone to let the audience listen to what is being said.

"He's speaking about how the G7 is launching a set of public policy principles for the retail central bank digital currencies, CBDC's. Central Bank Digital Currencies could be a digital version of money. A bit like a digital banknote that could be used..."

Guest: *"That's the guy who runs our economy in the UK, named the Chancellor of the Exchequer, and here is the article, 'Bank of England tells ministers to intervene on digital currency programming,' and here's a quote from the article. This isn't the telegraph, the one he pulled up, but it was behind the paywall. So, I'll just read the quote. 'Digital cash could be programmed to ensure it is only spent on essentials or goods, which an employer or government deems to be sensible.'"*

Best Business News Reports: *"So, here's the exact article that he's talking about. Quite literally, the title says, 'Bank of England tells ministers to intervene on digital currency programming. And what you can see, is giving the issuer control over how it is spent by the recipient. This is what I'm talking about when I say that nasty is coming to money. Ultimately, the central bankers will say who you can transact with, what* *you can purchase, when you can purchase, and if they don't like you, they don't like your ideas, they don't like past purchases you made ... maybe they think you're fat and you shouldn't buy candy. If they think that you gamble too much, maybe they don't want to allow you to pay for public transportation to go to a casino. It is totalitarian control over your financial life. If you don't have the freedom to transact, you're not free."*

And that's exactly the plan. But that's only the first thing switching to the seemingly innocuous "digital currency" will do.

Second, "digital currency" will control "how long" you can buy.

Narrator: *"In Digital Currency News: Yuan comes with an expiry date: Spend, or it will vanish." China is exploring an expiration date for its upcoming digital yuan, or DCUP, which means, the currency will expire, if not used within a certain timeframe. The digital yuan is programmable, to the point that the currency can be made to expire, thus forcing consumers to use it up by a certain date. This is a twist on an obscure, conventional monetary policy innovation, named Gesell currency: expiring money, which gives the issuing government a heightened degree of control over money velocity. If domestic consumption can be tightly controlled, then it's a way to not just increase the volume of consumption, but to control the variant of demand of goods that China produces. The digital yuan permits a new method for surveilling the population. Creating new data, which can be tracked by authorities."*

And again, that's the communist system that Klaus wants to bring to the planet, which as you saw, also includes an "expiration date" on your new "digital money."

So much for saving up so you can run and escape this prison planet. Yeah, that's exactly what you won't be able to do once it gets implemented, and that too, is a part of the plan.

But that's not all. **Third, "digital currency" will control "approved behavior" that is allowed to buy.**

CBN News Reports: *"China is pushing ahead into a cashless society. It's creating a digital currency to replace paper money and coins. It will also give the communist party total knowledge of how the Chinese people are spending their money. That opens the door for unprecedented government control. George Thomas has the story."*

George Thomas: *"The Chinese were the first in the world to invent paper money back in the 7th century. Now more than 1400 years later, China is again on the cusp of creating a new form of government currency, that some say could pose a serious economic threat to America and the West."*

CNA Insider Reports: *"China is about to launch one of the most revolutionary financial projects in the world. It's turning its physical coins and banknotes digital. Unlike most other cryptocurrencies like bitcoin."*

Erik Bethel, Fmr. U.S. World Bank Official: *"It's not cryptocurrencies. They are not so-called staple coins. In effect they are national, physical currency of a country, just represented in a digital form."*

CNBC Reports: *"Bitcoin, near record highs, brought to $23,000 ..."*

George Thomas: *"He says, while the world fixates on private cryptocurrency, like bitcoin."*

Newscaster: *"To begin with, the yuan isn't a payment system. It's actual money."*

George Thomas: *"Beijing is busy building a digital version of its own currency, the yuan, to control its citizens, and eventually threaten the dominance of the U.S. dollar."*

Erik Bethel: *"They pretty much created all of the building blocks that will allow a Central Bank digital currency to flourish."*

George Thomas: *"Yaya Fanusie, a former economic and counterterrorism analyst at the CIA, says, China's goal is to replace cash with a digital currency that is controlled by the communist government's central bank."

Yaya Fanusie, Former CIA Analyst: *"China has said for a while now that it pretty much expects to be a cashless society in the future. So, the idea is that cash notes, coins, will no longer be around, and the people will be using digital currency that will be in their wallets."*

George Thomas: *"That digital currency will also be issued by the government bank allowing what Congressman Michael McCall, the top Republican of the House Foreign Affairs Committee says is unprecedented access to people's financial transactions."*

Congressman Michael McCall: *"This will give them data, based on behavior and how they spend."*

George Thomas: *"And giving Beijing the power to track that spending in real time."*

Erik Bethel: *"There will be a point where the Peoples Bank of China is going to be able to look inside every single transaction and what everyone does, 24 hours a day, 7 days a week."*

George Thomas: *"Which means if you are a human rights activist or a Christian, authorities can now use this new technology to punish you if you engage in activities that they consider anti-government."*

Yaya Fanusie: *"This technological ability is something that the government has never had before. They always had to go to companies to say, 'Cut off this person.' Now the Chinese government, I think, at the proverbial flick of the switch, can make people fall in line by cutting off their access to money."*

George Thomas: *"The U.S. and other companies doing business in China, will be required to use the government's new digital currency payment system."*

Rep. Mike Waltz, (R) Florida: *"The Chinese government says, countries like Burma, Iran, North Korea and others who do business in that Chinese digital currency, will also allow China and those countries to work around one of our most powerful tools, which is sanctions."*

George Thomas: *"Based on history, Waltz believes that China is only too happy to share the technology with other world regimes that seek to enhance their own surveillance capabilities over their citizens."*

Rep. Mike Waltz: *"Know, that if those other countries - Africa, the Middle East and elsewhere - can dominate their people in line with the Chinese version of government, that data then comes back to Beijing, and so they will literally, through facial recognition, then be able to monitor the globe."*

CBN News Reports: *"Well, if you have ever wondered about some passages in the Bible, like how can a government restrict the population, so that you cannot buy or sell unless you have a particular mark, well, this is the answer. This is where we are literally being set up for that kind of government control."*

And that's again why we're doing this study. It's so obvious this is the "digital" Mark of the Beast financial system, that will be fully implemented in the 7-year Tribulation by the Antichrist that God warned about in Revelation 13, nearly 2,000 years ago!

And this again, is why other people who also have eyes to see and ears to hear, are blowing the whistle on this, "financial prison planet" that Klaus Schwab and the Global Elites are building for us, or should I say, the Antichrist.

Narrator: *"Central Bank Currency will control your life. Where you live, what you eat, where you travel, everything! Absolute control! You might be looking at me, thinking, who is this crazy conspiracy theorist? But don't take this from me. Take it directly from the head of the Bank for*

International Settlements. And fair warning, the clip that you are about to watch, is a bit disturbing."

Bank for International Settlements: *"With cash, and there is a huge difference there. For example, in cash we don't know, for example, who is using a 100 dollar bill today. We don't know who is using a 1,000-peso bill today. A key difference in the CBDC is that the central bank will have absolute control on the rules and regulations that will determine the use of that expression of central bank liability. And also, we will have the technology to enforce that. Those two issues are extreme."*

Narrator: *"You heard it directly. Absolute control. And the way that this would work is that in a cashless society the government's digital currency as a primary form of payment, it is very simple for a government to block a transaction or freeze your money. We don't have to imagine, because we can look directly at China and what has been going on over there for the last several years. China has a social credit system. Citizens will be given points or taken away based off of their behavior. If, for example if someone donates blood, or participates in charity work, they will be given points and rewards, like access to a free gym. Or shorter wait times in hospitals. But on the opposite side, if someone doesn't visit their aging parents, or they cheat in an online game or they spread rumors on the internet, they will be punished, and they lose certain privileges. For example, exclusions from flights or train tickets. Restricted access to public services...."*

One Chinese citizen: *"So, I tried to purchase a first-class ticket, but I was told my credit was too low to buy first class tickets."*

"No access to private schools and public shaming. It's really scary. And the reason that certain regions in China are able to do this program successfully, is because certain regions in China are nearing cashless societies."

Headline News: *"China's fully cashless society a step closer after two private banks end services for banknotes and coins."*

"The primary form of payment is digital, with popular apps like WeChat and Alipay. If you can control someone's money, you control their life. It's really scary and unfortunately, it's likely only going to get worse. China is at the forefront of CBDC."

Headline News: *"China to extend CBDC trial to most populous Province, Guangdong, the others report." "Official explains why China CBDC should not be as anonymous as cash." "China begins next phase of CBDC testing with e-CNY payment for payment transport."*

"They have been testing CBDC in several regions in China, and eventually when CBDC controls the entire country, China will have absolute control. There will be no running away. Everything that a user spends will be tracked, and money will be frozen or blocked at any moment. Now we're not talking about illegal activity. We're talking about activities that are simply frowned upon by the government. And China is not the only country working on this CBDC. More than half of the countries in the world are working on the CBDC and will likely grow over time.

I'm over here on the Atlantic Council CBDC tracker, and it shows all the countries around the world, and where they are currently standing with CBDC. We can see those who have already launched, those in pilot, those in development and many in research. If we look at the United States, they are currently in the research stage. In the First Crypto Regulatory Framework from the White House, they clearly outline that they are exploring a U.S. CBDC. But eventually it will be here. It's not just about the U.S. Many of you watching are not from the U.S. You are from different parts of the world, and CBDC's are coming.

So, what can we do to stop it? The answer is – NOTHING! They will be here. Some this year, some next year, some within the next five years."

Headline News: *"Israel, Norway and Sweden central banks, partner with BIS to explore CBDC payments."*

"When that happens, it's absolute control over your money."

Rich Planet TV Reports: *"The UK government will soon be introducing fundamental changes in how money works. The changes being formed by central banks around the world, including the UK central bank, The Bank of England. These changes, once introduced, will affect everyone."*

"So, what are these changes really about? The changes being proposed will mean that you will no longer have full control of your spending. In fact, what they are planning is the replacement of money. It is something fundamentally different. Therefore, it's not just cash they want to remove from the economy. It is money itself. Pay Attention!! Because if the new money system is allowed to happen, it will be very difficult to reverse and could mark the beginning of the end of human freedom.

The name of the new system is, Central Bank Digital Currency, or CBDC. It sometimes has other names, such as smart money. Here's how it works. Just imagine John wants to buy his daughter a birthday present from Argos. His mobile phone has a smart money wallet app on it, from which he pays 50 pounds for the product. The app communicates directly with the Central Bank of England and the money is transferred from his digital wallet to Argos' digital wallet in less than a second. The transfer of funds occurs at the time of purchase. And the transaction is recorded and approved by the centralized computer system on a centralized blockchain. A blockchain is a special computer program that records information very reliably and cannot be amended.

The centralized computer system runs continuously and can deal with hundreds of transactions per second as they occur throughout the entire continent, processing all of the public's purchases being made by millions of digital wallets. This sounds fantastic, and it's so much simpler and quicker than the old system. But there is a fundamental difference, which is that old transactions are centralized in real time, as they happen. In other words, one system will be able to know about every single digital transaction in the economy as the transactions occur. This is the critical difference with the new digital monetary system that everyone needs to be aware of. All transactions are centralized in real time, as they happen.

The people who are planning this new system have made it clear that it will be useful, in their eyes, to use Artificial Intelligence (AI), algorithms in real time to block certain public transactions for a range of different reasons. So, what does this mean for John? Let's just say there was another lockdown, and the government wants to stop the public from moving around the country. With this new system they could introduce a change which would mean John's wallet would only work if he was located within a certain distance of his own home. Argos is two miles from John's house, and he decides to go and buy his daughter a birthday present. He attempts to pay 50 pounds for the product with the app. The app communicates directly with the Bank of England's computer system, and the system rejects John's payment before it is made, because the system knows John is two miles from his own home and John's wallet is limited to spending within just one mile. John cannot now buy anything, unless he moves closer to his own home. His money is now useless if he wants to go anywhere.

Why doesn't John just use cash? That would be a good solution for John, as long as cash is still in use. So, how might this new system be introduced?"

Rich Planet TV Reports: *"The Prime Minister called an emergency meeting today to discuss the unprecedented slide in the economic recession in the UK and global economies. Inflation is out of control. And high interest rates are causing thousands of house repossessions. All of the over-the-counter cash purchases are now frozen and millions of people face losing their life savings as a number of banks are declared insolvent. The government and the Bank of England are accelerating the introduction of a new central bank digital currency, which all bank customers in the UK will be able to receive in exchange for their existing money, which in many cases is now unobtainable for mobile accounts. The governments say the new digital money will help the economy recover from recession. What we use to bail out, public and corporate money* currently held in millions of bank accounts, by banks, are at the point of collapse."

John: *"The ATM machine says, 'Cash unobtainable from this account.' It's frozen our money."*

Daughter: *"That can't be right. How much cash do we have?"*

John: *"We've got 120 pounds, and when that's gone, we have nothing."*

Daughter: *"I can't believe that the bank has frozen our money."*

John: *"We have 25,000 pounds in our account and no way of getting it back."*

Rich Planet TV Reports: *"Download your CBDC wallet app today and get bonus digital pounds free. If you transfer your bank funds into your digital wallet now, you will receive free digital pounds for each account you exchange. You can then spend from your digital wallet by using your phone app, exactly like a debit card. Download the free app now from the UK government website or the app store."*

John's wife: *"John, we need to download the digital wallet thing. See if we can get it in."*

John: *"We've got no other option. Well, it's transferred, and it's given us some bonus money. I can't believe it."*

John's wife: *"How do you know it will work?"*

John: *"It works, Luv. Everyone is using this money now. I'm going down to Tesco to try it out."* And he goes to the store.

Rich Planet TV Reports: *"Recent figures show that the public sees the cash comped in the last twelve months. Experts say that it is due to the success and sheer convenience of the new CBDC digital money. But the* *government has announced that all cash will be phased out completely over the next three years."*

John: *"I can't remember the last time I used cash. It seems so cumbersome and old fashioned, fiddling around with coins every time you want to buy something. It's much easier now."*

THREE YEARS LATER

John: *"Have you seen the remote control, Luv?"* As he is digging in the chair for the remote, he finds paper money. *"Look what I found. Remember these?"*

John's wife: *"What are you going to do with that?"*

John: *"Well, I don't know."*

John's wife: *"Why don't we keep it. I'll put it in a picture frame."*

Rich Planet TV Reports: *"Recent data from the annual climate change conference has revealed that there needs to be a drastic reduction in fossil fuel use to help protect against climate change. The government has announced that petrol and diesel use for all individuals in the UK will be purchased by using smart money. Each unit will be limited to a purchase of 15 liters per week, after which the wallets will be prevented from making any further purchases in that week.*

Growing concerns over obesity and bad health will be tackled by using the smart money network. The government proposes to limit the number of sugary items that the smart money can purchase in any given month."

John: *"What?!"*

Rich Planet TV Reports: *"Experts say that the new pandemic, which is ten times more contagious and deadly than Covid-19 Coronavirus, can only be defeated by minimizing all human contact and staying home as* much as possible. In order to enforce this, all digital wallets will only work within one mile of the address of which they are registered. Shopping times will be staggered so that you can only make purchases for a two-hour period each day. All non-essential purchases will be rejected.

The government, in a move to delay growth in the economy, is trying to ensure that all benefit money sent out to the public is spent within an appropriate time period. From the 1st of August, all benefit payments including the new social credits, should be spent within two-months of receiving them. Benefit monies will expire and be of no use if not spent within the two-months period."

John: *"They have put a shelf life on money."*

Rich Planet TV Reports: *"Vaccination uptake on the latest pandemic is now at 95%. Anyone who has not been vaccinated will have restrictions placed on their wallet. For the 5% unvaccinated, spending will only be allowed at certain times and only one mile from home. Certain goods, such as alcohol, travel tickets and such purchases will not be available for those who have not been vaccinated. And their digital wallets will not work outside the UK.*

Concerns are growing for people who grow their own food outside of government approved companies. The government will be restricting the purchase of all feed and other farming products to anyone who is not a registered farmer."

John: *"What are they doing that for?"*

Rich Planet TV Reports: *"The government is trying to reduce the amount of red meat people eat in their diet, for environmental and health reasons. Digital wallets will only be allowed to purchase eight ounces of red meat per week.*

In order to protect the environment, the government is introducing limitations on the amount each wallet will be able to spend on the following products: aerosol cans, coal, meat, chocolate, fish and coffee.

In a move to encourage good behavior, the government is awarding digital currency direct to your wallet if you report on anyone who is breaking any lockdown rules. All reports on individuals expressing extremist views may, in turn, have restrictions placed on their wallets."

John: *"What does that mean, extremist views?"*

Narrator: *"If you give up your cash, you will give up freedom for yourself, and you will give up the freedom of generations to come. It's not the convenience of the new money that is important. What is important, is the fact that centralized administration of smart money could be used to control every aspect of your life."*

And that's what the Bible calls the coming Mark of the Beast system, and that's exactly what Klaus Schwab and the gang are building right before our very eyes, around the globe, in all countries, with the Covid-19 Plandemic as the trigger to start it, and the excuse to implement it.

Boy have we been duped! And lest there be any doubt this new, seemingly innocuous "digital currency" is going to be used to usher in total Global financial tyranny that the Bible says will one day be used by the Antichrist and False Prophet to control all the "buying and selling" on the whole planet, here again, are these same Global Elites talking about how this change to a single, global digital currency is going to help create a Global Government at the, wait for it, World Government Summit back in 2022.

Dr. Pippa Malmgren, Economist, Former U.S. Presidential Advisor: *"Well, it might be a little bit late for that. I remember talking to an Australian diplomat about this break between the U.S. and China. and he said, both sides are going to say, 'Whose team are you on?' And he said,* our job is to make sure the question never arises. But the question has arisen. So, I think we have to go deeper. It's not about the U.S. versus China. It's about what underpins the World Order. It's always the financial system. I was very privileged. My father was the advisor to Nixon when they came off the gold standard in '71, so I was brought up with sort of an inside view. I learned how very important the financial structure is to absolutely everything else.

What we are seeing in the world today, we are on the brink of a dramatic change, where we are about to, and I'll say this boldly, we are about to abandon the traditional system of money and accounting and introduce a new one. The new accounting is digital. It means having an almost perfect record of every single transaction that happens in the economy, which will give us far greater clarity over what's going on. But I see our superpowers introducing digital currency. The Chinese were the first, and the U.S. is on the brink. We are moving in the same direction and the Europeans are committed to that as well.

The question is, will that new system of digital money and digital accounting accommodate the competing needs of all the citizens of all these locations? Because that is the only measure of whether a World Order really serves."

Listen to this: *"My country was the first, where they made cash illegal. 2016, digitalization was forced in the country. 8:00 in the evening, announced at midnight, cash was illegal, the big notes, and 70% of the economy crashed. This digitalization is now going all over the world, and there's a war on cash, because cash is merely a medium of exchange. It has no value in of itself. It's just a promise. You read the dollar note. It says, 'I promise to pay the bearer,' even when it's digital, even a credit card, you know you're giving rents to the global financial system. But, when it's cryptocurrency in the hands of algorithms and in the hands of big tech, they will do what is happening in China. Create a social credit system to decide a new cost system. And you might have also followed this while all that has been happening.*

The founder of the WEF wrote a book, called 'The Great Reset,' on how to deal with the Covid-19 crisis. And everything that is unfolding is part of The Great Reset."

In other words, this push for a "digital currency" is all part of Klaus Schwab, the World Economic Forum, and these Global Elites' plan to use the Covid-19 Plandemic as the catalyst and/or global crisis, to usher in this "reset" of the "global economy."

And this new "digital currency" will help create that One World Government, a One World Economy, and a cashless society that requires biometric body parts to activate that the Bible calls the Mark of the Beast system.

It's as plain as you can get. All the pieces are falling into place! And as dumb and dangerous and deceptive as all this is, as you've been seeing, while we're all being apathetic or distracted, it's already being launched around the whole planet.

Chapter Fifteen

World Economic Forum & the Digital Scoring System

But once again, don't worry! They've come to our aid to alleviate our so-called unfounded fears over this total financial control of our individual livelihood by this new "controllable" and "programmable" "digital currency."

You see, there's nothing to be afraid of, because it's just the new "Social Credit Score System" you've been hearing about. Or the new "ESG or Environment Social Government System" that will help save the planet from blowing up! And you don't want that to happen, do you?

Yeah, right! Let's expose that relabeling lie as well! Starting with the "Social Credit Score System." What is that all about?

Narrator: *"China's Social Credit Score System. Now a lot of people either try to make excuses for it, or they try to talk about how bad it actually is. I'm here to tell you that it's probably not what you think, but, in fact, it's probably much worse than you think. Everyone tries to make this comparison between China's social credit system to the episode of Black Mirror, or the one that is basically in a utopian future where* *everyone has this app, and they are basically rated on their popularity. Whether people like them and they are rated on a 5-stars, and they are segregated as such.*

For example, a car rental company won't rent to people below a certain score. People will judge you for being below a certain threshold, not inviting you to events. Some might keep you from jobs. But all this is based on the ability of everybody else being able to rate each other. So, it's not really the same as China's social credit score system.

In China, nobody is rating each other. Another misconception that I would like to get out of the way first, comparing it to the credit score system in the U.S., like FICO. Most people are familiar with the financial credit score that rates your financial trustworthiness. It's intended to give creditors an indication of risk, and how likely you are to pay or repay your loan commitment. However, outside of transactions, of that bad credit score does not prevent you from seeing your family or enrolling your kids in public school. In China, an individual's finance, social media activities, credit history, health records, online purchases, tax payments, legal matters and people you associate with, in addition to images gathered from China's 200,000,000 surveillance cameras and facial recognition software. By the way, do the math. That is one surveillance camera for every 7 citizens.

So, what I want to talk about today is actually how your social credit score is rated, what it means for you, how you gain and lose points and how the tier system, that caste system that they created, actually affects people in China. I actually found the framework in the document used by the Chinese government, to roll out their social credit system. So, keep in mind that this is how the social credit system is being experimented with, and eventually how it was rolled out in other areas. So, this is in its purest form.

The government basically handed out 1,000 points to its citizens. They are kept by local communist party officials. This is their baseline. So, you can either go above 1,000 or below 1,000. But basically, before we talk about what gives and takes away points, I want to tell you how their tier system works. So, it's very ironic that in China, a communist country, people are rated based on their credit worthiness. Right? So, they have this tier system, this caste system, that puts people either really high up or really low. The highest tier is called AAA. Of course, that is the best. It is called the model of credit worthiness. If you have 1,050 points or higher it means you went above the baseline. You get some benefits, right? The second tier is called AA for exceptional credit worthiness. This has basically the same benefits as AAA, but the next level is the A credit worthiness. This one comes with three flavors, A+/A/A-. This is when you are kind of hovering around what they handed out in the beginning. This is usually to your benefit. You get to be entered on a list that you use as a model in publicity. You give the government the ability to show you as a model citizen. For publicity, wow!

You get priority school enrollment and other social assistance. This is scary. It's a huge Chinese social program that they have. You have to get an A to get priority assistance in these things. School enrollment is supposed to be completely non-competitive in terms of what school you go to outside of your grade. So, now it's changing to that if you are not a good model citizen, your kids don't get to go to good schools. Which is terrifying. You get preferential care with employment, social assistance. You get preference over equally qualified competitors and attention, so this is in jobs and work and things like this. Oh, and by the way, I'm not talking about some secret speculation. These are official documents that say if you are an A, you get treated like a better person.

The next is relatively credit worthy. That's when you dip below 1,000. You are locked into it for two years. What happens now, if you are a B, you are probably going to get lectures and visits from government officials, and they are going to tell you how you can improve your score. You are going to be locked into probation for two years. Now, when you drop down to a C, that's when you're at 600-849 points, you are locked in there for three years before you move up to even a B. More visits from officials. They are going to be watching you to make sure you are watching your behavior. They are going to be scrutinizing you in your daily life. You're on a list now. Now this list won't go to the public with all the information - address, age, what you did wrong - but it will go to other government officials. So, they say, it will go to a limited audience.

Now, when you drop to the lowest tier that is a D. This is called Not Credit Worthy. Basically, it's like you are emitting gasses and are untouchable. You are locked into level D for five years. When you are locked into D, you are talking about officials coming to visit you all the time. They can cancel any government funding that you have. Not just temporarily suspend it, they are canceling the government subsidies. You go on a blacklist, and this is public. All of these will go public. So, it goes public, publicly disclosing the information on their untrustworthiness list. They can revoke all of your titles. If you have a PhD or a scientific discovery, whatever, you will have that erased. You can't get a loan, and you can actually lose your job over this. So, if it is tied to what happened, or what you did to be untrustworthy, according to the government, they can actually completely get rid of your qualifications and strip away your job.

So, you are locked in there for five years but what you have to understand is that there are all kinds of direct judgment factors. So, the Chinese government actually says that if you commit an intentional crime, this brings you to the bottom of the list. It's not like some sort of sliding scale. If you went out there and did something bad on purpose, you would just go straight down to D.

Now, let me make this super clear. If you are a political dissident, or you speak out against the government, you're screwed either way. The communist party of China will just lock you up or disappear you. This is not a country where there is a rule of law. It's more of a system to coerce and influence future behavior, and to standardize it for greater and ultimate control over the population.

So, now that you know all of these tiers, I wanted to break it down and make it super easy as to the ways you can gain or lose them. There are a thousand different ways you can gain or lose points. I will just highlight a *few picked at random. I want to take the average Zhou, and we're going to make two of them. We are going to make Good Zhou, and we're going to make Bad Zhou. They are both going to start with 1,000 points. We are going to go through some of the things that they are going to do that are good, and some that are bad, with the same baseline and see where they end up.*

If you overdraft on your credit card or your bank, it's minus 10 points. If you return lost money, and that is probably money to the government, by the way, that's plus 10 points. If you use WeChat, forums, blogs, or any other internet technology, or just say, the internet, that is minus 50. That's just negative information according to the government. If you disseminate false speech, insight, or cause trouble in groups, however, not like person to person, that's minus 30. So, sending a message literally on social media knocks you down 50 points, and if you do it in a WeChat room, it's minus 30.

If you report illegal conduct, such as people participating in superstition of Chinese religions, unlawful construction, and environmental pollution or participation of a cult organization, that's a plus 10. So, basically, you're a rat. You get a plus 10. If you don't accept the investigations from the officials, who are trying to look into why you're breaking laws and breaking rules, and why you're losing social credit points, if you don't allow them to collect evidence on you, there's another minus 20 points. If you are part of the community, which everyone is in China, basically everyone has a communist party head, and if you go around and help them get information on all the people who are staying there - keep in mind that you can't just randomly stay in a random place, you have to register. It's a very archaic system that still exists.

If you go around and get that information about who is currently there, and report back to the Chinese Communist Party, you get a plus 30 points. Tax evasion is minus 100 points. Seriously though, the entire system practices tax evasion, and it's led by the tax officials. It's just kind of how it works. If you help the community to solve a major dispute between neighbors, it's plus 10 points. You have to take some pressure off the top.

If you get a traffic stop, if you get a fine between 500 and 2,000 RV, which is really easy to do - it's like you go a tiny bit over the speed limit, because of the speed cameras everywhere in China. It's minus 10 points. Also, if you get a parking ticket twice, that's minus 10 points as well. If you set off firecrackers, dance in a square (like the old women like to do) without filing a permit, playing with a spinning top, using a high-pitched radio horn, causing noise, raising animals that interfere with other people's lives, that's minus 5 points. If you had been to China, you might know why they would consider a law like that. Illegally holding classes, that's minus 50 points. If you're teaching people anything, it's minus 50 points. They don't want people to have any underground meetings.

If you help the cops capture criminals or provide evidence, basically ratting them out, you get 20 points on that one. If you violate the reproducing planning policy, meaning you break the two-child policy, and you have three children or you don't allow the government to sterilize you, which does actually happen in the government reproducing planning buildings throughout the countryside, that is minus 40 points. So, if you have an extra kid, bye-bye, social credit.

If you donate organs, unpaid, plus 100 points. And I assume you have to donate organs of family members first, because I'm pretty sure you shouldn't be donating organs of people you don't know or your own. I guess if you are donating your own organs, I imagine you wouldn't have to care about your credit score if you weren't alive. Unauthorized renovation of houses, minus 5. If you receive a national level award, plus 100 points. So, I wonder if my Presidential Physical Fitness Award would count.

If you make a tombstone that is too big, like if it exceeds the area and height limit, minus 100 points. And that's crazy. Your kid joins the army, plus 5 points. Now this one is interesting. In the constitution of China, you have the ability as a citizen, to petition directly to the government if you have a grievance that is not being resolved, right? Grievance to the government doesn't mean that you can go out protesting. You have to go file a petition letter. Now what happens is, if you submit a petition to a small town, maybe your hometown, instead of taking it to the next bigger city, it will be minus 10 points for not petitioning to higher officials. If you petition to a higher provincial level, it is minus 20 points, and if you petition directly to Beijing, it is minus 50 points. If you have a problem that you need solved, and you need the government to help you, if you go to Beijing to petition, you literally lose 50 social credit points, even though it's in the constitution. Think about that for a second. They just literally want people's problems to be confined to their areas so they can micromanage and control them. If your kid receives a recreational award or sports award, you're going to get a plus 20 credits. Like Timmy wins a state championship for his football team, your credit score just went up.

Another way to lose points is if you receive criticism. There's this thing called self-criticism in China. You work in the party, or you work in a company, if you do something wrong, or the boss thinks you did something wrong, you have to deal with self-criticism. Self-criticism is where you have to make a statement in front of everybody and tell why you were wrong. That's minus 5. If they circulate it, actually put it in the newspaper that so-and-so was bad because of this or that - if that happens in the city newspaper, it's minus 10. If it goes to another bigger city, circulated there, then that is a minus 30.

I think you can see the trend here. It's kind of like how the Chinese media works. It goes into stages: super local, higher, higher, higher, higher. The higher up you go, the worse it is for your social credit score.

Now, if you look at the tallies, you can kind of understand how this works. What it looks like to me is that the government is really using this social credit system as ultimate control, almost like a Jason Bourne's Majority Report system, that people will be too scared to do anything in the future. They'll know what to avoid. Because when I look at the crimes, or the things that really take away points on this social credit system, there are things that are against the government, that are speaking out against the government, that are critical against the government. Less so, things that actually should be changed within the Chinese society. And it's kind of disappointing. The big focus here, are your kids being good? Are you being good? Are you loyal to the government?

And that's the way I see a lot of dictators around the world. If they were to read in the framework of this, they would be salivating over this. It goes much further than public shaming for jaywalkers, because China likes it when this comes out. Oh, look this jaywalker got publicly shamed. Around the world, yeah, I can't believe you jaywalked like this. But the implications are much more than that. The shaming behavior is one thing. This is more than shaming bad behavior. This is shaming actual potential dissidents. And people want to speak out and have freedom. This is the end. There was no freedom to begin with, but this kind of deletes the gray area that made China what it was.

Although this system was beneficially going to work in 2014, what leader could have come up with something like that? Unlike media portrayals of some App to see if someone has been good or bad, based on the government, the reality of what the social credit score is, is much more complicated, much more sinister. At the same time, China has paid for nationalist disinformation that you might see trolling around in comic sections. They want the rest of the world to think that either it's exactly the same as a FICO credit score, or a handy tool to punish criminals. It's much bigger than that."

And that's the system that Klaus and the gang want to bring to the whole planet, and this is why Klaus stated on tape that he thought "China was a model country." This is the model he wants to bring.

And that's why whistleblowers are starting to sound the alarm on what this Social Credit Score System will really allow these Global Elites around the world to do to us, if it gets implemented like China, as this man shares.

Dr. Zelenko: *"Let's look back at China. China just created a central bank, the digital Yuan. Then they banned every other currency. Then they linked the social credit system to cryptocurrency. Which means, if the*

Chinese government, who controls the central bank, doesn't like what you say, they could restrict, limit or outright deny you the ability to transact. So, now I don't have to put a bullet in your head. I'll just prevent you from buying bread."

And that's why we need to speak up as fast as we can about this. But, hey, no worries. Klaus Schwab and the gang of Global Elites have relabeled this Chinese Social Credit Score System, again, just in case you catch on to this evil empire sweeping the planet!

You see, you don't need to worry. It's merely the new ESG Scoring System. Huh, doesn't that sound much better? Yeah, right! It's the exact same thing, as this man shares.

WHAT IS AN ESG RISK SCORE?

Narrator: *"The ESG score is an acronym that stands for Environmental Social and Governance score. The ESG Risk score gauges a company's performance on ESG issues and exposure to ESG related risks. They are calculated against a set of ESG metrics and may be expressed on a number scale from 0 to 1, 0 to 10, 0 to 100, or through a letter ranking system. For the scores themselves and surrounding context, fill in the picture of a company's performance on environmental, social and governance issues. Some scoring reports also even have a controversy ranking. Which I find shocking, since one man's controversial company is another man's company that stands by its principles.*

WHO ARE THE ESG RATING AGENCIES?

Several third party providers, including agencies and research and analysis firms, evaluate companies on ESG performance, and determine independent ESG scores for investment decisions in comparison against peers. Some agencies include Bloomberg, ESG Data Services, Corporate Knights Global 100, Sustained Analytics, ESG Risk Ratings, Dow Jones, Sustainability Index Family, Thompson Reuters Esq. Scores and Rep. Risk.

WHAT IS A GOOD ESG SCORE?

Methodology, scope, and coverage varies significantly among each agency. Bloomberg and Corporate Knights rate companies on a 100-point scale, for example. Thomas Reuters assigns a score of zero (worst) to one (best), with a corresponding letter grade. Rep Risk measures companies on a Rep Risk index of 0 to 100 and provides a Rep Risk rating of AAA to D.

HOW IS SCORE DATA COLLECTED?

Well, it's one of two ways. It's either self-reported, or it's from publicly available data sets. Depending on the agency, some exclude self-reported data and only rely on publicly available data in order to generate a score.

ESG: ENVIRONMENTAL CATEGORY

What constitutes the ESG environmental category? Environmental factors range from a company's greenhouse gas emissions to its treatment of animals. Common evaluation criteria include metrics on climate change, soil and water contamination, renewable energy and environmental policy.

ESG: SOCIAL CATEGORY

What constitutes the ESG social category? Social factors examine a company's business relationships with employees, suppliers, partners, shareholders and other groups throughout the supply chain. For example, are workers in a factory abroad treated ethically? Do employees earn a living wage? Are facilities regularly inspected and safe to work? Can employees take leave when they are sick, or for other personal reasons? Social scores might also reflect charitable contributions, customer interactions, community impact and policy influence.

ESG: GOVERNANCE CATEGORY

What constitutes the ESG governance category? Governance criteria evaluate legal and compliance issues in board operations. For example, does the company abide by all local, state and federal laws? Does company composition represent diverse backgrounds and perspectives? How does executive and non-executive compensation compare to the company's peers?

ARE ALL SCORES PUBLIC?

Some ESG scores and reports are publicly available. The Dow Jones score, for example, releases World and Regional Industries on top performing companies annually. Other ratings and reports, such as those from Bloomberg and Rep Risk, are created for investors about companies they want to invest in.

PRO ESG POINT-OF-VIEW

Those who are for the continued proliferation and use of ESG say, organizations with a good ESG risk score are thought to be better equipped to anticipate future risks and opportunities, more inclined to long-term strategic thinking, and to prioritize long-term value creation over short-term gains. Research increasingly shows that companies that adhere to ESG principles are low-risk investments and more resilient over time. For that reason, forward thinking boards stay informed about their company's ESG issues and activities. The various third-party organizations evaluate their efforts and their ESG risk scores.

CON ESG POINT-OF-VIEW

This all sounds very wholesome and enlightened, so what could possibly go wrong? Well, let's look at the other side. Throughout history, loans for individuals and companies were based solely on the risk of them paying back the loan, not with what their views on solar panels or Covid-19 mask mandates were. In fact, they were never based on anything related to their social or political views for that matter.

ESG, in my view, is not enlightenment and information. It is a cage for your mind and your financial freedom. I can easily see ESG being used as just another political tool to wield power over your thoughts and beliefs. An enforced compliance for government prescribed orthodoxy. Companies with views that are not politically correct will have a low score. Companies that produce technology that is not considered progressive, like a gasoline-powered car, will have a low score.

Companies that are not charitable to the right organizations at the right moment, depending on the political whims, will have a low score. Companies with a low score will have difficulty getting loans and expanding their business and will pay higher interest on the loans they're trying to get or currently have. But this score is not just about the score of the companies you invest in. This is the real danger: consider it guilt by association. If the ESG of all the companies you invest in is, let's say, a 3 out of 10, then guess what? It is very reasonable that the government investors, or a company that wants to hire you, can assume your ESG score would be about a 3 out of 10, assuming that this information becomes public.

Is it that hard to believe that a bank or a company could get hold of this ESG score and tell you clearly, that you are not a big fan of the environment, or social justice or government rules during a pandemic that are meant to protect people? So, you are not worthy of a job or a loan with us at this time. However, go to this other ESG repair agency and once your score is high enough, then we'd love for you to come back to us. Much like what happens today when people try to get a loan and are often pointed to a credit repair agency in order to raise their credit score. Same idea. This is the real danger with this, as it could definitely be used and abused for the wrong reasons. ESG scores will be used to abuse, sanction and discriminate individual liberty and beliefs."

Which is exactly what the Chinese Social Credit Score system does, so once again, this is the exact same thing, only called by a different name! How dumb do they think we are? All they do is relabel their dangerous deceptive tactics and repackage it, and we fall for it all over again!

The ESG Scoring system is the exact same type of digital-financial prison the Chinese are using! And that's why the new term for all these financial prison planet scoring systems, whatever label you want to give them, is "Technocommunism," or, in other words, a "digital-financial" form of communism!

And that's why these whistleblowers are sounding the alarm on this ESG Scoring System, as well, and what it will allow the Global Elites and Klaus Schwab and the gang to do to us. In short, it will destroy everything, as this reporter shares.

Tucker Carlson: *"So, because of the ESG, Germany is now rationing electricity. Because of the ESG, farmers are in a revolt in the Netherlands. But the saddest victim of the ESG, is Sri Lanka. Once a prosperous country off the southern coast of India, Sri Lanka has collapsed. Inflation is over 50% and food prices are up over 80%. This week, Sri Lanka's President and Prime Minister fled the country. Citizens stormed their residences, went through their sock drawers, and swam in their swimming pools.*

It was just a few years ago that the World Economic Forum published an article, entitled 'This is how we make Sri Lanka rich by 2025.' Well, if you search this article online, it's been deleted. Oh, weird, covering their tracks. But not very well. So, how does this happen? In April of 2021, Sri Lanka's leaders banned chemical fertilizers. Now 90% of the country's farmers use chemical fertilizer. So, what happened next? A third of Sri Lanka's farms shut down completely. Now what happens when farms shut down? Well, people starve. This is what the largest city in Sri Lanka looked like this week."

Hundreds of people are rioting in the streets, tearing down the barricade between them and the police. The police are spraying water and throwing tear gas into the crowd. But they can't stop the crowd from overtaking the city.

"That's what the Green New Deal looks like in Sri Lanka. Now I know what you are thinking. Pampered-lifestyle liberals living in the United States have destroyed something else. They did this to Sri Lanka, like what busing did to American education. Absolutely wrecked it and then walked away like nothing ever happened. That's the downside. People's lives were destroyed. It's happened a lot. But here's the good news. Sri Lanka has an almost perfect ESG score. Sri Lanka's score is 98 on the ESG scale. That is more than double what our score is here in the United States. We had better step up our efforts to shut down farms. Peter Earle is an economist who follows all this stuff. Peter, thanks so much for coming on. ESG seems like the kind of idea that winds up in the pictures you just saw. It seems inevitable for any place that applies it."

Peter Earle: *"Yes, definitely. Thanks for having me. What you see here is what is really happening in a lot of places, which is where you have ideologies, in particularly woke ideologies, replacing prices in markets. You get this sort of classic misallocations of resources."*

Tucker Carlson: *"So, Sri Lanka had a 98% ESG score. So, like, they won. Why aren't the people there happy? Just because they are starving to death. But are there other reasons? Don't they feel virtuous? Don't they feel good about themselves?"*

Peter Earle: *"It doesn't seem like it. No. I have a feeling that you have to have at least a minimum of 1,500 calories a day to really enjoy the fruits of this sort of actual atrocity of what is going on over there."*

And around the world, whether you call it the Social Credit Score system, or the ESG Scoring system, it's all the same thing, and none of it's good! And lest there be any doubt who's behind all this, here's a recent interview with Klaus Schwab, not only once again praising China's role in all this, but he admits this is all part of his plan for a "systematic transformation of the world."

Narrator: *"At the D20, you were there meeting some of the leaders, as well, Mr. Schwab. What do you make of the results? To finally put something as a statement. It seems quite positive with all the words that are included."*

Klaus Schwab: *"I think it's positive. It's already positive for the fact that everybody agreed about the statement, which we haven't had the last years. Now the base has been formed but we have to go one step further. We have to have a strategic move. We have to construct the world of tomorrow. It's a systemic transformation of the world so we have to define how the world should look like, which we want to come out of this transformation. Period. I respect China's achievements, which are tremendous over the last 40 years. I think it's a role model for many countries."*

Is this guy insane, or what? China is a role model? Not only with their tyrannical Social Credit Score System tied into their new "digital Yuan" currency, but all their other blatant violations of human rights and murderous, oppressive behavior. They're a role model? Are you nuts?!

But this is a part of the "systematic transformation of the world" that he and the World Economic Forum and the Global Elites are working on. Bring China's system to the planet. You know, Technocommunism!

Just re-label it with different names, for different areas of the world, and nobody will know. Shhhh! You liar!

Chapter Sixteen

World Economic Forum & the CBDC Currency

And speaking of liars, good thing this Chinese Technocommunism - this financial prison planet, this thought control system that Klaus and the gang want to bring to the world - will never happen here in America! Why, we would never go along with creating a financial-digital prison to enslave and control our individual livelihoods!

Oh, how I wish that were true! The sad fact is, it's already being put into place with Klaus Schwab's buddy, Joe Biden, Mr. Build Back Better himself, and his latest push for an American version of this digital-financial control system, called the CBDC or new Digital Dollar.

China has the "Digital Yuan." Now apparently, we get the new "Digital Dollar." Once again, relabel it all, and somehow it makes it all go away. Yeah right! But don't take my word for it. Let's see what this new proposed CBDC, or new "digital dollar," from the Biden administration really is!

Here's Rishi Sunak. You know, the new Prime Minister of England, Klaus's new trainee, or puppy dog, promoting CBDC currency as the greatest thing since sliced bread.

Rishi Sunak: *"Today, I am proud to say that under the UK's presidency, the group of the world's seven most advanced economies, the G7, is launching a set of public policy principles for retail, Central Bank Digital Currencies, CBDCs. Central Bank Digital Currencies could be a digital version of money, a bit like a digital banknote that could be used alongside physical notes and coins.*

Unlike most of the digital money people use daily today, it would be issued directly by a Central Bank, like the Bank of England in the UK. And governments and central banks across the world are working together, looking into what having a digital currency might mean in practice. This includes issues that people care about, such as ensuring users' money would be safe and secure, that it could work with other ways to pay, would be energy efficient and available to everyone. A potential CBDC would offer businesses and consumers new ways to pay in the future. It's all part of the wider story of digital innovation that has delivered benefits to millions around the world and in the UK. We're excited to be taking a leading role with G7 members in publishing this exploratory work, bringing money and finance into the 21st century.

You mean, converting the financial system of Western nations into the prison planet that Klaus is launching everywhere, modeled after China.

But maybe that's just the UK. This digital CBDC currency system isn't coming to America, is it? Unfortunately, as I mentioned earlier, it's already been put into play by Mr. Build Back Better, Joe Biden, Klaus's buddy, with a recent signed executive order, as you can see here.

"Executive Order 14067—Ensuring Responsible Development of Digital Assets was signed."

This was done March 09, 2022, and it basically calls for a "digital dollar," in which some are now calling "Biden Bucks," that will function as a CBDC currency system here in the United States.

And all it is, shocker, is another "relabeling" of the Chinese Social Credit Score System and the ESG System, where soon this will be our reality in America. "I'm sorry, Sir. Your card was declined due to your political views."

And it's so obvious where these "Biden Bucks," or America's version of a CBDC currency system, will lead us, just like in China, that several whistleblowers are blowing the lid off of this!

Narrator: *"Where were you on March 9, 2022, when President Biden signed the death warrant on American freedom? On that day, in a hush ceremony at the White House, without the approval of Congress, the* states, or the American people, Biden signed into law Executive Order 14067. Buried in this order are a few paragraphs titled Section Four. Section Four makes Executive order 14067 the most treacherous act by a sitting president in the history of our Republic. Section Four sets the stage for legal government surveillance of all U.S. citizens, total control over your bank accounts and purchases, and the ability to silence all the dissenting voices for good. In this new war on freedom, they aren't coming for your guns. No, they are thinking much bigger than that. They are coming for your money, and it's already started."

"Thanks to Section Four of Biden's order 14067, ordering urgent research in developing the digital dollar, I believe the U.S. dollar, the standard of the world since 1792, will be replaced by a new currency, the digital dollar. These new electronic currencies are called CBDCs, or 'central bank digital currencies.' I call this digital dollar, Biden Bucks, because I want him to take full credit for what I consider to be crimes. This is not like money in your online bank account. No, this is new and different. Every digital dollar will be a programmable token, like bitcoin or other cryptocurrencies, but there is a big difference.

Cryptocurrencies are decentralized digital currency. Instead, if it plays out the way I see it, Biden Bucks will have the full backing of the U.S. federal reserve. They will replace the cash that we have now, and it will soon be the sole, mandatory currency of the US. When Biden Bucks get rolled out, many experts, myself included, believe CBDCs will begin an era of total government control and surveillance. This would dramatically extend the power and influence of the federal government, essentially acting like a new type of spyware. With Biden Bucks, the government will be able to force you to comply with this agenda. And if you don't, they can turn off your money.

It won't be like freezing your bank account. It will be so much easier. Because Biden Bucks will be 'digital tokens' programmed at the source – it could be 'turned on or off' at will, with just a keystroke. And they could be reprogrammed at any time. With Biden's secret surveillance running the show, the anti-freedom implications are almost limitless. For example,

Biden Bucks could be programmed to allow only certain kinds of purchases. Imagine what this new world could look like. You want to keep an internal combustible engine car? Your digital dollars suddenly won't pay for gas. Instead, you could be forced to buy an electric vehicle. That's just the tip of the fascist iceberg.

They can force you to get vaccinated. They can force you into solar. They can force you into using less water or heat. They can force you to eat fake, plant-based, meat. They can control where you are allowed to travel. They can stop you from purchasing certain items, like guns, ammo, or survival supplies. They can control to which candidate you are allowed to donate. They will know every single place you spend your money. Forever! Every single aspect of your life could be controlled if they controlled your money. In fact, I fully expect them to implement a social credit system like in China. If you say the wrong thing on social media, buy the wrong thing, subscribe to the wrong news channel, give money to the wrong candidate, your rating drops.

Suddenly, your Biden Bucks are frozen, and they have disappeared from your account. This is already happening in China. There, with a low social score, who are officially labeled untrustworthy, they can take away your ability to travel, restrict your internet access, deny your family the best schools and jobs. They can even take away your pets. I'm not kidding. All of this is going on today. So, that's China, a communist, oppressed country.

Could this really happen in a democracy? Just ask the truckers in Canada because that is exactly what happened to them. When Prime Minister Trudeau was granted special emergency powers during the peaceful trucker's protest over the forced vaccination law, he ordered all the banks to freeze the accounts of the protestors and anyone who aided them in any way. And it wasn't just a threat. That fascist froze the bank accounts of non-violent protestors. He locked up over $6 million in private accounts for protesting a forced vaccination law. The truckers were fully violated in their sovereign human rights. Think about that. They protested his *policies, so he took away their money. Do you think our current government would love to do that? Me too.*

Under the Biden Bucks, we will lose many of our God-given American rights and will be replaced by total government surveillance and control. For almost all Americans, this will be the death of freedom forever. I'm pretty skeptical."

Neil Kashkari: *"I keep asking anybody, anybody, at the Fed, outside the Fed, to explain to me what problem this is solving. I can send anybody in this room $5 with Venmo, right now. So seriously, what is it that a CBDC can do that Venmo can't do? And all I get is a bunch of hand waving. 'Well, maybe it's better for financial inclusion.' Maybe? Is there any evidence that it is? And then they say, 'What about China? They're doing it.' Well, I can see why China would do it. If they want to monitor every one of your transactions, you could do that with a central bank currency. You can't do that with Venmo. If you want to impose negative interest rates, you could do that with a central bank digital currency, but you can't do that with Venmo. If you want to directly tax customers' accounts, you can do that with a central bank currency, but you can't do that with Venmo. So, I get why China would be interested. Why would the American people be for that?"*

Finance News Reports: *"The most important thing today are credible sources. And we listen to Jim all the time. What is your concern on Executive Order 14067, which was just signed, by Biden and company only a few months ago? What is your concern? 14067."*

"Yeah, it has a number of parts. And the thing with, well, executive orders, or, for that matter, legislation, I can say you have to read the fine print. You do, but you have to actually consider the hidden agendas. Like, I can read it. Anyone can read it. It's a public document. But what's behind it? That is, where are they going with it? And that's really where the urgency comes in."

"It's basically an order that accelerates the U.S. movement towards a central bank digital currency, so-called CBDC. These are happening all over the world. Beijing already has on their passport, prototype stage. They kind of rolled that out during the Winter Olympics. You know, last February. I believe the Bahamas has a digital currency. And a few other countries are already going in that direction. Europe is the European Central Bank; it is very far along. The U.S. and the Federal Reserve, because they all of a sudden accelerated it, and they said, 'We got to move fast on this. We got to catch up.' And that's what 14067 was about. But, so okay, so that's kind of what you get from the meeting. But what's the hidden agenda?

Well, first of all, just a little background. Central bank digital currencies. It's still the dollar. So, a digital dollar is still a dollar. A digital Chinese yuan is still a yuan. A digital euro is still a euro. So, it's not a new currency, but it is a new payment channel. And it is a new form of currency, if you want to think of it that way, even though it's still the dollar, and it goes hand-in-hand with getting rid of cash.

But, what else? And this is the key, and this is why we are sounding the alarm a little bit on executive order 14067. So, once it's digital, a couple of things. First of all, they know your whereabouts now. They already know your whereabouts from your iPhone. Unless you turn your iPhone off, and not just turn it off. Put it in what's called a Faraday sack, which is a special woven fabric of metallic weave that blocks radiation. And they do the same thing with your E-Z Pass and other stuff. But unless you do that, then they know where you are through your iPhone or your Samsung or whatever. So, they already know your whereabouts. We have facial recognition software. You go, 'I'm going to wear a mask and sunglasses and put my hat down.'

Okay, they have gait recognition software - gait, meaning how you walk. It's like a fingerprint. So, even if you're wearing a mask, they see you walking down the street. That's Kim, or that's Robert or Jammer, as the case may be. So, they already know a lot. And they know your whereabouts. But now they are going to know what you're buying, right?

Because every product has a, you know, SKU, a stock keeping code, a stock keeping unit code, you know, with a QR scan, digital scan. So, they are going to know what you're buying. And this digital currency is programmable, meaning they can block certain purchases, or not.

So, let's say you donate money to Elise Stefanik. She's an up-and-coming Republican member of the Republican leadership in an upstate district in New York. Or have you donated money to Donald Trump? Well, they might well know that first of all. And you might find that your account's frozen, or let's say, they want to. See, right now, if you work in, you know, you're an employee, the technical term defined, you get paid, and you get a W-2 at the end of the year, but they withhold payment, or you get paid every two weeks or whatever.

The employer withholds taxes from your wages, and then you file your W-2, your tax return. You reconcile. Maybe you get a refund, or maybe you owe a little bit. But they got the money up front through withholding. But that's not true for independent contractors and professionals. Doctors, lawyers, architects, you know, landscaping. So, anybody who's not a W-2 employee doesn't have withholding. They've got to pay their taxes. What if they could just take it out of your bank account? Or pay your doctor. You put the money in this bank, and I'm just going to take, you know, some number, 20% out of your bank account every month. And yeah, we'll send you a statement, a 1099 to file your tax return. Either you owe, or you get a refund.

But no more honor system. In other words, no more waiting 'til your end. We're going to take it out of your bank account. Or what if it's from a stimulus. It's not a stimulus, but we'll call it that. We're going to put a countdown clock on your bank account, and if you don't spend 10% in the next 30 days we're going to deduct that much. So, it's 'you use it, or you lose it.' Now you say, 'I worked hard, I made this money, it's in the bank, but you are telling me that if I don't spend it, I'm going to lose it anyway. So, I might as well go spend it.' And of course, the idea is to stimulate the economy.

But the point is, the number of things you can do from surveillance to identifying your political preferences, withholding taxes, account freezes, account seizures, time limitations on your money. Your money's a countdown clock. It expires after a certain period of time, etc. I could go on and on. But you get the point, which is, it's not your money anymore. I've always told people, 'You put your money in the bank, it's not your money, it's the bank's money, and they will give it to you when they feel like it.'

Well, this is that same idea on stilts. Now the government's involved; and while it's easier, faster, cheaper about payments, it's also easier, faster, cheaper, for surveillance, confiscation, and account freezes. And then people say to me, after I explain it, 'Oh, that would never happen.' It's already happening. It's already here."

Dan Bongino, Fox News Reports: *"The Feds just admitted, they want a future federal currency. They are not being anonymous. They want to know what you are spending your money on. That means total control for them. Listen, I have been warning you over and over, and now the Feds are saying the quiet part out loud. They want the digital currency. Ladies and Gentlemen, this is the biggest surveillance tool you will ever see in human history. They are now saying the quiet part out loud about the creation of a central bank digital currency. Take a listen."*

Jerome Powell, Federal Reserve Chairman: *"So, we will not be anonymous. It would not be an anonymous instrument. We would be looking to balance privacy protection, identity identification - which has to be done, of course - in today's traditional banking system."*

Dan Bongino: *"You just heard him say, don't listen to me. Joining me now is Cryptocurrency expert, and the author of 'Undressing Bitcoin,' Layah Heilpern. Layah, thanks so much for joining us. You've been sounding the alarm about these central bank digital currencies, me as well. It's a big concern. This is the ultimate surveillance tool, isn't it?"*

Layah Heilpern: *"Absolutely, and it isn't even the worst of our problems. It's the fact that it's going to be programmable. Because it's digital, it means the money can be programmed, and it can be spent in any way in which the central bank or the government decides. So, one of my particular concerns is the WEF, because they are creating a carbon allowance. That means each individual will be given a set amount of credit, or whatever it is, carbon that they are allowed to emit, and how do they implement that? Through their central bank digital currency. So, if I buy too many plane tickets or if I buy too much meat, those things are supposed to be very bad for the environment. My money, when I go to pay with my card, can then be declined.*

So now they are literally controlling how we can and cannot spend our money. It's important to realize that the money can expire. So, the central bank loves to print lots and lots of money, which causes inflation, so we can get to a point where they say, instead of printing money, you have to spend at least 10% of your savings in the next three months. If you don't spend that money in the next three months that money is going to expire. And if you can't save money, then you can't build long-lasting generations of wealth. You are always going to be a slave to the system. And I don't really think people understand the severity of this. Money is literally the energy that fuels your life. If you don't have freedom of money, you don't have freedom of anything. You talk about the 2nd Amendment. They don't need to get rid of the 2nd Amendment, they can just, say, freeze your money so you cannot go buy a gun. So, again, this is the most tyrannical form of government that we will ever see. When you control the money, you control the world."

And that's precisely the plan from Klaus Schwab, the World Economic Forum and all these Global Elites, including Mr. Build Back Better, Joe Biden, to do to us! It's a coordinated global effort with the Covid Plandemic as the trigger to get it started, as well as the excuse to put it all into play.

We have not only been duped, but this is treason in high places, even here in the United States of America. Which is why many are sounding the alarm on what Biden is doing. He's selling out our country, as you can see here.

"**Biden Bucks: The Dangers of Digital Currency.**"

"One of the most horrifying things is coming down the pipeline. I refer to digital currency. A digital currency would, in effect, be the end of America."

If you think the term *"digital concentration camp" sounds extreme and over-the-top, think again. If the government decides to punish you, you're toast.*

You can't pay your power bill, so your electricity is shut off. You can't pay your water bill, so your water is shut off. You can't buy gas, so you can't drive. You can't pay your rent or mortgage, so you're evicted. You can't pay your property taxes, so your (paid-for) home is seized. You can't buy food. Forget medical care; that's out of the question.

This cascading series of events can happen, literally, at the push of a button. You won't be jailed, but you won't have to be. Your life will become a living hell when Biden Bucks are rolled out. This is not hyperbole.

And this article shares :

"Waiting In The Wings For An Economic Collapse - The Digital Dollar."

Imagine if there was no cash. It would be impossible to hide even the smallest transaction from government eyes. Something as simple as your morning trip to Starbucks wouldn't be a secret from government officials.

Here's what we could potentially see if a 'digital dollar' starts being used on us on a widespread basis.

1.) To protest governmental limits on personal freedom, liberty activists stage a peaceful protest around the nation's capital.

That nation's leader, wanting to quell the protest and protect his power, instructs his Minister of Economic Control to reduce the protesters' CBDC balances by 50 percent every day until the protest ends. The protest ends shortly after the message pings on the CBDC smartphone app.

2.) Economic growth is lagging, and the economists in the federal government suspect it is because consumer spending isn't strong enough. People are saving their money, rather than spending it. To fix this problem, the Ministry of Economic Control announces a new year-long, negative interest rate for all CBDC accounts. Unspent balances of CBDC will be reduced by 10 percent every month. As a result, no one saves, everyone spends, and the economists have saved the economy.

3.) You're at the grocery store picking up some ribeye steaks, because some friends are coming over for a barbecue.

When you get up to the counter, there's a problem. The cashier says the payment isn't going through. You check the CBDC app on your smartphone. There is an alert: 'You have exceeded your monthly carbon credit usage. Please remove the following items from your grocery cart in order to proceed.'

4.) You want to pick up a new firearm for hunting season, so you swing by the local sporting goods store.

But when you go to transfer CBDC credits for the purchase, you're denied. The trusty CBDC app explains: 'We've detected activity on your social media accounts that suggests you are at risk of causing harm to yourself or others. You are prohibited from purchasing a firearm for one year.'

Once we open the door to this sort of tyranny, there is no telling where it could potentially end.

And I agree. Which is why Robert Kiyosaki, investment guru and author of the finance book "Rich Dad, Poor Dad," also had some choice words for Biden's Executive Order 14067, that puts all this into play.

"It's the most treasonous act in U.S. history and the creation of Central Bank Digital Currencies, or CBDC, is communism in its purest form."

And that's exactly why this former communist is warning us of the same thing!

Fox News Reports: *"Police in China wrapping up protestors outside of the nation's central bank. Their crime, they want their own money, after their accounts were frozen due to covid protocols. Our next guest, who survived Mao's Marxist cultural revolution and immigrated here to the United States from China, she said this should be a warning about the evils of communism and the growing threat of totalitarianism that we face here. This is their money. Their bank accounts have been frozen since April. They need money to survive. They put it in the bank, and now they can't get it. What is your reaction to this? Many were seen beaten because of this."*

Xi Van Fleet, survivor of Mao's revolution: *"Yes, obviously this story tells us that China is in financial crisis. But this is not just about bank wrongs story, since the people could not get their money out of the bank. This is very difficult for Americans to imagine, that you put your hard-earned money in the bank, to be told later, sorry your life savings just vanished. And the government refused to step in. I want to use this horrific incident to remind Americans that China is not a normal country. It is a communist country through and through.*

Ever since its founding in 1949, communists do not respect private property, they do not respect human rights and human lives. These people are not fighting for a political right, they are merely fighting for the right to their own money. And their petition was met with such overwhelming force. You can see that some of the people are handicapped, older people, children, and even pregnant women.

I also want to talk a little bit about the Covid passport. Ever since the pandemic, everyone has to have an app on their phone. If your code is red, it means you are Covid-19 positive and you cannot leave your home. Ever since April, many people who went to the bank and demanded the withdrawal of their money from their account, their code turned to red. So, this is just horrible that the Chinese government went against ..."

Fox News Reports: *"Even if they didn't have covid? They were just trying to get their money."*

Xi Van Fleet: *"No, no, yes, it's total control. Weaponized passports, covid passports, Americans should pay attention!"*

I would say so! But good thing they're not going to cram down on us a Covid-19 passport, like they did with the Chinese. Yeah, that's coming next, as we'll see in a second, with the new "digital currency" tied into a new "digital identity" or "digital passport."

You won't be able to travel to go get your money, whether the red code Covid indicator is true or not. It's just another layer of communist control. You know, Technocommunism.

Which is why this article calls Biden's treasonous executive order, that he did in secret, for what it really is.

"Nightmare on G20 Street: Biden Delivers US To A Chinese Social Credit System."

Why? Because that's all this is,

once again, relabeled for our gullible consumption. These guys are masters of deceit. They're liars!

And lest you doubt this financial, communist prison planet, controlling every aspect of our individual livelihood, isn't going to go global and be all tied together, think again.

Here's the Bank of International Settlements manager, Agustin Carstens, talking about what the emergence of CBDC's will allow him and the rest of the Global Elites to do to us. We saw a little piece of it earlier.

Agustin Carstens: *"Our analysis on CBDC, in particular for the general use, we intend to establish the equivalence with cash, and there is a huge difference there. For example, in cash we don't know who is using a one hundred dollar bill today. We don't know who is using a one thousand peso bill today. A key difference in the CBDC is that the central bank will have absolute control on the rules and regulations that will determine the use of that expression of central bank liability, and also, we will have the technology to enforce that. Those two issues are extremely important, and that makes a huge difference with respect to what cash is."*

But it's not cash anymore as we understand it. It's digital. And straight out of the horse's mouth you heard him say this switch to Biden Bucks, here in America, or the new CBDC currency, will allow "The Central Bank will have absolute control that will determine the use of that digital money, and we will have the technology to enforce that." That is, Artificial Intelligence, or AI.

Can I translate that for you? All these new relabeled forms of "digital currencies" around the world, including CBDC's in America (the Biden Bucks), will allow these Global Financial Elites, and Klaus Schwab and the gang, the ability to control all the "buying and selling" on the whole planet, and create a One World Government, and a One World Economy and a cashless system.

Where have I heard that before? Oh, that's right. That's God's warning for us in the Book of Revelation from nearly 2,000 years ago! What we're seeing is, with Klaus' help, the rise of the actual Antichrist Kingdom!

And for those of you who don't know, The Bank for International Settlements (BIS), "was established to collect and disburse Germany's World War I reparation payments." But by WW2, it was the primary war spoils money laundering operation for the Nazis.

And the irony is, today it's effectively the World Central Bank, or the Bank of Central Banks. The BIS is the controlling node for all other central planning entitles, such as The Fed, the ECB, or European Central Bank, the BOJ, or Bank of Japan, and on and on it goes.

It literally controls most of the transferable money in the whole world, which it uses to drive sovereign governments into debt on behalf of the IMF for purposes of control."

And lest there be any doubt that Klaus Schwab, the World Economic Forum, is behind all this, here's another whistleblower blowing the lid off that as well.

Guest: *"This is developing within the Biden Administration. Putin and Russia are a threat. But we actually have a bigger problem here with the CCP. It's far more powerful than Russia, far more organized, far more centralized control, and are far wealthier. And the military is far stronger. I'm going to the real elephant in the room. It's the increasing power of the CCP, China. With China's influence of operations, having been responsible for a lot of this idea, where lockdowns were our solutions, it was the first nation to initiate lockdowns, and then Italy and Europe followed after China, and then the rest followed after that. Mark Singer has written an extensive book on this, tracing step-by-step with these influence operations. Where the CCP have been encouraging a draconian response to Covid-19 and all of the technocracy that is eventually going to* arise in the form of checkpoint Charlie's society and central bank conditions."

Joe Rogan: *"They have been encouraging other nations to implement these. How do they get away with that? How do these other nations comply? They comply because of influence?"*

Guest: *"Influence operations from funding. Intelligence operations."*

Joe Rogan: *"And because of that, they are willing to impart laws they would not normally do. The governments that are being influenced. The governments like, whether it's Great Britain or the United States. These governments are being influenced, in your mind?"*

Guest: *"With the help of the agenda coming from other actors, such as the WEF and their teams, penetrating capitalists across the world, as Klaus Schwab said. There are some supernatural interests here that exist above the nation-state, working to define the future in a certain direction."*

And Klaus Schwab, the World Economic Forum and the Global Elites are behind it all. Which is why this article is calling it what it is.

"BEWARE: Biden's 'Build Back Better' Socialism Bill IS the 'Great Reset.'"

They're all working together, that is, Klaus Schwab and his political puppets, like Biden. And this is why Klaus and the World Economic Forum, and his Global Elites keep pushing, not only the Covid Plandemic crisis, but the Ukrainian crisis, because they're both manufactured ongoing crises to create the ongoing, never-ending excuses, to "reset" the whole financial system around the planet to create a digital prison planet system, as you can see here.

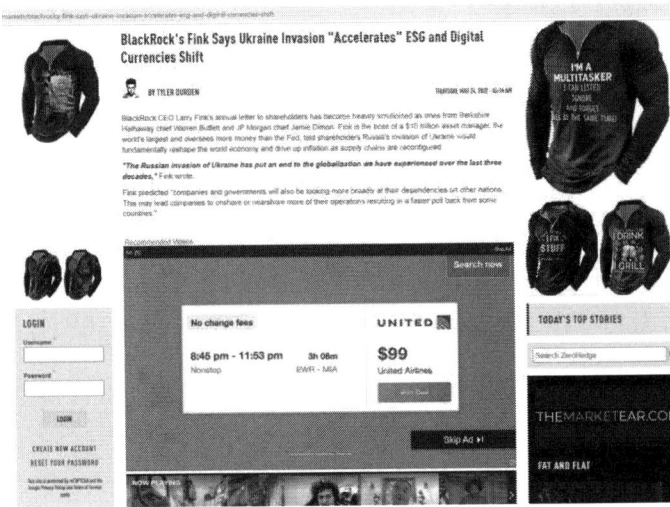

"BlackRock's Fink Says Ukraine Invasion 'Accelerates' ESG and Digital Currencies Shift."

Shocker! It's the old communism tactic "create a crisis so you can manage the outcome" and you keep these "crises" coming and going until you get the job done, which is to "reset" the whole world's economies into a digital, controllable one, by deliberately crashing the whole system.

Which is why many people are wondering why Mr. Wannabe False Prophet himself, Pope Francis, and the Vatican are also doing this.

"Collapse Incoming? Pope Francis Orders Holy See to Transfer All Assets to Vatican Bank."

Gee, I wonder why he's doing that? Do you know something we don't know? Surely, you're not in on this as well. Yeah, right! Of course, he is, as this guy shares.

"Does this have anything to do with the Pope's announcement that the world is already in a third world war? Is this just a coincidence?"

Not at all. Nothing's by chance folks. Not with these people. It's all preplanned, prepared, foisted upon us with fancy, relabeling deception.

Chapter Seventeen

World Economic Forum & the Global Biometric Passports

But speaking of deliberate crises, to deliberately create a collapse, to create an excuse for a digital currency, there's just one missing detail in this evil, deceptive, financial prison planet that Klaus Schwab, the World Economic Forum, and the Global Elites are building for us, if it's truly going to become the same one that the Antichrist will use during the 7-year Tribulation.

And that is, at some point, this digital financial prison system has to go "biometric" as well, specifically with the body parts of the "right hand" or forehead."

Revelation 13:16-17: "He also forced everyone, small and great, rich and poor, free and slave, to receive a mark on his right hand or on his forehead, so that no one could buy or sell unless he had the mark."

But hey, good thing we don't see any signs of Klaus Schwab and the gang doing that as well to us, right? Forcing a "biometric identity" upon us! Yeah, right! It's almost like they're following a script or something! This really is the next step in their deceptive, evil, financial prison planet they're creating for us, or should I say, the Antichrist!

In fact, they're promoting this new "digital identity" for everyone in one of their ongoing "crisis" areas, called Ukraine, which nobody seems to be talking about.

New State Services Available on "DIIA" Portal

UA Reports: *"Get a Covid passport or child's birth certificate, and apply for an unemployment grant, register an individual business, or order a car number plate. Those many services and otherwise, are now available for Ukrainians to receive, in a pair of clicks without leaving home. Thanks to DIIA Portal and its application. More than 11 million citizens are already using the DIIA platform for services, but the ministry of digital transformation is not about to stop. The agency has set a goal to make Ukraine the most comfortable state in the world."*

Mykhailo Fedorov, Deputy Prime Minister: *"Our vision of the most convenient state in the world, is crystallized through certain goals. The first goal is 100% public services digital. We want to digitize all available services by 2024. Make them online and introduce the principle that if services do not exist online, they cannot exist offline."*

UA Reports: *"Seven more options have recently been added to the deal list. Instead of hours spent in lines and dozens of papers to recalculate one's pension, one need only about half an hour to do this via smartphone."*

Maryna Lazebna, Minister of Social Policy of Ukraine: *"In order to calculate or recalculate the pension, one will need to fill out a survey, upload the necessary documents and apply. The liberalization of this process is particularly important in a pandemic to help seniors to prevent the additional risk of infection while standing in lines. Therefore, we know for us this will save lives."*

UA Reports: *"In addition to pension-related services, one can also apply for subsidies on the portal in a few clicks. No other country in the world has yet repeated the success of the Ukrainian DIIA."*

Claude Wild, Ambassador of Switzerland to Ukraine: *"Ukraine is the first country in the world that launched digital passports, and legally equated them to ordinary paper documents. And business registration in Ukraine has one of the fastest procedures in the world. That is why Ukraine is becoming a digital transformation model for many other European countries."*

Oh, there's that word again. So, while we are all focused on Russia, Russia, Russia, bad guys to Ukraine, that "crisis" is being used to turn Ukraine into a 100% totally digitized country, including a "digital identity" or "digital passport." And just like China, this will be the "model" for the rest of the world to follow real soon.

Makes you wonder if this is why Ukraine's President Zelensky is smiling and chumming up with Klaus here.

What a bunch of lying deceivers! We just thought it was about a supposed war against Vladimir Putin's evil aggression, when in reality, Ukraine is a "digital testbed" for Klaus and his gang and his evil Global Elites.

This is their next step. They want to create a "universal digital, global passport," with all our Covid-19 information and other identity factors on it, to tie us into their digital-financial prison planet.

In fact, here is the World Economic Forum promoting just that.

Uplink Reports: *"This app could help revive global travel and large events during the pandemic. Enabling people to visit countries, conferences, and sports events safely. Users will have their blood screened at an approved CovidPass laboratory before being issued with a secure QR health visa code via their phone. They can present at airline check-in, borders, or event entrances. The digital passport doesn't include tracing technology, preserving data privacy while saving time and money. CovidPass's creators say that by using blood test data, it's 100% reliable and could ensure only non-infectious people travel across borders, while monitoring access to concerts, conferences, and pilgrimages.*

It uses real-time, automated epidemiological dates and blockchain technology that could help countries manage future waves of Covid-19, or other epidemics without the need for a total lockdown. CovidPass plans to launch in September. It commits to mandatory carbon offsetting for each of its passengers to preserve the environmental benefits of reduced air travel during the crisis. Global travel and tourism have been devastated by the pandemic. International arrivals are predicted to be down by 78% in 2020. Airline passenger demand may not recover until 2024.

While millions of jobs in tourism are at risk, the virus has pushed back events worldwide, including the Tokyo Summer Olympics. But CovidPass could help revive tourism and entertainment securely and safely."

There it is again, from The World Economic Forum themselves, pushing this "digital Covid passport," from the get-go, almost like it was part of the plan from the very beginning. But don't worry. They won't track you with it! Did you see that? You liars! It uses "real-time, automated technology." Of course, it's going to track you, in real time!

But an "external," digital passport to identify you anywhere on the planet, is just the first step. Again, you could lose that "external," digital passport, then what would you do? You're shut out of their system! Or dare I say, they wouldn't be able to "track," I mean, "identify" you wherever you go, in order to give you minute-by-minute permission or lack thereof, for your everyday, individual livelihood. What will you do?

Well, this is why they've already moved to stage two of this "universal, global, digital identity" that connects you to their global, financial prison planet. Just like the Bible warned about, they're now promoting "biometric" digital ID's.

South China Morning Post Reports: *"Imagine showing your Covid passport with just a flash of your arm. This Swedish company says it has a chip that can hold information about your vaccination status. It's so small, you can embed it into your arm. The chip uses pre-existing technology that the firm was already developing. Stockholm-based Epicenter, has been working on human-compatible tech for years."*

Hannes Sjoblad, Chief Disruption Officer, Epicenter: *"Implants are a very versatile technology that can be used for many different things. And right now, it is very convenient to have a Covid passport always accessible on your implant."*

South China Morning Post Reports: *"The chip uses near-field communication (NFC). It can send data to any NFC-compatible device, such as a smartphone. The technology is not new but use in humans has grown popular in the last decade. The first person to have a microchip implanted was Keven Warnick in 1998, but the firm made headlines this year when staff had passkeys implanted in their hands. It's also known for throwing parties when employees get chipped."*

Oh, and they're promoting that in China. I wonder why.

But hey, do you see the convenience there? You could lose your "external," digital Covid passport, but not if it's on the "inside" of you! If you get the "chip" in your "hand," maybe at one of these parties they have, you'd never have to worry about being shut out of the global, financial prison planet system ever again. Wouldn't that be great? Yeah, that's exactly what they want!

These guys are sick! They're lying megalomaniacs, rolling out this satanic, digital plan step-by-step hoping no one will catch on to what they're really doing.

But this promotion of "biometric" implants for digital identity purposes is nothing new. Here's a recent promotional video from Walletmor, again, encouraging people about the so-called benefits, including financial benefits, of getting one of these implants in your "hand."

Ashleigh Banfield, @TVAshleigh: *"When was the last time you wrote an actual check or bought something with cash? Swiping or tapping our card and our apps are just the easiest way to spend money, or the safest way, unless we misplace our phones or our wallets and then it's a nightmare. It is hard to misplace your hand, however. And soon, your hand may be all you need to buy anything you can afford, and many things that you can't. Because a company called Walletmor is developing a very teeny, tiny chip (see it in the X-ray, that should creep you out) that are like the ones you find in credit cards or debit cards, and the chip gets embedded just under your skin, and makes your whole hand a credit card. Joining me now is Wojtek Paprota. He is the CEO and founder of Walletmor. Okay, Wojtek, this is so futuristic and out there. Walk me through how it actually works."*

Wojtak Paprota: *"Well, first of all, thanks for having me. Let's look at the chip, a super small part that you can use wherever payments are accepted. So, it's exactly the same. It's a technology called, New Field Communication, so therefore, it can be used only for Near Field Communication payments. It's exactly the same as your credit card."*

Ashleigh Banfield: *"Do you have it?"*

Wojak Paprota: *"Yes, of course. The X-ray that you saw was my hand."*

Ashleigh Banfield: *"Show me your hand. Is it possible to see it at all? It's just barely, barely standing out, right? Looks a little like a scar?"*

Wojak Paprota: *"Yeah, you can see I'm pumping it a little bit."*

Ashleigh Banfield: *"That's crazy. Did you have a doctor insert it?"*

Wojak Paprota: *"Yeah, that's part of the deal. We are only building the implants. When it comes to installations, we want the whole experience to be as safe as possible, so therefore, we built a national partnership in Europe and the U.S., so if you are ordering an implant from our site, it's shipped to you, and then you schedule an appointment with one of the specialists, who will just set it up for you."*

Ashleigh Banfield: *"So, do you use it? Do you just go up to a cashier and say, 'I'll just tap my hand, and if that's the case, what's the reaction from the salesclerks?"*

Wojak Paprota: *"Of course, I've been testing it myself since the very beginning. I was the first person to get it installed, and the reactions are pretty wild. But in most cases, it turns out to be a positive conversation, as long as I explain how it works and what's actually inside."*

Yeah, especially if I can combine my Covid passport with it, and all my other digital ID's, so I can just waltz around in this new digital, financial prison planet that Klaus and the gang are creating for me. And all I need to "interact" with it all, or even "buy and sell," is my hand. Sound familiar?

Yeah, it's the Mark of the Beast system! In fact, that really is the plan. To have literally "everything" tied together into these "digital, implant, biometric, identities" as you can see here.

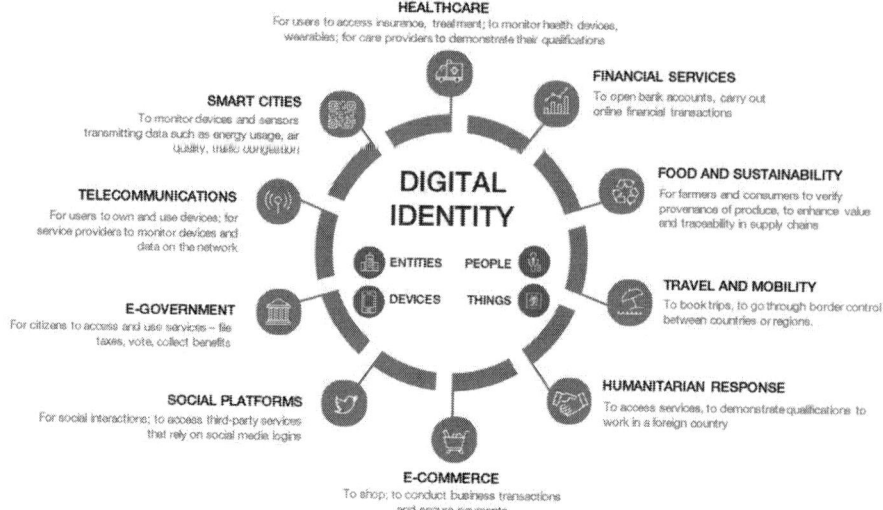

It will connect you to entities, people, devices, and things, including your healthcare, your financial services, your food, travel, humanitarian response, (that is, if you want to travel to another country), E-commerce online purchases, social platforms, telecommunications. And don't forget, that's being tracked like a rat wherever you go in their new smart cities.

That's their picture, folks, not mine. That is, The World Economic Forum. This is where all this push for a "biometric global, digital identity" scheme is headed. This is their plan for total control of the planet.

Klaus Schwab, the World Economic Forum and all these Global Elites are using the Covid-19 Plandemic and all these other crises they create, to not just tie the world economies all together digitally, for purposes of control, but to also tie their new digital currency directly to people individually, biometrically, to control them as well in their hands or foreheads. There will be no escape. This is what the Bible calls the Mark of the Beast system.

And we are being pressured to go along with it all, as these whistleblowers share!

Martin North, 10TP News Reports: *"Australia's banks want you microchipped! What's all this rubbish?"*

John Adams: *"Only a couple days ago, I got an email from one of our viewers who was deeply concerned that they had received an email campaign from their bank, an Australian bank, I'm told, who is putting a deal out there as to whether their customers want to be microchipped. The argument was that by being microchipped, it could drive efficiency for customers in terms of their interaction with their financial system. So, we're going to get into this, because this is a very big, shocking revelation. In fact, we have been on a crusade, you and I, for many years, about economic freedom, freedom in general, not being surveilled by government, surveilled by big banks, and that's obviously why we fought the cash ban.*

And we were successful in saying that we want to engage in commerce without you knowing what we're doing. And now we have at least one bank in Australia saying to the customers, 'How about we put a microchip into your hand,' so that any time you want to do banking, supposedly it's more convenient. But in reality, the bank will have all sorts of information implanted into someone's hand. This is completely nuts. And this is just another example of again, a couple years ago, when someone would suggest something along these lines, it's a conspiracy theory. And we always hear when dangerous ideas first pop up, it's conspiracy theories, but then somehow, they become reality. And the concern is that rather than having a full open debate about where this whole agenda is going, it is a quiet, slow, creeping set of events.

Where obviously, the issue is, if they were to say, they as the establishment - big business, big government, big tech - if they were to say at the public at large, 'Okay, this is the end state that we want to take you in.' I think most people say, 'No way, I don't want to live in that world.' So, they can't tell us, forthrightly. So, what they are trying to do is, slowly but surely, take baby steps, so that we don't notice. And they take it to the destination that they want to. And obviously, in the content of our last show, about the World Economic Forum, that's why a lot of Australians, people around the world, have very large concerns about where is the world headed.

This whole notion that an Australian bank would say to its customers, 'We want to do a survey, and we want to see if you would voluntarily be microchipped.' Completely nuts."

Martin North: *"Well, it is crazy. I happen to know a few things, internationally. I know there is a company in the U.S. who is arguing that people are already using mobile phones today, and they have biometrics on those mobile phones. You know, fingerprint or face identification, whatever, and what that basically means, is that you've already got a connectivity to do with your personal and your functionality, so why not just take the next step, which is basically, chipping. Chip in your arm and who needs a mobile phone anymore. And of course, there are a few high-tech people, who actually have already gone down the route and actually have chipped themselves. Using it as part of their own experiments.*

But the idea of pushing this more generally into the population, and I can't help but say, 'Well, just have a chip, and you have central bank digital currency. Put those two things together and what have you got?"

John Adams: *"Indeed. So, Martin, just so we can demonstrate to our audience that we're not making this up, let's actually put slide one on the screen. So, the viewer who sent this to me, her name's Lisa, I just want to quote from this email, because I think there is something that is fundamentally wrong. If we just look at the second sentence in the first paragraph, it says, 'Considering how much closer we are with technology, it makes sense for the next step to be keeping it inside our bodies with microchips, right?'"*

THE IRISH INQUIRY
ICONOBLAST – ONE TO ONE

Sara Haboubi, Presenter, Ryland Media Reports: *"Melissa, welcome to Iconoblast – One to One. Thank you for joining us today. You were on the Iconoblast Roundtable, and what you said had everybody pretty spellbound. And we have had tremendous feedback from those who watched that show. People really wanted to know about what you were talking about. And obviously, the key message that you were giving about the vaccine passports. So, what's going on?"*

Melissa Cuimmei, Independent Investor: *"They're not vaccine passports. They are data passports. They are participation passports. There is no medical reason behind these. If I had come to you two years ago and said, 'Here's what the government wants to do. They want to give everybody a chip. They want to put all your medical data, all your financial data on that chip. That would be your complete ID, and they can control you, or shut you out of society from that ID. Or they can put a quantum tattoo on you, so they can remotely medicate you. That sounds absolutely insane. That's the road we are going down right now."*

At least some people in Australia and Ireland are warning about this! They want us all microchipped, and Covid-19 was the trigger!

And lest you doubt this microchipping of the whole planet, with biometric technology, to create a Universal ID, is not a part of the plan, this is why people are also warning that this "digital identity" system will also be connected to the previous mentioned "digital currency" systems - the Social Credit Score System, the ESG System, the CBDC Systems - for even more purposes of total control of the planet, as seen here. **"Digital ID Will Merge Your Identity & Reputation into Trust Scores."**

And this is why:

"**Governments Worldwide are Working in Lockstep to bring in Digital I.D. & Social Credit System as EU agrees to Expand Online Censorship with 'Digital Services Act'**"

And I quote, from that article, *"Hillary Clinton and Barack Obama both lobbied for the EU to back the censorship bill, known as the 'Digital Services Act,' on Thursday, April 21st, 2022."*

They're still behind the scenes, messing things up! They're all in it together!

And this is also why,

"**G20 Pushes Vaccine Passports for ALL Vaccines for All Future International Travel: Only "Then You Can Move Around"**"

Total global control with this "biometric identity scheme," as you can see here.

Speaker at B20: *"So let's have a digital health certificate, acknowledged by WHO. If you have been vaccinated or tested properly, then you can move around. So, for the next pandemic* *instead of stopping the movement of the people 100%, which stopped the economy globally, you can still provide some movement of the people. Indonesia has agreed, other countries have agreed, to have this digital certificate using the WHO standard, and when we have the next worldwide assembly in Geneva, to enter it into the International Health Regulations, so, that hopefully, for the next pandemic, we can still see some movement of the people, some movement of the goods and movement of the economy."*

Won't that be great for the "next plandemic?" How many times have you got to say that. What are you "planning" on, down the pike? Sounds like they're not done with the plandemics. Covid-19 was just the beginning, just like Klaus said.

But in the "next one," the plan is to give everybody a "digital health certificate" that the World Health Organization identifies and agrees with, to determine who gets to travel around in the "next plandemic" and not get locked down, so the economy won't collapse again.

What a set up! You liars! And of course, the people who don't get "locked down" or "locked out" of the financial system, are those who "obey" their mandates, including vaccinations. Pretty slick, isn't it? And for even more proof of that lying scheme, this is also why,

"The WHO Treaty Is Tied to a Global Digital Passport and ID System."

Shocker! It's all tied together. What a setup, step-by-step! They've had this in the works for a long-time, folks. Don't be fooled!

And this article makes it about as blunt as you can get.

"Universal Vaccine Passports Plan Unites the World."

There it is! And you got to make sure you got enough money for this, and they do.

"World Bank Creates $1 Billion Fund for Vaccine Passports."

And don't forget who's going to build it.

"Deutsche Telekom to build global COVID vaccine verification app for WHO."

And don't forget you need an operating system for this, which is precisely why Bill Gates is involved in all this. He's going to make a ton of money off all this! Which is why he's working with Klaus Schwab and the World Economic Forum and the Global Elites saying things like this.

Bill Gates explains why digital financial inclusion should be 'universal.'"

Of course! That way you'll make a ton of money, "universally" over all this!

And that's why Gates has been calling for a Global ID2020 for a long time now.

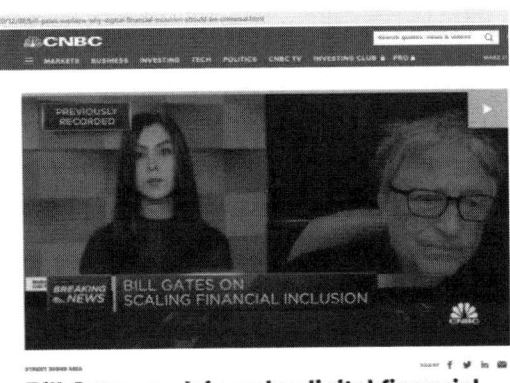

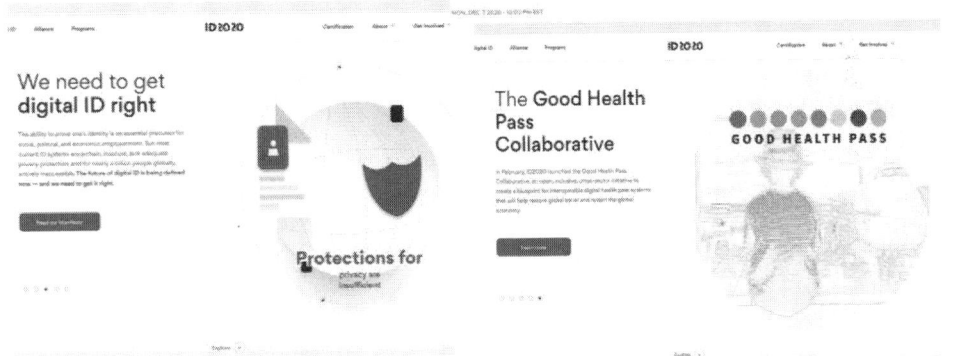

"We need to get it right," and "Everybody needs a Good Health Pass."

You know, like what Hitler did. He put out the "Gesundheit Pass Medical Card" for his people, because he didn't have microchips like Bill and Klaus and the gang do today!

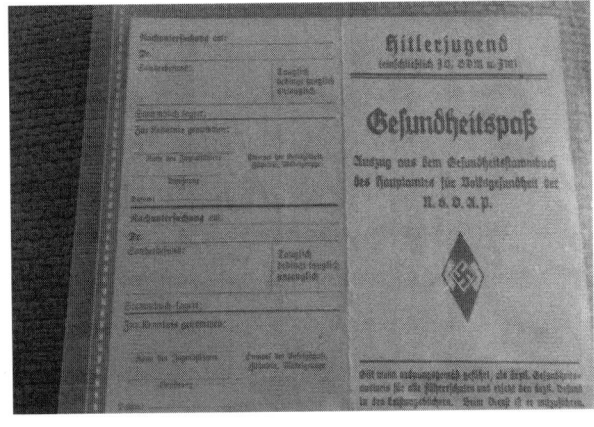

But hey, we still say "gesundheit" today, don't' we? When somebody sneezes? But we thought it meant German for "God bless you," when it really was Hitler's health control scheme. Once again, nothing new under the sun. Klaus's Nazi background keeps coming into play here!

And for even more proof that this is Bill Gates' Hitlerian scheme to get even more rich, by providing the computing platform to run all these digital IDs around the whole planet, this is why we also see his company Microsoft, involved in this.

"Microsoft, the ID2020 Alliance, universal digital identification and you."

Notice again, it's "universal," which is why Bill Gates is also saying we will all soon have this biometric reality.

"Bill Gates believes the electronic tattoo will become reality."

You know, a "mark" on your body. Which is why this guy is saying this about Bill Gates and his deceptive, greedy, Hitlerian behavior.

Jeremy Loffredo, New York Reporter: *"India is known as the most populous democracy in the world. It's also the home to the largest digital-biometric ID system in the world. According to a report from Reuters last* week, tens of millions of children in India are at risk of being excluded from school next year, because they are not linked up to India's digital ID system. Aadhaar, India's federally operated, bio-digital ID system, collected the names, fingerprint scans and eye scans of 1.2 billion Indians.

According to the report, India's 2009 Right to Education, provides the legal right to free education to all children, six to fourteen years old. But, apparently, only children willing to submit to invasive biometric recording and tracking are able to enjoy their own rights. Professor Sinha, at the university, told Reuters that requiring the digital ID for public schools, 'puts the onus on the citizen, and makes it much harder for them to access these rights.'

The report references an 11-year-old girl who had been barred from going into the 6th grade because she did not have the Aadhaar biometrical digital ID. Her parents made several attempts to get her one, but, between the hoops and the behemoth bureaucracy, she fell through the cracks. Now, she has to learn to read and write at home using the newspaper. Without Aadhaar, we have no other options, her mom said.

But Aadhaar is more than just a system that coerces people to submit their biometrics to receive their own rights. It's actually a giant social credit system wanted by political heavyweights and global leaders. Not much Western attention has been put on the Aadhaar system because it has been overshadowed by their geopolitical foe, China, and its social credit system.

According to the Huffington Post, which received documents under India's RTI Act, or Right to Information Act, the Indian government has integrated data collected by Aadhaar to establish a 360-degree database that automatically tracks citizens when they move between cities, change jobs, or buy new property.

Bill Gates, of all people, explained that the Aadhaar systems is a huge asset for India and branded the creator of the system, Nandan Nilekani, a partner of the WEF, a hero."

Bill Gates: *"My friend, Nandan Nilekani, is one of India's best-known entrepreneurs. He led the creation of the world's largest biometric ID system."*

Nandan Nilekani: *"Aadhaar is the world's largest digital ID system and entirely based using biometrics to ensure uniqueness. Our enrollment was very simple: name, address, date of birth, sex, email, ID, and phone number, if you wish, and the biometrics. The ten fingerprints of both hands. The iris of both the eyes and a photograph."*

Jeremy Loffredo: *"Despite the dystopian possibilities, selected officials in the U.S. are trying their best to force a giant biometric digital ID system on the entire population under the guise of equity. Illinois Congressman, Bill Foster, recently introduced the Digital Identity Act, which calls for the public sector, namely Homeland Security, to work with the private sector to build a giant digital biometric ID infrastructure in the United States. Congressman Foster explained the Gates funded vaccine ID initiative, ID2020, that collects biometric information on all citizens, could be leveraged by the private sector to generate profits."*

Congressman Bill Foster: *"Once the government has taken that essential step of taking those biometrics, there will be huge opportunities for the commercial sector to leverage there. They are trying to get this all started. I recently introduced a bill with four bipartisan co-authors on the bill. HR8215, the Improvement Identity Act. If enacted, this bill will take a number of steps to really prioritize the development of digital ID in this country."*

Jeremy Loffredo: *"Foster is trying to push this through under the guise of equity, by explaining that the system will make it easier for unbanked individuals, apparently a new marginalized group, to access financial services, cloaking the invasive ID system in WOKE language. In a House Committee on Financial Services hearing in July, Elizabeth Renieris, warned that biometric digital ID programs like Aadhaar are being used as giant surveillance tools establishing social credit systems."*

Elizabeth Renieris, Founding Director, Notre-Dame-IBM Technology Ethics Lab, University of Notre Dame: *"We must avoid building visual ID systems infrastructure in a way that would further stand and entrench the surveillance state, as do the national identity systems in India and China. For example, the Aadhaar system in India. That single identifier is able to track your activities, all facets of your life - your employment, health, school, pretty much everything you do - and so that's another area where you can't obtain autonomy over specific domains of your life."*

Jeremy Loffredo: *But it's this all-encompassing aspect of the system that makes people like Bill Gates so adoring of it. Addressing policymakers of the achievements of Aadhaar, Gates explained the usefulness of the social credit systems."*

Bill Gates: *"Over time, all of these transactions will create a footprint, so when you go in for credit, the ability to access your history - that you have paid your utility bills on time, you've saved up money for your children's education, all of those things in your digital trail - accessed in an appropriate way, will allow the credit market to properly score the risk."*

Jeremy Loffredo: *"Gates is trying to bring the Aadhaar social credit system, that he is so fond of, to the rest of the world. Gates, as part of the World Bank, launched their ID4D project with the declared purpose of bringing the Aadhaar approach to other countries. To date, the World Bank has invested $1.5 billion into the ID4D Initiative, with the official aim of creating an identification system using 21st century solutions. According to their 2021 annual report, ID4D is currently helping 49 national governments establish digital ID systems for 470 million people."*

And it's spreading around the world, including here in America, and Bill Gates stands to become one of the richest people ever, because of it. What a scam! They're all a bunch of liars!

And lest you think Klaus Schwab and the World Economic Forum is not behind all this, along with Bill Gates, this is why the World Economic Forum is promoting this on their website as well.

"What Does a Good Digital ID Look Like?"

Because that's the plan for all of us. And this is why this article tells it for what it is.

"Great Reset in Action: World Economic Forum's Communist 'Digital Identity' Scheme."

There it is again. This is all it is, folks! And I quote, "The WEF's digital identity scheme is laying the foundation for a global social credit system that will give them the power to control citizens and punish those they deem 'untrustworthy.'"

In other words, those who don't obey whatever they tell you to do, like the Antichrist.

"In February 2022, Klaus Schwab's World Economic Forum (WEF) released a new report, 'Advancing Digital Agency: The Power of Data Intermediaries,' which lays out their plans for the creation of The Fourth Industrial Revolution, a fusion of the 'physical, digital and biological world.'

The unelected WEF globalists have capitalized on Covid-19 and are using the 'vaccine passports' to lay the foundation for widespread digital identity adoption. This is just one more part of The Great Reset in action."

Or what the Bible calls, the Antichrist Kingdom in the 7-year Tribulation!

"These passports, by nature, serve as a form of digital identity. Such a digital identity can be used, among other things, to access your health insurance treatments, monitor health devices and your phones, open a bank account, and carry out financial transactions."

You know, your "buying and selling."

"With your digital pass, you can book trips and go through customs with it. You will also be able to use such a digital ID for shopping, social media, voting, filing tax returns and collecting benefits." Everything!

"According to the WEF report, digital identity schemes include biometrics such as national identifier numbers."

Gee, I wonder if they're going to use 666. Is this crazy or what? All, right here, before our very eyes, and the Bible is the only book on the planet that's been warning about it for 2,000 years now! No wonder the enemy doesn't want you to read that book! Again, if you're not saved, you better get saved now! Ask Jesus to forgive you of your sins before it's too late! This is not a game!

But as you can see, the day is coming when all the Global Elites are going to have the power to not only identify and microchip you, but shut your chip off if you don't obey. And they've been using lies and deceit by creating "crises" for a long time to get the job done, as this whistleblower shares.

Narrator: *"This is Aaron Russo, a filmmaker and former politician. To his left is Nicholas Rockefeller, of the infamous Rockefeller banking and business dynasty. After maintaining a close friendship with Nicholas Rockefeller, Aaron eventually ended the relationship, appalled by what he had learned about the Rockefellers and their ambitions."*

Aaron Russo: *"I got a call one day from a woman I knew, and she said, 'Would you like to meet one of the Rockefellers?' I said, 'Sure, I'd love to.' And we became friends. He began to divulge some things to me. He said to me one night, that there was going to be an event, and out of that event you're going to see that we are going into Afghanistan. So, we have two pipelines from the Caspian Sea. We are going into Iraq to take the oil, and establish peace in the Middle East, and then we are going into Venezuela and try to get rid of Chavez. You're going to see guys going into caves, looking for people that they are never going to find. He's laughing about the fact that there is a war on terror. There's no real enemy. He's talking about how having this war on terror, you can never win it, because it's an eternal war. So, you can always keep taking people's liberties away.*

I asked, 'How are you going to convince people that this war is real?' He said, 'The media. The media can convince everybody that it's real. You keep talking about things, you keep saying it over and over, and eventually people believe it. You created the Federal Reserve in 1913 through lies. You created 9/11 which is another lie. With 9/11 you are fighting the war on terror, and that equaled going into Iraq, which was another lie. And now they are going to do Iran. So, it's one thing leading to another, leading to another.'

I would say, 'What are you doing this for? What's the point of this thing? You have all the money you could ever want. You have all the power. You're hurting people. It's not a good thing.' And he would say, 'What do you care about the people for? Take care of yourself. Take care of your family.' Then I asked, 'What are the ultimate goals here?' His answer was, 'The goal is to get everybody in this world chipped with an RFID chip, to have all the money put on those chips. And if anybody wants to protest what we do, or violate what we want, we just turn off their chip.'"

Warned about over 15 years ago now. If only we had listened. But as you can see, it's all coming to pass!

And shutting you off with your "forced biometric chip" is just the beginning of the nightmare from these guys, if we allow them to create this digital prison planet, that Klaus Schwab, the World Economic Forum, Bill Gates and all the other Global Elites and bankers are salivating over and creating for us for a long time now.

Here's some further insight.

"New insight on Klaus Schwab's 'You will own nothing and be happy': How AI and the Internet of Things will control everything you do in life."

"Bill Gates' Microsoft may have been the first to lure people into this trap, with his Windows Operating System and Office Suite. You buy it. They own it. If you don't continuously update the software, feeding Microsoft data on your usage with each new update, you eventually lose it. It won't work anymore. The same goes for your iPhone.

Now it is happening with vehicles, and not only with luxury add-ons such as heated seats. You buy it. They own the software to block certain features. You have to pay them to unlock those features.

And it's about to get worse: By 2026, the federal government has mandated that all vehicle manufacturers include a remote 'kill switch' in every vehicle that leaves their factories. Now, we're talking about not just a seat that won't heat, but a car that potentially won't run.

Then you really won't own that car at all, because as soon as your social credit score dips below a certain level, the government can just flip the kill switch and your car has been rendered inoperable.

This strategy will soon be extended to your house as well. Builders are building 'smart houses' within 'smart cities' and 'smart meters' with little chips that interact with the power grid, monitoring not only how much power we're using in real time, but where exactly that power is drawing from. Every appliance made over the last 20 years or so contains a chip that talks to the smart meter and tells the power company everything it needs to know about where your electric power usage is coming from.

If you have guests at your house, your water supplier can tell by how many times the toilet flushes and the dishwasher runs, how many living souls are staying there and for how long. Think of the possibilities.

In the so-called 'green economy,' being pushed by the WEF, governments will at some point implement quotas on energy usage. If you have exceeded your monthly allotment for water or electricity, citing the latest climate change regulations, they automatically shut off the spigot, or maybe they will shut off certain appliances that have been overused by an 'irresponsible' citizen that routinely exceeds his assigned carbon footprint. I can hear it now: 'Three strikes and you're out! No more power for you! No more water!'

They are setting us up for the new, resource-based digital economy of The Great Reset, where you will truly own nothing and learn to like it.

And if you can't learn to be happy living in such a society, if you complain too much and too loudly, there's a special place set aside for such people. It's called the gulag.

Aldous Huxley, author of the 1932 dystopian novel, 'Brave New World,' also foresaw the coming technocracy.

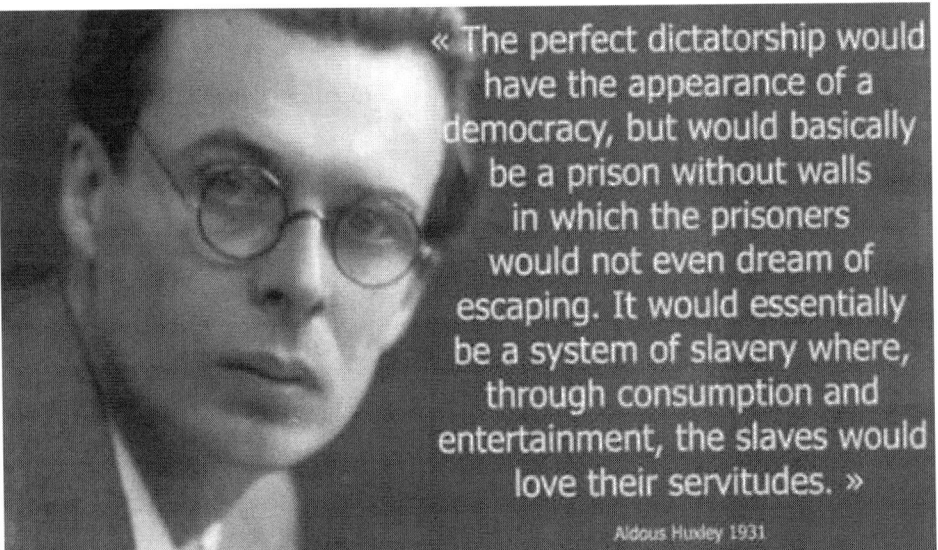

Huxley wrote: *'The perfect dictatorship would have the appearance of a democracy, but would basically be a prison without walls, in which the prisoners would not even dream of escaping. It would essentially be a system of slavery where, through consumption and entertainment, the slaves would love their servitudes."'*

So now you have it. The true meaning of "you will own nothing and be happy."

And pretty soon, if we do nothing and give into all this, this will become our new prison planet reality that Huxley warned about, even here in the United States of America.

Narrator: *"What I am going to talk about is facial recognition, is the title of the talk. Is it a digital identity, or is it a dictatorship? So, that's really the topic. How I am going to break down the presentation, I'll introduce* *what is facial recognition and how cameras are being installed all around the world to build a seemingly innocuous prison for everybody. It's going to be an open-air concentration camp, is what is being built. From there, I'm going to introduce smart cities, and how the LED lights that are being set up on smart poles around the world, and how they can be used against us, and what my intuition and research have gotten me to this point, with the LED lights and their implications with the sensors that are attached to them.*

From there we make a connection to the actual digital ID and how it is implemented in situations like shopping, accessing the internet, how you will be moving around in the world, and it will all tie into the smart cities and the facial recognition. I'll have some pictures of what Carrie was talking about, the things in Montana, that I've been capturing. I'd say, it's less when I've seen pictures of what is coming out of Canada and Australia. I think the smart cities there are much further ahead than in America. But it is happening very quickly. So, with that, I'm going to start my presentation.

FACIAL RECOGNITION
Digital Identity or Digital Dictatorship?

How Facial Recognition Works: Like if you have an iPhone, for instance. You pick up your iPhone, and it gets unlocked. What is really happening is that there is a 3D camera inside the phone and that projects back 30,000 or 60,000 dots, probably in the new ones, on your face and, depending on the contours and the depth of your face that pattern gets distorted and there's an invisible light or infra-red camera in there that takes a picture of that face and then it will decode the exact one to the face, kind of builds a symbolic equation inside, which is your unique identity for you. And that's how iPhones are unlocked. And this is very beneficial, right? It's quick and it has your security.

And like most technologies, that have been sold to us over the last two or three decades, they sell it as a carrot, for convenience, for safety and security, and it's to catch terrorist and bad guys – child molesters and thieves and such. So, we are given cameras, installed cameras, and we buy this stuff. It is okay as a society at large. But by the end of this presentation, you will see how their tricks are coming - by using this specific kind of technology. Many documentaries have been coming out over the past few years of how oppressive China has become - When Big Brother meets Big Data.

Facial recognition in China is used to control the behavior of people through a social credit system. I was in China for a conference in September 2019, and the number of cameras at every intersection, outside buildings, inside restaurants, it's just amazing. So, here's an example of this intersection. It has facial recognition cameras, license plate readers, and anywhere you go, there are TV screens that are doing facial recognition. They identify you, scoring you, and they even have an app, where they tell you what your social score is.

So, this app, combined with the AI algorithms, they are able to control your behavior. It has become a compliance society in China. And this is what is happening in America already, although they haven't given us the app. The narrative from all these documentaries, and little snippets they have on TV and the news, is that China has gone red, and we and the rest are free. There is no privacy and freedom, but we in the West are free. There is a social credit system to control people, which is true. What they have not said is that cameras per capita today in the U.S., 2022, is more than in China. We have 50 million cameras installed, connected to the internet, and installed, compared to 200 million in China, but the population ratio is much different.

London has 73 cameras per 1000 people. London is way ahead, as of this presentation. So, the infrastructure is in place, and it is expanding by the day, here in the West. By 2025, $2 trillion will have been spent on infrastructure and surveillance for smart cities. And the number is going to be $6.9, almost $7 trillion by 2030. That is where the money is going. So, while they are diluting the dollar, they are installing infrastructure with printed dollars.

So, what I call it is, when the world was sleeping and Covid-19 was announced, lockdowns began, all over the world, quarantines in place, and while everyone was watching 'fear TV,' they were installing cameras and smart cities infrastructures. By the end of 2022, there will be one billion surveillance cameras in the world. And these are not just surveillance cameras. They are data collection cameras, to watch everything about every person. That's the kind of system that is being put in place.

In the old days, surveillance was done by people looking at TV screens; human eyeballs were used. But that doesn't happen much anymore. What we have is basically AI security guards that will be (are) watching us at every moment with smart cameras. So, no humans are necessary, and all the intelligence has disappeared between the age of the camera and the cloud. So, know that whenever you are in front of these cameras, all the feed has been collected and you are being analyzed. You are being analyzed, you're being logged in, they are listening, and they are learning, and then they are scoring. So, that's how it works.

So, when are we not alone? Pretty much never, from the moment we leave our house until we return at night. Everywhere you go there are cameras looking at you. Even inside your car. Here is a picture of a Panopticon. A circular prison. This is from the late 1920s in Rhode Island on the East Coast, where you have the prison guards in the center and you have all these prison cells around, so no prisoner is left alone in a sense. They can be watched from anywhere. So, we in a sense, are in a Panopticon, where AI, along with computer vision and cameras, have locked us symbolically and practically inside a prison cell. And you are being watched in everything you do.

About five or six years ago, I started hearing the capital word, Internet of Eyes. I was kind of scratching my head, why would they bring that up. But today everything is clear. We have cameras on the streets, in automobiles. You have facial recognition cameras, satellite cameras watching us. We have drones, license plate readers, cameras in railroad stations, airports, etc. Even at home, by using devices from companies - like Microsoft,

Google, Samsung, Facebook, Zoom, Amazon, and Apple - we are helping Big Brother. If you are on a Zoom call, all the conversation is being recorded by Zoom and going to China.

So far, I have talked about facial recognition and cameras set up in the camera architecture. Here is a picture of smart lights on smart poles that are flooding the beautiful dark sky in Montana, and I bet all over the world. I live in a place in north Montana with not many people, but you see lights going up on freeways like crazy around here. Why do we need that? These are key points for smart cities. Initially, the way they are setting this is that you are going to have these smart poles, and you can add on all sorts of interesting sensors for your security and convenience. But, in reality, they are going to be surveillance devices. They are going to have radar, they are going to have face recognition cameras, they are going to have loudspeakers for instructions just like in China. They will have LED screens for instructions. Many of these smart poles and smart lights meet the specifications where the top of these lights are drone-charging stations. Where, when drones are flying around with police vehicles and they are running out of charge, they can sit on top of a smart pole and get a charge so they can continue their surveillance. These drones are going to have radar as well as cameras on them.

This is the kind of surveillance that is being set up, as we speak. Everyone should be observant as to what is coming to your towns and cities, even villages. I started looking further into the smart LED lights and the cameras that either use LED lights or lasers to project light onto your face. They use diffusers that diffuse the light so that it doesn't cause any harm. A lot of the streetlights that I am seeing right now don't have diffusers. It's blue lights from 450 to 490, I don't want to get too technical, but it's really not good for your health, lawn health or animal health.

So, I started to dig a little deeper. I was driving through this little town, Pablo, Montana, population 2000+. There used to be no streetlights, and now if you go there, there are over 100 streetlights on the freeway corridor. Think about it. They are selling these LED lights for global warming benefits, energy efficiency. They had zero lights. Now they have *hundreds of those lights. Think about that. It's really horrible about what is happening to our towns and cities and freeways. Someone in Canada sent me picture of the lights there. They have a new kind of light, an LED Incapacitator. Homeland Security had funded a company back in 2007, also known as Puke ray, where you can project different frequencies of light and interchange it really, really quickly. What it can do is cause sickness and can eventually cause death. It can cause spinal damage and other damage that a doctor would know better than I do.*

These are the kinds of technologies and weapons systems that are being installed all over the world. They do it slowly, and they do it at night and people get used to it. Now, how does this all connect? It's this concept called Digital Identity, that I came up with a while ago. This is a diagram from a 2018 WEF paper that I was reading. The digital identity is all about entities, people's devices, and things. Everything has to have an entity, a digital entity. What is this all about? This digital entity will be able to access your health care, your benefits, telecommunications, internet logins, when you want to buy food, when you want to log into social platforms, for anything you want to do in life. They want you to identify with a digital identity. And how is that supposed to happen? Through your face. Your face will be the key to unlocking life with your digital identity. But how are they going to use this to enslave humanity?

Because it's going to be linked to a new kind of currency, and that currency is going to be given through UBI, Universal Basic Income. Everybody is going to get carbon credit. Effectively, you will have a social score for your compliance and behavior, and they may also have your jab status. This is a perfect way for this AI system to control people and make them comply with whatever it wants to be done. This new system is already there in so many countries, the central bank, and the new currency.

Ukraine was the first country to roll out the UBI. They showed you the war mongering going on back in April, but what they were doing was unrolling the new system. It is already done. And they also have an app. The WEF said it's a new chapter in the social contract. The social contract that none of us has accepted or signed up for. This is the most important piece of information that will tie everything up. The big strategy is digital prison. It has nothing to do with your true identity. How are they going to implement this? There is a concept called zero trust. You might see it as ZTNA, 'zero trust network access.' So inside security, in companies where security is in servers and software, they are implementing zero trust for networks and for IOS sensors and all devices.

So, what is going to change is implicit allow – default deny. So, think of this, if you go to the internet and you log in, once you log into your computer, you generally can access most of your applications without further permission. But that isn't implicit-allow. What is going to happen is zero trust will come before 'deny.' That means, 'We don't trust you, and for everything you want to do, you have to prove that you are you, and you have to have your credit scores valid. So, how are they going to do this to us? Through digital ID and facial recognition. So, even when you are online, any time you want to go to a new application, it's authenticating you. This camera is going to be on all your devices, all the time. AI is looking at your face, tracking your eye movements.

And then the next version of the bureaucrats will be looking at all the data you are inputting or outputting. There will be no privacy left in any communications. So, this is what the world is going to look like with digital ID, and your life will be like a bunch of locks all day long, from the moment that you wake up until the time you sleep. You will be unlocking with your face. And this is how it's going to be. Here is someone shopping at a Walmart, somewhere in the U.S. They have these lighted, screen doors. All the contents of the food, all the bottles, all the shopping is behind these doors.

With the face ID, your digital ID, to get you access, you may be able to unlock these doors. There will be a face recognition camera on top of these doors, and if this woman's credits have not expired or if they have expired, she may have already had too much beef for the month, the door won't open. If she's had too much sugar, then the orange juice door won't open. And that is how it is going to be implemented. And it will be through the central banking currency, which is smart contracts. And I might add that a lot of companies are doing this but are being set up as a service. They are making money in real time, 24/7, by looking at faces. So, each time your face is in front of a camera, the chain of corporations are making money in real time, all the time.

What else will these smart cities and digital identities be used for? For access control, 'geofencing.' Think of this as an invisible fence around people or robots, beyond which you cannot go. They are going to 'geofence' the world. So, where, and how far you can fly will depend on your digital identity. How far you can drive. How far you can walk. Who you can communicate with. What music you can listen to. Who you can speak with. Everything has the potential to get geofenced, and it will. It's already started. If you go on Facebook or Instagram, they lock you out. Your information may not be shown to your followers if you have a thousand followers, or if you only have a hundred followers that will see your information. That is geofencing in the midst of us.

So, basically, the digital ID is being sold for security and privacy, and inside the Trojan Horse is actually the digital ID and face recognition which is going to mean all of our total control and compliance. This is very important to understand. In the second half of April, stakeholders from the WEF announced that now the global internet is a multi-stakeholder internet. Basically, they have taken over the internet. Again, it was announced by the Department of State, and we are going to live in a zero-trust world, going forward. And it's very possible that, in fact, I'm pretty sure that if you connect the dots, if you don't take your jabs, you won't have access to communications in the future. Because your digital ID won't unlock the internet access. It's all related to the cameras and face recognition.

There is a company named Clearview AI. Peter Steel, one of the original investors, is also a big investor in PayPal. He has also been funding a lot of pre-crime companies, and they are collecting tens of billions, with a target of $100 billion within the next two years. They already rolled out programs in Santa Clara, California, New Orleans, and spreading to more, doing this pre-crime, like in the movie, 'The Minority Report.' This *will be used for stakeholders. These other companies, which are touted as public, have private partnerships. Basically, private companies in the name of PPP, and they are pushing 'no identity left behind,' and it's for diversity, equity, and inclusion - buzz words that I think most people should be familiar with by now.*

But what they are trying to push is video selfies of yourself combined with your driver's license and password and benefits with the state, whether you have employment benefits or medical benefits, and this is how they are going to suck up with retirees and unemployed people to the digital ID system. But once you are in the digital ID system, you will be refused a lot of things in the world.

So, in summary, cameras and facial recognition, which is sold to you under the name of security and privacy, will result in a digital identity, which will be linked to a central banking type of financial system, and once we accept this as a civilization, this will be the final lockdown for humanity. So, I want you to understand, that once we accept a digital identity as a society, or as an individual, GAME OVER for humanity. So, we must resist this."

And I would agree. It's common sense, or at least you think it would be! But this is all part of this deceptive, satanic package, under the guise of safety and security and convenience, that Klaus and the gang are selling us. It's game over for humanity and the beginning of the Antichrist kingdom the Bible warned us about!

In fact, China has already started implementing these kind of Antichrist Draconian surveillance measures.

"Beijing Residents Forced to Wear Regime-Issued Electronic Bracelets if You Traveled Out of the City – Will Track Your Location and Monitor Temperature."

And as you can see here, this is the effect.

"Chongqing City, August 24th. 2 am. The authorities switched the color of all residents' QR code Covid app to orange and you need to take Covid test to turn it back to green. Tonight, all 30 million residents lined up the whole night to take a mandatory Covid test."

Why? Because otherwise, you're going to be "shut out" of their system, like Aaron Russo warned about over 15 years ago, what they were building for us. China is just ahead of the game!

But don't worry, after they deliberately crash the system, they'll come in and promise you that UBI thing. You know, that "Universal Basic Income," that's going to be "digital" with "biometric," and everything will be just fine.

No, actually, it will be the beginning of the end, as this man shares.

"They are going to say, the only way to sort this out is to have people given a guaranteed income. And the guaranteed income – I was writing this in the books way before it was ever mentioned publicly, but now it's everywhere – we will give you a guaranteed income, which will be a pittance, to pay for the necessities of life, to pay for the basics of life. But you're only going to get it if you do as you're told. If you are a dissident against the system, or if you're challenging the system and questioning the system, you ain't going to get it. And, oh, by the way, if you don't accept it, how else are you going to earn a living? We've destroyed everything else. That's the idea. And it's unfolding before our eyes, if only people would care to look at a very fast rate. But, and I keep coming back to this, but it can only happen if people acquiesce to it."

In other words, if you stick your head in the sand and act like it's not really happening. Folks, it's high time we speak up and take action, which is why we're doing this documentary.

But if you stir all this together, and you read the Bible, you will see this is clearly the long-prophesied rise of the evil, satanic, Antichrist system that God warned us about nearly 2,000 years ago that would come to the planet one day. We need to stop trusting in man and start listening to God, as this man shares.

Narrator: *"I want you to pay close attention to every single detail I am about to show you in this video. From the Today Show, this is Melinda Gates from the Bill and Melinda Gates Foundation. Around her neck is an inverted cross, which they use as a symbol in the rejection of Jesus Christ. I mean this woman is actually wearing a satanic symbol which means, 'I reject Jesus Christ.'*

And these are the people we are depending on to save the world from a global pandemic. This is exactly why God warned us in the book of

Jeremiah 17:5, *'Cursed be the man that trusts in man and makes flesh his arms and whose heart departs from the Lord.' In too many scenarios, we bring evil upon our own selves, because, instead of appealing to God for his wisdom and protection, we are running to human beings to save us, using their vast wealth and their intellectual resources. And we don't even know if they have good intentions."*

Melinda Gates: "Well, the pledge is to get 120 million women access to contraceptives by the year 2020. And the whole idea is to put this back on the global agenda. It hasn't been on the forefront of the health agenda for a very long time. And it's never been done in a way that it's really women centric."

John MacArthur: "William Pitt, a well-known name in the U.S. history said this, 'The necessity, i.e., public health, common good, is the plea of every infringement of human freedom. It is the argument of tyrants. Get people afraid, and they will do whatever you want. A fearful society will always comply. Panicking people will always believe anything."

Bill Gates: "The second time I saw him was March, after that, March 2017, in the White House. In both of those two meetings, he asked me if vaccines were a bad thing because he was considering a commission to look into the ill effects of vaccines. And I think somebody, I think his name was Robert Kennedy, Jr., was advising him that vaccines were causing bad things. I said, 'No, that would be a bad thing. Don't do that."

John MacArthur: "'Trust us,' said the government. 'We truly have your best interest at heart. All we want to do is help keep you safe.'"

Fox News Reports: "They say this could be a long war, measured in years, and I think everybody understands why this is happening, but is this sustainable? What do you say to those families that, 'Hey, we can't afford to pay $4.85 a gallon for gas for months, if not years,' to say it's not sustainable."

"The word from the President was a clear articulation of these stakes. This was about the future of the liberal World Order, and we have to stand firm."

Narrator: "Bill and Melinda Gates have been working on a plan with major world leaders for quite some time now."

Bill Gates: "Melinda and I picked, by in the year 2000, where we first got going."

Narrator: "But what exactly have they been working on for over two decades? The WEF engages the foremost political, business, cultural and other leaders of society to spread their global, regional and industry agenda. Their goal, based on their website, is to shape the world into a unique, institutional culture: A One World Government, a One World Culture, a One World Religion, and a One World King.

You can call me crazy if you want to, but I can tell you, that all of this fits right into the plan of the Antichrist. The final Antichrist that the Bible talks about in **Revelation 13**."

John MacArthur: "We are headed toward a One World Global Government, with one massive, monstrous, leader."

Narrator: "Listen carefully to what the President of the WEF has to say about their goal, and the prospects for the world."

Klaus Schwab: "Just to be clear, the future is not just happening. The future is built by us, by a powerful community, as you here in this room. We have the means to improve the state of the world."

Narrator: "Well, it's certain that these people are influential and powerful, and they have money beyond anything. However, there is something very important that they need to do before this whole plan can be unraveled. Now listen very carefully to the King of England's proposal at their annual meeting."

King Charles: *"Here, we need a vast, military style campaign to marshal the strength over the global, private sector. With trillions at its disposal, far beyond global GDP, and with the greatest respect beyond even the governments of the world's leaders, it offers the only real prospect, offering fundamental, economic transition."*

Narrator: *"Just in case you think that you might be protected under some Constitutional law or some Amendment, the truth of the matter is, all of that can be thrown to the side if it presents a problem for these world leaders. It's exactly what happened in 2020. The Constitution of the U.S., or any country for that matter, does it protect us from anyone doing the schemes of the devil, or anyone puppeteered to work out his plans?"*

Joe Biden: *"Careful, and I mean careful attention to billions sustained liberal world order. The United States and Europe, at its core, was the bedrock of the success that the world enjoyed in the second half of the 20th century."*

Narrator: *"That is exactly why the Bible says in **Psalm 118:8**, 'It is better to trust in the Lord than to put confidence in man.' It is better to trust in the Lord than in people. It is better to trust in the Lord than in man. Instead of trusting in the Lord and trusting in His sovereignty, His infinite power, we turn to man to rescue us from our despair. Now think about it. All these billionaires and powerful men and woman, like Bill and Melinda Gates, all in one room every year for this annual meeting, and the best they can come up with is to play right into the hands of satan and his final antichrist.*

*The Bible says in **Jeremiah 17:9**, 'The heart is deceitful above all things, and desperately wicked: who can know it?' You cannot put your trust in men and certainly not these people. Now where is all of this going?"*

John MacArthur: *"This is the kingdom that satan is pulling together as the final attempt to dethrone God. It describes this kingdom as having powers as a leopard, a bear, and a lion, and what we find here, is that this monster is none other than the final antichrist. Even now, John says, there* *are many antichrists. This is the final one. He rises up out of the sea, out of the nations, he consolidates all world powers. This is globalism, symbolized by 10 horns as a number of his completion. He has seven heads. He has consolidated power and consolidated authority. He is a blasphemer, but a powerful one. And the dragon is satan. And the dragon gave the antichrist, in John's vision, his power, his throne and his great authority."*

Narrator: *"In the book of Revelation, specifically* **Revelation 13**, *we can see that those powerful people would think that they own the planet. They are operating exactly as the Bible is saying.* **Revelation 13:7**, *'And it was given unto him to make war with the saints to overcome them, and power was given him over all kindreds, and tongues and nations.'* **Revelation 13:8**, *'And all that dwell upon the earth shall worship him, whose names are not written in the book of life of the Lamb, slain from the foundation of the world.'*

In hindsight, most of us can clearly say the year 2020 was the year of revelation. That year, we saw what great lengths the governments of this world had to go through to get the people to bend to their will. The prize prospect of a One World Government, one military force to be beyond anything of mankind. And it's so powerful, the greed supersedes the limits of sovereign nations. All of this fits into the plans that the prince of this world had from the beginning. Which is to subjugate men, to then influence and totally control them. And in the Book of Revelation, says to have mankind worship him. The beast wants to be worshiped, but only God deserves our worship. But he wants the worship that is due to God alone. He is jealous, just as he was in the beginning, jealous of the Glory of God. So, what does he do? He concocts a plan to subjugate men to worship him and steal the Glory of God."

John MacArthur: *"We are headed toward a time when there is a global satanic kingdom. It consolidates all kingdoms of the world. It is under the final antichrist, designed by the devil himself. And the entire world follows him. The entire world."*

Narrator: *"The world has been desensitized for over 20 years into accepting anti-God concepts. The next step was the idea of sexual ideologies, with dozens of streaming platforms promoting immorality over and over again. Now we have a time that is not only prepared, but willing to enter the next phase. We are the pinnacle of satan's plan in human history. The technological events that we have made as humans on planet earth make this One World Government very plausible and easy. Anyone, and I would venture to say, nations can be controlled by the push of a button."*

And anyone on the planet can be prevented from "buying and selling." Boy, have we been duped. Stop trusting in man and start listening to God.

Chapter Eighteen

World Economic Forum & The Ultimate Losers

But speaking of deception, how are they going to get people to bow a knee to this obvious takeover of the planet with this digital Antichrist prison they're building for us?

Simple, they are, as we speak, also creating the so-called justification for it all. You know, another "crisis." Klaus Schwab, the World Economic Forum, the Global Elites, and their political plants all over the world, who are from Klaus Schwab's school of global leaders, are all deliberately crashing the whole economic system, as we speak, to become the excuse for them to ride in as our saviors, by instituting this Great Reset that will save the day and create a modern-day utopia.

Again, it's not the diabolical, deceptive, satanic, Antichrist, digital-financial Mark of the Beast system the Bible warned about. It's not that simple. It's going to be great, wink wink.

And Lord willing, we'll get into that next deceptive lie and much much more in our next documentary entitled, **"Klaus Schwab the Deliberate Destruction & the Coming Antichrist Kingdom."**

They're using the same lies and deceit that the Antichrist uses to create his soon coming kingdom. But we will also share with you some practical steps to take, in order to do something about all this. In short, JOIN THE RESISTANCE, will you?!

But before we go, I wanted to end with some good news. In fact, it's really great news in light of all that we've just seen. And that great news is this.

Believe it or not, there's one way, one surefire way, to get out of all this mess - that is, this satanic Antichrist Kingdom that Klaus Schwab and the gang are building for us and have relabeled The Great Reset, Agenda 21, Agenda 2030, and The Fourth Industrial Revolution.

And that one surefire way is to make sure you're a part of the winning team. The winning team is none other than Jesus Christ.

The Bible is very clear. Jesus Christ not only defeated satan on the cross, but He's coming back again real soon to put an end to all this evil and tyrannical oppression we're seeing, including the actual Antichrist and False Prophet themselves. Nobody's getting away with anything. These people, including Klaus Schwab and the gang, have simply been duped by satan himself, the ultimate loser.

But what's important to note, is that nobody automatically gets to be a part of this "winning team" with Jesus, nor can you earn your way to be a part of it. No amount of "good works," or so-called "good behavior," can get you on the team, because the Bible says, we've all been disqualified. None of us are "good enough."

Romans 3:23, 6:23: "For all have sinned and fallen short of the glory of God. For the wages of sin is death, but the gift of God is eternal life in Christ Jesus our Lord."

Now, if you're anything like I used to be, you certainly don't like being called a "sinner." In fact, you're probably thinking at this moment, "Well, I'm not that bad of a person. I'm pretty good."

Actually, it's pretty easy to demonstrate that you're not, and neither am I for that matter. This is what God's Ten Commandments were all about. They are God's X-ray showing us that we've really been disqualified to be a part of Jesus' winning team. In other words, we've sinned.

For instance, how many of you have ever lied, (which is the 9th commandment)? Go ahead and raise your hand. Okay, for those who didn't raise your hand, you just did, you lied. Because we've all done that at one time or another.

Or how about this one, the eighth commandment, you shall not steal. How many of you have ever taken something that wasn't yours without permission, ever once? Go ahead and raise your hand. Okay, you already told me you're a bunch of liars, so let's not commit another lie and not raise your hand.

Because the truth is, we've all stolen or taken something without permission that didn't belong to us. That's just two out of the Ten Commandments. How are you doing?

It's obvious, when you begin to see the X-Ray, that none of us can keep them. Which means we all fall short of the glory of God. We have sinned, and we're all disqualified from being a part of Jesus' winning team. We deserve to be separated from God forever, not placed on His team.

But the good news is, God is willing to give us the "gift of eternal life in Christ Jesus our Lord." In other words, if you would just receive His "gift" of eternal life "by faith" and call upon the Name of Jesus Christ and ask Him to forgive you of all your sins, then you too, can become a part of the winning team, and go into and be a part of the real utopia that's coming to the planet real soon. You don't want to miss it! In fact, Jesus tells us He's the only way to get there.

John 14:6: "Jesus answered, I am the way and the truth and the life. No one comes to the Father except through Me."

Romans 10:9-10: "For if you confess with your mouth that Jesus is Lord and believe in your heart that God raised him from the dead, you will be saved. For it is by believing in your heart that you are made right with God, and it is by confessing with your mouth that you are saved."

Be encouraged. It really is true. If you would entrust your life to Jesus Christ and call upon the His Name and ask Him to forgive you of all your sins, then you too will become qualified for the winning team, Jesus's team, the real team that's headed to the true, awesome utopia that's coming to the planet real soon. Again, you don't want to miss it!

And by the way, I'm not going there because I'm perfect. It's simply because I've been forgiven! I "received" this "good news" "by faith" almost 30 years ago when my eyes were "opened" to "see" what the enemy didn't want me to "see."

The fact is, we've been horribly lied to by these Global Elites, including Klaus Schwab and the World Economic Forum, Bill Gates, and the other Elites around the world. They lied to us about God's existence and Who Jesus Christ really is, to enslave us.

And that's why God's giving you this opportunity today, with this documentary and all the evidence within, to see the ruse that these Global Elites really are foisting upon us, so that you will escape their evil satanic prison planet and join the rest of us in experiencing the real, true utopia with Jesus for free. You just have to receive it.

So please don't miss it. Please, ask Jesus right now to forgive of all your sins and ask Him to save you, before it's too late. Join the team! The winning team! I hope to see you there.

This is your final warning. God Bless!

WE HAVE BEEN WARNED!

"Satan deceiveth the whole world," **Revelation 12:9.** There has always been a conflict between good and evil. Truth from deception, freedom versus control.

Barack Obama: "I want to be the president of the United States of America. Where we once were, we are no longer a Christian nation. Change has come to America."

HOW DO YOU DESTROY THE GREATEST NATION ON EARTH?

"Gradually, America was born a Republic. Limited government with moral values. Shifted to Democracy. Rule by majority, even if unconstitutional - lost control to Corporate Forces. Government influenced by wealth, power, and greed, accepted Socialism – Government control of property, goods, and services. Carefully manipulated Fascism – exalts the nation but destroys the individual."

IS A DICTATORSHIP NEXT?

"The agenda - power, world power, world order, New World Order."

George Bush, Sr: *"A world in which there is a real prospect of World Order."*

Barack Obama: *"What is at stake is a New World Order, a global citizenship."*

THE PLOT

Economic instability, government bailouts, government takeover, trillions in national debt, $12,775,007,863,719.47 – OUR NATIONAL DEBT. Your family share – $86,017.00 – The National Debt Clock. Media propaganda, mass deception, mortgage crisis, government cover-ups, false flags, police state, freedoms lost, the Constitution ignored, the Constitution omitted, the Constitution violated.

THE EFFECT? FULFILLMENT OF PROPHECY

Wars and rumors of wars, earthquakes, tsunamis, volcanos, hurricanes, devastations, flooding, famine, food shortages.

ARE YOU EXPECTING THE GOVERNMENT TO SAVE YOU?

Because iniquity shall abound, the hearts of men will fail them, addictions, infidelity, abuse, anger, anxiety, guilt, fear, depression, greed, excessive debt, pressure.

THE SOLUTION: THE ONLY SOLUTION: THE ONLY REAL SOLUTION:
ONLY ONE WAY OUT:
ONLY ONE CAN SAVE YOU

JESUS CHRIST!
THE SAVIOR OF THE WORLD

"That whosoever believes in me should not perish but have everlasting life."

THERE IS NO OTHER SOLUTION, NO POLITICAL SAVIOR.
THE DAY OF DECISION IS HERE.

"Behold, I come quickly, will you come unto Me? I am the Way, the Truth and the Life."

ARE YOU READY?

How to Receive Jesus Christ:

1. Admit your need (I am a sinner).

2. Be willing to turn from your sins (repent).

3. Believe that Jesus Christ died for you on the Cross and rose from the grave.

4. Through prayer, invite Jesus Christ to come in and control your life through the Holy Spirit. (Receive Him as Lord and Savior.)

What to pray:

Dear Lord Jesus,

I know that I am a sinner and need Your forgiveness. I believe that You died for my sins. I want to turn from my sins. I now invite You to come into my heart and life. I want to trust and follow You as Lord and Savior.

In Jesus' name. Amen.

Notes

https://www.youtube.com/watch?v=AWBRldjVzuM
https://www.cnbc.com/2022/03/24/blackrocks-larry-fink-who-oversees-10-trillion-says-russia-ukraine-war-is-ending-globalization.html
https://maloneinstitute.org/wef
https://www.weforum.org/communities/strategic-partnership-b5337725-fac7-4f8a-9a4f-c89072b96a0d
https://en.wikipedia.org/wiki/Tedros_Adhanom_Ghebreyesus#Early_life_and_education
https://t.me/covidtruthnet/2955
https://www.technocracy.news/un-wef-call-for-new-global-social-contract-with-no-one-left-behind/
https://www.technocracy.news/vatican-goes-full-technocracy-with-council-for-inclusive-capitalism/
https://twitter.com/WaltzingMtilda/status/1569105718304980992?t=_AhsUOPPt7fHOxwmpnZyJQ&s=19
https://www.youtube.com/watch?v=C3Q41dRoGlo
https://freedomfirstnetwork.com/2022/03/biden-confirms-hes-a-puppet-of-his-globalist-masters-theres-going-to-be-a-new-world-order?fbclid=IwAR0Se11PaJ6MhMtgUx_eM8BtlQ0ddO3MLsyVePJg_SaYxDYtxbNcZAER2PA
https://www.youtube.com/watch?v=_KBkXitNHJM
https://rairfoundation.com/exposed-klaus-schwabs-school-for-covid-dictators-plan-for-great-reset-videos/
https://www.vanityfair.com/news/2009/01/getting-to-know-klaus-schwab-the-man-behind-davos
https://leohohmann.com/2022/02/10/klaus-schwabs-puppet-young-global-leaders-revealed-trudeau-in-canada-buttigieg-in-u-s-macron-in-france-and-many-more/
https://rumble.com/vw93e5-mega-boom-schwabs-global-shapers-network-exposed.html
https://t.me/SantaSurfing/44264

https://www.younggloballeaders.org/
https://sonsoflibertymedia.com/the-world-economic-forum-the-great-reset/
https://www.lifesitenews.com/blogs/why-would-the-ukrainian-president-cite-justin-trudeau-as-an-inspiration/
https://newspunch.com/wef-hand-over-your-sovereignty-to-the-elite-or-die/
https://geopolitics.co/2022/02/22/world-economic-forums-young-global-leaders-revealed/
https://www.technocracy.news/world-economic-forums-young-global-leaders-revealed/
https://homunizam1.wordpress.com/2020/11/18/klaus-schwab-and-his-great-fascist-reset/
https://unlimitedhangout.com/2021/02/investigative-reports/schwab-family-values/
https://vigilantcitizen.com/vigilantreport/top-10-insane-wef/
https://www.technocracy.news/un-wef-call-for-new-global-social-contract-with-no-one-left-behind/
https://www.technocracy.news/vatican-goes-full-technocracy-with-council-for-inclusive-capitalism/
https://www.rebelnews.com/tags/world_economic_forum
https://www.weforum.org/agenda/2016/11/america-s-dominance-is-over/
https://thenewamerican.com/biden-administration-proposes-merging-u-s-with-mexico-and-canada/
https://amac.us/defeat-the-great-reset-to-save-american-freedoms/
https://sonsoflibertymedia.com/marxist-theology-a-trojan-horse-through-sustainable-development-goals/
https://www.thegatewaypundit.com/2022/10/no-borders-no-countries-biden-regime-calls-north-american-union-rep-matt-gaetz-responds/?utm_source=Email&utm_medium=the-gateway-pundit&utm_campaign=dailypm&utm_content=2022-10-15
https://sonsoflibertymedia.com/sustainable-debt-slavery/
https://vigilantcitizen.com/vigilantreport/top-10-insane-wef/
https://sonsoflibertymedia.com/the-world-economic-forum-the-great-reset/

https://www.thegatewaypundit.com/2022/08/update-saudi-prince-offers-glimpse-dazzling-500-billion-smart-city-future-will-nothing-happy/?utm_source=Email&utm_medium=the-gateway-pundit&utm_campaign=dailyam&utm_content=2022-08-02
https://twitter.com/PezntJournalist/status/1484578454204997632
https://en.wikipedia.org/wiki/Ursula_von_der_Leyen
https://twitter.com/WallStreetSilv/status/1585556920198471681?t=0qxe5QqEfiXqyOfmSxInrA&s=09
https://www.youtube.com/watch?v=COsL0IfvXsw
https://www.youtube.com/results?search_query=agenda+2030
https://www.youtube.com/results?search_query=great+reset
https://www.youtube.com/worldeconomicforum/videos
https://leohohmann.com/2022/11/23/smart-cities-worldwide-being-converted-into-open-concentration-camps-says-ex-silicon-valley-engineer-turned-whistleblower/
https://www.weforum.org/agenda/2016/11/8-predictions-for-the-world-in-2030/
https://www.amazon.co.jp/-/en/Nations-Headquarters-Limited-Cloisonne-Specifications/dp/B081RHR9TW
https://www.weforum.org/agenda/2016/11/america-s-dominance-is-over/
https://thenewamerican.com/biden-administration-proposes-merging-u-s-with-mexico-and-canada/
https://www.msn.com/en-us/news/world/communist-china-survivor-issues-warning-to-americans-socialism-is-only-the-first-stage/ar-AA11aoow?ocid=msedgntp&cvid=b9a67f8d45df2f5216cc79abe2cb5045
https://www.naturalnews.com/2022-11-02-democrats-beg-for-covid-forgiveness-after-destroying-the-lives-of-millions.html#
https://www.smartcitiesdive.com/news/for-his-new-smart-desert-city-billionaire-marc-lore-eyes-nevada-utah-and/628483/
https://www.breitbart.com/europe/2022/10/25/coup-complete-globalist-rishi-sunak-installed-as-prime-minister-of-the-united-kingdom/
https://en.wikipedia.org/wiki/Great_Reset

https://www.howestreet.com/2020/10/klaus-schwab-says-you-will-own-nothing-in-10-years/

https://sonsoflibertymedia.com/marxist-theology-a-trojan-horse-through-sustainable-development-goals/

https://www.thegatewaypundit.com/2022/10/no-borders-no-countries-biden-regime-calls-north-american-union-rep-matt-gaetz-responds/?utm_source=Email&utm_medium=the-gateway-pundit&utm_campaign=dailypm&utm_content=2022-10-15

https://www.weforum.org/agenda/2020/06/now-is-the-time-for-a-great-reset/

https://sonsoflibertymedia.com/sustainable-debt-slavery/

https://duckduckgo.com/?q=the+great+reset+america+will+no+longer+be+a+world+superpower&ia=web

https://www.infowars.com/posts/the-serial-killers-of-the-great-reset/

https://www.infowars.com/posts/the-serial-killers-of-the-great-reset/

https://sonsoflibertymedia.com/the-world-economic-forum-the-great-reset/

https://www.technocracy.news/un-wef-call-for-new-global-social-contract-with-no-one-left-behind/

https://www.thegatewaypundit.com/2022/08/update-saudi-prince-offers-glimpse-dazzling-500-billion-smart-city-future-will-nothing-happy/?utm_source=Email&utm_medium=the-gateway-pundit&utm_campaign=dailyam&utm_content=2022-08-02

https://www.technocracy.news/vatican-goes-full-technocracy-with-council-for-inclusive-capitalism/

https://www.forbes.com/sites/worldeconomicforum/2016/11/10/shopping-i-cant-really-remember-what-that-is-or-how-differently-well-live-in-2030/?sh=2c8bd3e17350

https://www.weforum.org/agenda/2021/08/covid19-long-term-effects-society-digital?utm_source=twitter&utm_medium=social_video&utm_term=1_1&utm_content=23444_5_ways_pandemic_rehape_lives_longterm&utm_campaign=social_video_2021

https://financialpost.com/investing/a-20-trillion-blackrock-vanguard-duopoly-is-investings-future
https://www.foxnews.com/world/world-economic-forum-chair-klaus-schwab-declares-chinese-state-tv-china-model-many-nations
https://www.facebook.com/walletmor/photos/a.181898776961837/623712232780487/
https://www.youtube.com/watch?v=2P5AL9rT_Ks
https://www.youtube.com/watch?v=0MCLmXV1O9M
https://www.youtube.com/watch?v=xNIWXDTdwvA
https://www.youtube.com/watch?v=HR0Jtokcfu4
https://www.youtube.com/watch?v=4qwYRVDJ4M0
https://www.forbes.com/sites/alexledsom/2020/09/30/amazon-is-now-scanning-your-hand-to-pay-for-groceries/?sh=3db02118385b
https://harbingersdaily.com/artificial-intelligence-taking-the-world-towards-the-perfection-of-global-tyranny/
https://beforeitsnews.com/awakening-start-here/2022/10/beast-system-is-happening-now-pay-with-your-hand-or-face-head-17570.html
https://www.thegatewaypundit.com/2022/03/bombshell-video-economist-world-government-summit-says-new-financial-world-order-shift-dramatic-new-direction/
https://bestlifeonline.com/tag/coronavirus/
https://news.yahoo.com/cash-coins-notes-money-cashless-society-card-payments-coronavirus-112834843.html
https://sonsoflibertymedia.com/heres-how-a-cashless-society-would-affect-day-to-day-life-2/
https://www.prophecynewswatch.com/article.cfm?recent_news_id=5684
https://www.prophecynewswatch.com/article.cfm?recent_news_id=5537
https://sonsoflibertymedia.com/world-economic-forum-pushes-chip-implants-for-children-comparing-them-to-eyeglasses-hearing-aids-video/
https://www.thegatewaypundit.com/2022/08/world-economic-forum-recommends-humans-become-cyborgs-implant-brain-chips-solid-rational-reasons-children-microchipped/?utm_source=Email&utm_medium=the-gateway-pundit&utm_campaign=dailyam&utm_content=2022-08-23

https://www.prophecynewswatch.com/article.cfm?recent_news_id=5674
https://www.zerohedge.com/economics/australias-central-bank-working-bis-launch-digital-currency-system
https://beforeitsnews.com/awakening-start-here/2022/10/beast-system-is-happening-now-pay-with-your-hand-or-face-head-17570.html
https://www.zerohedge.com/markets/blackrocks-fink-says-ukraine-invasion-accelerates-esg-and-digital-currencies-shift
https://www.thegatewaypundit.com/2022/03/bombshell-video-economist-world-government-summit-says-new-financial-world-order-shift-dramatic-new-direction/
https://www.investopedia.com/terms/d/digital-currency.asp
https://www.stridentconservative.com/digital-currency-unlimited-government-control-of-you-and-your-money/
https://rairfoundation.com/exposed-klaus-schwabs-school-for-covid-dictators-plan-for-great-reset-videos/
https://www.gizmohnews.com/tv/world-economic-forum-panel-on-the-value-of-digital-identity-for-the-global-economy-and-society-2039
https://sonsoflibertymedia.com/heres-how-a-cashless-society-would-affect-day-to-day-life-2/
https://twitter.com/WallStreetSilv/status/1585919311373225984?t=eW0bRSFb-RNrJZjAm0L_aQ&s=09
https://www.youtube.com/results?search_query=what+is+esg
https://www.youtube.com/results?search_query=esg+score+parody
https://harbingersdaily.com/are-sri-lankans-about-to-become-the-worlds-first-net-zero-refugees/
https://sonsoflibertymedia.com/bill-gates-social-credit-scores-are-an-asset-video/
https://www.bitchute.com/video/6GEXRvNYMFFB/
https://en.wikipedia.org/wiki/Environmental,_social,_and_corporate_governance
https://beforeitsnews.com/entertainment/2022/10/federal-reserve-announcement-6-large-banks-will-participate-in-pilot-climate-scenario-or-social-credit-system-2676249.html

https://www.2ndsmartestguyintheworld.com/p/how-technocommunism-will-institute
https://healthimpactnews.com/2022/is-sri-lanka-leading-the-way-into-the-new-world-order-or-is-it-showing-us-the-way-out/
https://spectator.org/mutual-funds-esg/
https://sonsoflibertymedia.com/nearly-2-billion-5g-base-stations-now-deployed-in-china-coming-soon-near-you-video/
https://www.technocracy.news/nightmare-on-g20-street-biden-delivers-us-to-a-chinese-social-credit-system/
https://t.me/SidneyPowell/3969
https://sonsoflibertymedia.com/cash-free-central-bank-digital-currency-roll-out-coming-in-december/
https://rairfoundation.com/beware-bidens-build-back-better-socialism-bill-is-the-great-reset/
https://www.prophecynewswatch.com/article.cfm?recent_news_id=5628
https://www.wnd.com/2022/08/biden-planning-protect-us-cash-beginning-dec-13/
https://kanekoa.substack.com/p/central-bank-digital-currencies-are
https://www.prophecynewswatch.com/article.cfm?recent_news_id=5667
https://sonsoflibertymedia.com/government-pushs-a-digital-dollar-so-it-can-seize-assets-at-will-enslave-humanity/
https://rairfoundation.com/great-reset-self-anointed-elitists-want-to-impose-global-socialism-must-watch/
https://sonsoflibertymedia.com/imf-chief-cbdc-should-be-used-alongside-social-credit-system-to-enslave-humanity/
https://www.ibtimes.com/kiyosaki-warns-about-eo-14067-calls-cbdc-creation-communism-its-purest-form-3578565
https://reclaimthenet.org/rishi-sunak-cbdcs
https://sonsoflibertymedia.com/social-credit-score-tied-to-central-bank-digital-currency-looms/
https://sonsoflibertymedia.com/the-coming-central-bank-digital-currency-must-be-resisted/
https://www.prophecynewswatch.com/article.cfm?recent_news_id=5751

https://rairfoundation.com/archbishop-pope-francis-is-a-zealous-cooperator-of-the-globalist-great-reset-plot-video/
https://reclaimthenet.org/australia-considers-centralizing-digital-id
https://reclaimthenet.org/nsw-wants-to-explore-biometrics-for-digital-id
https://www.thegatewaypundit.com/2022/07/beijing-residents-forced-wear-regime-issued-electronic-bracelets-traveled-city-will-track-location-monitor-temperature/?utm_source=Email&utm_medium=the-gateway-pundit&utm_campaign=dailypm&utm_content=2022-07-15
https://euroweeklynews.com/2022/03/06/bill-gates-believes-the-electronic-tattoo-will-become-reality/
https://www.theepochtimes.com/canada-partners-with-the-wef-to-unleash-digital-ids-is-the-us-next_4671688.html
https://www.reuters.com/business/healthcare-pharmaceuticals/deutsche-telekom-build-global-covid-vaccine-verification-app-who-2022-02-23/
https://www.prophecynewswatch.com/article.cfm?recent_news_id=5725
https://sonsoflibertymedia.com/g20-pushes-vaccine-passports-for-all-vaccines-for-all-future-international-travel-only-then-you-can-move-around-video/
https://articles.mercola.com/sites/articles/archive/2023/02/02/covid-lab-leak.aspx?ui=dfe05d4f2ed6f1d238e270a073e115e2f13728d5b7c8b944431eaf13671443b3&sd=20160215&cid_source=dnl&cid_medium=email&cid_content=art1HL&cid=20221130&cid=DM1296582&bid=1657574636
https://rairfoundation.com/great-reset-in-action-world-economic-forums-communist-digital-identity-scheme-video/
https://www.bitchute.com/video/A1i3YtzVzKXf/